Thinking Syntactically

Blackwell Textbooks in Linguistics

The books included in this series provide comprehensive accounts of some of the most central and most rapidly developing areas of research in linguistics. Intended primarily for introductory and post-introductory students, they include exercises, discussion points and suggestions for further reading.

Thinking Syntactically

A Guide to Argumentation and Analysis

Liliane Haegeman

Blackwell
Publishing

BLACKWELL PUBLISHING
350 Main Street, Malden, MA 02148-5020, USA
9600 Garsington Road, Oxford OX4 2DQ, UK
550 Swanston Street, Carlton, Victoria 3053, Australia

First published 2006 by Blackwell Publishing Ltd

7   2012

Library of Congress Cataloging-in-Publication Data

Haegeman, Liliane M. V.
    Thinking syntactically : a guide to argumentation and analysis / Liliane Haegeman.
        p. cm. — (Blackwell textbooks in linguistics ; 20)
    Includes bibliographical references and index.
    ISBN 978-1-4051-1852-1 (hard cover : alk. paper)
    ISBN 978-1-4051-1853-8 (pbk. : alk. paper)
    1. Grammar, Comparative and general—Syntax.
    2. Linguistic analysis (Linguistics)   I. Title.   II. Series.

    P291.H234 2006
    415—dc22
                                                                            2005010992

A catalogue record for this title is available from the British Library.

Set in 10/13pt Sabon
by Graphicraft Limited, Hong Kong
Printed and bound in Singapore
by Markono Print Media Pte Ltd

The publisher's policy is to use permanent paper from mills that operate a sustainable forestry policy, and which has been manufactured from pulp processed using acid-free and elementary chlorine-free practices. Furthermore, the publisher ensures that the text paper and cover board used have met acceptable environmental accreditation standards.

For further information on
Blackwell Publishing, visit our website:
www.blackwellpublishing.com

Contents

Preface and Acknowledgments

The title of this book is *Thinking Syntactically*. As the title suggests, the focus of the book is on "thinking about syntax." Syntax is the component of linguistics that is concerned with the way words are put together to form sentences. This book illustrates one way of thinking about sentence formation.

The Goals of the Book

Over the years, many types of syntactic theories have been developed in an attempt to explain how sentences are formed. An approach that has given rise to a lot of exciting discoveries is the one initiated by the American linguist Noam Chomsky in the 1950s and which is known as "generative grammar." One of the properties of generative grammar which I think makes it particularly attractive is that it uses a methodology modeled on what is used in the natural sciences. Thus, generative linguists try to "think" about syntax in a scientific way; they elaborate their analyses using a scientific methodology. The emphasis on methodology entails that, when confronted with a syntactic theory or a particular syntactic analysis, syntacticians do not have to accept the proposals as they are, unthinkingly and blindly. Rather, they can examine the logic behind the proposals, evaluate it, and decide on its merits. Ideally, then, learning generative syntax should imply learning this way of thinking about syntax. It should definitely not be rote learning. In practice, I feel syntax has often been reduced to rote learning, and that is why I have written this book.

The goal of the book is not to present all the intricacies of one syntactic theory. Rather, its aim is to reconstruct and to illustrate as explicitly as possible the thinking behind generative syntax. In other words, the aim is to illustrate how to "think syntactically." Generative syntax is not a spectator sport, where you sit on the sidelines and watch others perform. Rather, I would like to get you involved. I would like you to enter the world and the mindset of the practicing generative syntacticians, to think with them and follow the argumentation as it develops. For instance, sometimes when arguing in favor of one analysis over another, syntacticians will use arguments drawn from language data; such arguments are called empirical arguments. At other times, the syntactician will use arguments which themselves are drawn from the theory he or she is working in; such arguments are theoretical arguments. Ideally, these empirical and theoretical arguments should converge, but that is not always the case. In such circumstances, in order to evaluate one analysis over another, it is important to be able to assess the nature of the argumentation itself and to compare different arguments.

The result of working your way through this book should be that when you are confronted with syntactic analyses you are able to evaluate the arguments that have led to the analyses, to check the way the arguments have been built up, to examine the argumentation. Indeed, observe in passing that the kind of rigorous thinking explored here may well come in handy in everyday life, as, for instance, when you are deciding who to vote for, whether to buy a house or to rent one, or which job to apply for.

Another aspect that distinguishes this book from many introductions to generative syntax is the kinds of examples used. Very often, syntactic analyses are based on a small set of home-made examples, which seem to have little or no bearing on any kind of language that we meet in everyday life. Though this is a perfectly legitimate move and one that we will sometimes also adopt in this book, to the beginning students of syntax such an approach to language may look rather dry and totally irrelevant. Because of the exclusive use of artificial examples, a syntax course often seems to belong in a separate world, unconnected to the daily linguistic reality. In this book, there will be arguments based on home-made "artificial" examples, but in addition we will also be using a lot of attested examples mainly taken from recent journalistic prose. The reason for introducing such examples is to show how concepts that are relevant to syntactic theory are not outside the real world, but, rather, drawn from and part of the real world.

To my mind, thinking syntactically should not be confined to syntax classes. It should be a way of thinking that is available to you in your daily life, that makes you curious about linguistic phenomena, that makes you interested in the language used around you, and that even makes you more aware of the language you use yourself. I hope that having worked your way through this book, you will have acquired a new linguistic sensitivity, and that in everyday life you will recognize certain patterns discussed in the book and that you will also spot new and different patterns that would perhaps not be accounted for in the book. I hope that in the latter case you become so intrigued by these new data that you will try to figure out how these new data should be analyzed in terms of the system elaborated in this book.

In addition to the many attested examples, it will also often be necessary to construct our own examples in order to test certain hypotheses. In the final chapter of the book we will pay some attention to how such examples are constructed.

Though most examples discussed in this book are drawn from English, there is also material drawn from other languages. The goal is to show that just as we can think in a formal way about the structure of English, we can do the same for other languages. If you are a native speaker of a language other than English you are encouraged to think about your own language in similar terms as those laid out in the book.

The book does not aim at providing a complete survey of a particular theory. Rather, it shows that a theory is the result of a particular way of thinking. But the book also shows that the thinking is never finished. At the end of the book, we will have outlined some components of a theory about sentence formation, but as will become clear in the exercises throughout the book, there remain many questions and problems, and the theory presented is by no means complete. However, this is not only due to the limited scope of this introduction. Even if I had written a book twice as long, and even if I had been able to incorporate all the current proposals in syntactic theory, still, in a few months' time, if not sooner, there would have come along new proposals challenging some of the hypotheses presented here and invalidating others. Syntactic research is a continuous and continuing enterprise shared by many enthusiastic researchers across the world. If syntacticians really had already formulated an exhaustive and perfect theory of sentence formation, if there really were no questions left, then there would be no practicing syntacticians left, either.

The Organization of the Book

The exercises

The book contains five chapters, each elaborating a step toward the formulation of a theory of sentence structure. With each chapter comes a set of exercises. The exercise headings are accompanied by the abbreviations (T), (L), and (E). The abbreviation (T) stands for "tie in," and indicates that a particular exercise ties in with the material in the preceding chapter. Tie-in exercises are signaled by footnotes in the chapter. Whenever a footnote points toward an exercise, it means that the exercise can be tackled at that point in the chapter. The abbreviation (L) stands for "look ahead" and it signals that the material covered in the exercise will be taken up in a later chapter of the book. Look-ahead exercises also contain cross-references to the later point at which the material is tackled. The abbreviation (E) stands for "expansion" and signals that the material covered in these exercises goes beyond that covered in the book. Again references to further reading will be included in them. Since the material contained in T-exercises has been covered in the text, T-exercises will tend to be "easier" than L-exercises or E-exercises.

The format of some of the E-exercises and the L-exercises is quite different from the standard exercise format that you may expect to find in a textbook. In particular, some exercises are longer, they contain lots of text, and they look more like workbook sections. The reason why such discursive exercises have not been included in the main body of the text is that they are only intended here as additional illustrations of how certain issues are problematic and how they can be or have been pursued using the argumentation developed in the associated chapter. These discursive exercises typically will not offer an exhaustive or definitive treatment of the issues in question. Rather, they illustrate how a hypothesis is challenged and how it may have to be reworked in the light of new data or of new theoretical proposals.

When, having worked your way through a chapter, you want a quick rehearsal of the material in the chapter, you will probably mainly want to revise using the T-exercises. If you want to know what is to come later in the book, you could also try the L-exercises. If you want to discover more intriguing problems which go beyond the discussions in the present book, you should try the E-exercises.

The footnotes in the chapters and in the exercises also contain references to the scientific linguistics literature. However, for the student-reader many of the publications referred to will be too advanced and too technical and they should not be tackled until you have reached the end of the book. Some more accessible references are pointed out when they are available.

The chapters

The first chapter of the book offers an introduction to scientific methodology and how it can be applied to the study of syntax. Among other things, this chapter introduces the hypothesis that the meaning of a sentence is calculated on the basis of its component parts and their relations in the structure. This hypothesis about the mapping of form onto meaning will be one of our guidelines throughout the book. The first chapter also provides an overview of some patterns of question formation in English and French.

Chapter 2 introduces the key tools for identifying the constituents of a sentence. It is shown that two of the main constituents of the sentence are its subject and its verb phrase. The verb phrase is a constituent whose head is a verb. It is a "projection" of the verb. The verb denotes the action or state depicted by the sentence; it has a lot of descriptive content and it is called a lexical head. The projection of the verb is a lexical projection.

Chapter 3 shows how subject and verb phrase are related through a linking element, the inflection of the verb. This chapter introduces the hypothesis that the inflection of the finite verb heads its own projection. The inflection is a "functional" head; it does not have the same kind of descriptive content as a lexical head. Projections of functional elements are called functional projections.

In Chapter 4 we pursue one of the consequences of the hypothesis that the meaning of the sentence is worked out on the basis of its component parts and their structural relations. We will discover that for this hypothesis to be maintained, the sentences must have more than one subject position. We introduce the hypothesis that the subject is first inserted inside the VP and is then moved to the subject position outside the VP.

The final chapter of the book returns to question formation and we show how the system elaborated in the first four chapters of the book can be implemented to derive the word order in English questions. This chapter focuses on the importance of the movement operation for the formation of sentences.

A Note to the Teacher

This book targets introductory syntax classes. It could be the first step in a syntax program that will lead onto more theoretical work or it could be the starting point of a more empirically oriented approach with a generative basis. The exercises try to illustrate these two directions.

Though there are many exercises in the book, I hope that the exercises will also provide inspiration for additional exercises along the format of those in the book. This may be particularly relevant for teachers whose students are native speakers of languages other than English. Exercises in the students' own language can be provided modeled on those in the book. One type of exercise which is not provided in the exercise sections but is a natural spin-off from the way the book is written is to ask students to look for particular patterns in their own reading. From my own experience, though, I have found that it is important to define such research tasks rather narrowly, so that they can be tied to the teaching. The attested data in the exercises in this book can be taken as a guideline for the students' own search. Such research exercises can be devised both for English and for other languages.

References in footnotes of the text signal the relevant literature and they are intended to make up for the inevitable shortcuts that have to be part and parcel of a fairly basic introduction. Both older "classic" texts in the generative literature and more recent minimalist texts have been included.

The textbook should cover an introductory semester-long course in syntax. The chapters can also be the basis for self-study. The text can be complemented with additional readings, and suitable supplementary reading can be of various types. By way of illustration, I offer some suggestions here, but the choice will depend very much on the overall orientation of the linguistics program into which this book is being integrated. For instance, since a lot of the discussion hinges around functional structure and the subject, the course could lead up to a study of some of the recent discussions of the position of subjects or of verbs. Accessible overview papers on this area can be found in many of the syntax handbooks that have been published recently. McCloskey (1997), for instance, would be a very good follow-up to Chapter 4. Another possible extension would be to take the students beyond the proposals in the book and to explore the concept of "Predicate Phrase" (Bowers 2001). Yet another possibility would be to extend the discussion to the structure of the nominal projection, an issue which is not touched upon very much here. Bernstein (2001) could be the basis for such an extension. Some more advanced theoretical papers written against a Minimalist background might also be used, though these will probably require more input from the teacher.

The book might be suitably complemented with papers in neighboring areas of interest. For instance, the discussion of functional categories might be linked to papers on the question of language acquisition and on the question of how much of such structure is present in the early grammar. To mention but two examples, one might choose some of the papers in Clahsen (1996) or in Friedemann and Rizzi

(1999). The text could also be complemented with material on language variation or on creolization (cf. DeGraff (1997), and the papers in DeGraff (1999)). Alternatively, the course could be accompanied by papers on processing such as Frazier and Clifton (1989), or Gibson and Warren (2004) to mention one recent example.

The textbook should also enable the student to move easily on to introductory textbooks such as my own *Introduction to Government and Binding Theory* (1994) or Haegeman and Guéron's (1999) *English Grammar: A Generative Perspective*. The book could also lead onto any of the recent introductions to Minimalist syntax such as Andrew Carnie's (2002) *Syntax: A Generative Introduction*, David Adger's (2003) *Core Syntax*, Andrew Radford's (2004) *Syntactic Theory and English Syntax*, or Norbert Hornstein, Jairo Nunes, and Kleanthes Grohmann's (forthcoming) *Understanding Minimalism: An Introduction to Minimalist Syntax*.

Acknowledgments

This book owes a lot to my students and my colleagues. I mention in particular the *licence*, *maîtrise*, and *DEA* students at the university of Lille, who were a skeptical and challenging audience at first. They were the ideal audience to try out this material. Through them, I discovered the shortcomings of many textbooks, especially my own earlier ones. My students were the good-humoured, willing, and challenging testing ground for various parts of this book. Among my students, I mention in particular Elodie Gauchet and Virgine Marant, who pointed out some of the typos in Chapters 4 and 5.

Among the colleagues who encouraged me to write this book I mention David Adger, Siobhan Cottell, Ilse Depraetere, Eric Haeberli, Chad Langford, Philip Miller, Kathleen O'Connor, and Paul Rowlett. Thanks to David and Paul for comments on some sections. I thank Ruth Huart for providing the critical outside view that made me rethink textbook writing. Warm thanks also go to three anonymous reviewers for Blackwell: their encouraging remarks and suggestions helped reshape this book. I also thank Jacqueline Guéron for very useful comments on an earlier version and Artemis Alexiadou, Frank Nuyts, Eric Haeberli, Suzan Pintzuk, and Ur Shlonsky for help with the examples. Special thanks go to Katya Paykin-Arroues, who proofread parts of the final version, and to John Wakefield whose careful editing also improved the text a lot. I also thank Siobhan Cottell for being a patient friend who was there to listen when I needed a sympathetic ear, who encouraged me to write this book and who painstakingly provided detailed comments on a prefinal version. Siobhan helped me to devise ways of making this book more student-friendly. I hope she will not be too disappointed by the final version. Thanks to three people at Blackwell who made writing this book so much fun: Philip Carpenter, who certainly knows how to tempt his authors into writing books, and Ada Brunstein and Sarah Coleman who acted like my guardian angels. I also owe thanks to Etienne Vermeersch, who, about 30 years ago now, was the first to make me realize the importance of the difference between inductive and deductive thinking, and to David Lightfoot, Henk van Riemsdijk, and Neil Smith, who, also some time ago now, were the first to teach me how to think syntactically.

Finally, I thank Hedwig and Nelson for being there, and for preventing me from thinking syntactically all the time.

Thanks to Brian Robinson, Damien Laflaquière and Liu Zhaojing for pointing out some shortcomings in the text.

Liliane Haegeman
Gentbrugge

1 Introduction: The Scientific Study of Language

Discussion

Contents

0 Introduction: Scope of the Chapter

This chapter is an introduction: it sets the scene for the remainder of the book. The focus of our enquiry in this book is language and in particular we will be interested in the way that words are put together to form sentences. The study of sentence formation is usually referred to as **syntax**.

Syntax is a branch of **linguistics**. In this chapter we discuss the main properties of the methodology used in linguistics. We set the scene for the later chapters in that we will determine how we ought to go about it when studying syntax. The chapter is divided into three sections. In section 1 we discuss the methodological implications of the idea that linguistics is a scientific discipline. We will try to determine what the defining properties of scientific work are and to formulate some guidelines for our own work. Using the example of question formation in English, section 2 offers an illustration of the scientific methodology used in linguistics. Section 3 shows why, even when concentrating on the formation of English sentences, it is important to extend the data we examine beyond Modern English. Section 4 is a summary.[1]

1 Linguistics as the Science of Language

1.1 Linguistics as a science

1.1.1 SOME DEFINITIONS

Syntax, the area of study we are concerned with in this book, is a domain of linguistics. When we look up the word *linguistics* in a dictionary we find definitions such as the following:

---

[1] In this book footnotes will be used for the following purposes:

- to add various comments to the text – notes 2 and 6 of this chapter are examples;
- to refer to earlier or later sections in the book in which the issue under consideration or a related issue is discussed – notes 8 and 9 of this chapter are examples;
- to point the reader to relevant exercises – note 4 of this chapter is an example;
- to refer to the literature for more extensive discussion of issues dealt with in the text – notes 3 and 5 of this chapter are examples. In general the references will offer a more complete survey of the data and/or a more sophisticated theoretical analysis. The texts referred to will usually be more advanced and will probably not be accessible to the student-reader, at least not at the early stages of the book. When a text is itself introductory (and hence accessible) this will be signaled in the note.

Linguistics   (i)   The science of language(s), esp. as regards nature and structure. (*Concise Oxford Dictionary* (*COD*) 1976: 632)

(ii)   The study of human speech in its various aspects (as the units, nature, structure, and modification of language, languages, or a language including esp. such factors as phonetics, phonology, morphology, accent syntax, semantics, general or philosophical grammar, and the relation between writing and speech) – called also *linguistic science, science of language.* (*Webster's Third New International Dictionary of the English Language* 1981: vol. II, 1317)

(iii)   The study of language in general and of particular languages, their structures, grammar etc. (*Longman Dictionary of English Language and Culture* (*LDOCE*) 1998: 767)

The three definitions are similar, but careful readers may have observed that definitions (i) and (ii) contain the word *science*, and that the word is absent from definition (iii). Before we conclude that this means that the compilers of the *COD* and those of Webster's dictionary used to think that linguistics was a scientific enterprise but that those compiling the Longman dictionary no longer do, consider that in English other scientific fields of study are also referred to by words ending in *-ics*: physics and mathematics, for instance. The gloss for the ending *-ics* in the Longman dictionary is as follows:

-ics   1. The scientific study or use of ___: *linguistics* (the study of language), *electronics* (the study or making of apparatus that uses CHIPS, TRANSISTORS etc.), *acoustics* . . . (*LDOCE*: 1566)

In other words, combining Longman's definition (iii) of *linguistics* with its gloss for the ending *-ics*, we can conclude that the Longman dictionary makers also consider linguistics to be the scientific study of language.

Since dictionary makers try to reflect actual usage of language, linguistics can plausibly be defined as the science of language or the scientific study of language. However, while it is easy to provide such a definition of the discipline, it is much harder to go beyond that and to explain what it is that linguists do and in what way their work is supposed to be "scientific." Commenting on this point the English linguist David Crystal says:

Linguistics, indeed, usually defines itself with reference to this criterion [being scientific]: it is the scientific study of language. But this is a deceptively simple statement; and understanding exactly what anyone is committed to once he decides to do linguistics is an important step, an essential preliminary to any insight into the essence of the subject. What are the scientific characteristics that make the modern approach to language study what it is? (Crystal 1971: 77)

Before embarking on the study of syntax, which is the branch of linguistics that concentrates on the formation of sentences, we should try to clarify what makes a branch of study scientific. Once we have done that, it will be easier to understand why linguists in general, and syntacticians in particular, go about their work the way they do. Note that the brief presentation of our interpretation of the concept "science" is not at all an attempt to offer an introduction into the philosophy of science. Rather, by stepping back and reflecting for a moment on what we normally see as the defining properties of science, we can try to isolate the main features of the scientific method and then try to implement these same features when studying syntax.

Below are some definitions of the notion "science," taken from various written sources. Read them carefully and identify what you think the key concepts in these definitions are. Pay particular attention to concepts that occur more than once.

(1) Systematic and formulated knowledge, pursuit of this or principles regulating such pursuit. Branch of knowledge (esp. one that can be conducted on scientific principles), or organised body of knowledge that has been accumulated on a subject. (*COD*: 1066)

(2) Accumulated and accepted knowledge that has been systematized and formulated with reference to the discovery of general truths or the operation of natural laws; knowledge classified and made available in work, life, or the search for truth; . . . knowledge obtained and tested through the scientific method. (*Webster's Third New International Dictionary of the English Language* 1981: vol. II, 2032)

(3) Science is a hunt for order, explanation and regularity. It explains the anomalous by reference to the law it seeks to establish. (Hywel Williams, *Guardian*, 7.8.2002, p. 8, col. 7)

(4) Science, by definition, is the search for order in nature. (Newmeyer 1983: 41)

The concepts that occur frequently in the definitions above have been isolated and grouped:

knowledge (1), (2);
pursuit (1), hunt (3), search (2), (4), seek (3);
explanation (3);
laws of nature, natural laws (2), general truths (2), law (3);
order (3), (4), regularity (3), systematic (1), (2);
formulate/formulation (1), (2).

Not surprisingly, these extracts converge on the key concepts associated with science. They all agree that science aims at achieving knowledge and that science is an activity. Science is not an inert state of knowledge; science means doing something, engaging in some activity. Scientific activity is defined as a "search," a "hunt," a "pursuit"; in other words science is the active pursuit of a goal. Combining these two concepts we can say that the search undertaken by the scientist has as its goal "knowledge," but the kind of knowledge that is achieved is in itself dynamic. The goal of scientists is not merely taking note of and recording certain phenomena and thus "knowing" about them: scientists want to explain the phenomena they have observed. Explanation leads to understanding: scientists want to understand why the phenomena observed are the way they are.

1.1.2   EXPLANATION: AN EXAMPLE

To clarify the notion "explanation" let us look at an example. We start from the following very simple observation. Snow that has fallen overnight often turns into water during the day. We refer to this natural phenomenon as "melting": a solid matter gradually turns into a liquid. When dealing with such a natural phenomenon, scientists will not be satisfied with mere observation. They will want to understand it. They will want to explain why the snow has melted and why other solid matters, say, a glass or a plastic cup or the mud in the garden or the sand on the beach or the tarmac on the roads, have not melted at the same time and/or in the same manner. Scientists will also want to understand why snow melts on certain days, but does not melt on other days. In order to explain the phenomenon observed scientists will try to relate it to other phenomena. So the goal of scientists will be to find the cause of the phenomenon observed. For our example, a fairly plausible hypothesis could be that snow melts on a certain day because during the day the temperature has risen, and as a result the snow reaches the critical temperature at which it turns into water, its melting point. If that particular temperature is not attained, snow will not melt. Scientists might formulate the hypothesis that there is a causal link between temperature and the solid/liquid states observed.

Scientists will not stop at snow turning into water. They will view the melting of snow in more general terms; they will look at other solids and examine whether these also change into liquids when heated. Metals, for instance, such as iron or steel or copper, also melt, but they require a much higher temperature than snow. In order to find out whether particular metals melt or not, scientists cannot just patiently wait and hope to come across them melting. For instance, if the melting point of a particular solid matter is 100 degrees centigrade, this temperature cannot be met with in everyday circumstances, even on a hot day. To go beyond the mere observation of phenomena in the natural environment and to find out more about melting temperatures, scientists can resort to experiments: they heat solids to a certain temperature and observe and record what happens. While doing so, scientists rely on the generalized hypothesis that all solids will melt under certain well-defined conditions, namely when they reach a critical temperature, their melting point.

As mentioned, when trying to assess the melting points of individual matters, scientists do not just wait for things to happen. Rather, what they do is create the relevant circumstances that can trigger the process under examination, in other words they will run an experiment. But note that before doing the experiment, scientists must already have some idea what the relevant factors will be. For instance, if scientists think that heat is responsible for the melting process, they will apply heat to the material and they will keep all other elements constant. The experiment is guided by a **hypothesis,** namely that solids melt when heated to a critical point. The goal of the experiment is (i) to test the general hypothesis that all solids melt when they are at some particular temperature, and (ii) to identify the relevant critical temperature.

What scientists are doing is looking for **regularities** (here that all solids liquefy at a certain point), for systematic **patterns.** Scientists try to formulate **general laws** to cover the facts they observe. They are looking for **order.** In our example, these laws establish relations between temperature–matter–melting. We provide an **explanation** if we can account for the phenomena, if we can say that snow melts because the temperature rises above 0°C and that 0°C is the melting point of snow. On the other hand, a silver bracelet will not melt in the same circumstances because its melting point is much higher.

Scientists will not stop at the inventory of melting points. Having confirmed that a series of solids melt when heated to certain temperatures, they will then want to explain why different materials have different melting points. Again they will try to answer this question by observation, experimentation, and by forming hypotheses which they put to the test.

As a further step scientists will try to explain the difference in the melting points by looking more closely at the nature of the different materials under examination. Ultimately, they will devise an account which not only explains why the matters that have been observed melt at a particular temperature but they will also try to **predict** melting points for matters that they may come across in future. For instance, they will predict the melting point of a metal that consists of two parts zinc and one part copper. Note that this means in fact that by identifying a melting point for a solid matter scientists predict when the solid matter will melt and they also predict when it will not melt, i.e. when it remains solid. Once again, the prediction will be tested by experimentation.

1.1.3 LANGUAGE PHENOMENA: AN EXAMPLE

1.1.3.1 *Ambiguity*

The object matter that is studied in linguistics is language. If linguistics is a science, then we should not simply make an inventory of linguistic phenomena (i.e. language facts) and describe them but we also want to explain them. Let us just look at a simple point here to illustrate the nature of the task that awaits the linguist. Consider example (5a), taken from a British newspaper. How does this extract refer to the protesters? What kind of individuals would qualify as the relevant protesters?

(5) a Manchester's morning rush-hour traffic was brought to a near standstill yesterday as 150 black cab drivers staged a go-slow protest calculated to cause maximum disruption to commuters. (*Guardian*, 14.9.2000, p. 4, cols 2–3)

In the extract, the protesters are described by means of the string of words *150 black cab drivers*. What kind of individuals does this string pick out? The string of words *150 black cab drivers* has two interpretations or two **readings**: in one reading we are referring to 'those who drive cabs and are of a specific ethnic origin', and in the other we are referring to 'those who drive cabs which are of a particular color'. In both readings, the adjective *black* distinguishes the drivers in question from others: in the first reading the distinctive feature is the color of the driver's skin, and in the second it is the color of his cab. In example (5a) both readings are available.

Observe that the extract above is taken from a British newspaper. In Britain, taxis are indeed often black. But even in a context in which taxis tend to be a different color, say yellow, the string *150 black cab drivers* still potentially has the two interpretations described above. Linguistically speaking, the string is ambiguous regardless of which color taxis actually are.

The question arises why the string *150 black cab drivers* has these two interpretations. Are all strings of words necessarily ambiguous in this way? If not, what is the cause of the ambiguity of this example? Could it be the word *cab*, another word for *taxi*, that causes the ambiguity? To find out if the use of the word *cab* is at the basis of the ambiguity, we can experiment with the sentence and replace the word *cab* with the word *taxi*. Consider (5b): is this sentence ambiguous?

(5) b   Manchester's morning rush-hour traffic was brought to a near standstill yesterday as <u>150 black taxi drivers</u> staged a go-slow protest calculated to cause maximum disruption to commuters.

(5b) remains ambiguous. The presence of the word *cab* in (5a) as such is not the cause of the ambiguity. Does the presence of the numeral *150* have anything to do with the ambiguity? Or could the ambiguity be due to the fact that the noun *driver* is in the plural? Neither of these is probably at the basis of the ambiguity; to confirm this intuition let us again experiment with the sentences above. It is clear that both (5c), without the numeral *150*, and (5d), with a singular noun *driver*, remain ambiguous.

(5) c   Manchester's morning rush-hour traffic was brought to a near standstill yesterday as <u>black cab drivers</u> staged a go-slow protest calculated to cause maximum disruption to commuters.

  d   Manchester's morning rush-hour traffic was brought to a near standstill yesterday as <u>a black cab driver</u> staged a go-slow protest calculated to cause maximum disruption to commuters.

Can we reword the string *150 black cab drivers* and make it unambiguous? One option is shown in (5e):

(5) e   Manchester's morning rush-hour traffic was brought to a near standstill yesterday as <u>150 drivers of black cabs</u> staged a go-slow protest calculated to cause maximum disruption to commuters.

Table 1 Classification of examples

Number	Example	Ambiguous?
(5a)	*150 black cab drivers*	+
(5b)	*150 black taxi drivers*	+
(5c)	*black cab drivers*	+
(5d)	*a black cab driver*	+
(5e)	*150 drivers of black cabs*	−

At this point, we could inventorize our observations and come up with the classification in Table 1. Why is (5e) no longer ambiguous? And why are the other examples ambiguous? The ambiguity relates to the position of the adjective *black* in relation to the other words of the segment. In the ambiguous cases *black* precedes *cab driver(s)* and it may either be taken to modify a string *cab driver(s)*, in which case *black* refers to the ethnic origin of the driver(s), or it may be taken to modify the noun *cab*, in which case it refers to the color of the cab. We can show these relations by using **square brackets** as in (6).

(6) a   150 [[black cab] drivers]
     b   150 [black [cab drivers]]

Square brackets show the grouping of words into larger units: in (6a) *black* is combined with *cab*, giving the unit [*black cab*]. The meaning of the unit [*black cab*] is calculated on the basis of the combination of the meanings of its component parts, the words *black* and *cab*. The meaning of *black* combines with the meaning of *cab*: in this grouping *black* refers to the color of the cab. The unit [*black cab*] is then grouped with *drivers* to form a more comprehensive unit [[*black cab*] *drivers*]. The meaning of the resulting unit is again based on that of its component parts: (i) *black cab*, and (ii) *drivers*. With the grouping in (6a), *black cab drivers* denotes a driver of black cabs.

In (6b) on the other hand, *cab* is first combined with *drivers* to form [*cab drivers*]. The meaning of this unit is calculated on the basis of the meaning of its two component parts *cab* and *drivers*: here *cab drivers* denotes people who drive cabs. Then we combine the unit [*cab drivers*] with the adjective *black* to form [*black* [*cab drivers*]]. Again the meaning of *black cab drivers* is based on that of its component parts, (i) *black* and (ii) *cab drivers*. In the grouping in (6b), the adjective *black* modifies the unit *cab drivers*; *black cab drivers* now denotes cab drivers who are black.

The fact that two groupings of words are available for one string of words is the cause of the ambiguity of the string. So we explain the observed ambiguity by relating it to a particular cause: the internal organization or **structure** of the string.

The ambiguity in the relevant examples is said to be **structural**. This means that we must assume that the relations between words have an impact on their interpretation: the string *150 + black + cab + drivers* has two meanings because the words in the string can be combined with each other in two different ways.

To remove the ambiguity we can combine the words *black, cab, drivers* differently, as shown in (5e). In (5e) the adjective *black* precedes *cabs* and it does not precede the noun *drivers*. In this example the adjective *black* is related uniquely to *cab*, and only one reading is available, the reading corresponding to that of (6a).

(6) c   150 drivers of [black cabs]

The following extract confirms the potential for ambiguity of the example in (5a):

(7) a   A few years ago a newspaper article about the dangers of women riding alone in cabs brought a long and furious tirade from a reader incensed by the way the drivers had been racially described. In fact the article had been using the phrase "black cab drivers" to differentiate those working in hackney cabs from mini-cab drivers. (*Independent*, 13.10.2000, Review, p. 5, col. 2)

Example (5a) actually appeared in the context (7b). In that context, a reader confronted with the ambiguous sentence (5a) would immediately have been able to select the appropriate grouping of the words with the associated reading: in (7b) reference is made to "black cabs," making *black* distinctive as a color of cabs.

(7) b   More than 70 black cabs travelled under police escort from Manchester airport to the city, driving four abreast and slowing early morning traffic to a 10mph crawl. (*Guardian*, 14.9.2000, p. 4, cols 2–3)

Examine the caption in (8a) which was used to characterize a person on TV: in what way is it ambiguous? What could be the cause of the ambiguity?

(8) a   a tall rose grower (BBC 1 television, 31.7.2002 (News, South))

The person we are talking about, the "referent" of the string of words in (8a), could be either a person of any height who grows tall roses (8b), or a tall person who grows roses of any height (8c).[2] We can again relate the ambiguity of (8a) to the structure of the sequence of words: that is, to the different ways the words *tall, rose,* and *grower* can be combined. In (8b) and (8c) square brackets again represent the two structures. In (8b) we first combine *tall* with *rose*, giving the unit *tall rose*. In this unit the adjective *tall* modifies *rose*: it denotes the size of the rose. This unit is in

---

[2]   In the particular BBC broadcast the first reading was intended: the speciality of the particular gardener was growing tall roses.

turn combined with *grower*. The person denoted by this string of words grows tall roses. According to the grouping in (8c), *rose* first combines with *grower*, giving the unit *rose grower*. This unit denotes a person who grows roses. The adjective *tall* then combines with *rose grower*. In the second combination, *tall* modifies the unit *rose grower*, the adjective indicates the size of the rose grower.

(8) b   a [[tall rose] grower]
     c   a [tall [rose grower]]

Strings of words are sometimes ambiguous, and the ambiguity of the particular examples examined above was due to the organization of these words into larger units, their structure. In both the examples, *black cab drivers* and *tall rose grower*, the ambiguity is related to the sequencing of the combination of the elements. This means that the interpretation of a string of words is not merely the left-to-right sum of the interpretations of the individual words. It also depends on how the words are put together. We could think of a mathematical analogy here. The formula $(A - B) - C$ is not identical to the formula $A - (B - C)$. When $A = 6$, $B = 3$, and $C = 2$, for instance, the first equation equals 1, and the second equals 5. We can make this observation into a more general hypothesis and propose that in language, interpretation depends on the way the strings of words are composed, namely their structure:

(9) **Compositionality**
     The meaning of a string of words is determined **compositionally**; i.e. it is
     determined by its component parts and by their relations.

1.1.3.2   The data

Out of context, the string *150 black cab drivers* (5a) has two interpretations; the string *150 drivers of black cabs* (5e) does not. This is a **fact** of language. We offered a first explanation in terms of the grouping of the words contained in the string. Before we continue the discussion, it is useful to think again about the kind of language material we have been using. Did we restrict ourselves to observing the language material available? Or did we also use experimental facts?

Sentence (5a) is an **attested** example, it was found in a newspaper. As speakers of English we are able to interpret it and we can assign two interpretations to it. In other words, we use our intuitions about the interpretation of the string. The dual reading of the example is due to the fact that there is an ambiguous string in the sentence, *150 black cab drivers*. We have relied on material found, an attested sentence, but not only that: we also rely on our linguistic competence. As speakers of English, we can work with the observed material: we assign an interpretation to the strings of words, and, using our knowledge of the language, we are able to reformulate these strings and compare the interpretations of various strings. Sentence (5a) does not come with a warning that it is ambiguous. We rely on our intuitions about the language to decide on its interpretation.

Sentences (5b–e) are not attested examples. Relying on our competence as speakers of English, we have constructed these sentences ourselves, using (5a) as our inspiration. If we want to understand why a sentence is ambiguous, we will not just examine it as it is. We will play around with the example, to see whether we can construct similarly ambiguous sentences, or ones that are unambiguous. We **experiment** with the data, relying on our **competence** of the language.[3]

As linguists we will, among other things, want to look at data such as those in (5) and try to explain why examples (5a–d) are ambiguous and why example (5e) is not. We rely on our own intuitions concerning attested data, and also on experimental data (sentences which we construct ourselves).

Though attested data may be useful, we definitely cannot confine or research to them. In addition to playing around with attested examples, as we have done above, we can also just construct examples "out of the blue" and experiment with them. For example, the string in (10a), which is again ambiguous, is not an attested example. It is a constructed example which serves to illustrate once again how the different groupings of words lead to ambiguity:

(10) a   a Flemish language teacher
      b   a [Flemish language] teacher
      c   a Flemish [language teacher]

1.1.3.3   Predictions

Recall that one of the goals of a scientific approach is also to predict what is possible and what is not possible. For instance, the melting point of a metal predicts both at which temperature the metal will melt and when it will not melt. Similarly, when dealing with language data we want to elaborate predictions. For instance, taking our example above, we don't only want to account for the ambiguity of a particular example, but we also want to predict when strings of words will be ambiguous. Based on the attested examples in (5a–d) and in (8a) and on the constructed example in (10a) we could formulate a first hypothesis that a string of words composed of the sequence adjective – noun – noun may lead to ambiguity. The ambiguity of such sequences is due to the fact that the adjective either bears on the noun that it immediately precedes or it bears on the combination of the two nouns that it precedes:

(11) a   [[adjective noun] noun]]
      b   [adjective [noun noun]

Thus we generalize our findings and go beyond the description of some individual examples (attested or constructed) to formulate general principles. (11c–g) contains

---

[3]   On the use of intuitions and attested data see also the recent (and fairly accessible) discussions in Borsley and Ingham (2002, 2003), Stubbs (2002), Lehmann (2004), and the papers in Penke and Rosenbach (2004).

some additional constructed examples of the same sequence adjective – noun – noun and indeed these examples are also ambiguous.[4]

(11) c a French art student
     d an American literature teacher
     e an Italian restaurant owner
     f a Dutch bicycle maker
     g a trendy furniture designer

The example in (5e), which was not ambiguous and which we repeat here in (11h), does not display the relevant sequence. Here the adjective *black* preceded just the one noun *cabs*, which it modifies.

(11) h 150 drivers of black cabs

1.2 *How to go about it*

1.2.1 INDUCTION AND DEDUCTION

From the descriptions above we can also infer how not to proceed in scientific work. To reach the goal of explaining the data that we observe we cannot simply draw up a list of interesting observations. A mere list of phenomena does not lead to any understanding. When discussing an example such as (5a), for instance, we cannot satisfy ourselves with a mere anecdotal description of the example and how it may give rise to ambiguity and to misunderstanding (cf. (7a)). We should try to relate the observed language fact, the ambiguity of the example, to other language facts and to elaborate an explanation that goes beyond example (5a).

A starting point is identification and classification of the data, the material we wish to examine. We may, for instance, identify a set of ambiguous examples and oppose them to a set of non-ambiguous examples. Classification is followed by an attempt at explanation.

---

[4] Exercises 1, 2, and 3. Among other things, footnotes will be used to refer to the exercises. When a footnote reads "Exercise 1" this means that you can try Exercise 1 at that point in the chapter. You are advised to tackle the exercises at two points in time. First you can do each exercise at the point in the chapter when it is signaled by a note. The exercise will allow you to apply what you have just learnt and will provide more illustrations of the concept being discussed. You can also try to do the same exercise later on, when you have covered more ground. Doing this will ensure that you still remember the notions which you have learnt previously.

Sometimes a (partial) key will be provided in the exercises and additional discussion will be added under the heading "Key and comments." These supplementary discussions will alert you to specific points that have not been tackled in the main body of the text. In particular, sometimes such discussions will answer questions that you may have been wondering about.

When research starts from observation of empirical data, the procedure we adopt is referred to as **induction**. This type of approach is captured by Webster's dictionary in the following way:

NATURAL SCIENCE
A branch of study that is concerned with observation and classification of facts and esp. with the establishment or strictly with the quantitative formulation of verifiable general laws chiefly by induction and hypotheses. (*Webster's Third New International Dictionary of the English Language* 1981: vol. III, 2032)

By means of induction we attempt to uncover general principles (or "laws") that underlie the observed phenomena. We formulate hypotheses whose first goal is to account for the observed phenomena. Ideally, however, the hypotheses must always go beyond providing an account for what is observed. We also want to understand why we have observed just those phenomena and not others. We want to be able to predict which alternative phenomena COULD have been observed and which ones would NEVER arise. Put differently, we set out to define the bounds of what is possible.

In our melting point example discussed in section 1.1.2, scientists first observe and classify data in relation to the natural phenomenon of melting. At some point they will have established an inventory of melting points: for instance silver melts at 961°C, while gold only melts at 1063°C and platinum melts at 1769°C. As a second step, an attempt is made to provide an explanation for why silver melts at a lower temperature than gold. This difference will be related to the internal composition of the solid materials studied. A successful analysis should be able to account for the melting temperatures observed and it should also predict when solid matters will melt and when they will not melt. Similarly, when dealing with the ambiguity of (5a) we first classify a sample of language data with respect to their potential for ambiguity. The ambiguity is related to the internal composition of the data analyzed, in particular the ambiguous strings allow for two possible groupings of the sequence adjective – noun – noun. In so doing, we define the bounds of what is possible. We predict that *150 black cab drivers* is ambiguous, because it has the relevant structural property, and that *150 drivers of black cabs* is not ambiguous, because it lacks those properties. Thus, we go beyond the data observed and formulate predictions about what can arise and what will not arise.

When working on the linguistic examples we appealed to some hypotheses about language. For instance, we proposed that words are grouped, that language is structured. We needed these concepts to be able to isolate a string of words *150 black cab drivers*, from a sentence. We appealed to a general concept "**structure**" to refer to groupings of words in the string. But if we appeal to the concept structure, then we need to clarify at least two points. (i) We have to define the nature of linguistic structures, and (ii) we have to be able to make precise how "structure" is mapped into meaning or interpretation. In other words we have to elaborate a theory of language; we need a theory about how linguistic forms are structured and how these structures relate to interpretation. Such a theory will provide the framework for the discussion and explanation of the data examined.

Scientific work is guided both by **empirical** considerations (observation of data and experimentation) and by **theoretical** concepts. With respect to linguistics, the interplay between empirical data and theory is expressed very clearly in the following extract by the Dutch linguist Simon Dik:

> In linguistics, as in other sciences, there is an essential interaction between data analysis and theory formation: an adequate analysis of the data of some particular language is impossible without some general theoretical insight into the principles underlying the structure and functioning of language in general; on the other hand, an adequate development of general linguistic theory presupposes the meticulous analysis of the facts of particular languages. (Dik 1989: 33)

In our example above, we proceeded from the observation of empirical data to the formulation of a hypothesis which provides an explanation of these data. This way of working is called induction. The combination of several hypotheses about a certain domain of enquiry (here language) gives rise to a more comprehensive network of hypotheses, a **theory**.

Having formulated a set of principles that are part of a theory, scientists (and hence linguists) may also proceed to working "**deductively**." That means that they examine a particular component of their theory (that is the network of hypotheses). Their aim will be to examine how the hypotheses that have been formulated interact with each other. For instance, they may look for internal inconsistencies that arise when two hypotheses lead to contradictory predictions. They may also examine whether there is any overlap between the different components of the theory, when the same facts are explained by two different hypotheses. This type of theoretical work may lead to the reformulation of some components of the theory. Thus novel hypotheses may emerge from theoretically oriented work and these new hypotheses will themselves have to be tested on the basis of the empirical data. Once again the data examined may consist of attested language material or of constructed language material.

In science, experimental, data-driven work and theoretical work continuously interact. Hypotheses are formulated on the basis of the observed data and these hypotheses are integrated into the theory. The theory itself is examined and streamlined; theoreticians formulate predictions on the basis of the reformulated theories and their predictions are tested by observations and experiments.[5]

1.2.2 EXPLICITNESS, SYSTEMATICITY

In our list of essential concepts in the definitions (1)–(4), we also signaled the terms *formulate* and *formulation* ((1), (2)). Some extracts from the dictionary definitions of the verb *formulate* that are relevant here are given in (12):

---

[5] For a general discussion of the relative impact of induction and deduction in various present day approaches to linguistics see also Stuurman (1989).

(12) *formulate*   a   Longman   to express in an exact way
                    b   COD   set forth systematically
                    c   Webster   put into a systematized statement or expression

The definitions of *formulate* refer to expressing something systematically and in an exact way. Scientists have to formulate, i.e. to state, their basic assumptions, their hypotheses, their procedures, and their results precisely and explicitly. This will enable other scientists working in the same area to evaluate the work, to repeat experiments on which the research is based, and either to accept and implement (parts of) the findings contained in the work or to challenge them. To put it more succinctly: scientific research is "capable of replication and subject to peer review."[6]

In order to guarantee that their research can be replicated and reviewed by their peers, linguists also have to formulate their findings as precisely and explicitly as possible. Sometimes, mathematical types of formulae are used in linguistics. This is not really a requirement of scientific methodology, but it is a natural by-product of the wish to be as precise as possible. By using exact and generally unambiguous formulae, scientists ensure that there is clarity as to the interpretation of their statements.

Note that the term *formulate* implies a pre-requirement that scientists be able to define the terms they use. They must be able to describe their procedures, argumentation, etc. They cannot satisfy themselves with a vague description of results without, for instance, stating exactly how experiments were run and how the results were obtained. For linguistics, the same requirements of explicitness apply. Simply saying that (5a) has two interpretations and that this is due to the adjective *black* modifying either the noun *cab* or the noun *cab drivers* is not going to be sufficient. We must express quite precisely how the relation of modification is encoded in language. In our representation of the structure, we have tried to represent this by the squared bracketing convention, which is used to represent the grouping of words into units.[7]

Another point that comes up regularly in the definitions of the scientific enterprise is the concept **systematicity** (see definitions (1) and (2) and also (12c)). The linguist David Crystal (1971: 90) says: "The need to study phenomena using a procedure which is as methodical and standardized as possible is . . . obvious enough." He goes on to underline the importance of an underlying descriptive framework that provides the system in which the research is inscribed. Systematicity implies systemizing, i.e., looking at things against the background of a system. "Systemizing is the drive to analyse and explore a system, to extract underlying rules that govern the behaviour of a system" (Simon Baron-Cohen, *Guardian*, G2, 17.4.2003, p. 12, col. 1).

1.2.3   ELEGANCE, PARSIMONY, ECONOMY

It often happens that a number of scientists (or linguists) are simultaneously trying to account for a particular set of data and that each comes up with a different account

---

[6]   Citation due to Dr David Gosling, letter to the editor: *Independent*, 15.7.2004, p. 22, col. 2.
[7]   A very accessible preliminary discussion of requirements in scientific work is given in Crystal (1971: 77–127).

for these data. Scientists will often be seen to elaborate competing accounts. The question arises of how to choose between competing accounts. What would make one explanation or one theory better than another? Newmeyer says:

> Science, by definition, is the search for order in nature. Scientists take it for granted that their goal is to formulate the most elegant (i.e. the most order reflecting) hypothesis possible, consistent with the data, about the particular area under investigation. (Newmeyer 1983: 41)

Let us go back to our example of the melting of snow. The initial observation was that the snow that had fallen overnight may melt during the day. Scientists working on this issue and who observe that snow melts when the sun comes up might have proposed that the melting process is due to the length of exposure to sunlight. In other words, they explain the melting by two factors: (i) sunlight, (ii) time. Even though these scientists might also be able to account for the observed fact, snow melting during the day, their account is not as highly valued as the one we elaborated above because it invokes two factors, sunlight and time, rather than one, temperature. If two accounts cover the same sets of facts, then an account relying on one factor is better than an account that requires two. Ultimately, in fact, the account which accounts for the melting of snow relying on sunlight and time can be reduced to an account in terms of temperature, because sunlight will give rise to an increase in the temperature. But we know that sunlight as such is not essential for snow to melt: a sudden increase in the temperature overnight will also make snow melt. Explanations and theories should use as few rules/principles as possible to account for the data.

The idea that scientific explanation should be as simple as possible is not new, it is sometimes referred to as "Ockham's Razor," due to the English theologian and philosopher William of Ockham (c.1285–1349), who said that *entia non sunt multiplicanda praeter necessitatem* – 'entities are not to be multiplied unnecessarily.' This means that, all things beings equal, the simpler of two explanations is to be preferred. In the same vein, Newmeyer writes:

> Certain points, I think, are uncontroversial. One is that, given two theories that cover the same range of facts, the one in which the facts follow from a small number of general principles is better than the one that embodies myriad disparate statements and auxiliary hypotheses. Another is that it is methodologically correct to reduce redundancy within a theory, to reduce the number of postulates while preserving the scope of the predictions. (Newmeyer 1983: 41)

Einstein put it more succinctly:

> The grand aim of all science is to cover the greatest possible number of experimental facts by logical deduction from the smallest number of hypotheses or axioms. (Einstein 1954, cited in Abraham et al., 1996: 4)

In linguistics too, we will value an account with a smaller number of rules more than one which requires more rules to explain the same set of data.[8]

1.2.4   DOUBT

A final essential ingredient of scientific work is doubt. This statement may come as a surprise, since a search for knowledge and understanding would at first sight seem to aim at certainty rather than doubt. When we say that doubt is an important component in scientific work this means that we should always remain aware that our answers to problems and the knowledge we acquire are hypotheses. New insights or new developments in research may well mean that we must go back on what we think we know and revise earlier proposals. The journalist Tim Radford cites the scientist Tom McLeish:

> Doubt, expressed most potently 3,000 years ago in the biblical book of Job, is the greatest scientific tool ever invented . . . To do good science you have to doubt every-thing, including your ideas, your experiments, and your conclusions. (*Guardian*, G2, 4.9.2003, p. 12, col. 4)

1.2.5   SUMMARY

In this section we have looked at the idea that linguistics is a science and we have gone over the main properties of the scientific method. Science is based on the interaction of the observation of phenomena ("data") and theory. The observation of data may lead to theoretical proposals or hypotheses. This is described by the term induction. Sets of hypotheses, or theories, may themselves also lead to new hypotheses; this is referred to as deduction. We have also seen that scientific work is systematic and explicit. It aims at providing simple explanations for complex data. We have mentioned that one should not take for granted whatever results one has arrived at and that any kind of research implies that the researcher is willing to question and challenge the results of his or her own work.

In the remainder of this chapter we will illustrate the kind of phenomena, the data, that are dealt with in syntax. We will look at a set of language phenomena and we will try to describe the data and evaluate some explanations for them. In the later chapters of this book, we will elaborate step by step analyses of specific problems, focusing on the overall question of how a sentence is structured. We will try to show in as precise a way as possible how a hypothesis can be developed and evaluated in linguistics, and how the proposals elaborated will lead to the formulation of a more comprehensive theory. We will repeatedly show that once we have developed a certain hypothesis we need to examine its consequences and that we continuously need to reconsider and revise the results of earlier work. The role of doubt in scientific work will thus be made clear throughout the discussion. Note that though

---

[8]   For a concrete illustration of how the criterion of economy or simplicity can apply in syntactic theory see Chapter 2, section 2.4.2.

we will end up providing some interesting insights into language, in this book we are mainly interested in the process of the research, that is, how we have arrived at the results.

2   From Raw Linguistic Data to Generalizations: Word Order in English Questions

In this section we examine another concrete example of how we could go about analyzing language in a scientific way. We choose what looks like a well-known and very simple domain of enquiry, that of English question formation. The goal of the section is to show how even apparently simple linguistic phenomena require the greatest care when it comes to formulating hypotheses. It is important to bear in mind that the goal of this section (and indeed of this book) is not to elaborate a full-fledged and finished analysis of sentence formation, nor do we pretend to arrive at a complete explanation, but rather we try to illustrate one way we can "think" scientifically about language. What we will try to do is to "unpick" our thinking about a phenomenon, to dissect the argumentation into smaller building blocks. We will also show how we may compare various formulations.

In the discussion below it is important to actively try to do the thinking. When a question is raised in the text, first try to answer it before reading the account. It is important, then, to be an active reader who does not simply follow the text but who tries to carefully monitor each step of the discussion.

2.1   *Introduction: Sentence meaning and word meaning*

In the discussion above, we have introduced the idea that language somehow unites "form" with "interpretation." The "forms" of language are ultimately either sounds, or symbols on paper, "letters." Linguistic entities may be associated with interpretation. We say "may" because sounds as such do not necessarily have meaning. For instance, though the sound [a:] happens to correspond to a meaningful unit in many variants of English ("are"), other sounds [b] or [p] do not. Words, on the other hand, are meaningful units: *dog, cat, nose*, etc. are all words with an interpretation.[9] Some words may have the same meaning, for instance *cab* and *taxi*. Such words are said to be synonyms. Some elements may correspond to more than one meaning. A

---

[9]   In Chapter 3, section 3 we will discuss how the kinds of meanings conveyed by words may be made more precise. For instance, the verb *examined* in example (i) seems, at first sight, to contribute more to the message conveyed by the sentence than the auxiliary *have*.

(i)   The students have examined the documents.

classic example is the word *bank*, which may refer to a riverbank or to a financial institution.

Sentences consist of words, and the interpretation of a sentence is calculated (or "computed") on the basis of the combined meanings of the individual words. The words contribute their own meaning to the sentence, and the combination of these individual meanings provides us with the sentence meaning. Going back to (5a), for instance, if you replace the word *cab* by its synonym *taxi* the meaning of the sentence does not change. This is so because the contribution of *cab* to the meaning of the sentence is the same as that of the word *taxi*. If you replace *cab* by a word with a different meaning, say *bus*, then the meaning of the sentence will change:

(5) f   Manchester's morning rush-hour traffic was brought to a near standstill yesterday as 150 black <u>bus</u> drivers staged a go-slow protest calculated to cause maximum disruption to commuters.

Observe that (5f) remains ambiguous. In the sequence *black bus drivers* the adjective *black* might again refer to the ethnic origin of bus drivers, or it might set off black buses from other buses. The latter reading does presuppose that such a taxonomy of buses makes sense; one can easily imagine a context in which black buses might for instance be run by a low-budget company, or that they are specifically used for long-distance travel, etc.

Sentence meaning derives from word meaning. However, we have seen that the meaning of sentences is not simply attained by adding up the meanings of the individual words. The meaning of a sentence is also determined by how the sentence is assembled, how the words are put together. This was illustrated by the discussion of (5a). In order to account for the ambiguity of this example, we elaborated the hypothesis that words in a sentence are grouped; in other words, they form units, which we indicated by means of square brackets: we repeat (6a–b) here as (13a–b):

(13) a   150 [[black cab] drivers]
      b   150 [black [cab drivers]]

(13a) serves to show that in the sequence adjective – noun – noun, the adjective *black* is grouped with the noun *cab*: the string *black cab* is a unit inside the larger unit *black cab drivers*. In this structuring of the words, *black* modifies *cab*; *black* refers to the color of the cab. In (13b) the noun *cab* is structured with the noun *drivers*, and to this unit is added a specification of color. *Cab* narrows down the type of driver we are talking about. In (13b) *black* modifies *cab driver*; *black* indicates the ethnic origin of the drivers. So sentence meaning is based (i) on the meaning of the individual words, and (ii) on the way these words have been assembled into larger units. The technical term to refer to the way words are assembled into sentences is *syntax*, which is based on Greek συν ("*sun*") 'together' and τασσω (*"tassoo"*) 'put, arrange in a particular order'. In the next section we will explore further the idea that syntax determines sentence meaning.

2.2   Question formation

2.2.1   SUBJECT-AUXILIARY INVERSION

Consider the underlined sections in the following short extract: What does the punctuation mark "?" at the end signal? Suppose you replace the symbol "?" by the full stop. How would you minimally have to change the sentences?

(14)   She had meant to drive down to the quay and regain the yacht, but she now had the immediate impression that something more was to happen first. "<u>Which way are you going? Shall we walk a bit</u>?" he began . . . (Edith Wharton, *The House of Mirth*, 1998: 201)

We refer to the symbol "?" as a "question mark" because this symbol occurs at the end of a sentence which is used to ask a question. Sentences ending in a question mark convey that there is a certain amount of information which the speaker/writer doesn't have and he or she is trying to make the interlocutor supply that missing information. In the extract (14) the speaker ("he") asks two questions of his interlocutor ("she"). Let us isolate the questions in (14) and look at their form more closely.

(15) a   Shall we walk a bit?
      b   Which way are you going?

If we merely replace the question mark by a full stop and do nothing else, the sentences do not really work any more. There is something wrong with them; they are not really **acceptable** sentences of English. In (15c, d) below we use the asterisk (*) to signal that we find a sentence unacceptable. In fact, care must be taken here. Of course, the sequences of words in (15c, d) are as such not unacceptable, since they are perfectly natural questions (15a, b), but the problem with (15c, d) is that by removing the question marks and replacing them with full stops, we signal that the sentences should no longer be interpreted as questions. The asterisks in (15c, d) mean that these sentences become unacceptable if not interpreted as questions.

(15) c   *Shall we walk a bit.
      d   *Which way are you going.

To repair the sentences in (15c, d) we could propose the rewordings in (15e, f). These sentences can be used as **assertions**; they are not normally used as questions. The speaker does not indicate that he or she expects a response from the interlocutor; he or she simply affirms something. The sentences in (15a, b) are **interrogative** sentences, those in (15e, f) are **declarative**.[10]

(15) e   We shall walk a bit.
      f   You are going this way.

Compare the forms of (15c, d) and of (15e, f). We see that the sentences in (15e, f) begin with the pronouns *we* and *you*; these pronouns function as the **subjects** of the sentence. The subjects are followed by *shall* and *are*, elements referred to as **auxiliaries**. A provisional (and very approximate) characterization of auxiliaries, to be refined in Chapter 3, is that they are elements that are typically followed by a verb: *shall* is followed by the verb *walk*, *are* is followed by the verb *going*.[11] The examples above show that the relative positions of the subject and the auxiliary in a declarative sentence are different from those in an interrogative sentence. Consider the extracts in (16). Identify the questions. For each question locate the subject and the auxiliary.

(16) a   Eventually the waitress came out of the kitchen with a tray the size of a
           table-top . . . "Can I get you anything else?" she said. "No, this is just fine,
           thank you." . . . "Would you like some ketchup?" "No, thank you." (Bill
           Bryson, *The Lost Continent*, 1990: 159)
      b   The people of Toronto are not wearing masks . . . Are we taking precau-
           tions such as washing our hands? Of course. Are we stopping our lives
           because of this? Certainly not. (*Guardian*, 26.4.2003, p. 11, col. 6, letter to
           the editor from Michelle Lee, Toronto)
      c   What are my borrowing options? . . . How much can I afford? . . . Where
           do I begin? (*New York Times*, 28.4.2003, p. A22, advertisement Fleet)
      d   Can she be held accountable for the problems that today's nurses are grap-
           pling with? (*Washington Post*, 29.4.2003, p. F1, col. 2)

The declarative sentences contain no special marking of the declarative force, the interrogative pattern is signaled by the word order: the auxiliary precedes the subject. We might propose that the interrogative pattern is formed by changing the position of the auxiliary with respect to that of the subject. We refer to this process as **subject-auxiliary inversion**, abbreviated as **SAI**. Now how exactly does SAI work? In a declarative sentence we find the order in (17a), in a question we get (17b):

(17) a   declarative: subject – auxiliary
      b   interrogative: auxiliary – subject   (SAI)

----

[10]   In the following discussion we will often equate the concepts "question" and "interrogative
       sentence." This equation would have to be challenged in a more careful analysis and we should
       make a distinction between the two concepts. However in the framework of what we are
       trying to do in this chapter the distinction is not crucial. For a good and accessible discussion
       see Huddleston (1994).
[11]   Exercise 4.

Suppose we start from the order in the declarative sentence (17a) and try to attain ("derive" to use the technical term) the order in the question (17b). How can we relate the order in (17b) to that in (17a)? There are basically three options, which are schematically summarized in (18). (18) contains three hypotheses about how the order auxiliary – subject is formed or **derived**. The arrows are intended to show the **derivations**, that is, which constituent is moved and where it is moved. According to (18a), the auxiliary is moved to a position to the left of the subject; according to (18b), the subject moves to a position to the right of the auxiliary; according to (18c) subject and auxiliary switch places.

(18)   SAI

a	declarative sentence		subject	auxiliary	verb
	interrogative sentence	auxiliary	subject		verb

$\longleftarrow$

b	declarative sentence	subject	auxiliary		verb
	interrogative sentence		auxiliary	subject	verb

$\longrightarrow$

c	declarative sentence	subject	auxiliary		verb
	interrogative sentence	auxiliary	subject		verb

$\longleftarrow\longrightarrow$

How can we decide between these derivations? For examples like those in (16) it is not clear how to decide. The three alternatives will produce the same end result: the subject will end up to the right of the auxiliary. How could we differentiate the three alternatives? In order to find out which of the three hypotheses is preferable we will run an experiment. We will create a sentence in which the outcome of the three procedures in (18) would be different. Here's an idea. Suppose we had a declarative sentence in which something intervened between the subject and the auxiliary, then the outcome of the different operations in (18) would be distinct. Consider the following example:

(19)   These new shops definitely are doing well.

Let us try out the three derivations for SAI illustrated in (18) on the basis of example (19). Each derivation leads to a different pattern, as illustrated by (20). In (20a) the auxiliary moves to a position to the left of the subject; in (20b) the subject moves to a position to the right of the auxiliary; in (20c) the subject and the auxiliary switch places. The acceptable word order is that in (20a). What would you conclude with respect to the precise formulation of SAI?

(20) a   Are these new shops definitely —— doing well?

$\longleftarrow$

   b   *—— Definitely are these new shops doing well?

$\longrightarrow$

c   *Are definitely these new shops doing well?

The data in (20) show that SAI is an operation in which the auxiliary moves from a position to the right of the subject to a position to its left. We can now formulate a rule for the derivation of interrogative sentences in English as in (21a). To this we also add a specific formulation for deriving the order auxiliary – subject. (21b) makes explicit what the process of SAI involves.

(21) a   Interrogative sentences are formed by means of SAI.
     b   SAI: move the auxiliary leftward across the subject.[12]

To further test (21), we can invent additional examples with auxiliaries and check whether the corresponding questions would be formed by moving the auxiliary to the left of the subject. For example:

(22) a   The murderer has broken the window.
     b   The murderer was arrested last night.
     c   We really must go to that meeting.

The prediction of (21) is that questions corresponding to (22) will be as in (22′):

(22) a′   Has the murderer broken the window?
     b′   Was the murderer arrested last night?
     c′   Must we really go to that meeting?

(21) formulates a hypothesis for turning a declarative sentence into an interrogative sentence. Examples (22a′–c′) are compatible with this hypothesis. Observe that underlying the hypothesis is a much more general hypothesis that form (word order) and meaning are related. An additional underlying assumption in (21b) is that in SAI the position of the subject and that of the verb are themselves unaffected by SAI, only the auxiliary moves. SAI affects certain elements of the sentence but not others.

2.2.2   WHEN THERE IS NO AUXILIARY

We started out from the observation that sentences may serve to make a statement, in which case they are declarative, and they may be used to ask a question, in which case they are interrogative. The form of the sentence encodes the difference in interpretation: questions are formed by SAI, that is moving the auxiliary across the subject. The examples in (23) pose a problem for applying SAI (21). Why is that? How would we form the interrogative variant of the sentences?

---

[12]   Exercise 12 provides an additional specification concerning the application of SAI.

(23) a   He wants to buy a house this year.
     b   She wanted to become a policewoman.

The problem with (23) is that the sentences lack an auxiliary. Their interrogative form is given in (24):

(24) a   Does he want to buy a house this year?
     b   Did she want to become a policewoman?

Once again, we see that an element precedes the subject, *does* in (24a) and *did* in (24b). Let us experiment with these sentences. Could the added elements have occurred in the position to the right of the subject?

(25) a   He does want to buy a house this year.
     b   She did want to become a policewoman.

Observe that the additional element *do* is inflected. The form of the ending of the verb in (23) corresponds to that of *do* in (24) and (25): in (23a) the verb *wants* has the third person singular ending -*s*; in (24a) and in (25a) *does* is a third person singular of *do*. Similarly, in (23b) *wanted* is a past tense form of the verb; in (24b) and (25b) *did* is a past tense form of *do*. The present tense form and the past tense form of the verb are called the finite forms of the verb. When a sentence contains a finite verb it is called a finite sentence. In the examples in (24) and (25) a finite form of *do* is accompanied by a non-finite form of the verb *want*.

Apparently, both in questions and in declarative sentences, the elements *does* and *did* can occupy the same positions as elements such as *shall* and *is*, the auxiliaries. We will assume that *does/did* are also auxiliaries. So in interrogative sentences with *do*, an auxiliary element is used to signal interrogative force, and the positions of the subject and the verb (*want* in (24)) do not change.

Things are becoming complex here. When there is an auxiliary in the sentence we move that auxiliary to the left of the subject to form a question. When there is no auxiliary, we insert a form of the auxiliary *do* and invert that with the subject. Could we have inserted *do* in sentences with auxiliaries? If you form questions on the basis of the declaratives in (22), but by inserting *do* to the left of the subject, the resulting patterns are those in (26), none of which is acceptable.

(26) a   *Do we must go to that meeting?
         *Do must we go to that meeting?
         *Must do we go to that meeting?
     b   *Does the murderer has broken the window?
         *Does has the murderer broken the window?
         *Has does the murderer broken the window?
     c   *Did the murderer was arrested last night?
         *Did was the murderer arrested last night?
         *Was did the murderer arrested last night?

Table 2   English question formation

Sentences with auxiliary	Sentences without auxiliary
Subject-auxiliary inversion (21b)	Insert *do* in the auxiliary position Subject-auxiliary inversion (21b)

On the basis of the examples given, we could conclude that questions are encoded by SAI. If there is already an auxiliary in the sentence we invert that auxiliary with the subject, if there is no auxiliary available, we choose a variant of the sentence with the auxiliary *do*, and invert *do* with the subject. We sum up our findings in Table 2. Again, the formulations in this table rely on additional tacit assumptions. For instance, the instruction to "insert *do* in the auxiliary position" implies that a sentence has an "auxiliary position." In more general terms, this implies that we think of sentences in terms of particular positions or slots into which elements are inserted and that certain types of units belong to certain types of positions. In the next chapters we will make these assumptions more explicit.

Obviously, we also want to know why questions are formed using SAI. We want to know why we insert *do* in sentences without auxiliaries. And we want to know why we do not insert *do* in sentences with an auxiliary. We will attempt to formulate a first rough hypothesis, to be refined in later chapters. We will say that questions can be formed by subject-auxiliary inversion. We will further propose that this is because the position to the left of the subject encodes question force.[13] If there is no auxiliary in the sentence, *do* is inserted as a sort of saving device, to enable us to form the question. If there is an auxiliary in the sentence, inserting *do* is uneconomical, since we already have all the ingredients to form a question. We only insert *do* as a **last resort**. We return to this issue later, but it is important to signal here that while formulating the proposal above we have introduced yet another general hypothesis. The idea that we only introduce *do* as a last resort suggests that question formation is somehow guided by a principle of "**economy**," which says "Do not insert elements if you don't need them."

At this stage the discussion of question formation remains highly informal, but hopefully it can serve to illustrate how we proceed when elaborating hypotheses in syntax. We start from some data, either attested data or constructed data, or a mixture, and we move on to formulate one or more hypotheses to account for the data. Then we increase the size of the data set and we test our hypothesis, modifying it whenever necessary. While formulating our hypothesis we will probably introduce further theoretical assumptions. We can introduce additional assumptions to enable ourselves to formulate a general rule. For instance, we assume that there is a relation between linguistic form and meaning. However, we must remain vigilant:

---

[13]   For more discussion of this idea see Chapter 5.

we should be aware of any additional assumptions that we have been relying on and we should be prepared to examine these additional hypotheses themselves, possibly at some later stage. When evaluating a particular hypothesis, we examine its empirical coverage (the data which it can account for) and we also have to examine what additional assumptions we have been relying on. It will be important to keep track of any additional hypotheses because we need to make sure, for instance, that they do not lead to contradictions in our system.

2.2.3 LANGUAGE AND ECONOMY

The idea that we only introduce the auxiliary *do* as a "last resort" suggests that question formation is somehow driven by a principle of "economy": "Don't insert forms if you don't need them." If we adopt this principle, another question arises: Is the scope of the principle of economy confined to question formation or does it apply more generally?

Actually, keeping strictly to the use of English *do*, we have already come across examples in which *do* occurs in a non-interrogative form. Was the use of *do* essential in (25)? Or to put it differently: Are the sentences with *do* in (25) and those without *do* in (23) exactly equivalent? If inserting *do* in non-interrogative sentences did not make any difference, then the examples in (25) would contradict the economy principle we have hinted at. They would be **counter-evidence** for the principle of economy. However, when we study the relevant examples carefully we note that the insertion of *do* in (25) (as compared to the original examples (23)) has some inter-pretive effect, though it may be hard to pin down. Try to think of circumstances where (25a) with *do* would be appropriate. One might imagine this in a context such as the conversation in (27), in which doubts have been raised about Bill's intention to buy a house:

(27)   Speaker A: I think Bill has changed his mind about buying a house. He is redecorating his flat.
         Speaker B: He does want to buy a house this year. The redecoration of his flat is because he wants to add to its sales value.

The auxiliary *do* is inserted to strengthen an affirmation against a background in which some doubt has been raised about it. In (27B), the speaker uses *do* to counteract the doubt expressed by the preceding utterance. This suggests that the auxiliary *do* is not completely redundant in declarative examples and declarative sentences containing the auxiliary *do* are not in contradiction with the hypothesis that there is some principle of economy at work in language. Let us therefore maintain the hypothesis that economy is a guiding principle in the formation of sentences.

Consider the underlined examples of *do* in the following extracts. What effect does the presence of *do* have for the interpretation of the sentence?

(28) a   Photographers aren't allowed to alter their photos in a way that misleads you, from posing a photo to digitally deleting a stray hair or telephone wire.

The Post <u>does</u> allow photographers to do some things to their pictures. They can "enhance for reproduction," meaning they can adjust the colors slightly so they will print better on the paper's presses. (*Washington Post*, 10.12.2002, p. C14, col. 3)

b I am glad that Roy Grimwood points out the advantages our generation (1960s) has had from university and which, thanks to the Thatcherite legacy, we would deny others. However, while no doubt many graduates <u>do</u> earn extra because of their qualifications, it must not be assumed that all do. (*Guardian*, 7.12.2002, p. 11, col. 5, letter to the editor from Robert Bracegirdle, Rothley, Leicestershire)

In both examples, the underlined auxiliary (*does, do*) serves to oppose the affirmative content of the sentence to a denial explicit or implicit in the context. If we delete *do* we alter the meaning slightly in that we weaken the contrastive effect of the sentences.[14]

2.3 *From form to meaning: Subject-auxiliary inversion and question formation*

2.3.1 INTRODUCTION

We have seen that subject-auxiliary inversion (SAI) is used to form interrogative sentences in English. There is a relation between form, the position of the auxiliary in the sentence, and interpretation: SAI helps to show the difference between statements and questions. We have not been fully explicit, though, about the nature of the relation between SAI and interrogative interpretation. A more precise formulation is called for. Is the relation between SAI and interrogative interpretation a strict relation of cause and effect? Does the correlation imply that all English interrogative sentences are necessarily formed by SAI? Does the correlation mean that SAI necessarily gives rise to questions? Let us try to make the nature of the correlation more exact.

We are investigating a form–interpretation relation: the form concerns a particular word order pattern: SAI. We have interpreted it as a leftward movement of the auxiliary across the subject. What exactly is the relation between SAI and interrogative interpretation? There are a number of possible relations that might obtain. We will compare the statements in (29) and try to assess which kinds of sentences would be covered by each of the statements. Though the statements are similar, it will soon turn out that the linguistic data they cover differ considerably. The statements lead to different predictions.

---

[14] Exercise 7.

For more discussion of examples with *do* see also Chapter 3, section 1.2.3.2.

(29) a SAI can give rise to interrogative interpretation.
　　 b SAI always gives rise to interrogative interpretation.
　　 c Interrogative sentences can be formed by means of SAI.
　　 d Interrogative sentences are always formed by means of SAI.
　　 e SAI is always used to form an interrogative sentence, and interrogative
　　　　sentences are always formed by means of SAI.

We will test the impact of these statements below. For each statement we will first make explicit its predictions and then we will try to test these predictions on the basis of empirical data.

2.3.2   SAI CAN GIVE RISE TO INTERROGATIVE INTERPRETATION/ SAI ALWAYS GIVES RISE TO INTERROGATIVE INTERPRETATION

The discussion above has shown that statement (29a) is valid. How does (29b) differ from (29a)? (29a) is a statement about a potential ("can") use of SAI. If we think about it carefully, we will conclude that (29a) is equivalent to (30a): the predictions of (29a) and (30a) are identical. (29a) says that SAI CAN be associated with question interpretation.

(30) a Some sentences with SAI are interrogative.

To formulate (29b) we have removed the modal auxiliary *can* and we have added the adverb *always*. Compared to (29a), (29b) is stronger: it says that whenever SAI applies you create an interrogative sentence. (29b) does not imply a POTENTIAL outcome of SAI, it implies a DEFINITE outcome. (29b) is equivalent to (30b):

(30) b All sentences with SAI are interrogative.

Consider the underlined fragments in the examples in (31). Do they bear on the statements we are examining? Let us first examine if they are compatible with the formulation in (29a).

(31) a All he wants to know is <u>which boxes have I ticked on the forms he keeps giving me to fill in</u>. (*Guardian*, G2, 15.3.2001, p. 9, col. 8)
　　 b People ask <u>why was I not at Coniston when Bluebird was raised</u>, but I would have been far too emotional. (*Guardian*, 15.3.2001, p. 5, col. 8)

With respect to (29a) there is no problem: the underlined strings in (31a) and (31b) display SAI and they are interrogative.[15] The interrogative sequences in (31) have been integrated into a larger structure. Sentences that become part of larger sentences

---

[15]　We will see later that there is something special about the word order in these sentences (Chapter 5, section 2.6), but this point is not relevant to the current discussion.

are said to be **embedded** or **subordinate clauses**.[16] In (31a) the string *which boxes have I ticked on the forms he keeps giving me to fill in* is an embedded clause which is also interrogative, an embedded interrogative for short. Embedded questions are also called **indirect** questions, or **reported** questions. (31c) is an independent question or a **direct** question: the sentence is addressed by a speaker to an interlocutor and the speaker expects an answer from the interlocutor.

(31) c   Which boxes have you ticked on the forms he keeps giving you to fill in?

We can form additional examples of direct questions of our own, which will again be compatible with (29a):

(31) d   Why were you not at Coniston when Bluebird was raised?
     e   Have you done linguistics before?
     f   Would all linguists agree that linguistics is a science?

Let us return to (29b). How could we evaluate its empirical coverage? We have seen that the claim in (29b) is stronger than that in (29a). (29b) says that whenever you have SAI you have an interrogative sentence, i.e. a sentence that can be used as a question. (29b) is a general rule for the interpretation of SAI. We reworded (29b) in (30b) above. (29b)/(30b) implies that there is a necessary link between the pattern of SAI and the interrogative force of the sentence. How can we evaluate this type of general statement?

Let us think of similar general statements that are not about language. Consider the statement: "All swans are white." It is a universal claim about the color of swans. To prove the universal claim true it is not sufficient to find a number of white swans. Even having found thousands of white swans, we cannot be sure that the next swan might not be non-white. On the other hand, if we find just one non-white swan, we will have shown that the statement "All swans are white" is false. In other words, in order to evaluate a general statement, we do not really show the statement to be true, but we look for evidence to falsify it, for "**counter-evidence**."

Now we return once again to (29b)/(30b). What kind of data would count as counter-examples to the generalization? Relevant counter-evidence would be sentences that display SAI and which are not interrogative. Are there such sentences? To test the claim, we could try to devise sentences of our own with SAI and which are not interrogative or we could try to find attested examples that contradict the claim. In the first procedure, we rely purely on our intuitions as speakers of English. This procedure might appear risky and less objective than the second procedure where we could claim the evidence is "objective" because it exists independently. However, note that this is not necessarily true: even in the second procedure we still need to rely on our intuitions because as speakers we have to decide whether the function of SAI in the relevant sentences is or is not that of forming a question. We

---

[16]   We return to the form of embedded clauses in more detail in Chapter 5.

still need to interpret the evidence and for that, we need to rely on our intuitions. So whichever line of attack we use, our own intuitions are involved.[17]

Are there any sentences that display the SAI pattern and which are not interrogative? Consider the following examples: (32a) is constructed, (32b–c) are attested. Does SAI give rise to an interrogative interpretation in these examples? If not, what is the interpretive contribution of SAI in these sentences?

(32) a   Had I known you were coming, I would have baked a cake.
    b   The guests were being offered cushions to take with them should their free seats prove insufficiently comfortable. (*Guardian*, 1.7.2002, p. 4, col. 8)
    c   Had the money not been returned, the evidence would have pointed strongly to a conclusion that the NRCC "financed" the Forum. (*Washington Post*, 29.4.2003, p. A18, col. 3)

In (32a–c) SAI is used in conditional clauses. These examples can be paraphrased as in (33):

(33) a   If I had known you were coming, I would have baked a cake.
    b   The guests were being offered cushions to take with them in case their free seats should prove insufficiently comfortable.
    c   If the money had not been returned, the evidence would have pointed strongly to a conclusion that the NRCC "financed" the Forum.

Now consider the following examples:

(34) a   Not one word of evidence have they brought to support that. (*Guardian*, 11.12.2001, p. 4, col. 7)
    b   Within a year of Hague becoming leader, the party had a ballot of its membership to say that not within the lifetime of this parliament would Britain enter the Euro. (*Guardian*, G2, 13.5.2002, p. 7, col. 2)

In (34a) and (34b) the inverted auxiliary (*have, would*) is preceded by a negative element (*not one word of evidence, not within the lifetime of this parliament*). If these negative elements are removed from the initial positions, the SAI pattern is no longer possible (35). In (34a) and (34b) SAI seems to be caused ("**triggered**") by the presence of the negative element in initial position.[18]

(35) a   They have <u>not</u> brought one word of evidence to support that.
    b   Within a year of Hague becoming leader, the party had a ballot of its membership to say that Britain would <u>not</u> enter the Euro within the lifetime of this parliament.

---

[17]   See also the discussions in Borsley and Ingham (2002, 2003) and Stubbs (2002).
[18]   This pattern is sometimes called **negative inversion**. Exercise 6 of Chapter 5 is an exercise on negative inversion.

We conclude that SAI may give rise to question formation but that it is not exclusively used for that purpose. SAI may also be used to form conditional clauses and in sentences with negative elements in the initial position.[19]

We conclude from the discussion that (29b) and its paraphrase (30b) are not empirically adequate. If (29b)/(30b) were adequate we should not be able to create sentences like those in (32) and in (34), where SAI occurs in non-interrogative sentences.

2.3.3 INTERROGATIVE SENTENCES CAN BE FORMED BY MEANS OF SAI/INTERROGATIVE SENTENCES ARE ALWAYS FORMED BY MEANS OF SAI

Let us turn to the second set of statements, (29c) and (29d). They are repeated here, with (29a), for convenience's sake. First compare the formulation of (29c) with (29a). What makes them different?

(29) a SAI can give rise to interrogative interpretation.
     c Interrogative sentences can be formed by means of SAI.
     d Interrogative sentences are always formed by means of SAI.

Both statements imply a causal relation: some factor A gives rise to/causes some result B. To bring out the causal relation more clearly, let us try to paraphrase the statements using a conditional sentence, i.e. using the pattern "if A then B." (29a) corresponds to (36a), (29c) to (36b):

(36) a If we apply SAI to a sentence, it can become interrogative.
       SAI → question
     b If we want to form an interrogative sentence, we can use SAI.
       Question → SAI

The paraphrases reveal that the two statements differ in the way they conceive of the cause-effect sequence. Statement (29a) takes the form (the word order arising by SAI) as the starting point and conceives of the interpretation ("question") as the result of that form; statement (29c) takes the interpretation as the starting point and predicts the form that will be used to convey it. We have looked at the empirical adequacy of (29a)/(36a) already. What kind of examples would support (36b)? (36b) predicts that interrogative sentences may display SAI. The examples discussed in the preceding sections are compatible with the statement. Some of them are straightforward illustrations of (36b) in that they illustrate questions formed by means of SAI. Examples in which SAI does not lead to interrogative sentences are irrelevant because like (29a), (29c) does not make a general over-arching statement about the shape of interrogative sentences. It does not raise the "white swan" problem posed by (29b) that was discussed above.

---

[19] One may try to propose a more general explanation to account for why inversion applies in just these three environments. We will not do this here.

(29c) says that if we want to form interrogative sentences we SOMETIMES use SAI. By comparison, (29d) is much stronger. This is shown by the conditional paraphrase (36c):

(36) c If we want to form an interrogative sentence we always use SAI.

Both (29c) and (29d) concern properties of interrogative sentences. (29c) says that an interrogative sentence MAY display SAI. (29d) says that it MUST display SAI, or, put differently, that SAI is a NECESSARY property of questions. (29c) corresponds to (37a), (29d) to (37b):

(37) a Some interrogative sentences display SAI.
     b All interrogative sentences display SAI.

How can we test these statements? We have assumed that the validity of (29c) was confirmed by the fact that some interrogative sentences have SAI. To test (29d), would it be sufficient to be able to construct or to find interrogative sentences with SAI? Would sentences such as those in (32) and (34), in which SAI is used in non-interrogative sentences, be relevant? The answer to both questions is negative. Take the second point first. The fact that SAI may be used in sentences which are not interrogative does not bear on (29d). It is irrelevant to the issue since (29d) is only concerned with sentences that are interrogative. Secondly, finding or constructing examples of interrogative sentences which display SAI does not "prove" that interrogative sentences must always be formed by SAI. We need to show that all interrogative sentences are formed by SAI. Again we are in a position in which we have to test a universal claim. What then would be counter-evidence for (29d)? What we need to find is interrogative sentences (i.e. questions) without SAI. Do such data exist? Consider the examples in (38) and compare them with (31a, b):

(38) a All he wants to know is <u>which boxes I have ticked on the forms he keeps giving me to fill in</u>.
     b People ask <u>why I was not at Coniston when Bluebird was raised</u>, but I would have been far too emotional.

In (38a) the underlined string is an indirect question: (38a) reports a question uttered by the person referred to by the pronoun *he*. Similarly (38b) reports a question asked by people. The indirect questions in the underlined sections in (38a) and (38b) differ from those in (31a, b) in that they do not display SAI. The auxiliaries *have* and *was* follow their respective subjects. In fact, there is dialectal variation in terms of the form of embedded questions. For many speakers of English, the SAI pattern in the embedded interrogatives in (31a, b) is slightly unusual and the non-inverted pattern in (38) would be more usual. To form an (embedded) interrogative sentence, SAI is not required. Statement (29d) is too general: it does not allow us to predict that the underlined strings in (38a, b) also qualify as interrogative.

Would the examples in (38) pose a problem for statement (29c)? In other words, do they constitute counter-evidence to the claim that "some interrogative sentences have SAI"? Clearly not, (29c) leaves it open that there may be questions without SAI. The weaker formulation in (29c) is compatible with the data; as far as we can assess at this point, it is empirically adequate. The stronger formulation in (29d) is not empirically adequate because it would lead us to expect SAI always to apply in embedded questions, which is not the case. Because of these observations, we might wish to narrow down statement (29d) to apply only to direct questions. This is shown in (39a) and in its conditional paraphrase (39b):

(39) a   Direct questions are always formed by means of SAI.
     b   If you want to form a direct question you always use SAI.

The new formulations predict (39c):

(39) c   All direct questions display SAI.

At first sight, this universal claim may seem plausible, and we have found many examples that seem to confirm it. But consider the examples in (40). Are they direct questions? The answer is positive. Now let us locate the subject and the auxiliary and evaluate the empirical coverage of (39c):

(40) a   Which student will finish the exam first?
     b   How many images will be remembered or become symbols of the war in
        Iraq? (*Guardian*, G2, 16.4.2003, p. 11, col. 1)

(40) illustrates direct questions. In these examples, however, the subject is not preceded by the auxiliary. In (40a) the subject is *which student* and the auxiliary *will* follows it. Similarly, in (40b) the subject *how many images* is followed by the auxiliary *will*. In other words, these direct questions do not display SAI. So we cannot claim that all direct questions necessitate SAI.

If we turn to the last statement in (29) repeated below, it is clear that this cannot work either:

(29) e   SAI is always used to form an interrogative sentence, and interrogative
        sentences are always formed by means of SAI.

(29e) conjoins statements (29b) and (29d), both of which were independently shown to give rise to counter-examples. The counter-evidence raised against the independent statements also falsifies (29e). We could replace (29e) by a weaker statement, the conjunction of (29a) and (29c):

(29) f   SAI can give rise to interrogative sentences, and interrogative sentences can
        be formed by means of SAI.

2.3.4   VERBS AND INVERSION

Statement (29f) summarizes our findings, but unfortunately it is relatively weak and not very insightful. It says that interrogative sentences may display SAI and that we may find SAI in interrogative sentences. We do not claim a strong correlation between the form (SAI) and the interpretation (question) and we also do not claim to be providing an explanation. We know that the statement is an appropriate summary of the data, it is **descriptively** adequate. But disappointingly, we have not really made any predictions as to the difference between data which will be found and those that will not be found. (29f) is not a general rule or a law, since it allows both for cases in which SAI does not give rise to interrogative sentences and for cases in which interrogative sentences do not display SAI.

However, in the discussion we did actually come across a pattern that is much closer to a general rule than (29f). Recall our discussion of question formation with respect to examples without auxiliaries such as (23), repeated here as (41) for convenience:

(41) a   He wants to buy a house this year.
     b   She wanted to become a policewoman.

We said that in order to form a question with inversion we inserted *do*, "as a last resort." Apparently when there is no auxiliary in a sentence we cannot simply invert the verb with the subject to form a question: the examples in (42) are unacceptable.

(42) a   *Wants he to buy a house this year?
     b   *Wanted she to become a policewoman?

Recall that we discovered that SAI is used in some other contexts. In the examples in (32) in section 2, SAI was shown to be used to form conditional clauses and in (34) we found it used in contexts with a sentence-initial negative element. In the underlined conditional clauses in (43) there is no auxiliary. Would these contexts allow a verb to invert with the subject?

(43) a   <u>If I knew you were coming</u>, I could have baked a cake.
     b   The guests were being offered cushions to take with them, <u>in case their free seats proved insufficiently comfortable</u>.
     c   <u>If the money remained unaccounted for</u>, the evidence would have pointed strongly to a conclusion that the NRCC "financed" the Forum.

It is not possible to rephrase these examples using inversion of the verb and the subject:

(44) a   *<u>Knew</u> I you were coming, I could have baked a cake.
     b   *The guests were being offered cushions to take with them <u>proved</u> their free seats insufficiently comfortable.

c   *<u>Remained</u> the money unaccounted for, the evidence would have pointed strongly to a conclusion that the NRCC "financed" the Forum.

The underlined elements in (45) are negative. Would fronting that constituent entail inversion of the verb and the subject?

(45) a They brought <u>not a shred of evidence</u> to support that claim.
     b Within a year of Hague becoming leader, the party had a ballot of its membership to guarantee that Britain <u>never</u> enters the Euro.

Once again, even if the negative elements were fronted, the verbs would not invert with their subjects:

(46) a *Not a shred of evidence <u>brought</u> they to support that claim.
     b *The party had a ballot of its membership to guarantee that never <u>enters</u> Britain the Euro.

These data do allow the formulation of a "general law": verbs, as opposed to auxiliaries, cannot invert with the subject in interrogative sentences, in conditionals or as a result of a sentence-initial negative constituent.

(47)   Verbs that are not auxiliaries do not invert with the subject.[20]

(47) is general and it does succeed in defining the bounds of possibilities in that it radically excludes sentences such as (42), (44), and (46). The statement allows us to predict that we will never find such sentences and that if we construct them they will be unacceptable.

    (47) raises questions. First we need to try to define auxiliaries and we need to make explicit how they differ from non-auxiliaries. We turn to this point in section 2.4.[21] Second (47) is still only a generalization of facts, (47) is not an explanation. We should not stop here but we should ask ourselves why it is that auxiliaries invert with the subject and verbs do not, in other words why they differ in their **distribu-tion**. The question is like asking ourselves why snow melts in the sunshine and glass does not. We will return to an explanation of the difference in distribution between auxiliaries and verbs in Chapter 3, section 3.4.

2.4   A brief discussion of definitions

We have mentioned that scientific research has to be explicit. Being explicit means, among other things, that the terminology used is transparent, that terms are defined

---

[20]   Exercise 11 deals with an apparent counter-example to (47).
[21]   We will come back to the distinction in Chapter 3, section 3.4.

clearly and unambiguously and that they are used in a systematic way. Obviously, in the preceding section we have not been fully explicit ourselves: we have not defined all the terms that we have been using, we have used some terms relying on a previous understanding of them, in a rather vague pre-theoretical way. This is because we all come to the task with some terminology and we have implemented that in order to be able to start dealing with some data. This type of approach is just about acceptable as long as we bear in mind that we have not yet defined our terms and that sooner or later (and preferably sooner rather than later) we will define the technical terms used.

In this section we briefly look at two terms that we have been using in a pre-theoretical sense and we will try to make them precise: these terms are **auxiliary** and **verb**. What is a verb? Consider the following examples and identify which words you think are verbs:

(48) a They bought books for their children.
    b They wrote novels about the war.

Probably you will pick out the words *bought* and *wrote*. Why do we call these words verbs? Often verbs are defined as words denoting an action. Using this definition as a guideline, which words would you identify as verbs in (49)?

(49) a His actions seemed incoherent.
    b Her friends' complaints remained secret.

In (49a) the word *actions* denotes actions but it will not normally be considered a verb. Similarly in (49b) the word *complaint* may be said to denote an action, but it is not a verb. On the other hand, words like *seemed* in (49a) and *remained* in (49b) are normally classified as verbs even though they do not denote actions. Why do we classify *seemed* and *remained* as verbs, with *bought* and *wrote*? What do these words have in common? What these words share is that they have a set of forms that differentiate them from the words that are not classified as verbs. For example, verbs have a form referred to as the "past tense"; *bought* in (48a), *wrote* in (48b), *seemed* in (49a), and *remained* in (49b) are all past tense forms. We experiment with the sentences in (48) and in (49) and remove the past tense form of the verbs. What does the difference in verb form do? Does it have an interpretive effect?

(50) a They <u>buy</u> books for their children.
    b They <u>write</u> novels about the war.
    c His actions <u>seem</u> incoherent.
    d Her friends' complaints <u>remain</u> secret.

While the sentences in (48) and (49) situate the state of affairs they denote in the past time sphere, those in (50) situate it in the present time sphere. The *-ed* ending of the past tense form here serves to indicate that the situation described by the sentence is not to be situated in the present. The form *remained* is composed of two units: the verb *remain*, and the inflectional ending *-ed*. *Remain* means roughly 'stay', *-ed* means roughly 'not situated in the present/situated in the past'. Both components are units of form; they can be used in other circumstances: *remain* does not need to be associated with *-ed*, and *-ed* combines with other verbs than *remain*. The units *remain* and *-ed* themselves are units of meaning and they cannot be decomposed into smaller units with identifiable meanings. We call such units **morphemes** and we will say that *-ed* is an **inflectional** morpheme. The morpheme *-ed* is also called a **bound** morpheme because it can never be used on its own; it must be attached to another morpheme. *Remain* is a free morpheme: it can be used on its own.

Often grammarians will refer to the verb forms without *-ed* in (50) as the present tense. But note that there is in fact no real tense marking at all in the form of the verb. The past tense ending *-ed* is not replaced by a specific ending for the present, the form *remain* is simply the base form of the verb. In the present tense, the verb gets a special ending only in examples with third person subjects such as those in (51).

(51) a She buys books for her children.
      b She writes novels about the war.
      c His action seems incoherent.
      d Her friend's complaint remains secret.

The so-called present tense and the past tense are said to be **finite** forms of the verb. In the examples in (52a, b) the verbs *buy* and *write* combine with the ending *-ing*.

(52) a She is buying books for her children.
      b She is writing novels about the war.

-ing is also an inflectional morpheme. In (52a, b) it serves to create the so-called present participle of the verb, which follows *is*, itself a finite form of the auxiliary *be*. This auxiliary cannot be followed by the finite forms of the verb (present tense or past tense) (52c, d) and we have to use the *-ing* form. The *-ing* form of the verb is a **non-finite** form. Finite forms vary for tense (*is* is a present tense, *was* is a past tense), non-finite forms do not vary for tense.

(52) c *She is buys books for her children.
      d *She is writes novels about the war.

Observe that the past tense ending (*-ed*), the third person singular ending (*-s*), and the *-ing* ending typically are attached to verbs. They are not found on other categories such as nouns, such as *cat*, or *girl*.[22] So we can identify verbs by looking at their **morphology**, at the kinds of inflectional morphemes they combine with.

---

[22] When we find the *-s* ending on a noun it is used either for a plural (*cats*, *girls*) or to form a genitive (*cat's*, *girl's*). We assume that plural *-s* and genitive *-s* are different entities.

The uninflected base form of the verb may typically be found in contexts such as these illustrated in (53):

(53) a She will buy books for her children.
 b To write a novel about the war would be hard.

Buy and *write* in (53) do not have any endings. Even though the subject in (53a) is a third person, *she*, the verb could not possibly be marked with the *-s* ending, nor could we replace *buy* by the past tense form.

(53) c *She will buys books for her children.
 d *She will bought books for her children.

Typically, words like *will* and the infinitive marker *to* are followed by the uninflected base form of the verb. This base form is also referred to as the infinitive of the verb. We can also use this **distributional** information to identify a verb: if a word can follow the auxiliary *will* or the infinitive marker *to*, then that word will be a verb.

To find out if a word qualifies as a verb, we can check whether it has the morphological and distributional properties of verbs such as *buy* or *remain* in the examples above: that is to say we examine whether the word can associate with the typical verb endings (*-s*, *-ed*, *-ing*), and whether it can occupy positions typically occupied by verbs. Identify the verbs in the following example (which corresponds to example (31a) in section 2). You may obviously experiment with the sentence to check whether the items that you have identified as verbs have the various forms we have been talking about.

(54) a All he wants to know is which boxes have I ticked on the forms he keeps giving me to fill in. (*Guardian*, G2, 15.3.2001, p. 9, col. 8)

In (54a) *wants* is a verb. For one thing it has the third person ending *-s*, and it can also be used in a past tense. In the non-finite form *want* can be used after *will* or after *to*:

(54) b All he wanted to know is which boxes have I ticked on the forms he keeps giving me to fill in.
 c All he will want to know is which boxes have I ticked on the forms he keeps giving me to fill in.
 d All he seems to want to know is which boxes have I ticked on the forms he keeps giving me to fill in.

Other verbs in (54a) are *know*, *have*, *tick*, *keep*, *give*, *fill*. Recall that (54a) contains an indirect question signaled by the inversion of the auxiliary *have*. Using the formal criteria set out above, words that are referred to as "auxiliaries" are also verbs. The auxiliary *have* displays the morphological and distributional properties of a verb:

(55) a He <u>has</u> ticked the boxes.
    b I <u>had</u> ticked the boxes.
    c <u>Having</u> ticked the boxes, I handed in the form.
    d I will <u>have</u> ticked all the right boxes.
    e I expect to <u>have</u> ticked the wrong boxes.

(56) illustrates the so-called progressive use of *be*: the auxiliary *be* is used in combination with the present participle to express (roughly) an ongoing activity.[23]

(56) a The teacher <u>is</u> meeting the students.
    b The teacher <u>was</u> meeting the students.
    c The teacher has <u>been</u> meeting the students for a while.
    d The teacher will <u>be</u> meeting the students.
    e I expect to <u>be</u> meeting the students.

Morphologically and distributionally, auxiliaries are a subclass of verbs. Why then do we not just call them verbs? We saw in the preceding sections that auxiliaries have distinctive distributional properties that set them apart from the other verbs. Typically, auxiliaries can **invert** with the subject – for instance in interrogative sentences, in conditional clauses, or if a negative element has been fronted.[24] In the same circumstances, non-auxiliary verbs do not invert with their subjects.

    There are further properties that set apart auxiliaries among the class of verbs. Auxiliaries can be followed immediately by the negation marker *not*, and they can also contract with *not*. Ordinary verbs like *meet* do not invert with the subject and the use of the negation marker *not* in a finite sentence gives rise to the insertion of the auxiliary *do*.

(57) a The teacher is meeting the student.
    b <u>Is</u> the teacher meeting the student?
    c The teacher <u>is not</u> meeting the student.
    d The teacher <u>isn't</u> meeting the student.

(58) a The teacher met the student.
    b *<u>Met</u> the teacher the student?
    b′ <u>Did</u> the teacher meet the student?
    c *The teacher <u>met not</u> the student.
    c′ The teacher <u>did not meet</u> the student.
    d *The teacher <u>meetn't</u> the student.
    d′ The teacher <u>didn't meet</u> the student.

---

[23] Exercises 5 and 6.
[24] Exercise 12 shows that not every sequence consisting of auxiliary *be* + subject instantiates SAI.

In what follows we will occasionally (re)define some traditional terms.[25] Since auxiliaries are verbs, it is difficult to set up the opposition shown in (59a). We need to differentiate verbs that are not auxiliaries from those that are. The terms that are usually used for this opposition are given in (59b, c).

(59) a   auxiliary   ↔   verb
     b   auxiliary   ↔   lexical verb
     c   auxiliary   ↔   full verb

The term *auxiliary* is related to a Latin verb *auxiliare*, which means 'help'. Informally, we could say that auxiliaries "help" the lexical verb that follows them. The term "full verb" suggests that auxiliaries, in contrast to full verbs, are "not full." Full verbs have a lot of descriptive content: a change of full verb in a sentence may radically change the action referred to in that sentence. A change of auxiliary will not alter the action referred to, but it will perhaps shift the action in time or make it less plausible. The term *lexical* is related to the word *lexicon*. The lexicon of a language is its dictionary, the list of its words. The list of what we call lexical verbs is open ended. We can add new lexical verbs to the language. Recent English words are *pedestrianize, download, digitize*, etc. Verbs are **open class** words (and so are nouns, adjectives, and adverbs). On the other hand, auxiliaries belong to a **closed class**. We do not normally expect people to start creating new auxiliaries.[26]

3   Language and Languages

3.1   *Going further afield: Comparative syntax*

We have discovered that the distribution of English auxiliaries differs from that of English lexical verbs. Section 2.4 briefly discusses how to set off the two subclasses of verbs by looking at their distributional properties. The question arises why lexical verbs cannot invert with their subjects in questions and why auxiliaries can. Before we can address this question, though, we must check how general this restriction on inversion is.

In the introduction to this chapter we said that linguistics is the scientific study of language. Language as an abstract concept manifests itself through individual languages: English, French, German, etc. We have discovered that English verbs do not invert with their subjects in questions. Before trying to account for this restriction, we might do well to check whether this ban on verb inversion is general. The reason why we should do this is the following: if we discover that the ban on inversion is universal, i.e. if it applies to all languages, then we can try to explain it by a very

---

[25]   For a general discussion of the complexities of defining word classes such as verbs and auxiliaries see for instance Aarts and Haegeman (forthcoming).

[26]   We return to the oppositions in (59) in Chapter 3, section 3.4.

powerful linguistic principle, one that will not vary cross-linguistically. On the other hand, if we discover that subject-verb inversion is banned in English but is possible in other languages, then we know that we must provide a flexible explanation, one that can be adjusted to the properties of the individual languages. In other words, the following possibilities could be considered:

(60) a   There is a universal ban on inverting the verb with the subject.

     b   There is a language specific ban on inverting the verb with the subject. The ban applies in the following languages: English, . . .

To account for a **universal** pattern, we will have to invoke a universal principle that rigidly applies to all languages. If there is no such universal pattern, we will have to devise a **parameter** along which languages may vary. We will then try to relate the observed cross-linguistic variation to specific properties of individual languages. In what follows we will try to assess which of the two statements in (60) is correct.

3.1.1 FRENCH

Consider the French examples in (61) and their word-for-word glosses in English. Verbs and auxiliaries are given in bold. It is clear that for many of the examples, the word-for-word glosses would not qualify as English sentences. In the light of the discussion above, what conclusions could we draw with respect to inversion in French? Would you say that French is more "liberal" than English in its use of inversion? Or is it more restricted? Motivate your answer.

(61) a   **Achetait**-elle le journal tous les jours?   A-t-elle **acheté** le journal?
        bought she the paper all the days   has she bought the paper
        'Did she buy the paper every day?'   'Has she bought the paper?'

     b   **Ecrit**-elle des romans?   A-t-elle **écrit** des romans?
        writes she novels   has she written novels
        'Does she write novels?'   'Has she written any novels?'

     c   **Vient**-il demain?   Est-il venu hier?
        comes he tomorrow   is he come yesterday
        'Is he coming tomorrow?'   'Did he come yesterday?'

     d   Que **dit**-il?   Qu'a-t-il **dit**?
        what says he   what has he said
        'What does he say?'   'What has he said?'

The English versions of the examples in the left most column read as in (62).

(62) a   Did she buy the paper every day?

     b   Does she write novels?

c   Does he come tomorrow?
d   What does he say?

With respect to the position of lexical verbs, French seems to be more liberal than English in that such verbs invert with the subjects, as do auxiliaries. Let us refer to a pattern in which the full verb inverts with the subject as subject-verb inversion, or **SVI**. Languages differ with respect to whether they allow SVI: English doesn't allow SVI, French does.

3.1.2   GERMAN AND DUTCH

We conclude that the difference in inversion patterns distinguishes French from English. French is a Romance language, English is a Germanic language. Could it be that this difference accounts for the difference observed here? Perhaps Germanic languages in general never allow SVI. Let us look at some Germanic languages like German or Dutch. Do they allow verbs to invert with their subjects? If we turn to German, we find that there too the verb can precede the subject. Verbs and auxiliaries are in bold.

(63) a   **Kaufte** sie jeden Tag die Zeitung?   **Hat** sie jeden Tag die Zeitung **gekauft**?
         bought she every day the paper   has she every day the paper bought
         'Did she buy the paper every day?'   'Has she bought the paper every day?'

     b   **Schreibt** sie Romane?   **Hat** sie Romane **geschrieben**?
         writes she novels   has she novels written
         'Does she write novels?'   'Has she written any novels?'

     c   **Kommt** er morgen?   **Wird** er morgen **kommen**?
         comes he tomorrow   will he tomorrow come
         'Is he coming tomorrow?'   'Will he come tomorrow?'

     d   **Was** sagt er?   **Was** hat er **gesagt**?
         what says he   what has he said
         'What does he say?'   'What has he said?'

Similarly, the Dutch examples in (64) display SVI:

(64) a   **Koopt** zij elke dag de krant?   **Heeft** zij de krant elke dag **gekocht**?
         bought she every day the paper   has she the paper every day bought
         'Did she buy the paper every day?'   'Has she bought the paper every day?'

     b   **Schrijft** zij romans?   **Heeft** zij romans **geschreven**?
         writes she novels   has she novels written
         'Does she write novels?'   'Has she written any novels?'

   c **Komt** zij morgen?   **Zal** zij morgen **komen**?
      comes she tomorrow   will she tomorrow come
      'Is she coming tomorrow?'   'Will she come tomorrow?'

   d Wat **zegt** zij?   Wat **heeft** zij **gezegd**?
      what says she   what has she said
      'What does she say?'   'What has she said?'

From the **comparative** data above we conclude that there is **cross-linguistic variation** with respect to the possibility of SVI. This means that postulating a universal ban on SVI would lead to the wrong predictions. Any attempt at explaining the ban on SVI in English will have to take into account specific properties of that language.

3.2 *Going back in time: Diachronic variation*

We have shown the relevance of using comparative data for linguistics research. On the basis of the small sample of languages discussed in the previous section, we concluded that the ban on inverting English verbs with subjects should not be stated as a "universal law of language." Languages vary with respect to their word orders. Even if we are mainly (or only) interested in English, it is still useful to introduce the comparative angle, because this will mean that we can situate the English data in a wider perspective and we know what kind of explanation to look for.

    Could we conclude that the ban on verb inversion is an inherent rule of English? Consider the data from Old English (or Anglo-Saxon) in (65). Auxiliaries and verbs are in bold. Do auxiliaries invert with their subjects in questions? Does Old English have verb inversion?

(65) a Hwi **sceole** we oþres mannes **niman**?
       why should-1PL we another man's take
       'Why should we take what belongs to another?'
       (Ælfric, *Lives of Saints*, 24, 188, Haeberli 2000: 110)

    b Hwi **noldest** ðu hyt **secgan** me?
       why NEG+would-2SG you it say me
       'Why would you not tell it to me?'
       (*Gen*, 31.27, Kroch and Taylor 2000: 152)

    c Hwilcne oþerne sige **sceolde** ure drihten **syllan**?
       what other victory should-3SG our Lord give
       'What other victory should our Lord give . . . ?'
       (*ÆLS*, 31.128–9, Pintzuk 1991: 53)

d Hwæt **sægest** þu, yrðling?
   what say-2SG you, peasant
   'What do you say, farmer?'
   (*Acoll*, 22, Van Kemenade 1987: 138)

e Hu **begæst** þu work þin?
   how beget-2SG you work your
   'How do you carry out your work?'
   (*Acoll*, 22, Van Kemenade 1987: 138)

f To hwæm **locige** ic buton to ðæm eaðmodum?
   to whom look-1SG I except to the humble
   'To whom do I look except to the humble?'
   (*CP*, 41.299.18, Fischer et al. 2000: 54)

In each of the examples (65d–f) a full verb inverts with the subject. Old English seems to behave more like German, Dutch, and French than like Modern English. In particular, Old English displays SVI in questions. Why should that be? In order to understand this, we would have to examine Old English in more detail to detect what property or properties will set it off from present-day English and what makes it more similar to French or to Dutch and German.[27]

When we consider the historical development of a language we engage in what is called **diachronic linguistics**. We examine earlier stages of the language and compare them with later stages. Obviously, since there are no native speakers of Old English we have to turn to attested material.

3.3 Comparative data: Conclusion

We conclude that languages vary with respect to inversion patterns. Inversion affects full verbs in some languages but not in others. This is summarized in Table 3. A

Table 3 Inversion patterns: classification of languages

Language	SAI	SVI
Modern English	+	–
Old English	+	+
French	+	+
German	+	+
Dutch	+	+

[27] We will attempt to offer an explanation for the difference in inversion patterns between Old English and Modern English in Chapter 3, sections 1.2.4.2, 1.2.4.3, and 1.2.4.4.

classification like that in Table 3 is only a first step in our research. Remember that our aim is to formulate the "laws" of language. In the next chapters we will, among other things, try to explain why languages differ in this particular way.

4 Summary

This chapter sets the scene for the remainder of the book. We have first discussed the properties of the scientific method. One core concern is that science presupposes that we aim at providing an explanation of data. We set out to provide general accounts for particular data. We try to attain this goal by formulating hypotheses that relate sets of empirical data in terms of cause and effect. Such hypotheses lead to the elaboration of theories, sets of interacting hypotheses. The hypotheses and the theory also allow us to make predictions about what will be possible (the data that we may find) and what will be impossible (the data that we should never find).

It is important to formulate the empirical observations and the hypotheses that account for them as precisely and explicitly as possible. The importance of precise and explicit formulation is illustrated in a discussion of the relation between a formal property of English – subject-auxiliary inversion – and an interpretative property – interrogative force. It has become clear from the data that we cannot strongly correlate SAI and interrogative force: not all examples displaying SAI are interrogative and interrogative force does not always lead to SAI. Any formulation of that correlation must refer to potential rather than general links between form and meaning.

One empirical generalization about English that does emerge from the discussion was that verbs do not invert with their subjects in English. In the final part of the chapter, we saw that this generalization cannot be stated as a universal linguistic ban on subject verb inversion and that in many languages, including earlier stages of English, verbs do indeed invert with their subjects.

In the discussion of the relation between form and meaning we have underlined the importance of structure, that is, the way that words are combined to form units and sentences. Our discussion of inversion patterns implies that we think of sentences as containing particular positions or slots into which elements are inserted and that certain types of units belong to certain types of positions. In the next chapters we will explore these underlying assumptions about sentences structure and we develop an explicit and systematic theory of the structure of sentences.

Exercises

Contents

Introductory note to the exercises

The exercises in this book will be accompanied by the abbreviations (T), (L), and (E). The abbreviation (T) stands for "tie in," and it serves to signal that a particular exercise ties in with the material in the preceding chapter. Such tie-in exercises are signaled by footnotes in the chapter. The abbreviation (L) stands for "look ahead" and it signals that the material covered in the exercise will be taken up in a later chapter. The abbreviation (E) stands for "expansion" and it signals that the material covered in the exercise goes beyond that covered in the book. Since the material contained in them has been covered, T-exercises will tend to be "easier" than L-exercises or E-exercises. Sometimes exercises will combine tie-in elements with new material that is to be treated in a later chapter, in which case we will label them as (T, L). Alternatively they may partly be exercises of the material in the chapter to which new material is added. Such exercises are labeled (T, E).

Some of the E-exercises will include longer discussion of particular points. Exercises 11 and 12 of this chapter are examples. The reason why the discussion in these exercises is not included in the main body of the text is that the exercises are intended only as illustrations of how research topics can be pursued in linguistics. Using the argumentation developed in the text, the discussions show how particular issues can be picked up and developed further. These "discursive exercises" typically will not offer an exhaustive or definitive treatment of the issues in question. Rather, they illustrate how an analysis can be called into question and may have to be reworked in the light of new data or of new theoretical proposals. Recall that scientific theories are not static. A scientific theory is not a painting that you can admire but that essentially is "dead" in that nothing in it can alter. Science is a search, it is active and alive.

> In any branch of science there are only two possibilities. There is either nothing left to discover, in which case why work on it, or there are big discoveries yet to be made, in which case, what the scientists say now is likely to be false. (Nigel Calder, author of *Magic Universe: The Oxford Guide to Modern Science*. Cited in the *Guardian*, 3.6.2004, p. 6, col. 2)

Exercise 1   Exploiting multiple meaning (T)

(1)   The following is a letter to the editor published in *The Guardian* (13.9.1997, p. 8). Discuss the interpretation of the extract.

Branching out
I was amazed to read in your article about Marc Bolan (The King and I, September 11) that "... a headstone is to be erected by the tree that killed him." I presume you will be giving full coverage to this example of arboreal largesse and perhaps you will even print extracts of the tree's speech?
Francis Quinn, 52c James Street, Cookstown, Co. Tyrone, BT80 8LT.

Discuss how the potential for multiple interpretation is exploited in the following extracts.

(2)   A couple of hunters are out in the woods when one of them falls to the ground. He doesn't seem to be breathing. The other whips out his mobile phone and calls the emergency services. He gasps out to the operator: "My friend is dead! What can I do?" The operator, in a calm soothing voice says: "Just take it easy. First, let's make sure he's dead." There is silence, then a shot is heard. The guy's voice comes back on the line. He says "OK, now what?" (*Guardian*, G2, 20.12.2001, p. 4, col. 6; "The world's funniest joke?")

(3)   A man spots a farmer standing in a field in the rain. "Why?" he asks. The farmer replies: "I am trying to win a Nobel Prize. You get one for being out standing in your field." (*Observer*, 10.10.2004, p. 19, col. 5)

(4)   My most vivid memory of him and us students was waiting for a train at Victoria and telling jokes in the manner of "Will the people who took the train

on platform seven please bring it back?" (*Guardian*, 22.11.2002, p. 9, col. 6, letter to the editor from Edward Lynton)

(5) "George Best was a fantastic football player and he would have been even better if he'd been able to pass night-clubs the way he passed the ball," Docherty said of the errant star. (Based on *Guardian*, 31.7.2002, p. 3, col. 4)

(6) Mr Howard said that under Labour a teacher is assaulted every seven minutes (as in the old joke, "and he's getting pretty damned sick of it"). (*Guardian*, 1.7.2004, p. 2, col. 7)

(7) a I have always found the advice on medicine bottles to "keep out of reach of children" to be advice well worth following. (*Guardian*, 18.2.2002, p. 13, col. 4, letter to the editor from David Carter)

   b Another unintended message: Marks and Sparks' advice to its customers, as printed on all their plastic shopping bags, is: "To avoid suffocation, keep away from children." (*Guardian*, 18.2.2002, p. 13, col. 4, letter to the editor from Dick Brown)

Exercise 2   Ambiguity (T)

The following passages are extracts from published written material. In each of the extracts some segment gives rise to more than one interpretation and could potentially lead to misunderstandings. Sometimes the ambiguity is highlighted in the passage because it is exploited by the author, but in most cases the ambiguity may well go unnoticed because the context of the extract will privilege one reading rather than the other. Discuss the ambiguities that arise in the examples and identify the linguistic elements that give rise to the multiple interpretations. After you have dealt with the examples one by one try to classify them in terms of the cause of the ambiguity.

(1) Jackie Child's youngest daughter was just two when she was jailed for manslaughter nine years ago. (*Guardian*, G2, 27.7.2001, p. 10, col. 1)

(2) "Have a fag."
   "You're making me into a smoker, Mrs Anthony. Thanks, I will. But you should try to cut them down, they aren't too good for you."
   "Twenty a day since I was twenty-five and seventy yesterday," said Mrs Anthony.
   "Seventy! Gracious, you'll be . . ."
   "Seventy years of age yesterday."
   "Oh, seventy. Isn't it time you had a rest then?"
   (Muriel Spark, *Memento Mori*, 1977: 54)

(3) If you feel threatened in a taxi, firmly ask the driver to stop and get out. (based on *Guardian*, G2, 7.3.2003, p. 7, col. 2)

(4) Perhaps they hadn't intended to kill, only confront him jointly, threaten and shock. But the French cook's knife had been handy, lying on the table maybe. (Ruth Rendell, *An Unkindness of Ravens*, 1994: 213)

(5) "I can't get used to wearing my engagement ring yet. The other day I even scratched my nose with it because it's so big – the ring I mean." (based on "Diana, a tribute." *Sunday Times Supplement, Style*, 7.9.1997, p. 11)

(6) In the survey, 200 couples were asked to keep reading diaries for three weeks. (*Guardian*, 27.5.2002, p. 8, col. 8)

(7) What funny story about your life do you tell your grandkids (if you've got any)? Do you mean, if I've got any funny stories, or any grandchildren? As it happens I have three grandchildren and no funny stories. (*Independent*, interview Gore Vidal, 11.8.1999, p. 7, col. 6)

(8) We need more robust measures. (Headline, *Guardian*, 29.11.2003, p. 20)

(9) Error lets bad meat trader off the hook. (Headline, *Guardian*, 24.5.2004, p. 6, col. 7)

Comment on the interpretation of the underlined sections in the following passages:

(10) a Since 2003 individual drivers have also been subject to a licensing regime and it is a source of some satisfaction to <u>drivers of black cabs</u> that many <u>mini cab drivers</u> and firms have struggled to comply. "The mini cabs are in dire straits," claimed Mr. Oddy. "In reality people need moving around London and mini cabs don't to the same sort of work <u>black cab drivers</u> do." (*Guardian*, 3.9.2004, p. 14, col. 6)
     b Rhys Jones lived in the penthouse and a swimming pool was built in the basement. "<u>Black-cab drivers</u> ask me if he still lives there," says Ellis. (*Observer Magazine*, 25.7.2004, p. 38, col. 3)

Discuss the orthography in (10b).

Exercise 3   Time specifications and their interpretations (T)

Discuss the interpretation of the underlined time specifications in the following examples.

(1) Tony Blair admitted that he had run into "tough times" <u>in recent months</u> <u>yesterday</u>. (*Independent*, 5.9.2003, p. 2, col. 1)

(2) Mr Straw decided to appoint a panel of independent doctors to examine General Pinochet <u>on January 5</u>. (*Guardian*, 13.1.2000, p. 1, col. 3)[1]

(3) We found out that he had been given a scholarship to the RAF <u>just after the</u> <u>accident</u>, which was an awful timing. (*Guardian*, 19.5.2001, p. 4, col. 8)

(4) Men who use internet chatrooms to "groom" young girls for sex were warned that they face long jail terms <u>yesterday</u>. (*Guardian*, 16.10.2003, p. 5, col. 1)

(5) George Carey, the Archbishop of Canterbury, formally made the long anticip-ated announcement of his plan to retire from office <u>in the autumn</u> <u>yesterday</u>. (*Guardian*, 9.1.2002, p. 3, col. 1)

Exercise 4   Auxiliary (T)

In section 2.2.1 of the chapter we roughly defined auxiliaries as follows:

> A provisional (and very approximate) characterization of auxiliaries, to be refined in Chapter 3, is that they are elements that are typically followed by a verb.

Discuss the appropriateness of the definition on the basis of the following examples:

(1)   James is definitely writing another novel.

(2)   Has James already finished his novel?

(3)   He hasn't talked to his publisher yet but he will soon.

(4)   I promised I would get you a present and get you a present, I will.

(5)   The baby is asleep in its cot.[2]

---

[1]   For discussion of this example see also Chapter 2, section 1.1.
[2]   See also Exercise 5.

Exercise 5   Copula *be* (T)

On the basis of (1) show that *be* is an auxiliary when followed by the progressive participle:

(1)   The baby is sleeping in its cot.

Consider now (2):

(2)   The baby is asleep.

In this example *be* relates a subject, *the baby* and an adjective *asleep*. The adjective expresses a property of the subject and this use of the adjective is often referred to as **predicative**. Copula *be* links a subject and a predicate. In (2) copula *be* is not followed by another verb. Examine the morphological and distributional properties of *be* when used as a copula. Does copula *be* behave as a lexical verb or as an auxiliary? Provide arguments for your answer.

Exercise 6   Copula *be* and other linking verbs (T)

Consider the examples below.

(1)   Mary was very tense.

(2)   Mary seemed very tense.

(3)   Mary remained very tense.

(4)   Mary became very tense.

(5)   Mary looked very tense.

In each of these examples we basically ascribe a property 'very tense' to the referent of the name *Mary*. The link between the property and the subject is established by means of the words *was, seemed, remained, became, looked*. What is the category of these words? Are they auxiliaries or full verbs? Motivate your answer.

Exercise 7   "Emphatic *do*" (T)

Consider the underlined occurrences of *do* in the following examples.[3] Can we eliminate *do* and preserve a grammatical sentence? It turns out that if we eliminate

---

[3]   See also Chapter 3, section 1.2.3.2 for discussion.

do we must attach the inflection that is associated with *do* to the verb itself and the resulting sentences will be acceptable. Looking at the contexts in which the sentences with *do* are used, try to identify a common contextual factor that relates all these examples.

(1) I don't remember much of anything she said in the church foyer or what I uttered back. She had that dazzling effect on me. Truth is, she still does. What I <u>do</u> recall is that she invited me to a holiday party two nights later at the mutual friend's place. (*Chicago Tribune*, 22.12.2003, section 13, p. 9, col. 1)

(2) Coleman, who describes himself as a "semi-professional punter", gave evidence at a trial in Southampton in October 2001 and his statements to the court then will form the basis of the case against him. It is still not clear if he will turn up for the 10 a.m. hearing at the club's headquarters in London, but the feeling at Portman Square yesterday was that he would indeed appear to defend himself . . . If Coleman <u>does</u> appear this morning, the Jockey Club may also wish to inquire about another part of the evidence. (*Guardian*, 22.1.2003, p. 14, cols 1 and 2)

(3) On Tuesday Clarett disputed the contention of university officials that he had failed to file the proper paperwork that would have allowed him to attend the funeral . . . Each side is right, Clarett <u>did</u> fill out the papers but filled them out too late to receive tickets to fly home. (*New York Times*, 2.1.2003, p. D1, col. 1)

(4) Jackson is hardly a virgin forest. Like most of the state's redwood land, it has been logged intermittently since about the middle of the 19th century . . . But the forest <u>does</u> have thousands of acres of 80- to 100-year old redwoods. (*San Francisco Chronicle*, 28.11.2002, p. A34, col. 1)

(5) I'm probably more benevolent towards Mr Livingstone than a lot of people and I actually <u>do</u> think he's very brave in trying congestion charging. (*Guardian*, 3.1.2003, p. 3, col. 4)

(6) People close to Senate leader Tom Daschle say he should be considered a possible candidate, but many Democrats say they would be surprised if he <u>does</u> run. (*Atlanta Journal-Constitution*, 1.12.2002, p. A6, col. 5)

(7) But that's the trouble with middle-aged men these days: they're so busy trying to convince the world that they really <u>do</u> like Eminem that they have forgotten several decades of their past. (*Los Angeles Times*, 26.11.2002, p. E13, col. 3)

(8)   In the new report, mice that were fed only every other day – but could gorge on the days they <u>did</u> eat – saw similar health benefits to ones that had their diet reduced by 40 percent. (*Washington Post*, 29.4.2003, p. A3, col. 5)

(9)   We were told journalism is a science. It didn't make sense then nor does it now. But it <u>does</u> make sense that we were learning a profession. (adapted from *Washington Post*, 29.4.2003, p. A22, col. 4)

(10) When it was first established in 1900, the Nobel committee clearly thought [the Peace Prize] should be awarded to people who really <u>did</u> believe in peaceful solutions and non-violence. (*Guardian*, 7.12.2002, p. 10, col. 1)

Exercise 8   Contextually related ellipsis (L)

As shown by examples (2) and (7) in Exercise 2, material from a sentence may sometimes be omitted or deleted. The omitted material can usually be recovered from the context. In the following examples locate all instances of ellipsis. Identify which material has been omitted. Indicate the ellipsis by means of the symbol Ø and consider which element immediately precedes it.[4]

Example
I asked him to write the report but he wouldn't.

- I asked him to write the report but he wouldn't Ø.
- Omitted material: *write the report.*

Ø is preceded by the contraction of the auxiliary *would* + negation.

---

(1)   He wants to be the boss. In Silver Spring yesterday, he was. (*Guardian*, 23.10.2002, p. 1, col. 5)

(2)   When he first ran for office four years ago, Gov. Gray Davis vowed to save California's old-growth forests. He hasn't, as Moloney sees it, and she wants him to live up to that long-ago campaign promise. (*Los Angeles Times*, 26.11.2002, p. B7, col. 2)

(3)   A lot of prisoners lie and say they are sorry about something when they are not. (*Guardian*, 17.1.2003, p. 1, col. 30)

---

[4]   We will be looking at the relevance of ellipsis for determining structure in Chapter 2, section 1.6.

(4) This study compared complications in 552 ARF patients in the intensive care unit at four academic hospitals, 326 of whom received diuretics on a particular day and 226 who did not. (*Los Angeles Times*, 26.11.2002, p. F7, col. 1)

(5) Whitelaw had given his word to be loyal to her, and he was. (*Guardian*, G2, 11.9.2002, p. 4, col. 4)

(6) Sometimes I feel like I would like to crawl away and hide. But I will not. (*Guardian*, 11.12.2002, p. 1, col. 2)

(7) I have never been to Australia, but a friend who has assures me that Moody is quite correct. (*Guardian*, Sport, 14.12.2002, p. 4, col. 3)

(8) After all, Francesca's hardly news any more. We are all trying to forget her. As if we could. Although we should. I can't. (Francis Fyfield, *Undercurrents*, 2001: 50)

(9) We're also keen to have a meeting with all parties and find out what's gone wrong, because it's obvious something has. (*Guardian*, 13.12.2002, p. 15, col. 4)

(10) Under government policy, Cubans who make it to shore are generally allowed to stay, while those who do not are sent back to their homeland. (*New York Times*, 28.11.2002, p. A26, col. 2)

Exercise 9   Substitutes for units containing a verb (L)

In the previous exercise we saw that to avoid repetition, a string of words is sometimes omitted.[5] In examples (2), (4), (6–10), the omitted strings contained a verb. For instance: (8) has 3 ellipsis sites:

(1) a   We are all trying to forget her. As if we could Ø. Although we should Ø. I can't Ø.

The symbol Ø stands for *forget her*:

(1) b   We are all trying to forget her. As if we could forget her. Although we should forget her. I can't forget her.

In each case, the ellipsis site is preceded by an auxiliary: in (i) the relevant auxiliaries are *could, should, can't*.

[5]   For the role of substitution in syntactic analysis see Chapter 2, section 1.3.

In the examples below the repetition of a string of words is avoided not by omitting it but by substituting one word or a short string of words. The substitutes are underlined in the examples. Identify which strings have been replaced by the underlined words:

(2)   When he was named chief by Mayor James K. Hahn, Bratton told The Times that he wanted to establish close ties with prominent leaders in the city's minority communities. In <u>doing so</u>, he said, he would be better able to keep local leaders informed of police action and reduce the likelihood of communities "exploding in anger." (*Los Angeles Times*, 26.11.2002, p. B10, col. 5)

(3)   Is there anything that can prevent Hurricanes? To date, science and tech-nology have not given us the ability to <u>do so</u>. (*Chicago Tribune*, 3.1.2004, section 1, p. 28, col. 1)

(4)   Can stout shoes save you during a nuclear attack? They might <u>do</u>, providing you shake the radioactive dust from them before going inside. (*Guardian*, G2, 1.4.2004, p. 15, col. 4)

(5)   I believe that if I were to continue to play for Zimbabwe I would <u>do so</u> only by neglecting the voice of my conscience. (*Guardian*, Sports, 17.3.2003, p. 6, col. 2)

(6)   Your leader (Local voters must use their power, April 30) is right. <u>So</u> they must, but why then stop at suggesting the proportional representation that alone can make it worthwhile to vote? (*Guardian*, 5.5.2003, p. 19, col. 4, letter to the editor from Prof. George Hutchinson, Southampton)

(7)   During the appearances, Bratton rejected the idea of flooding South Los Angeles streets with officers. <u>Doing so</u> would probably raise the ire of a community with a long history of confrontation with police rather than solve any problems. (*Los Angeles Times*, 26.11.2002, p. B1 + 10, col. 1)

(8)   The national primary care research and development centres at Manchester and York universities, which carried out both this study and 1998's, acknow-ledge that not all the doctors who say they want to leave will. But previous research has shown that many will <u>do so</u>. (*Guardian*, 3.1.2003, p. 1, col. 1)

(9)   We save life first and we do the rest if we possibly can. The priority is to save life. If we can put the fire out, we will <u>do so</u>. (*Guardian*, 14.11.2002, p. 1, col. 4)

(10) I'm sure that neither of them could have murdered Brooks. It's a physical impossibility, knowing about dates and times. But *she* could have <u>done</u>. Ellie

Smith could have <u>done</u> – if only just. (Colin Dexter, *The Daughters of Cain*, 1995: 330)

(11)   "What was your accent like?" "Southern Welsh; You can still hear the trace of it, mind you." "<u>So</u> you can," said Isobel. (Muriel Spark, *The Bachelors*, 1963: 101)

Exercise 10   Substitution by *so* (L)

In Exercise 9 we have seen that strings of words containing a verb may be replaced by *do* (4), (10), and by *do so* (2), (3), (5), (7), (8), (9).[6] *Do* and *do so* in fact always replace a string containing a verb. In examples (6) and (11) of Exercise 9, a string of words containing a verb is replaced by *so*. The relevant part of (11) is repeated below:

(i)   "You can still hear the trace of it." "<u>So</u> you can," said Isobel.
       So = *still <u>hear</u> the trace of it*.
       Hear is a verb.

Examine the examples below. Could we generalize the pattern illustrated in (i) and say that *so* always substitutes for a string of words containing a verb?

(1)   We have counselled against the war, but once it's a reality the story moves on and <u>so</u> will we. (*Guardian*, G2, 17.3.2003, p. 7, col. 4)

(2)   The towns [Paula Radcliffe] has lived in (Nantwich, Bedford and Lough-borough) are the epitome of Middle England. And <u>so</u> is she. (*Guardian*, 17.12.2002, p. 13, col. 1)

(3)   Willie Whitelaw on a meeting with the West German interior minister: "He's very keen on terrorism. <u>So</u> am I." (*Guardian*, G2, 11.9.2002, p. 5, col. 4)

Exercise 11   Classifying examples: Locative
inversion (E)

In this exercise we return to the classification of inversion patterns. The exercise is longer and more discursive than the preceding exercises. It probably is also slightly more demanding. The goal is to carry further the kind of investigations started

---

[6]   For the role of substitution in syntactic analysis see Chapter 2, section 1.3.

in the chapter and see where that would lead us. In this particular exercise we will discover that English has more than one type of inversion. Here we look at patterns in which a verb appears to the left of the subject. Exercise 12 ties in with Exercise 11.

Recall that we discussed the derivation of word order patterns in which the subject of a sentence is preceded by an auxiliary. Let's start from (1a) below. Identify the subject and replace it by a pronoun. Does the example contain any auxiliaries? Is the auxiliary immediately followed by a full verb? Using SAI, form a direct question based on (1a).[7]

(1) a   This startling insight will naturally emerge from doing the syntax course.

The subject of the sentence is *this startling insight.* The sentence refers to a future event, futurity being signaled by the auxiliary *will*, which is followed by the infinitive of the verb. The various modifications suggested above are illustrated in the following sentences:

(1) b   It will naturally emerge from doing the syntax course.
    c   Will this startling insight naturally emerge from doing the syntax course?

Observe that when we apply SAI, we only move the auxiliary *will* in front of the subject; we cannot also move the verb *emerge* in front of the subject, regardless of whether we take the adverb *naturally* along:

(1) d   *Will emerge this startling insight naturally from doing the syntax course?
    e   *Will naturally emerge this startling insight from doing the syntax course?

Observe finally that we can also apply SAI to (1b), whose subject is a pronoun:

(1) f   Will it naturally emerge from doing the syntax course?

Now consider (2a). What is the subject? Is there an auxiliary? How would we form a direct question?

(2) a   This startling insight naturally emerges from doing the syntax course.

The subject of (2a) is again *this startling insight,* there is no auxiliary. We can replace the subject by a pronoun. When we want to ask a question we apply SAI, inserting the auxiliary *do* as a last resort.[8]

(2) b   It naturally emerges from doing the syntax course.
    c   Does this startling insight naturally emerge from doing the syntax course?

---

[7]   See Chapter 1, section 2.3.2.
[8]   See Chapter 1, section 2.2.2.

Again, we can also apply SAI with *do* insertion to (2b), with a pronominal subject:

(2) d <u>Does</u> it naturally emerge from doing the syntax course?

Observe that in order to ask a question we cannot invert the verb with the subject:

(2) e *<u>Emerges</u> it naturally from doing the course?

This is because in English full verbs do not invert with subjects. This was expressed in generalization (47) in the discussion section of the chapter, repeated here as (3):

(3) Verbs that are not auxiliaries do not invert with the subject.

Consider the position of the underlined verb in the following example in the light of the generalization in (3):

(4) a From behind detail of courses and qualifications <u>emerges</u> the progressive con-
       viction that no one can ever learn enough. (Based on *Guardian*, 14.2.2002,
       p. 9, col. 1)

In (4a) the verb *emerges* precedes the subject. We note that the subject itself is long and complex (*the progressive conviction that no one can ever learn enough*). At first sight we might think that example (4a) constitutes counter-evidence to our generalization in (3). If this were true we would have to re-examine the data and somehow weaken our generalization.

   However, closer examination of (4a) reveals that this example must be treated as a separate pattern. This can be seen if we compare this sentence with those in (1) and (2). Recall that in the cases of SAI illustrated above, a subject could be replaced by a pronoun (1f), (2d). If we try to replace the subject by a pronoun in (4a) the result is unacceptable:

(4) b *From behind detail of courses and qualifications emerges it.

To facilitate further comparison with the examples in (1), let us modify example (4a) slightly. We do this by inserting the auxiliary *will* in (4a), thus locating the event in the future. The resulting order is as in (4c) and not that in (4d):

(4) c From behind detail of courses and qualifications <u>will emerge</u> the progressive
       conviction that no one can ever learn enough.
    d *From behind detail of courses and qualifications <u>will</u> the progressive con-
       viction that no one can ever learn enough <u>emerge</u>.

We see that in this example the subject is preceded by both the auxiliary and the verb. Recall that this order was not possible with respect to our typical examples of SAI: (1d) and (1e) were unacceptable.

Table 1   Two inversion patterns

	SAI	Inversion type in (4a)
Can the subject be a pronoun?	yes	no
Will the order be auxiliary – subject – verb?	yes	no
Will the order be auxiliary – verb – subject?	no	yes

If you compare the inversion patterns in (1), (2), which we identify as instances of SAI, and the variations associated with example (4), there are a number of differences to note. In the routine examples of SAI as applied to (1a), the subject can be a pronoun (1b), and only the auxiliary *will* precedes the subject (1c). In (4a), the subject cannot be a pronoun (4b), the subject follows both the auxiliary and the lexical verb (4c). We summarize the differences in Table 1.

The inversion pattern illustrated in (4a) has a restricted distribution. One typical manifestation is that illustrated here, in which the first component of the sentence is a locative element, here *from behind detail of courses and qualifications.* The pattern in (4a) is often referred to with the term **locative inversion**.[9] In such patterns, the subject has to be relatively heavy; as we have seen, a pronominal subject is not possible.[10] The subject is found in a position towards the end of the sentence, where it is highlighted.

Identify the locative inversion patterns in the following examples. Compare their properties with those summarized in Table 1. Can the subject be replaced by a pronoun? For examples without any auxiliary, try inserting one (with appropriate change of verb form): what is the resulting word order? For examples with an auxiliary, comment on the relative position of auxiliary, subject, and verb.

(5)   On the credit side of South Africa's balance sheet goes the 8.4 million people who now have access to clean water, 3.8 million with electricity, and 1.46 million who have new homes. (*Guardian*, 24.5.2003, p. 11, col. 2)

(6)   Behind the celebrations and enthusiasm lies a project marked by controversy. (*Guardian, Life*, 18.3.2004, p. 2, col. 1)

(7)   From this has stemmed the bad manners and casual crime we see today. (*Independent*, 20.8.2004, p. 12, col. 2)

---

[9]   For a description of locative inversion see Emonds (1976: 34–7), Coopmans (1989), Hoekstra and Mulder (1990), Bresnan (1994), Culicover and Levine (2001).

[10]   In Chapter 5, Exercise 15 we will see that in French inversion, postverbal pronouns pattern differently from postverbal NPs. As this is the very last exercise of the book, this is not the right moment to tackle it!

(8) Through the door rushes his estranged brother, Turley, running for his life.
     (*Guardian*, *Review*, 20.3.2004, p. 13, col. 5)

Exercise 12   Classifying examples: Predicate inversion (E, L)

In this exercise we examine the classification of inversion patterns. The exercise is similar to Exercise 11 in that it is longer and more discursive than Exercises 1–10. The idea is again that we carry further the kind of investigations started in the chapter and see where that would lead us. In particular we will find confirmation that English has more than one type of inversion, a point already shown in Exercise 11, and we will discover that not all patterns in which an inflected form of *be* appears to the left of the subject are cases of SAI. This exercise ties in with Exercise 11.

Recall that we have discussed the derivation of word order patterns in which the subject of a sentence is preceded by an auxiliary. Let us start from (1a). Identify the subject of the sentence and replace it with a pronoun. Does the example contain any auxiliaries? Is the auxiliary followed by a full verb?

(1) a   Cost is complicating matters.

The subject of (1a) is *cost*; we replace the subject by a pronoun in (1b):

(1) b   It is complicating matters.

Apply SAI to the example in (1a, b) to form a direct question.[11] What is the resulting order? As you can see we have straightforward sequences of auxiliary – subject:

(1) c   Is cost complicating matters?
    d   Is it complicating matters?

When we apply SAI, we cannot also move the verb *complicating* in front of the subject:

(1) d   *Is complicating cost matters?
    e   *Is complicating it matters?

Let us now turn to (2a). How does it differ from (1a)?

(2) a   Cost will be complicating matters.

---

[11]   See Chapter 1, section 2.3.2.

The difference between (1a) and (2a) is that the state of affairs expressed by the latter sentence is situated in the future. This is achieved by means of the auxiliary *will*. By adding *will* to (1a) we create a sentence with two auxiliaries: the modal auxiliary *will* and the non-inflected form of *be*.[12] Identify the subject and replace it with a pronoun. The subject of the sentence is *cost*. We can replace the subject of (2a) with a pronoun.

(2) b It will be complicating matters.

Apply SAI to the examples in (2a, b) to form a direct question.[13] What is the resulting order? As you can see we again have straightforward sequences of auxiliary – subject:

(2) c Will cost be complicating matters?
    d Will it be complicating matters?

Observe that when we apply SAI, we must move only one auxiliary: it is not possible to move two auxiliaries across the subject (2e), nor is it possible to move both auxiliaries as well as the full verb (2f):

(2) e *Will be cost complicating matters?
    f *Will be complicating cost matters?

Let us formulate this in terms of a general principle:

(3) SAI moves only one auxiliary across the subject.

We can summarize the various patterns as in Table 2 below. Consider the examples in (4): the underlined subject is preceded by the verb *be*. Is *be* an instantiation of copula *be* or of auxiliary *be*? What arguments could you offer in support of your analysis?

(4) a Complicating matters is cost. (*Washington Post*, 10.12.2002, p. A16, col. 1)
    b Helping to run the house were a cook, a housemaid and a manservant. (Carol Shields, *Jane Austin*, 2001: 123)

Identify the participles associated with the auxiliaries. We find that in the examples the participle (*complicating, helping*) precedes its auxiliary. Restore the sentences to a more neutral word order in which the subject precedes the auxiliary and the verb:

(5) a Cost is complicating matters.
    b A cook, a housemaid and a manservant were helping to run the house.

---

[12] We will discuss sentences containing more than one auxiliary in more detail in Chapter 3, section 4.
[13] See Chapter 1, section 2.3.2.

Table 2 SAI

Can the subject be a pronoun?	yes
One auxiliary	
Order will be auxiliary – subject – verb?	yes
Order will be auxiliary – verb – subject?	no
Two auxiliaries	
Order will be auxiliary – subject – auxiliary – verb?	yes
Order will be auxiliary – auxiliary – subject – verb?	no
Order will be auxiliary – auxiliary – verb – subject?	no

The initial element of the examples in (4) is a string of words containing the participial form of the verb (*complicating, helping*). Given that they display the order auxiliary – subject we might conclude that the examples in (4) are simply examples of SAI.

However this conclusion would be rash. We first examine (4a). Try replacing the subject in (4a) by a pronoun. The resulting sentence is no longer acceptable.

(5) c   *Complicating matters is <u>it</u>.

The examples in (4) and in (5) contain just one auxiliary *be*. To examine if they really illustrate SAI we could also try to test our generalization in (3). What would happen if there was a sequence of auxiliaries, as in our earlier examples in (2)? Recall that principle (3) summarizes our finding that SAI moves only one auxiliary to the left of the subject. Try adding the future maker *will* to (5a), replacing the present tense form of *be* by *will be*.

(6) a   Complicating matters <u>will be</u> cost.

Observe that if we insert a future marker *will* in example (4a), the resulting order is that in which both *will* and *be* precede the subject *cost*. If we apply SAI as described in (3) above, then only the auxiliary *will* should precede the subject. But in (6), if only the auxiliary *will* precedes the subject while *be* follows it the sentence is unacceptable:

(6) b   *Complicating matters <u>will</u> cost <u>be.</u>

If you return to the main properties of SAI as summarized in Table 2, you will see that the inversion which is illustrated in (4) is quite different from SAI. We summarize the differences in Table 3. In the discussion above, identify which examples provide evidence for the various properties. Because of the differences between the two patterns, we will not consider the examples in (4) as illustrations of SAI. This means that the term SAI is restrictive: not every sequence in which an auxiliary precedes

Table 3   Two types of inversion

	SAI	Examples in (4)
Can the subject be a pronoun?	yes	no
Two auxiliaries		
Order is auxiliary – subject – auxiliary?	yes	no
Order is auxiliary – auxiliary – subject?	no	yes

the subject is automatically an instantiation of SAI. If you examine the properties of (4b) along the lines outlined above you will conclude that that example too is not an instantiation of SAI.

The patterns illustrated in (4) are often referred to as **predicate inversion**. In predicate inversion patterns the predicate, the string of words that would follow *be* in the neutral order, precedes *be*, and the subject, which would precede *be* in the neutral order, follows *be*. Examples (7)–(10) also illustrate predicate inversion. Restore the sentences in (7)–(10) to the more neutral order, in which auxiliary *be* is preceded by its subject:

(7)   Hurting the industry's ability to raise fares is the fact that the big airlines are putting more seats back into the skies to battle the rapid expansion of the budget airlines. (*Wall Street Journal*, 29.3.2004, p. A6, col. 6)

(8)   Sitting next to her in the remote cabin was 71-year old Elisabeta Sigilyetova, one of the last living speakers of a rare dialect of Khanty, a regional tongue nearly overwhelmed by Russia's Slavic majority. (*Wall Street Journal*, 26.3.2004, p. A1, col. 4)

(9)   Enjoying the festivities at the Sterling Fire Department's Patton Hall are, clockwise from above, Robyn, Blocher's dog, Winston, 5, Melanie Howard and Cosmo, 2, and, from left, Scott Morrison, Blocher, Cinston, and Blocher's father, Bill Blocher. (*Washington Post*, 25.3.2004, "Loudoun", p. 1, col. 1)

(10) Tucked away in the back of the booth of Haboldt & Company, a Paris dealer, is perhaps the best old master drawing here. (*New York Times*, 8.3.2004, p. E5, col. 6)

We return to the patterns illustrated in (4) and in (7)–(10) in Exercise 23 of Chapter 4.[14]

---

[14]   For discussion see Birner (1992), Birner and Ward (1992), Emonds (1976: 34–43), den Dikken and Næss (1993), Heycock and Kroch (1997).

2 Diagnostics for Syntactic Structure

Discussion

Contents

0   Introduction

In this chapter we start our systematic analysis of the structure of sentences. We will first elaborate some techniques for discovering sentence structure, so that, whenever we formulate a hypothesis about a particular structure, we can test this hypothesis using a well-defined set of analytical tools. We will decompose English sentences and demarcate their core constituents. The current chapter mainly concentrates on the position of the verb in the structure of the sentence. In the next chapters, we also turn our attention to the relation of the subject to the sentence and to the verb. Once we have determined what the components of the sentence are, we can formulate a hypothesis concerning the derivation of the sentence, that is, the way sentences are built up from such components. This will be further worked out in Chapters 3, 4, and 5.

Throughout the discussion, two kinds of data will be used. On the one hand, we use attested examples. Sometimes, we will manipulate these examples to clarify structural relations. In order to test our hypotheses we will often also create our own examples. When using attested data, we are acting like scientists doing field-work. We discover phenomena and we examine them in their natural settings. When creating our own examples, we are like scientists who conduct experiments in their laboratories.

On the basis of our observations and of our experiments, we will formulate a number of general hypotheses about how sentences are internally organized and how they are put together. These hypotheses will guide us in later sections.

The chapter is organized as follows: Section 1 develops a series of tests for identifying strings of words inside a sentence as units or constituents. Section 2 focuses on constituents containing a verb and examines two competing hypotheses about the composition of verbal constituents or, to introduce the technical term, verb phrases. According to one hypothesis, the verb phrase contains the verb and the auxiliaries of the sentence; according to the alternative hypothesis, the verb phrase contains the verb, its complements, and its adjuncts. We will show that the second hypothesis is both empirically and theoretically preferable.

While discussing the structure of sentences, we will elaborate the far-reaching theoretical proposal that all syntactic constituents are the result of combining or merging two constituents, and that constituents are hierarchically organized around a head. The head first combines with its complement. The resulting constituent then combines with the specifier. The need to postulate a specifier as one essential part of the constituent will initially be motivated on the basis of our analysis of the structure of the noun phrase in section 3. Head, complement, and specifier are the three core components of the phrase. Phrases may be further augmented by means of adjoined constituents. Section 4 summarizes the chapter.

1   Diagnostics for Structure

1.1   *Structure and meaning*

The discussion of the first chapter of this book was based on the hypothesis that language is two-faced: it unites form and interpretation ("meaning"). This hypothesis is trivially correct in the sense that words have a form and a meaning, but we have also seen that the arrangement of words into a sentence in itself is meaningful in that it also contributes to the interpretation of the sentence. Consider the underlined string of words in (1). What kind of information ("meaning") does it contribute to the sentence? Could you replace the underlined words by just one word?

(1)   Mr Straw decided to appoint a panel of independent doctors to examine General Pinochet <u>on January 5</u>. (*Guardian*, 13.1.2000, p. 1, col. 3)[1]

The string of words *on January 5* provides information about a date, or, in more general terms, about 'time'. The date given, *January 5*, refers to the time of some action or event. Which event is this? In fact, upon reading our example carefully, it seems that there are three possible ways of relating *on January 5* to the sentence: (i) *on January 5* may denote the time of Mr Straw deciding, (ii) it may denote the time of appointing, or (iii) it may denote the time of examining. (1) is three ways **ambiguous**: one string of words has three interpretations. The ambiguity does not reside in a lexical ambiguity of any one of the individual words in the string *on January 5*. These words have a constant meaning in this example, whichever the interpretation chosen. Let us look more closely at each of the three readings.

In the first reading, Mr Straw decided to do something, and his decision was taken on January 5. On January 5, what did Mr Straw decide to do? The answer to this question is that he decided to appoint a panel of independent doctors to examine General Pinochet. The string of words *to appoint a panel of independent doctors to examine General Pinochet* is a unit that functions as the object of the verb *decided*. The string of words *on January 5* itself is not part of the answer to the question as to what Mr Straw decided, it is not part of the object of *decide*:

(1) a   Mr Straw decided
         WHEN? – [on January 5]
         WHAT? – [to appoint a panel of independent doctors to examine GP]

In the second reading of the sentence, Mr Straw decided to do something and this activity would take place on January 5. To the question what Mr Straw decided to do, the answer would now be "to appoint a panel of independent doctors to

---

[1]   Cf. sentence (2) in Exercise 3 of Chapter 1.

examine General Pinochet on January 5." In this reading of (1), the string *on January 5* is part of the answer to the question of what Mr Straw decided, in other words it is part of the object of *decide* and it specifies the time of appointing. The time of Mr Straw's decision-making itself is now not specified. In this reading, the object of *decide* is the string *to appoint a panel of independent doctors to examine General Pinochet on January 5*. To the question when he will appoint the panel the answer is that he will appoint them on January 5. To the question who Mr Straw will appoint on January 5 the answer is: "a panel of independent doctors to examine General Pinochet." For this second interpretation, we can represent the relations between the elements of the sentence informally as in (1b). In (1b) *on January 5* is part of the object of *decided*. Recall that in (1a) above, the string *on January 5* was not part of object of *decided*.

(1) b   Mr Straw decided
        WHAT?
        [to appoint a panel of independent doctors to examine GP on January 5]
        to appoint
            WHEN? – [on January 5]
            WHO? – [a panel of independent doctors to examine GP]

Finally, in the third reading, the string *on January 5* specifies the time of the examining. We are not told when Mr Straw took his decision, nor are we told when the appointment will take place, but we are told on which date the appointed panel will examine General Pinochet. In this reading, Mr Straw again decided to do something. To the question what Mr Straw decided to do, the answer would again be "to appoint a panel of independent doctors to examine General Pinochet on January 5." In the third reading of (1), the time of the decision-making is not specified. The direct object of *decide* is the string *to appoint a panel of independent doctors to examine General Pinochet on January 5*. The string *on January 5* is part of the object of *decide*, but in the third interpretation it does not specify the time of appointing. *On January 5* specifies on which date the panel will examine General Pinochet. The answer to the question who Mr Straw will appoint is "a panel of independent doctors to examine General Pinochet on January 5."

(1) c   Mr Straw decided
        WHAT?
        [to appoint a panel of independent doctors to examine General Pinochet on January 5]
        to appoint
            WHO? – [a panel of independent doctors to examine General Pinochet on January 5]
        to examine
            WHO? – [General Pinochet]
            WHEN? – [on January 5]

(1) thus has three interpretations which arise from the three different relations that the string *on January 5* can have with the remainder of the sentence. As mentioned, the string *on January 5* itself does not change its meaning in the three interpretations. *On January 5* denotes a temporal specification, the fifth day of the month of January. What changes is the way this temporal specification is integrated into the sentence. In (1c) *on January 5* specifies the timing of *examine General Pinochet*; in (1b) it specifies the timing of *appoint a panel of independent doctors to examine General Pinochet*; in (1a) *on January 5* specifies the timing of *decided to appoint a panel of independent doctors to examine General Pinochet*. The different meanings come about by the way the unit *on January 5* is hooked onto the sentence; in other words, the different meanings come about by the various ways by which the sentence can be assembled. The three readings of *on January 5* are due to the structural relations in the sentence, its **syntax**. Ambiguities which arise through different structural relations are **structural ambiguities**.

The ambiguity that arises in (1) is not an exceptional phenomenon. This type of structural ambiguity is fairly frequent in actual usage, even though it rarely leads to problems of communication. In a particular communicative setting, the reader/hearer of ambiguous sentences will be able to pick out the appropriate reading easily.[2] Sometimes, though, a writer/speaker may deliberately exploit the potential for ambiguity created by the syntax. The following extract illustrates this point:

(2)   I went to the National Gallery today, but it brought back painful memories of B., so I went back to Soho and paid two pounds to watch a fat girl with spots remove her bra and knickers <u>through a peephole</u>. I watched her through a peephole. She didn't remove her underclothes through a peephole. Query: are there night classes in syntax? (Sue Townsend, *Adrian Mole: The Wilderness Years*, 1993: 248–9.)

Let us look at (1) once again. Our discussion of this example implies that a sentence is not put together at one go but that it is assembled step by step from smaller units. The different readings of (1) can directly be related to the way the sentence is assembled. In particular, we can relate the ambiguity of (1) to the timing of hooking the unit *on January 5* onto a particular part of the sentence. In (1c), the string *on January 5* belongs with *to examine General Pinochet*. We could say that when assembling the sentence, the string *on January 5* is hooked onto the string *to examine General Pinochet*, creating a unit *to examine General Pinochet on January 5*. The resulting unit is then hooked up to *a panel of independent doctors*. In turn, the resulting unit *a panel of independent doctors to examine General Pinochet on January 5* is hooked onto *appoint*, and finally the result is itself hooked up to the verb *decided* and its subject *Mr Straw*.[3] (3a) schematizes the steps of the assembly process to create the reading in which *on January 5* modifies *examine*.

---

2   See Sperber and Wilson (1986) for an account of this type of disambiguation.
3   This sketch is provisional. We return to the various steps in this chapter and in Chapters 3 and 4.

(3)　(i)　to examine General Pinochet + [$_{\text{UNIT1}}$ on January 5]
　　　　⇒[$_{\text{UNIT2}}$ to examine General Pinochet [$_{\text{UNIT1}}$ on January 5]]

　　(ii)　a panel of independent doctors + UNIT2
　　　　⇒[$_{\text{UNIT3}}$ a panel of independent doctors [$_{\text{UNIT2}}$ to examine General Pinochet [$_{\text{UNIT1}}$ on January 5]]]

　　(iii)　appoint + UNIT3
　　　　⇒ [$_{\text{UNIT4}}$ appoint [$_{\text{UNIT3}}$ a panel of independent doctors [$_{\text{UNIT2}}$ to examine General Pinochet [$_{\text{UNIT1}}$ on January 5]]]]

　　(iv)　Mr Straw decided + UNIT4
　　　　⇒[$_{\text{UNIT5}}$ Mr Straw decided [$_{\text{UNIT4}}$ to appoint [$_{\text{UNIT3}}$ a panel of independent doctors [$_{\text{UNIT2}}$ to examine General Pinochet [$_{\text{UNIT1}}$ on January 5]]]]]

In order to achieve the reading in (1a), we assemble the sentence rather differently. When we link the string *to examine General Pinochet* with the string *a panel of independent doctors* we do not yet integrate *on January 5*. The temporal specification only comes in later, when we are putting together *decide* with the remainder of the sentence.

(4)　(i)　a panel of independent doctors + [$_{\text{UNIT1}}$ to examine General Pinochet]
　　　　⇒[$_{\text{UNIT2}}$ a panel of independent doctors [$_{\text{UNIT1}}$ to examine Greneral Pinochet]]

　　(ii)　appoint + UNIT2
　　　　⇒ [$_{\text{UNIT3}}$ appoint [$_{\text{UNIT2}}$ a panel of independent doctors [$_{\text{UNIT1}}$ to examine General Pinochet]]]

　　(iii)　Mr Straw decided + UNIT3
　　　　⇒[$_{\text{UNIT4}}$ Mr Straw decided [$_{\text{UNIT3}}$ to appoint [$_{\text{UNIT2}}$ a panel of independent doctors [$_{\text{UNIT1}}$ to examine General Pinochet]]]]

　　(iv)　UNIT4 + [$_{\text{UNIT5}}$ on January 5]
　　　　⇒[[$_{\text{UNIT4}}$ Mr Straw decided [$_{\text{UNIT3}}$ to appoint [$_{\text{UNIT2}}$ a panel of independent doctors [$_{\text{UNIT1}}$ to examine General Pinochet]]]] [$_{\text{UNIT5}}$ on January 5]]

In representation (3), the unit *on January 5* is deeply integrated into the sentence; it is combined early on (in step (i)) with the verb *examine*. In representation (4), the same unit is added at the final stage of the construction of the sentence (in step (iv)). The brackets used in the schematic representations above reflect the level of integration: in (3) *on January 5* is followed by 5 right-hand brackets; in (4) by only 2 such brackets.

The displays in (3) and in (4) are imprecise. For one thing using labels such as UNIT1, UNIT2 suggests that all these entities are similar in nature, though they make different contributions to the interpretation of the sentence. Also the representations are very difficult to read. They are a complex ways of showing the history of how the sentence is put together and how the interpretations are arrived at. In the remainder of this chapter we will elaborate a more precise and transparent way for representing the structure of sentences and we will also provide tools to determine the structural units.

1.2   *Intuitions about structure*

In section 1.1 we talked about structure in a fairly intuitive and loose way. We appealed to our linguistic awareness as speakers of English to informally represent some of the structural units that build the sentence with the different interpretations associated to the sentence. We indicated these units by bracketing, [. . .]. Units of form, i.e. sequences of words, such as *on January 5*, are taken to correspond to units of meaning, the string *on January 5* is a time specification.

Consider a sentence such as (5a). Going by your intuitions as to who does what and when, how would you identify the major meaningful units in this sentence? Represent each unit by using square brackets ([$_{\text{UNIT}}$ . . .]).

(5) a   The customer in the corner will order the drinks before the meal.

Probably, you will have bracketed the string as in (5b):

(5) b   [$_{\text{UNIT}}$ The customer in the corner] will order [$_{\text{UNIT}}$ the drinks] [$_{\text{UNIT}}$ before the meal].

Square brackets will from now on be used to demarcate units of structure. We don't have to label each set of brackets as "UNIT": the very presence of the brackets means that the string of words contained in the brackets is a unit.

(5) c   [The customer in the corner] will order [the drinks] [before the meal].

In (5c) the brackets identify three units or **constituents**: (i) *the customer in the corner*, (ii) *the drinks*, (iii) *before the meal*. There is no indication as to how the auxiliary *will* and the verb *order* are integrated into the sentence. In Chapter 1, section 2.2.1, we saw that auxiliaries tend to associate with a verb. We might propose that the auxiliary *will* in (5) forms a unit with the verb *order*. On this assumption, we could formulate the hypothesis that the assembly of the sentence is as in (5d).

(5) d   **Hypothesis A**
         [The customer in the corner] [will order] [the drinks] [before the meal].

But others might say that the bracketing in (5d) is counter-intuitive because the verb *order* should first be assembled with the string *the drinks*, which is the direct object of the verb and which refers to the entity affected directly by the action expressed by the verb. If you use the verb *order* you expect to find a direct object: 'order what?' 'Ordering' is an activity that implies there will be some entity being ordered. This relation between *order* and *the drinks* is independent of the presence of the auxiliary *will*: we can use the string *order the drinks* also in the absence of an auxiliary such as *will*:

(5) a′   The customer in the corner orders the drinks before the meal.

The close relationship between *order* and *the drinks* is not revealed in the bracketing in (5d). How could we represent this relationship between the verb and its object? The bracketing in (5e) is meant to show that the verb *order* and the unit *the drinks* are first assembled to form a unit.

(5) e **Hypothesis B**
[The customer in the corner] [will] [order [the drinks]] [before the meal].

Let us compare (5d) and (5e) and try to make more explicit the claims that the two alternative bracketings make. Having clarified this issue, we will examine the predictions of these claims more carefully.

In the diagrams below we use another format to represent how sentences are built up. This format is called the **tree diagram** format: like bracketing, it schematizes how sentences are formed from smaller units. The tree diagrams below correspond to the bracketed representations above, but they allow us to read off more easily how the various parts of the sentence are put together.

According to one representation, (5d)/(5d′), when assembling the sentence, we first assemble the auxiliary *will* and the verb *order*, and then we combine the resulting unit with the other constituents: the subject *the customer in the corner*, the direct object *the drinks*, and the time specification *before the meal*. In the tree, a triangle associated with a constituent is a device to show that the internal make-up of the unit in question is not relevant to the current discussion.

(5) d′

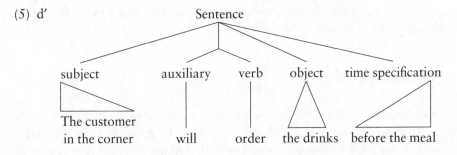

According to the alternative in (5e), the assembly proceeds differently. Here, the verb *order* is first assembled with its object, *the drinks*. Then we combine the resulting unit with the auxiliary *will*, with the time specification *before the meal*, and with the subject *the customer in the corner*.

(5) e′

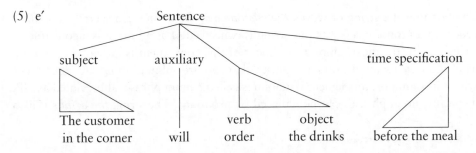

These structural representations have different implications. For instance, starting from the root of the structure "Sentence," to reach the object *the drinks* in (5d') you go directly from the root to the unit *the drinks*. This means that, starting from Sentence, the subject *the customer in the corner* and the object *the drinks* are both equally accessible. On the other hand, to reach the object *the drinks* in (5e'), we first have to enter into the unit *order the drinks*. In (5e') the subject *the customer in the corner* is more readily accessible from the root "Sentence" than the object. From Sentence it takes one single step to reach the subject; it takes two steps to reach the object. The subject is presented as an **immediate** constituent of the sentence, the object is presented as an **ultimate** constituent of the sentence: it is a component of the sentence by virtue of being a component of the unit *order the drinks*, which is itself an immediate component of the sentence. (5e') introduces a subject-object asymmetry, it suggests that the relation between the sentence and the subject is more immediate than that which exists between the sentence and the object. Conversely, according to (5e') the object has a closer relationship with the verb than the subject, since verb and object together form a constituent that excludes the subject.

In what follows we will evaluate the two hypotheses by examining their consequences. Intuitively, both have some appeal, so we cannot simply rely on intuitions to discard one or the other. We will investigate whether there are any criteria that could be used to distinguish between the two ways of integrating the verb into the sentence. In other words, we are trying to elaborate diagnostics for syntactic structure.

In order to elaborate diagnostics for structure, we will look at attested examples to see if the language itself perhaps provides any indications that a particular string of words acts as or is perceived as a unit.

1.3   Substitution

Anaphoric elements, such as, for instance, pronouns, are elements that can be used to replace strings of words.[4] This is illustrated in (6). The pronoun *he* in (6b) refers to the subject, *the customer in the corner*, in (6a), and the pronoun *them* refers to the object *the drinks*. The constituent that is replaced by a pronoun is its **antecedent**.

(6) a   <u>The customer in the corner</u> will order <u>the drinks</u> before the meal.
     b   <u>He</u> will pay for <u>them</u> later.

The fact that the string of words *the customer in the corner* can serve as the antecedent of a pronoun suggests this string is conceived of as a unit; it is a constituent. At first sight, the most important element of this constituent is the noun *customer*. The noun *customer* denotes the entity that we are talking about. A constituent whose most important element is a noun is called a **noun phrase**, abbreviated as **NP**. Typically, noun phrases can be replaced by pronouns. The string *the drinks* is also

---

[4]   See Chapter 1, Exercises 9 and 10.

a constituent: it can be replaced by the pronoun *them*. Because the most important element of the constituent is *drinks*, the plural form of the noun *drink*, the constituent *the drinks* is also a noun phrase.

Before the meal is another constituent, it can be replaced by a word such as *then*. The string *before the meal* contains a noun phrase, *the meal*, which can be replaced by *it* (cf. *before it*). *Before the meal* combines a preposition, *before*, with an NP; it is a **prepositional phrase** (PP). Other examples of prepositional phrases are *in the garden*, *for his brother*, *after the war*, etc.

Depending on their core elements, constituents will be of different types: constituents belong to **categories**. The core element of the constituent, which determines its category, is called the **head**. An NP contains a noun (N) as its head, an NP is **headed** by an N.

Based on this conception of constituency, a **verb phrase** is a constituent whose head is a verb. For our test sentence we have elaborated two hypotheses for the identification of the verb phrase (VP): according to (5d) the VP is *will order*, according to (5e) the VP is *order the drinks*. Let us see if substitution of strings containing a verb can help us choose between these hypotheses. Examine how substitution affects verbal units in the examples in (7):

(7) a If I had wanted to hurt someone, believe me, I would have done. (Elizabeth George, *Missing Joseph*, 1993/1996: 172)
    b If Sir Alex wants to sign somebody he can do. (*Guardian*, 31.12.2002, p. 14, col. 1)[5]

In these examples the verb *do* serves to replace a verb and its object. In (7a) *done* = *hurt someone*; in (7b) *do* = *sign somebody*. If a verb and its object can be replaced together, this suggests that the relevant string of words is a unit, a constituent.

Consider (8). What does the pronoun *he* refer to? What does the string *do so* stand for?

(8) The home secretary is under an obligation to examine any evidence of discriminatory treatment. He can only do so through assessment, examination of facts, communication with people and rational arguments and actions. (*Guardian*, 9.9.2002, p. 11, col. 3)

In (8) the pronoun *he* refers to *the home secretary*, an NP. *Do so* stands for *examine any evidence of discriminatory treatment*, i.e., a verb + its direct object.[6]

With the examples in (7) and (8) as your models, try to replace a string of words containing the verb *order* in our test sentence (6a) above. In (9), we give some possible results.

---

[5] Note that the substitution illustrated in (7) may not be accepted by all speakers of English. In particular, speakers of British English accept it more easily than American speakers, and even among British speakers there is variation.
[6] See also Chapter 1, Exercise 9.

(9) a   The customer in the corner will order the drinks before the meal but in order
        to <u>do so</u> before the meal he will first need a wine list.

    b   The customer in the corner will order the drinks before the meal but in order
        to <u>do so</u> he needs a wine list now.

    c   If the customer in the corner wants to order the drinks before the meal he
        can <u>do</u>.

Do so in (9a) stands for *order the drinks*. Let us return to the representations for the
sentence which we are examining. Representation (5d′), based on hypothesis (5d), is
not really compatible with the substitution in (9a). According to (9a) the string
order the drinks acts as one constituent: it can be replaced by *do so*. But in (5d′) the
verb *order* does not form a constituent with the object *the drinks*. The constituent
that contains the verb is the string *will order*, it is composed of the verb and the
auxiliary. On the other hand, representation (5e′), based on hypothesis (5e), represents the verb and the object *order the drinks* as forming a unit. The most important
element in this unit is a verb (*order*): it tells us what kind of action is going on. A
constituent whose most important element is a verb is a **verb phrase** or **VP**.

Compare (9a) with (9b) and (9c). Which constituents are substituted for in
(9b) and in (9c)? In these examples, the substitution process also affects the time
specification *before the meal*. *Do so* in (9b) and *do* in (9c) stand for *order the
drinks before the meal*. Is this type of substitution predicted by hypothesis (5d)
and representation (5d′)? Clearly not, since, as we have just seen, according to (5d)
the auxiliary *will* and the verb *order* are taken to form a constituent, but the object
the drinks and the time specification *before the meal* are not represented as being
part of that constituent.

However, hypothesis (5e) and its representation (5e′) also do not predict that the
substitutions in (9b, c) are possible. If substitution identifies constituents, i.e. strings
of words that act as units, then the string *order the drinks before the meal* must be
a constituent. (5e′) does not offer a basis for this substitution: the time specification
is not part of the constituent containing the verb. In order to ensure that the unit
containing the verb, or the VP, contains the time specification as well, we should
integrate the time specification into the constituent headed by the verb, the VP.
What we want is something like (5f). We have labeled all constituents according to
their category.

(5) f

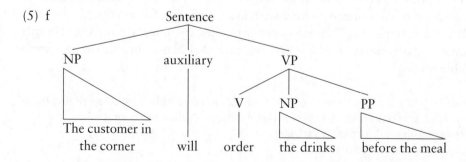

In this representation, the string *order the drinks before the meal* as a whole is represented as a VP. From the point labeled VP, three lines link down to three constituents: the verb *order*, the object *the drinks*, and the PP *before the meal*. In the tree diagram representation, a point in which a number of lines come together is called a **node**; nodes are given labels to indicate their category. The lines linking nodes in a tree to their constituents are called the **branches** of the tree.

Compare (5f) with (5d') and with (5e'). Does (5f) have more of the properties of (5d') or is it closer to (5e'). To answer this question you should assess the implications the tree would have for the relations of the various constituents to the sentence.

You will probably conclude that like (5e'), (5f) establishes an asymmetry between the subject and the object, linking the object more closely to the verb than the subject, and conversely, relating the subject more directly to the sentence as a whole. The trees (5e') and (5f) differ in the way in which they treat the time specification, that is, the PP *before the meal*. According to (5e'), the time specification remains completely outside the VP (*order the drinks*); in (5f) the PP *before the meal* is fully integrated into the VP. We can ask ourselves what the advantages of (5f) are. And also: does it have any drawbacks?

Recall that we assume that syntactic structure determines interpretation. Let us consider the claims made by the different representations above for the interpretation of the relevant strings. When comparing (5f) and (5e'), we observe that in (5e') the verb is assembled with the object, the temporal PP is not part of the resulting verb-object unit. (5e') represents the verb and its object as having a closer relationship than that which holds between the verb and the time specification. Such an asymmetry between the object NP and the temporal PP seems intuitively plausible: the action described by the sentence is 'ordering drinks'. The time of that action is additional information that does not alter the nature of the action: ordering drinks before a meal or during a meal remains the same kind of activity. (5f) suggests that the verb is assembled with its object and with the time specification at the same time. Such a representation of the structure of the sentence fails to reflect any asymmetry between the object NP and the time PP. In (5f) the hypothesis seems to be that the time PP is automatically part of the VP.

What predictions do the representations make for substitution? One prediction of (5f) is that whenever you replace a constituent containing the verb (= a verb phrase), this will automatically affect the PP *before the meal*. Or, phrasing the prediction differently: it should not be possible to simply replace a unit consisting of the verb *order* and its object *the drinks*. Is this prediction correct? If you turn back to the examples of substitution in (9), you will conclude that (5f) is incompatible with (9a), while (5e') is compatible with this example.

Having already discarded (5d'), we still have a problem to define what should be the appropriate representation of the sentence. We find ourselves in a sort of paradox. To account for the substitutions in (9b, c), we would favour (5f). To account for the substitution in (9a), we would favour (5e'), because the latter representation captures the closer relation between verb and object. What we need then is a more articulated representation with a VP that singles out the verb and the object, excluding the PP, and which at the same time allows the verb, the object, and the PP to be a unit. This can be achieved if we assemble the VP step by step: first we assemble the verb and its object, then we assemble the resulting unit with the time specification:

(5) g

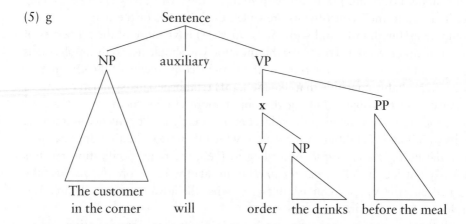

(5g) combines the good points of (5e′) with those of (5f). Substitution can pick either the unit x, composed of [V + NP], (as in (5e′)) or the unit labeled VP, composed of [V + NP + PP], (as in (5f)). (5g) introduces a **hierarchy** internally to the VP: the object is "closer" to the verb than the time specification.

What kind of label should we give to the constituent *order the drinks*? Its core element is a verb, and substitution is by means of *do* or *do so*, typically verb phrase substitutes. This suggests that this constituent is also a VP. The structure we end up with has what is called a **layered** VP. First, we construct the **core** VP, the central layer containing the verb and its object. Then we extend this layer with a time specification by adding the PP *before the meal*, creating a larger constituent. If we assume that the structure of a sentence is related to its meaning (as we have to do in order to account for structural ambiguity), then the layered VP should feed into the interpretation. Such a layered structure implies that a time specification is less central to the activity expressed by the verb than the object. This consequence of the structure mirrors our intuitions about interpretation: a time specification such as *before the meal* does not define the kind of activity denoted by the VP, but it merely provides accessory information on the timing of that activity.

In (5h) we provide both the tree representation and the labeled bracketing representation for the structure of the sentence. In the latter, the labels in the left-hand corners identify the category of the constituent. (5h) contains two nodes labeled VP, one immediately above the other. What is the head of the lower VP? What is the head of the higher one? For both constituents, the related head is the verb *order*. It is not the case that there are two distinct VPs in this structure. Rather, we have one core VP augmented with an extra constituent, the time specification. The time specification is not central to the information conveyed by V. It can be omitted.

(5) h **Hypothesis B (revised)**
The diagram

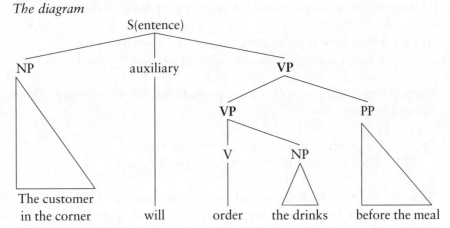

Labeled bracketing
[s [NP The customer in the corner] [will] [VP [VP order [NP the drinks]] [PP before the meal]]].

The argumentation above introduces two kinds of motivations for adopting the layered structure with the double VP node. On the one hand, the representation is motivated on **empirical** grounds: we have shown the need for introducing the layered structure by looking at substitution data. The structure is also motivated by the general hypothesis that the structure of a sentence is related to its interpretation. The latter is a **theoretical** hypothesis; we could also say that the second argument is **conceptual**, since it follows from the way we have conceived our theory. Both types of argumentation contribute to the analysis. When formulating an argumentation, it is important to be able to identify which type of reasoning has been used.

1.4 Movement

In a neutral sentence, the subject typically precedes the verb and the object follows it. The preverbal position of the subject and the postverbal position of the object are called their **canonical** positions. Identify the direct objects in the sentences in (10). You will observe that objects do not always occupy their canonical positions. Some objects have been moved to a different position. Try to restore any displaced objects to their canonical positions.

(10) a Baxter said that he had been using a *Sinex* liquid decongestant . . . but then spotted the *Vicks* inhaler when shopping in Park City, and bought it since he preferred to use it. "The British one, I have been using since I was about nine." (*Guardian*, 22.3.2002, p. 3, col. 1)
   b The news, when it comes, he seems to take well enough. (*Guardian*, G2, 26.7.2002, p. 2, col. 1)

As you can tell, two direct objects have been shifted to the beginning of the sentence.[7]
If we restore them to their canonical positions we arrive at the following:

(10) a′ I have been using <u>the British one</u> since I was about nine.
     b′ When it comes, he seems to take <u>the news</u> well enough.

The underlined strings of words in the primed (10a, b) are constituents. They can be
replaced by pronouns.

(10) a″ I have been using <u>it</u> since I was about nine.
     b″ When it comes, he seems to take <u>it</u> well enough.

Typically, constituents can be moved around in the sentence. Consider (11a). What is
the subject related to the verb *think*? What is the subject of *are just a vast conspiracy
to divorce you from ordinary life*? Do these subjects occupy their canonical positions?

(11) a A lot of the elements that surround you in the job, you sometimes think
         are just a vast conspiracy to divorce you from ordinary life. (*Guardian*,
         26.4.2002, G2, p. 6, col. 4)

In (11a) the subject of the verb *think* is the pronoun *you*; it occupies its canonical
preverbal position. The subject of *are a vast conspiracy* is the noun phrase *a lot of
elements that surround you in the job*. This subject is not in the expected position,
to the immediate left of *are*. It has apparently been shifted leftward. We can restore
it to its canonical position as follows:

(11) b You sometimes think <u>a lot of the elements that surround you in the job</u> are
         just a vast conspiracy to divorce you from ordinary life.

Identify the displaced constituent in (11c), identify its category, and restore it to its
canonical position:

(11) c Our dustmen arrive too early for me to check, but our fishmonger and his
         staff in Petersfield all wear ties (Letters, October 22) and very smart they
         look too. (*Guardian*, 23.10.2002, p. 9, col. 5, Letter to the editor from
         David Dew, Horndean, Hants)

In this example the string *very smart* has been fronted, its canonical position is to
the right of the verb *look* (*they look very smart too*). *Very smart* has as its main
component the adjective *smart*. A constituent headed by an adjective is an **adjective
phrase** or **AP**.

---

[7] For the interpretive effect of preposing constituents see Ward (1988) and the references cited
there. See also Reinhart (1981), Authier (1992), Rizzi (1997).

Let us return to our initial example (5a). Is it possible to displace the direct object or the time specification?

(12) a The drinks, the customer in the corner will order before the meal (but the dessert, they will order later).
      b Before the meal, the customer in the corner will order the drinks.

In English, the order in which the subject precedes the verb and the object follows it is the unmarked word order.[8] Fronting of a constituent gives rise to a special or **marked** word order, i.e. an order that deviates from the neutral order. We assume that creating a pattern that deviates from the normal neutral word order is an additional operation. Recall that we proposed that language is guided by a principle of economy. In Chapter 1, section 2.2.3, we proposed that units are only inserted if they have some impact on the interpretation of the sentence. We illustrated this hypothesis by the discussion of the use of the auxiliary *do*. We could extend the application of the principle of **economy** by proposing that operations that rearrange constituents also have to be associated with some particular interpretive effect. If they were not, then, by virtue of the principle of economy, there would be no point in performing the operation. In other words, a non-neutral or marked order will be associated with some difference in interpretation. For instance, the fronted object in (12a) gives rise to some contrasting effect: we contrast *the drinks* and *the dessert*. When we front a time specification (12b), we organize the information in the sentence according to temporal information. In the following examples, the authors are exploring the possibility of fronting constituents. Identify the fronted constituents. Restore them to their canonical position. What is the category of the fronted constituents?

(13) a "They must talk about it, and talk about it they must," he said. Food for thought, there! It's a phrase that could add a measure of gravity to any press conference. "We must do this, and do this we must." (Simon Hoggart, *Guardian*, 29.1.2003, p. 2, col. 5)
      b But I was still a long way from figuring out what my goal was. I told the governor [of the prison] that I wasn't sure how I was going to manage it – but manage it I would. (*Guardian*, G2, 15.5.2003, p. 7, col. 4)

---

[8] The unmarked order is the neutral word order. Marked word orders are less neutral in that they carry some specific communicative effect. For instance, the word order in sentence (ia) is unmarked: the object NP *this book* follows the verb *like*. In (ib) fronting of the object NP *this book* gives rise to a marked word order. This example could be used, for instance, if the speaker wants to contrast the book under discussion with another book.

(i) a I didn't like this book very much.
     b This book, I didn't like very much (but that one I really enjoyed).

For discussion of the concept of markedness and its relation to interpretation see de Hoop, Haverkot, and van den Noort (2004). For the interpretive effect of preposing constituents see Ward (1988).

In (13a) the author fronts *talk about it* and *do this*, and in (13b) *manage it* is fronted. Since these strings are constituents whose most important element is the verb, they are verb phrases:

(13) a′   "They must talk about it, and [$_{VP}$ <u>talk about it</u>] they must," he said. Food for thought, there! . . . "We must do this, and [$_{VP}$ <u>do this</u>] we must."
      b′   I told the governor [of the prison] that I wasn't sure how I was going to manage it – but [$_{VP}$ <u>manage it</u>] I would.

Let us return to our test example, (5a). On the basis of the structural representation of the sentence, we should be able to predict how VP fronting will apply. In representation (5h), there are two nodes labeled VP: the core VP and the augmented VP including the temporal specification. Try fronting either of these. You will find that both operations give an acceptable result:

(14) a   Order their drinks before the meal, they will.
      b   Order their drinks, they will before the meal.

The data in (14) provide empirical support for the structure in (5h). Would the fronting data in (14) be compatible with the other representations that we had envisaged, that is (5d′), (5e′), and (5f)? Adopting (5d′) would pose a problem: in that representation there is no constituent containing the verb and the object (14a) or the verb, the object, and the time specification (14b). (5e′) fares slightly better in that it allows (14b) but it does not allow (14a). Conversely, (5f) allows (14a) but not (14b). So (5h) represents a better hypothesis about the structure of the sentence.

1.5   *Question formation*

Invent an answer to the questions in (15):

(15) a   Who have you invited to the party?
      b   Who has invited you to this meeting?
      c   What have you bought?
      d   An Indian meal or fish and chips. Which do you prefer?

When you think up answers to the questions above, it is quite possible that you will come up not just with one word but with a string of words. The relevant string of words functions as a unit in the communicative exchange: it provides the answer to the question. An answer to a question will fill in the missing information that is represented in the question by words such as *what, who, which*. As discussed in section 1.3, strings of words that are replaced by one word are constituents. For instance, take (15a). A possible answer could be:

(16) a My friends from college.

Question (15a) implies that 'you have invited someone', and it signals that the speaker doesn't know who the invitee was. (16a) supplies the missing information: it supplies a replacement for the interrogative word *who*. Questions which ask for a replacement of an interrogative constituent, are called **constituent questions**: the answer to such questions supplies the missing constituent. Because most interrogative words in English begin with *wh*, such questions are also called ***wh*-questions**, and interrogative constituents such as *who*, *what*, etc. are called ***wh*-constituents.**[9]

(16b) inserts the answer to (15a) into the sentence. Compare the form of question (15a) and the form of the answer (16b):

(16) b I have invited [my friends from college].

(15a) differs from (16b) in a number of ways. (i) In (15a) the direct object is realized as a *wh*-constituent, *who*. (ii) This (interrogative) direct object of the verb *invited* does not occupy its canonical position but it takes up an initial position. (iii) There is an application of subject auxiliary inversion (SAI, see also Chapter 1, section 2.2). Of particular relevance to the current discussion is the observation that in the answer the interrogative constituent of the question is replaced by the constituent (here *my friends from college*). We can conclude that another technique for identifying constituents is to examine whether the strings of words that are taken to be constituents can serve as answers to questions.

Formulate constituent questions to target each of the underlined constituents in our test sentence:

(17) a <u>The customer in the corner</u> will order <u>the drinks</u> <u>before the meal</u>.

Recall that we also identified a constituent centered around the verb. How is the VP questioned in (18)?

(18) a I think that would be the worst thing in the world for him, a family holiday. What's he going to do? Sit on the beach? (Based on *Guardian*, G2, 29.7.2002, p. 4, col. 3)
   b What is Sylvia to do? What are we all meant to do? Hang our cars from the trees? Throw them away? (*Guardian*, G2, 28.4.2003, p. 9, col. 3)
   c "We need fewer people." "What would you do? Eliminate people?" (Based on a cartoon in *Washington Post*, 29.4.2003, p. C12)

As you can see, verb phrases can function as targets for *wh*-questions. In our test sentence (5a), repeated in (17a) above, we identified a core VP (*order the drinks*)

---

[9] We look more carefully at the fronting process involved in the formation of *wh*-questions in Chapter 5.

and what we called an augmented VP (*order the drinks before the meal*). Using the examples in (18) as a model, try to formulate questions targeting either of these VPs. Based on (17a) you could form either of the following questions:

(17) b   What will the customer in the corner do before the meal?
      c   What will the customer in the corner do?

Wh-questions confirm that the strings *order the drinks* and *order the drinks before the meal* are constituents: each string can be the answer to a *wh*-question.

1.6   Deletion/ellipsis

Consider the following fragments. In the second part of each extract some material has been omitted. The site of the ellipsis is to the right of the underlined words. Supply the words that have been omitted. On what basis can you recover the omitted material?[10]

(19) a   It is up to us other teams to take steps to rectify our performance defi-
          ciency, and <u>we will</u>. (*Guardian*, 8.10.2002, p. 15, col. 7)
      b   When he first ran for office four years ago, Gov. Gray Davis vowed to save
          California's old-growth forests. <u>He hasn't</u>, as Moloney sees it. (*Los Ange-
          les Times*, 26.11.2002, p. B7, col. 2)
      c   After all, Francesca's hardly news any more. We are all trying to forget her.
          As <u>if we could</u>. Although <u>we should</u>. <u>I can't</u>. (Francis Fyfield, *Undercurrents*,
          2001: 50)
      d   I saw Mr Clark stand up, throw a punch at Mr McAlpine, kick the table
          over, jump at him on the ground, and start choking him, before two chefs
          came out of the kitchen and pulled them apart . . . We have an open-plan
          kitchen, and so my staff jumped in and separated them; I wouldn't like to
          think what would have happened if <u>they hadn't</u>. (*Guardian*, 11.11.2002,
          p. 9, col. 4)
      e   All in the name of a pretence that, with just a little bit more time passing, all
          obstacles will miraculously recede. <u>They won't</u>. (*Guardian*, 6.5.2003, p. 16,
          col. 2)
      f   Only those who were in the room know the absolute truth of this story.
          <u>No one else probably ever will</u>. (*Washington Post*, 25.3.2004, p. D3, col. 5)
      g   If we could charge more money, <u>we would</u>. (*Wall Street Journal*, 29.3.2004,
          p. A6, col. 6)
      h   Everyone says you can't be scientific and fun, but we think <u>you can</u>. (*New
          York Times*, 8.3.2004, p. C5, col. 2)

---

[10]   See also Chapter 1, Exercise 8.

In these examples a constituent that is recoverable from the preceding context has been omitted. For instance, in (19a) we can recover the string *take steps to rectify our performance deficiency* from the preceding sentence. In each of the examples, the auxiliary is retained and a constituent centered around the verb is omitted. We restore the omitted strings in (19'):

(19') a <u>We will</u> [$_{VP}$ take steps to rectify our performance deficiency].

      b <u>He hasn't</u> [$_{VP}$ saved California's old-growth forests].

      c As <u>if we could</u> [$_{VP}$ forget her]. Although <u>we should</u> [$_{VP}$ forget her]. <u>I can't</u> [$_{VP}$ forget her].

      d I wouldn't like to think what would have happened if <u>they hadn't</u> [$_{VP}$ jumped in and separated them].

      e <u>They won't</u> [$_{VP}$ miraculously recede].

      f <u>No one else probably ever will</u> [$_{VP}$ know the absolute truth of this story].

      g <u>we would</u> [$_{VP}$ charge more money].

      h <u>you can</u> [$_{VP}$ be scientific and fun].

Let us once again turn to representations (5d') and (5h). By adopting (5h), we can straightforwardly describe the processes applying in (19) as an illustration of verb phrase ellipsis. If we adopt (5d') we cannot describe the process in (19) as VP ellipsis: in (5d') the auxiliary and the verb form a constituent and the object remains outside this constituent.

Taking (20a) as a basis, how could VP ellipsis be applied to B's reply?

(20) a Speaker A: The customer in the corner will order the drinks before the meal.

          Speaker B: Actually, I wouldn't be so sure that he will order the drinks before the meal.

The application of VP ellipsis to (20a) is given in (20b), where the symbol [$_{VP}$ ∅] stands for the omitted VP.

(20) b Speaker A: The customer in the corner will order the drinks before the meal.

          Speaker B: Actually, I wouldn't be so sure that <u>he will</u> [$_{VP}$ ∅].

1.7 Focalizing a constituent

1.7.1 THE CLEFT SENTENCE

In the following examples, a special word order pattern is used which has the effect that one constituent is promoted to the foreground while the remainder of the sentence is backgrounded.

(21) a   It was <u>the prison chaplain's wife</u> who first gave me an inkling that I might
         have a talent for writing. (*Guardian*, G2, 21.4.2003, p. 2, col. 1)
     b   Ford directed many films but it is <u>for Westerns</u> that he will be remembered.
         (*Guardian*, 21.4.2003, p. 310, col. 4)

Both examples contain the pattern *it is X who/that Y*. In this pattern, the element
in the position of X is highlighted. It is presented as prominent information. The
elements in Y are backgrounded. Consider for instance (21a). We can paraphrase it
with (21a′).

(21) a′ The prison chaplain's wife first gave me an inkling that I might have a
         talent for writing.

The word order in (21a′) is neutral. (21a′) does not give the same prominence to the
constituent *the prison chaplain's wife* as the original example, (21a). The information conveyed by the two variants is similar: both sentences communicate that at
some point in the past the prison chaplain's wife gave the speaker the idea that he
might be a good writer. Sentences (21a) and (21a′) describe the same event. Could
you imagine a situation in which (21a) is true and (21a′) is false? This is not
possible. If (21a) is a true statement, then (21a′) will also be true and vice versa.
The effect of the rewording in (21a) is "presentational": we reorganize the way the
information is presented. In (21a) the writer highlights that the initial trigger for
the speaker's writing was the chaplain's wife.

    The wording of (21a) serves to focus on a particular constituent and to back-
ground the remainder of the sentence. The pattern where we focus on a constituent
using the *it is X who/that Y* pattern is called a **cleft** sentence. Clefting is a way of
reorganizing the information in a sentence, backgrounding some information and
foregrounding the focal information. As you can see, clefting foregrounds or focuses
on a constituent: in (21a) the NP *the prison chaplain's wife* is singled out or focused
on; in (21b) the PP *for Westerns* is focused on.

    Given that clefting promotes one constituent to the foreground, we can use the
pattern to identify constituents. Apply clefting to our test sentence. Again you will
find that it serves to isolate constituents: in (22a) the NP *the customer in the corner*
is focused, in (22b) the PP *before the meal* is focused on, and in (22c) the NP *the
drinks* is focused on.

(22) a   It is [$_{NP}$ the customer in the corner] who will order the drinks before the meal.
     b   It is [$_{PP}$ before the meal] that the customer in the corner will order the drinks.
     c   It is [$_{NP}$ the drinks] that the customer in the corner will order before the meal.

Recall that we have been entertaining two hypotheses for the representation of the
sentence: either the auxiliary and the verb form a constituent (23a), or else the verb
forms a constituent with its object. On the basis of additional evidence, we elaborated the latter option and proposed that the VP was layered (23b).

(23) a **Hypothesis A**

[$_S$ [$_{NP}$ The customer in the corner] [$_{VP}$ will order] [$_{NP}$ the drinks] [$_{PP}$ before the meal]].

b **Hypothesis B (revised)**

[$_S$ [$_{NP}$ The customer in the corner] [$_{AUX}$ will] [$_{VP}$ [$_{VP}$ order [$_{NP}$ the drinks]] [$_{PP}$ before the meal]]].

The cleft patterns in (22) do not bear on (23a) and (23b), because clefting of the type illustrated here does not affect the VP.[11]

1.7.2 THE PSEUDO-CLEFT SENTENCE

Consider the effect of the rewordings in the paired sentences in (24)–(27).

(24) a I don't need the equivalent of another car loan.

b What I don't need is the equivalent of another car loan. (*Chicago Tribune*, 22.12.2002, section 15, p. 3, col. 1)

(25) a You are seeing the biblical law of reciprocity in Prince George's Country.

b What you are seeing in Prince George's Country is the biblical law of reciprocity. (*Washington Post*, 29.4.2003, p. A7, col. 2)

(26) a She needed someone to talk to.

b What she needed was someone to talk to. (*Washington Post*, 29.4.2003, p. B1, col. 2)

(27) a They will force them underground.

b What they will do is force them underground. (*Guardian*, 9.7.2002, p. 8, col. 8)

(28) a Contacting his relatives will cause mayhem in his family.

b What contacting his relatives will do is cause mayhem in his family. (Adapted from *Guardian*, G2, 11.4.2003, p. 11, col. 3)

As was the case for the clefting paraphrases discussed in section 1.7.1, the content of the paired sentences is near identical. Both sentences in (24), for instance, convey that 'there is no need for the equivalent of another car loan'. As was also the case for the clefting paraphrases, the two sentences have the same truth conditions. If (24a) is a true statement, then (24b) will also be a true statement. The difference is again one of presentation and focus. (24b) serves to highlight one informational

---

[11] This is not quite correct: in Hiberno English, the variant of English spoken in Ireland, VPs can be clefted. (Cottell 2002: 111)

(i) Q. What are the women doing?

A. It's playing backgammon that they are.

unit, here the NP, *the equivalent of another car loan*, and it does so by splitting this constituent off from the remainder of the sentence using a paraphrase with *what*. The pattern displayed here is referred to as **pseudo-clefting**. Identify the focused constituents in the (b)-examples (26)–(28). What is their category?

(26) b′   What she needed was <u>someone to talk to</u>.

(27) b′   What they will do is <u>force them underground</u>.

(28) b′   What contacting his relatives will do is <u>cause mayhem in his family</u>.

In (26) the focused constituent is an NP. In (27) and (28) it is a constituent centered around a verb, a VP (*force them underground, cause mayhem in the family*). Do examples (27) and (28) bear on the choice between representations (23a) or (23b)? What would (23a) predict with respect to pseudo-clefting of a VP? And what would be the predictions of (23b)?

   Using examples (27) and (28) as models, let us also apply pseudo-clefting to our test sentence. Could (23a) constitute a basis for pseudo-clefting of a verb-centered constituent? That is, can we use pseudo-clefting to highlight the VP as represented in (23a)? The answer is that it is not possible to pseudo-cleft the VP as represented in (23a):

(29) a   *What the customer in the corner will do the drinks before the meal is <u>will order</u>.

On the other hand, (23b) has two constituents labeled VP: *order the drinks*, the core VP, and *order the drinks before the meal*, the augmented VP including the time specification. Try pseudo-clefting either of these. Either VP can be focused by pseudo-clefting.

(29) b   What the customer in the corner will do before the meal is <u>order the drinks</u>.
    c   What the customer in the corner will do is <u>order the drinks before the meal</u>.

Once again, the layered VP hypothesis of (23b) allows us to predict that pseudo-clefting will affect a constituent centered around the verb, containing the direct object and possibly the time PP. If we adopt representation (23a), it is hard to account for the fact that the verb and the constituents to its right can be treated as one constituent and undergo pseudo-clefting. In (23a), the verb is taken to form a constituent with the auxiliary and the object and the time PP are separate constituents.

   Identify the highlighted constituent in the following examples. Do the examples bear on the choice between (23a) and (23b)?

(30) a   In the Lower 48 states, people consider reindeer as pets, so the last thing they would do is <u>eat them</u>. (*Chicago Tribune*, 22.12.2002, section 1, p. 16, col. 1)

b All Pastor Edgar Chacon wanted to do, he says now, was protect the children. (*Los Angeles Times*, 26.11.2002, p. B4, col. 4)

c All we can do is do it well. (*Guardian*, 1.11.2002, G2, p. 9, col. 2)

As before, in (30) we focus on a verb-centered constituent, containing the verb, its object, and an additional specification of manner in (30c). The sentences in (30) are again best compatible with a representation like (23b).

1.8 Co-ordination

As units of structure, constituents can be manipulated in various ways. So far we have illustrated that we can replace a constituent by a shorter form (1.3), that we can move a constituent around (1.4), that a constituent can function as the answer to a question (1.5), that we can omit a constituent (1.6), and that we can highlight a constituent by clefting (1.7.1) or by pseudo-clefting (1.7.2). Sometimes, we may decide to link two constituents together. To do this we **co-ordinate** them, i.e. we link them by means of a **co-ordinating conjunction** (*and, or, but*).

(31a) contains two sentences. There is some redundancy in this passage. Identify the overlapping parts between the sentences. Reword the passage to express the information in (31a) in a more compact way, using only one sentence.

(31) a The customer in the corner will order the drinks before the meal. He will also order the dessert before the meal.

We can condense the information in (31a) into one sentence by co-ordinating the object of the first sentence, the NP *the drinks*, and the object of the second sentence, the NP *the dessert*, thus turning these two NPs into one constituent: *the drinks and the dessert*. To do this, we use the conjunction *and*. As a result of the co-ordination, the constituents form one single constituent, as represented by the outer brackets surrounding the co-ordinated NPs:

(31) b The customer in the corner will order [[$_{NP}$ the dessert] and [$_{NP}$ the drinks]] before the meal.

What type of evidence could we provide that the string *the dessert and the drinks* in (31b) is one constituent? One way of showing that the string *the dessert and the drinks* is one constituent is by asking a constituent question targeting just this string (31c). The string can also be replaced by a pronoun (31d).

(31) c <u>What</u> will the customer in the corner order before the meal?

d The customer in the corner will order <u>them</u> before the meal.

Since the co-ordinated constituent can jointly be replaced by a pronoun, *them*, this suggests that the string is an NP, which is the result of co-ordinating two NPs.

How could (32a) be expressed more economically by using co-ordinated structures?

(32) a   The customer in the corner will order the drinks before the meal. He will also order the dessert before the meal. He will also order the coffee before the meal.

In (32a) there are three constituents that function as the object of *order*: *the drinks, the dessert, the coffee*. They can again be co-ordinated. When we have more than two elements to co-ordinate there are two options, illustrated in (32b) and (32c).

(32) b   The customer in the corner will order the drinks and the dessert and the coffee before the meal.
     c   The customer in the corner will order the drinks, the dessert, and the coffee before the meal.

Underline all the co-ordinated constituents in the examples in (33), and identify the category of each of the co-ordinated constituents.

(33) a   Det. Insp. Smith told lies in one of his reports and to the enquiry. (*Guardian*, 15.7.2003, p. 1, col. 7)
     b   Being in Europe does tend to mean that public transport is functional, that public health care is not considered a dangerous pipe-dream, and that education is valued. (Adapted from *Guardian*, 9.12.2002, p. 12, col. 3)
     c   Among the larger issues here are why this happened at all, who allowed it to happen and why the law reinforcement establishment refused to intervene even after it was clear that a great injustice was occurring. (*New York Times*, 28.4.2003, p. A25, col. 1)
     d   Many parents with children in these schools have felt the impact and seen the point. (*Guardian*, 17.7.2002, p. 2, col. 3)
     e   They are also re-equipping six Iraqi hospitals that were looted and building a plant in Basra. (*New York Times*, 28.4.2003, p. A11, col. 6)
     f   He has made its programs newsworthy and kept the institution afloat. (*New York Times*, 28.4.2003, p. A25, col. 4)
     g   Jones said urban sprawl and heightened environmental concerns were imposing increased limits on U.S. military activities in Western Europe and driving up costs. (*Washington Post*, 29.4.2003, p. A6, col. 3)
     h   Boyle testified that she told Malvo four times that he could be silent or see an attorney but that Malvo continued to talk about the shootings in a relaxed, almost convivial way, laughing about Buchanan's slaying and other shootings. (*Washington Post*, 29.4.2003, p. B1, cols 3–4)

In (33) we find the following illustrations of co-ordination:

(33) (i) PP co-ordination
- [PP in one of his reports] + [PP to the enquiry] (a)

(ii) NP co-ordination
- [NP urban sprawl] + [NP heightened environmental concerns] (g)
- [NP Buchanan's slaying] + [NP other shootings] (h)

(iii) sentence co-ordination
- [S that public transport is functional] + [S that public health care is not considered a dangerous pipe-dream] + [S that education is valued] (b)
- [S why this happened at all] + [S who allowed it to happen] + [S why the law reinforcement establishment refused to intervene even after it was clear that a great injustice was occurring] (c)
- [S that she told Malvo four times that he could be silent or see an attorney] + [S that Malvo continued to talk about the shootings in a relaxed, almost convivial way, laughing about Buchanan's slaying and other shootings] (h)

(iv) VP co-ordination
- [VP felt the impact] + [VP seen the point] (d)
- [VP re-equipping six Iraqi hospitals that were looted] + [VP building a plant in Basra] (e)
- [VP made its programs newsworthy] + [VP kept the institution afloat] (f)
- [VP imposing increased limits on U.S. military activities in Western Europe] + [VP driving up costs] (g)
- [VP be silent] + [VP see an attorney] (h)

Do the co-ordination data in (33) bear on the choice between Hypothesis A (23a) and (revised) Hypothesis B (23b) for the structure of the VP? In particular, would Hypothesis A in (23a) lead us to expect the patterns of VP co-ordination displayed in (33)? The answer is negative. In (33d), for instance, co-ordination affects two constituents consisting of a verb and the object. Crucially, the auxiliary remains outside the co-ordinated structure.

Recall that the revised hypothesis B in (23b) allows for layering inside the VP: the verb and the object form a core VP, which then combines with less central material, the time specification in our earlier example. If VPs can co-ordinate, then we predict that for our test example two types of VP co-ordination are possible, one affecting the augmented VP, one affecting just the core VP. Discuss the relevance of the co-ordinations in (34) for this prediction.

(34) a The customer in the corner will order the drinks before the meal and accompany his guests into the dining room.

b The customer in the corner will order the drinks and choose the dessert before the meal.

In (34a) the co-ordinated strings are *order the drinks before the meal* and *accompany his guests into the dining room*. Once again, the first co-ordinated constituent contains the verb, the object, and the time specification. This confirms that the string *order the drinks before the meal* is a constituent. (34b) confirms that the string *order the drinks* is also a constituent, since it is co-ordinated with *choose the dessert*. The data in (34) offer further support for the layered VP in (23b).[12]

2   The Verb Phrase and the Sentence: A First Exploration

2.1   *Starting point*

Recall that in the previous section we were led to choose between two representations of sentence structure, repeated in (35). The label S abbreviates the label "Sentence."

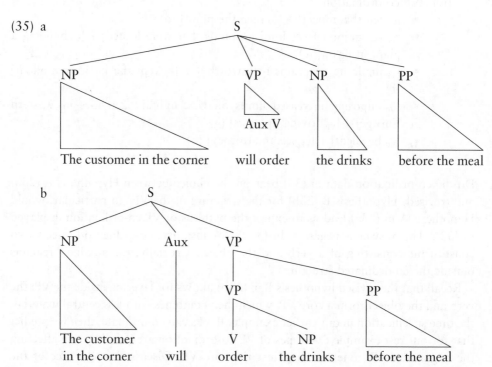

(35) a

b

While (35a) is "flat," (35b) introduces hierarchical levels of structure. The structure in (35b) is more "articulated": the constituents of the sentence have different

---

[12]   Exercises 1A, 3, 4, 5, 6, 8, 9, 19.

relations between each other. There are two important differences between the representations:

(i) (35a) presents the subject NP and the object NP as being on equal footing; (35b) creates a **subject/object asymmetry**. From the root S it takes one single step to reach the subject NP, it takes three steps to reach the object NP.[13]

(ii) Conversely, in (35b), the object is contained in the VP, the subject is outside it. This means that in (35b) the object has a closer relationship with the verb than the subject.

(iii) (35a) presents the direct object and the temporal PP as being on equal footing. In (35b) the object and the verb form a separate unit, the core VP; the temporal PP is added to the periphery of that same VP.

2.2 The relation between the auxiliary and the VP

Representation (35a) follows from the intuition that there is a close relationship between the auxiliary and the verb. This relationship is not captured in (35b), in which the auxiliary has a symmetric relation with subject and VP. Consider the underlined co-ordinating conjunctions in (36). For each conjunction, identify the co-ordinated constituents. Does either of the structures in (35) allow us to predict the co-ordinations in (36)?

(36) a   Parents of the 53 Dartmouth swimteam members are pressing administrators and college trustees for the team's reinstatement, <u>and</u> are asking for help from Dartmouth alumni and donors. (Adapted from *Boston Globe*, 4.12.2002, p. A3, col. 3)

   b   Stop and search isn't working <u>and</u> won't work. (*Guardian*, 9.11.2002, p. 11, col. 6, letter to the editor from Marc Cohen)

   c   State officials say Massachusetts may eliminate a prescription drug program that covers 80,000 elderly, <u>and</u> is considering a variety of other cuts and restrictions. (Based on *New York Times*, 28.4.2003, p. A21, col. 2)

   d   Three high-rise towers would wall off the stadium from the skyline <u>and</u> would drastically shrink the center field park. (Based on *New York Times*, 28.4.2003, p. A22, col. 1)

   e   We believe that such a proposal could seriously undermine the voucher program <u>and</u> could potentially harm the millions of low-income people assisted with housing vouchers. (*Washington Post*, 29.4.2003, p. A8, col. 2)

---

[13]   In Chapter 5, sections 3.2.3.1, 3.2.3.2, 5.2.2, and 5.3.2.2, we will discuss a number of subject/object asymmetries in connection with question formation and relative clause formation.

The constituents co-ordinated by the underlined conjunctions in the above examples are isolated in (37):

(37) a   [are pressing administrators and college trustees for the team's reinstatement]
         + [are asking for help from Dartmouth alumni and donors]
     b   [isn't working]
         + [won't work]
     c   [may eliminate a prescription drug program that covers 80,000 elderly]
         + [is considering a variety of other cuts and restrictions]
     d   [would wall off the stadium from the skyline]
         + [would drastically shrink the center field park]
     e   [could seriously undermine the voucher program]
         + [could potentially harm the millions of low-income people assisted with housing vouchers]

The problem arising for both representations in (35) is that the co-ordinated constituents in (36) correspond to the combination of the auxiliary, the verb and its complements and other specifications. But in neither of the representations in (35) do these strings form a constituent: (35a) does combine the auxiliary with the verb, but neither the direct object nor the temporal specification is part of the VP. In (35b) the auxiliary and the VP do not form a constituent.

Based on our test sentence we can create sentences such as the following, raising a similar problem for the representations in (35):

(38) a   The customer will order the drinks before the meal but may pay for them later.
     b   The customer will order the drinks before the meal and is waiting for the wine list.
     c   The customer in the corner has just taken his seat and will order the drinks before the meal.

According to representation (35a), to be able to operate on a constituent that contains the auxiliary, the verb, and the additional material, we would have to take the complete sentence (S). The sequence VP + NP + PP is composed of three autonomous constituents, but these constituents do not exhaustively form a bigger constituent. In (35b), the problem is identical: the sequence Aux + VP does not form a constituent without the subject NP.

The attested data in (36) and the experimental data in (38) both lead to the conclusion that Aux and the components of the VP in (35b) must also form a constituent together. Let us adjust the tree accordingly. Rather than having the ternary structure in (35b), in which three branches start from the S node, we need a **binary** branching structure, as in (39): for the time being we do not give a specific label to the constituent formed by the auxiliary and the VP. We return to this point in section 3.1 and also in the next chapter.

(39) a [s [NP The customer in the corner] [CONSTITUENT [AUX will] [VP [VP order [NP the drinks]] [PP before the meal]]]].

b

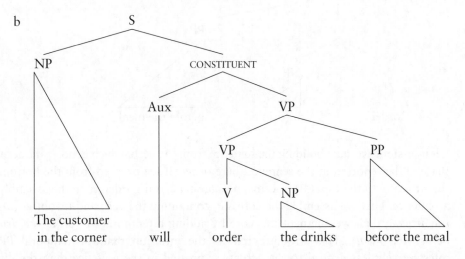

This structure splits the sentence into two parts, the subject and a second constituent, which we could loosely refer to as the "predicate."[14] The subject "specifies" or delimits the domain of application of the predicate. That is to say: the predicate tells us what kind of action is taking place, and the subject says to which entity this action is applied. The role of the auxiliary is to link the VP and the subject. The auxiliary also qualifies the validation of that link: for instance, the auxiliary may specify that the link will only be validated in the future (*will*), or that the validation is situated in the past (*has*), etc.

The structures in (39a, b) give rise to an immediate question. Not every English sentence contains an auxiliary. We will have to devise a way of representing the structure of sentences such as (39c).

(39) c The customer in the corner ordered the drinks before the meal.

We return to this issue in Chapter 3, section 1.2.

2.3 *Layered structures*

2.3.1 COMPLEMENTS VS. ADJUNCTS IN THE VP

Recall that we proposed that the structure of the VP is layered. In (40) we repeat the structure we arrived at based on our experimental sentence.

---

[14] Exercises 2 and 10.

(40) a   [$_{VP}$ [$_{VP}$ order [$_{NP}$ the drinks]] [$_{PP}$ before the meal]]

   b

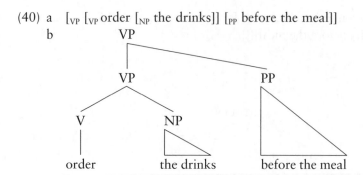

Let us assume we start building the sentence from the verb, which denotes the activity that will be reported in the sentence, here *order*. If we proceed from the bottom of the structure to the top, (40b) seems to suggest a certain ordering in the assembly of a sentence. First we assemble the core VP, containing the verb and its object (*order the drinks*); then we augment this core by adding a temporal PP (*order the drinks before the meal*). This structure reflects the intuition that the temporal PP is interpretively less central to the activity expressed in the sentence than the direct object. The PP *before the meal* does not serve to define the kind of activity expressed by the VP; it simply provides accessory information on the timing of that activity. The PP is more peripheral to the VP: the core VP consists of the verb and the object. That core VP is assembled first.

In traditional terms the verb *order* is a **transitive** verb. The verb *order* **selects** the object *the drinks*, in that it requires that there be a complement and it determines the type of complement that is required, here an NP. We call the constituent selected by the verb a **complement**. The time PP is not a complement of *order*; the verb *order* does not select a time specification, it does not require that there be a time specification, nor does it require that a time specification in the sentence be of a particular category. Material that is not selected is attached outside the core VP. The temporal PP is said to be **adjoined**; a constituent that is adjoined to another constituent is also called an **adjunct**.

(40) c

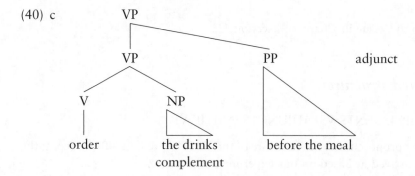

The nature of the process that puts together the core VP is slightly different from that of adjoining the time PP to it. When we assemble the core VP we combine a head, the verb, which is one word, with a phrase, the NP object. The resulting unit denotes a particular type of action. The head selects the complement. When we adjoin the adjunct, we assemble two ready-made phrases: the "finished" core VP and, in our example, the adjunct PP. The adjunct, though part of VP, is not fully integrated into its core and it does not serve to differentiate a particular action from another one. Verbs do not select time specifications, and if there is going to be a time specification this can be expressed in different ways.

To use a metaphor: we can compare adjoined constituents to, for instance, the garage that is built next to a house. Garages are "external" to a house. If you say that you are "in" the house, you will not normally be thought to be in the garage. On the other hand, if you sell a house you will also sell the garage with it. And moreover, the presence of a garage will mean that the house is worth more. But garages remain extras: in order to qualify as a house, a building does not need a garage; if you demolish the garage that goes with a house, the house itself remains a house.

The structure in (40c) is elaborated for the VP. We can generalize (40c) to all constituents, proposing that for each type of head we distinguish its complements, the constituent selected by the head in question, and which, together with the head, forms the core constituent, from the adjoined constituents, peripheral elements which may but need not be added. We use the labels X , Y, and Z as variable labels that stand for any category type (N, V, P, etc.). In (41), the constituents YP and ZP will be formed according to the same schema: they will have a head (Y, Z), and may have a complement and/or an adjoined constituent.

(41)

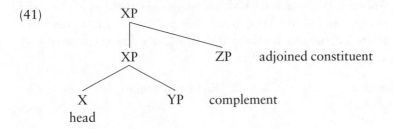

2.3.2 DIRECTION OF ADJUNCTION

Identify the VPs in (42). Do the verbs select a complement? Are there any adjoined constituents? What is the category of the adjoined constituents? Discuss the difference between (42a) and (42b). Draw the structure for the VPs.

(42) a One of the most controversial takeovers in British sporting history was awaiting a government decision last night. (Based on *Guardian*, 13.3.1999, p. 1, col. 1)

b One of the most controversial takeovers in British sporting history was last night awaiting a government decision. (*Guardian*, 13.3.1999, p. 1, col. 1)

In (42a) *last night* is an adjoined constituent; it follows the verb and it is realized by an NP. In (42b) the same constituent precedes the verb. To allow for both the order adjunct – verb and the order verb – . . . – adjunct, we can enrich our structure by allowing both **left-adjunction** and **right-adjunction**. Using our earlier architectural metaphor, garages may be built to the right of a house or to its left.

(40) d   Right-adjunction   Left-adjunction

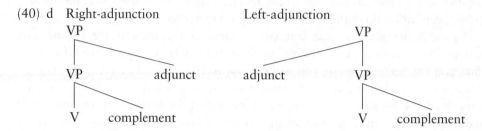

Among our earlier examples, (19e) also illustrated left-adjunction. We repeat it for convenience in (43a). We can reword the example and replace the left-adjoined adjunct by a right-adjoined one as in (43b).

(43) a   All in the name of a pretence that, with just a little bit more time passing, all obstacles will [$_{VP}$ miraculously [$_{VP}$ recede]].
      b   All in the name of a pretence that, with just a little bit more time passing, all obstacles will [$_{VP}$ [$_{VP}$ recede] miraculously].

This example is of interest because the core VP does not contain any complement. This is so because the verb *recede* does not select a complement. *Recede* is an **intransitive** verb. Adopting the format in (40d) we assign the structures in (43c) and (43d) to the VPs in (43a) and (43b). Though *recede* is just one word, we represent it as constituting a core VP, because we want to show that the adjunct *miraculously* is not part of the core VP but is adjoined to it.

(43) c   Left-adjunction   d   Right-adjunction

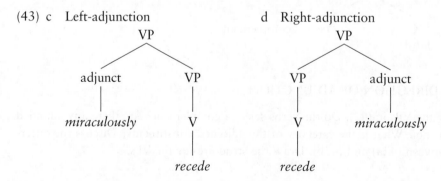

Identify the co-ordinated VPs in the following example:

(43) e   We budget for shows with the expectation that it will increase the gaming revenue and in turn pay for the show. (*New York Times*, 28.4.2003, p. B5, col. 4)

As you can see, the second co-ordinated VP *in turn pay for the show* contains a left-adjoined PP, *in turn*.

(43) f   [$_{VP}$ in turn [$_{VP}$ pay for the show]]

Finally, exploiting our metaphor once again, it is also possible to build a garage both to the right and one to the left of a house. In the same way, we can also adjoin constituents both to the right and to the left of a VP. (43g) is a constructed example with one adjunct to the right and one to the left, both adjuncts can also appear on the left (43h) or on the right (43i).

(43) g   They will <u>carefully</u> analyze the financial situation of the company <u>later on</u>.
     h   They will <u>later on carefully</u> analyze the financial situation of the company.
     i   They will analyze the financial situation of the company <u>carefully later on</u>.

Our hypotheses of VP-layering and of adjunction can account for these word orders. Observe that examples such as those in (43g–i) also show that a VP may be augmented by more than one adjunct.[15]

2.3.3   OV ORDERS?

The data we have encountered lead to the hypothesis that adjunction may either be to the right or to the left of the VP. When the object of a verb was located in the VP,[16] then it was always found to the immediate right of the verb. This follows from our structure: the complement of a head appears to its right. We may however wonder whether this is the only option. Having introduced both left-adjunction and right-adjunction, should we also allow for the complement to occur either to the right or to the left of the verb in the VP? In other words, do we also have to allow for the following structure for the core VP?

(40) e   **Hypothesis: Object-Verb patterns in English**

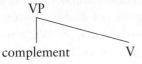

How do we find the evidence for or against this hypothesis? We could look for examples of this type in which the object remains in the VP but occurs to the

---

[15]   Exercise 14. We will return to multiple adjuncts in Chapter 3, section 2.1, and in Exercise 3 of Chapter 3.

[16]   The object can be moved out of the VP to an initial position, as shown in section 1.4. This fronting operation is also used for forming constituent questions that bear on the object. Clefting (section 1.7.1) and pseudo-clefting (section 1.7.2) may also rearrange the position of the object with respect to the verb. For a discussion of movement see Chapter 5.

immediate left of the verb. Now, suppose we do not find any such examples, even after an intensive search using sophisticated computer technology. Would that definitely mean that such structures are to be excluded on principled grounds? Though the total absence of relevant examples could well be taken to suggest that certain structures are ill conceived, we cannot be totally sure about this conclusion. It could also be that the relevant data are rare for other reasons, for instance, because they are stylistically extremely marked. Not finding the relevant example is suggestive but not conclusive. Recall from the discussion in Chapter 1, section 2.3.2 that the fact that we have never seen a black swan would not mean that they cannot exist.

   To check the validity of a hypothesis we can also try to conduct an experiment. To do this, we create our own examples, corresponding to the pattern in (40e) and check their status. We either simply create new sentences out of the blue that illustrate the pattern that we are interested in, or we modify the examples that we are currently working on. Find the NP complement in (42) and place it to the immediate left of the verb – is the result good or bad? Try the same using our test sentence. What do you conclude? It seems to be the case that in English the complement of the verb cannot be inserted to the immediate left of the verb.

(44) a   *One of the most controversial takeovers in British sporting history was [$_{VP}$ [$_{VP}$ [$_{NP}$ a government decision] awaiting] [$_{NP}$ last night]].

   b   *One of the most controversial takeovers in British sporting history was [$_{VP}$ last night [$_{VP}$ [[$_{NP}$ a government decision] awaiting]]].

   c   *The customer in the corner will [$_{VP}$ [$_{VP}$ [$_{NP}$ the drinks] order] before the meal].

We decide that such sentences "are not English." The word orders illustrated here are not allowed by the structure of the language. The grammar of English does not allow the structure in which the object occurs to the immediate left of the verb. When an unacceptable structure is ruled out because the grammatical system of the language does not allow it then we call it **ungrammatical**. In the preceding discussions we have often labeled strings as unacceptable, without saying that they were ungrammatical. This was mainly because at the point of discussion we were simply interested in observing that these strings were not correct. When we say that an unacceptable string is ungrammatical, we suggest an explanation for why it is unacceptable. In what follows we will use the labels unacceptable and ungrammatical indiscriminately. This is because we are interested in unacceptable sentences precisely because they give us an insight into the grammar.

2.3.4   BASE POSITIONS AND MOVEMENT

While adjuncts may apparently be left-adjoined and right-adjoined to the VP, the complements of V are inserted to the immediate right of V.[17] Does this mean that a

---

[17]   Exercise 18.

direct object of a verb will always be found to the immediate right of the verb? Recall the examples in (10), repeated here as (45):

(45) a   The British one I have been using since I was about nine. (*Guardian*, 22.3.2002, p. 3, col. 1)
   b   The news, when it comes, he seems to take well enough. (*Guardian*, G2, 26.7.2002, p. 2, col. 1)

In these examples the objects *the British one* and *the news* do not occupy a position next to the selecting verb. Restore these "dislocated" objects to their canonical position. Could the objects appear in a position immediately preceding the verb?

(45) c   I have been using the British one since I was about nine.
   d   When it comes, he seems to take the news well enough.

Once again you would not be able to put the object in a position to the left of the verb.

(45) e   *I have been the British one using since I was about nine.
   f   *When it comes, he seems to the news take well enough.

We have to allow for constituents such as the direct object to occupy various positions in the sentence. On the other hand, the object is closely related to the verb. We proposed that the object must first combine with V to form a core VP before adjoined constituents are added to the VP by the assembly process. One possible way of thinking about the sentence-initial position of the object illustrated above is to say that the object is first inserted in the position to the right of V but that it may subsequently be moved away from that position. To allow for the construction of sentences such as (45a, b), while at the same time excluding patterns such as (45e, f), we will have to restrain the **landing site** of a moved constituent: movement of constituents apparently targets designated positions.[18]

2.4   Deductive approaches

2.4.1   HEAD AND PROJECTION

So far we have encountered constituents belonging to various categories: NP, VP, AP, PP. The label of the constituents (NP, VP, etc.) was determined by the category of the head (N, V, etc.). Let us formalize this procedure by explicitly defining the category of the constituent in terms of the category of its head:

---

[18]   We turn to some aspects of this issue in Chapter 5.

(46) a   **Head hypothesis**
        The category of a constituent is determined by the category of its head.

(46a) is a general hypothesis about structure: it applies to all the material we have discussed so far and, being general, it will also apply to new material. If we discover a new type of head X, then by (46a) we deduce that this head will project a constituent of type XP:

(46) b   XP

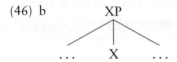

        ...   X   ...

(46) is thus not simply a summary of our findings so far. It goes beyond the observations and generalizes what we have found to all constituents. The effect of the generalization is to **restrict** the way we will analyze any new data we may come across in future; following (46a) we assume that all structure is headed. In postulating (46a), we draw the bounds of possible representations more narrowly. Based on (46a) we **predict**, for instance, that there will never be any structures of the type in (46c):[19]

(46) c   *   XP

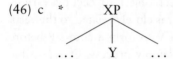

        ...   Y   ...

This also means that if we did come across a constituent that seems to require representation (46c), we should rethink our analysis of that particular constituent or, alternatively, we would have to rethink our theory.

2.4.2   BINARY BRANCHING

Let us compare some of the tree structures discussed so far, focusing simply on the geometry of the **branches**, the lines that compose the trees. For instance, let us compare the way these lines are organized in (5e′), repeated here as (47a), with the organization in (39b), repeated here as (47b).

---

[19]   There is a huge literature concerning the general format for syntactic structure known as "X-bar theory." For first proposals see Chomsky (1970), see also Jackendoff (1977) for a first fully elaborated account. For a critical evaluation of various implementations see also Kornai and Pullum (1990).

(47) a

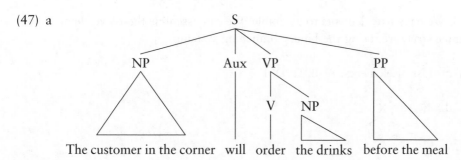

The customer in the corner will order the drinks before the meal

b

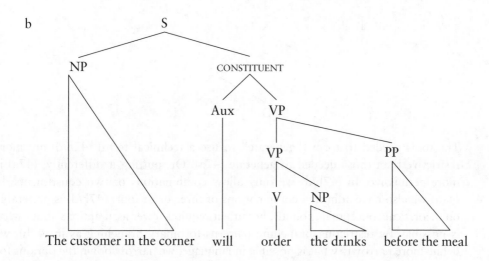

The customer in the corner   will   order   the drinks   before the meal

(47a) and (47b) display different types of combinations. In (47a) the root **node** S splits up into four separate branches. S **dominates** four immediate constituents: (i) the subject NP, (ii) the auxiliary, (iii) the VP, and (iv) the PP. The same tree also contains instances of a node dominating just two constituents; for instance, the VP node dominates the verb and the object NP. If we removed the time specification from the sentence, we would end up with yet another type of composition, since the root S would then dominate only three constituents. (47a) suggests that the types of nodes in a tree are unconstrained: we can have binary branching nodes (V + NP in (47a)), or ternary branching nodes (if we omit the time PP from (47a)), or even four-way branching nodes (S in (47a)). This wealth of options is in sharp contrast with the restricted branching pattern in (47b): here all the nodes dominate just two constituents. (47b) only has **binary branching** nodes. (47b) is more **restrictive**.

Let us think about the branching patterns in more general terms. What we are concerned with in this book is "syntax," that is: putting units (here units of language) together, or assembling units. It is trivially true that in order to assemble elements, you need at least two of them. In fact, in order to assemble elements, you do not need more than two of them. If you do have more than two elements to put together, you can still use a binary combination system to assemble them. Consider

(47c). We have five elements to assemble. We can assemble these five elements into a simple structure, using the binary branching system:

(47) c   List of elements: A, B, C, D, E

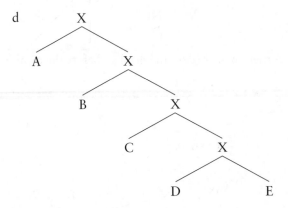

The tools needed to form (**"generate"** to use a technical term) (47b/d) are more restrictive than those needed to generate (47a). Or, putting it differently, (47a) is more permissive. In (47b/d) we only allow combinations of two constituents; in (47a) we also have admitted combinations of three or four. (47b/d) is preferable on theoretical/conceptual grounds, because it requires fewer assumptions about what is possible. By restricting branching patterns to binary branching as in (47b), we define more narrowly what is possible in language, we narrow down the options for combining constituents to combinations of just two constituents, or binary combinations. (47b/d) thus once again will correspond better to Einstein's description of the goals of scientific research given in Chapter 1, section 1.2.3:[20]

> The grand aim of all science is to cover the greatest possible number of experimental facts by logical deduction from the smallest number of hypotheses or axioms. (Einstein 1954, cited in Abraham et al. 1996: 4)

For (47a) we need at least three types of branching. For (47b) we only need binary branching: each constituent grouping, each syntactic unit, combines two constituents. Thus a theory including (47b) is more elegant and economical than one that includes (47a), the latter having more tools available.

(47b) is supported both by empirical evidence (the evidence provided by applying the constituency tests to data as discussed in this chapter) and by theoretical arguments. Let us therefore postulate that all linguistic structure is based on binary branching.[21] From now on, when we try to derive structures of sentences we will

---

[20]   See also the discussion of "Ockham's Razor" in Chapter 1, section 1.2.3.
[21]   Exercise 11.

work with the hypothesis in (48).[22] Once again, (48) is a theoretical hypothesis which, though inspired by a set of empirical data, goes beyond these data.

(48) **Binary composition hypothesis**
       All syntactic structure is binary.

From now on, our analysis will be guided by (48), a theoretical principle formulated to restrict our theory. When theoretical interest guides the way we look at data we adopt a **deductive** methodology. In such an approach the hypotheses that constitute a theory form the basis of the deduction, but again what we deduce will be a general principle and once again this principle will be tested by observation, or, if possible, by experiment. Our theory about syntax, about putting words together to form sentences, proposes that all syntax, all "putting together," is ruled by binary combinations; all syntactic branching will be binary.[23] (48) says that syntax is the combination of two elements. A constituent is formed by the fusion or the **merger** of two constituents; that newly formed constituent can be merged with yet another constituent to form another constituent etc. Concretely, the **derivation** of our example sentence proceeds as follows:

(49) a   assemble core VP   = V + NP
       b   assemble augmented VP   = VP + PP
       c   assemble "CONSTITUENT"   = Aux + VP
       d   assemble sentence   = NP + CONSTITUENT

Recall that the assembly of the core VP (49a) is different from the assembly of the augmented VP (49b). In the former case we assemble a head and an element that is selected by that head to form a phrase. In the second type of assembly we combine two phrases which are already themselves fully formed. We have seen that we need both types of procedures in order to differentiate obligatory complements and optional adjuncts.

2.5   A short note on binary branching and word structure

We have so far only dealt with the assembly of sentences (and only a small sample of possible sentences), but we might generalize our proposals to say that the binary branching hypothesis in (48) is a general hypothesis about structure in language. In other words, the hypothesis would be that ALL linguistic units are built up by combining two elements.

---

[22] As briefly discussed in Exercise 7, co-ordinated structures raise a problem for the binary branching hypothesis. For some sophisticated proposals on how to deal with co-ordination see Camacho (2003), Goodall (1987), van Oirsouw (1987).

[23] In generative linguistics, the binary branching hypothesis was elaborated by Richard Kayne (1984).

Words are smaller units of language than sentences; words are themselves combined into phrases to form sentences. Let us briefly look at English words. Does the internal structure of words conform to the binary branching format? Consider the underlined words in (50). Do they have internal structure? What are their components? How are the components assembled?

(50) a   Anthrax was hard to <u>weaponize</u>. (*Guardian*, 15.10.2001, p. 5, col. 2)
    b   [The powder] was not, however, "<u>weaponized</u>" – genetically modified to be antibiotic-resistant. (*Independent*, 22.10.2002, p. 5, col. 3)
    c   Among those countries are nations that have tested the <u>weaponization</u> of those chemical and biological agents. (*Guardian*, 10.10.2001, p. 2, col. 8)

The root common to the words *weaponize, weaponized,* and *weaponization* is the noun *weapon*. On the basis of the noun *weapon* we create the verb: *weaponize* (50a), meaning "turn something into a weapon," "use something as a weapon." This verb can be inflected: in (50b) we find its past participle *weaponized*. In (50c) we create a noun, *weaponization,* on the basis of the verb *weaponize*. It is clear that in the examples illustrated here, the process of creating new words is based on binary branching: it is summarized in the structures in (51):

(51) a

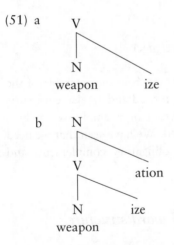

Consider the underlined words in the following extracts. Describe the process by which they are formed:

(52) a   The current State Department reaction to criticism by the <u>hawkish</u> commentator Newt Gingrich offers examples of weak and strong vituperation. (*New York Times*, 28.4.2003, p. A25, col. 5)
    b   [He was] conscious of the discomfort at Washington's growing <u>hawkishness</u>. (*Guardian*, 26.4.2003, p. 6, col. 3)

Discuss the interpretation of the adjective *undoable* in the following examples:

(53) a This task is undoable: we don't have the people and we don't have the time.

 b This knot is undoable; all we need is a fine needle and a lot of patience.

The adjective *undoable* has two interpretations: 'which cannot be done' and 'which can be undone'. In the same way that sentences can have different interpretations as a result of being structurally ambiguous, the ambiguity of *undoable* can be related to its internal make-up, its structure:

(53) c [$_A$ un [$_A$ [$_V$ do] able]]   vs.   [$_A$ [$_V$ un [$_V$ do]] able]

By adopting the binary branching hypothesis for all structural relations we have elaborated a simpler theory than if we allow for all types of branching. We need only one type of combination: structure is formed by putting together ("**merging**") two constituents. As mentioned, a theory that uses only binary branching is to be preferred over a theory that has both binary branching and ternary branching.[24]

3 Specifiers

3.1 Noun phrases

3.1.1 A BINARY BRANCHING STRUCTURE FOR NPS

Consider the NP *the teacher of English*. We will try to develop a structural representation, using as our guidelines the theoretical concepts elaborated so far.[25] In particular, we assume that all structure is headed and all structure is binary branching. This means that, for instance, representation (54a) will be excluded on theoretical grounds.

(54) a

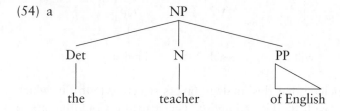

---

[24] Exercises 16, 17.

[25] This is a first approximation of the structure of NP. The structure would have to be revised in a number of ways in the light of further developments of the theory. We do not go into this area but refer the reader to the existing literature. For a first introduction see Haegeman and Guéron (1999: chapter 4). For more detailed and more advanced discussion see also Bernstein (2001).

The label "Det" in (54a) stands for "determiner." The term is used provisionally as a cover term for articles such as *the, a* and for elements that seem to occupy the same position in the NP, such as demonstratives.[26]

In principle, either (54b) or (54c) would respect the binary branching hypothesis; we again use the label CONSTITUENT as a provisional label:

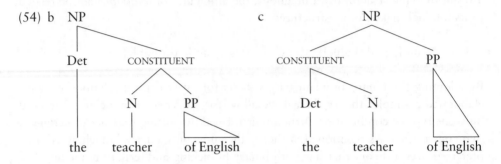

(54) b NP

Which of these should we adopt? In order to choose between the two structures, we can use theoretical considerations as well as empirical ones. Ideally, the two kinds of argumentation should converge and lead to the same conclusion. Consider first the noun *teacher*, which is morphologically related to the verb *teach*. In the NP *the teacher of English*, the relation of the noun *teacher* to the PP *of English* is similar to that between the verb *teach* and a direct object in the sentence, cf. (54d):

(54) d

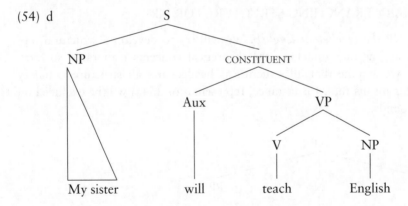

Tentatively, we could conclude that this analogy favors structure (54b), in which the N *teacher* first merges with the PP *of English*. The structure would be one in which the determiner *the* is outside the resulting constituent [N + PP]. Is there any evidence that the unit *teacher of English* is a constituent? And if so, what kind of constituent would it be? Do the data in (55) shed light on this question?

---

[26] Below we will replace this label by a more adequate label for the position occupied by such elements. For the importance of the determiner in the structure of the NP see Abney (1987), Bernstein (2001), and the references cited. These publications are advanced and should only be tackled after you have finished this book.

(55) a   This teacher of English has arrived today but that one arrives only tomorrow.
  b   John's teacher of English is British and Mary's is American.

(55a) contrasts two NPs: *this teacher of English* versus *that one*. The opposition is expressed by the demonstratives *this* and *that*. The component *teacher of English* is not contrasted and in the second part of the co-ordinated structure the string *teacher of English* is replaced by the word *one*. The fact that one word, *one*, can substitute for a string of words suggests that the string, *teacher of English*, is a constituent, a conclusion compatible with representation (54b), though not with (54c).[27]

The same conclusion is reached if we examine (55b). Here the non-contrastive part of the NP is deleted:

(55) c   John's teacher of English is British but Mary's Ø is American.

If we assume that ellipsis affects constituents (as argued in section 1.6), then again this example is evidence for the structure in (54b).

We have argued for the structure in (54b) on the basis of *one*-substitution and of ellipsis. If we adopt structure (54b), the question arises as to the nature of the CONSTITUENT N + PP. How does it relate to the determiner? If we pursue the analogy with VP, i.e. the hypothesis that N is the head of the constituent [*teacher of English*] in the way that V is the head of [$_{VP}$ *teach English*], then we ought to conclude that the constituent N + PP is an NP. On the other hand, it is not an ordinary NP. *Teacher of English* does not have the same distribution as other NPs: it cannot function as an object (56a), nor can it function as a subject (56b).

(56) a   *I met teacher of English.
  b   *Teacher of English arrived late today.

What minimal "correction" would save the unacceptable strings in (56)? To enable the string *teacher of English* to freely occupy subject and object positions we need to add a determiner, such as *a, the, this, that*. How could we characterize the interpretive effect of adding these elements? How do *the teacher of English* and *teacher of English* differ in meaning?

(57) a   I met a/the/this/that teacher of English.
  b   A/the/this/that teacher of English arrived late today.

The string *teacher of English* denotes a property of the entity that we are referring to. In other words, we attribute to that entity the characterization that he/she 'teaches English'. To pick out an entity with the relevant property (to "refer" to such an entity), we need to use a determiner. By inserting the indefinite article *a* we signal

---

[27]   For discussion of *one* substitution see also Panagiotidis (2002, 2003).

that there is at least one entity that has the property 'teacher of English', and that this entity is being introduced in the discourse. By inserting the definite article *the* we signal that one such entity with the relevant properties is already familiar in the discourse: speaker and hearer can identify the entity of the type 'teacher of English' we are talking about. In other words *a* and *the* serve to specify reference: these elements help us pick out the entity to which we attribute the property 'teacher of English'. Observe that we only use one such determiner:

(57) c   *a this teacher of English

Determiners specify the reference of the NP. We insert them in a position labeled **specifier,** as in (58). Because the combination *teacher of English* cannot on its own function as a complete NP, while at the same time it is a constituent headed by an N, we will label it N′ (N-prime), corresponding roughly to a partial NP.[28]

(58)

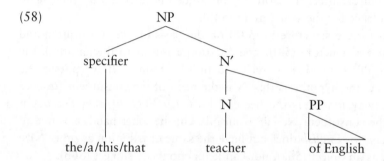

At this point, the specifier position is new to our structures. So far we have been operating without it. If we do introduce this concept in the NP, we should show that it is really required. We should, for instance, show that a specifier is distinct from a complement and from adjoined constituents. Once we have motivated the specifier position in the NP, we have to address the question whether there could be a similar specifier position in other constituents, such as VP and S. If the answer to that question is positive, we will want to know which elements occupy the specifier positions. If the answer is negative, we have to determine why specifiers are restricted in their distribution.

3.1.2   SPECIFIERS IN THE NP

3.1.2.1   *Specifier–head agreement*
The specifier position in the projection of the noun has some properties that set it apart from other constituents in the NP. First, look at the form of the demonstratives in the following English examples: how do we account for the different forms?

---

[28]   The intermediate level N′ is also sometimes referred to as "N-bar."

(59) a this   teacher   of English
     b these   teachers of English
     c that   teacher   of English
     d those   teachers of English

As you see, the form of the demonstrative depends on the form of the head noun: a singular N *teacher* goes with the forms *this/that*, a plural N *teachers* with the forms *these/those*. The specifier **agrees** with the head in terms of the number **feature**. The same pattern is found in French:

(60) a ce   professeur   d'anglais
        this (SG) professor (SG) of English

     b ces   professeurs   d'anglais
        these (PL) professors (PL) of English

French singular nouns also match with the demonstrative for the feature gender, as shown by the following examples:

(60) c ce   cours   d'anglais
        this (MASC) course (MASC) of English
        'this English course'

     d cette   leçon   d'anglais
        this (FEM) lesson (FEM) of English
        'this English lesson'

Cours ('course') is a masculine singular noun; it is accompanied by the masculine singular demonstrative *ce*. *Leçon* ('lesson') is a feminine singular noun; it is accompanied by the feminine singular demonstrative *cette*.

French articles also match a singular head noun in gender (60e, f) and number (60g):

(60) e <u>un</u>   cours d'anglais   *vs.*   <u>une</u>   leçon   d'anglais
        a (MASC-SG) course of English   a (FEM-SG) lesson (FEM-SG) of English
        'an English course'   'an English lesson'

     f <u>le</u>   cours d'anglais   *vs.*   <u>la</u>   leçon   d'anglais
        the (MASC-SG) course of English   the (FEM-SG) lesson (FEM-SG) of English
        'the English course'   'the English lesson'

     g <u>les</u>   cours   d'anglais   *vs.*   <u>les</u>   leçons   d'anglais
        the (PL) courses (PL) of English   the (PL) lessons (PL) of English
        'the English courses'   'the English lessons'

The constituent in the specifier position of the NP agrees with the head noun. Let us formulate the hypothesis that agreement relations are realized through specifier–head relations. Consider the following examples: how is agreement encoded in the sentence?

(61) a The teacher of English is arriving today.
     b The teachers of English are arriving today.

Agreement obtains between the subject NP, *the teacher(s) of English*, and the inflected auxiliary, *is/are*. We return to the relevance of this observation in section 3.1.2.3, and also in Chapter 3.

3.1.2.2 *Prenominal genitives*

Examine the underlined NPs in the following extracts. The head nouns are preceded by genitive forms of NPs. Can the genitive NP preceding the head N be replaced by a pronoun? How could we characterize the semantic relationship of the prenominal genitive NP to the associated N? Can the head nouns of the underlined NP, which are preceded by the genitive NP, also be preceded by a determiner that specifies the reference of the head noun (a demonstrative or an article)?

(62) a One of the most controversial takeovers in British sporting history was last night awaiting a government decision after the Monopolies and Mergers Commission delivered its verdict to ministers on whether <u>Rupert Murdoch's bid for Manchester United Football Club</u> should be allowed. (Adapted from *Guardian*, 13.3.1999, p. 1, col. 1)
     b Instead, the reminder of the best of Labour came in <u>Estelle Morris's speech</u>. (Adapted from *Guardian*, 4.10.2002, p. 7, col. 1)

The prenominal genitive NPs *Rupert Murdoch's* and *Estelle Morris's* can be replaced by pronouns (*his, her*). We cannot add a determiner to the underlined NPs:

(63) a *<u>the</u> Rupert Murdoch's bid for Manchester United Football Club
        *Rupert Murdoch's <u>the</u> bid for Manchester United Football Club
     b *<u>the</u> Estelle Morris's speech
        *Estelle Morris's <u>the</u> speech

If we wanted to use a determiner then we would have to remove the prenominal genitive NP:

(63) c the bid for Manchester United Football Club by Rupert Murdoch
     d the speech by Estelle Morris

In our examples, a prenominal genitive NP and the determiner specifying the reference of the head noun cannot co-occur. Either we use a prenominal genitive or we use a determiner. The prenominal genitive and the determiner are said to be in **complementary distribution**. To rule out that a genitive NP preceding a noun co-occurs with a determiner related to the same noun, we could propose that the genitive NP and the determiner are inserted in the same position. We have proposed that determiners occupy a particular position of NP labeled specifier. Let us postulate that (i) each syntactic position can contain only one constituent and (ii) that there is just one specifier position in the NP. If prenominal genitive NPs occupy the specifier position of NP, we correctly predict that an NP contains either a prenominal genitive or a determiner.[29]

In the examples above the nouns *bid* and *speech* can be related to the verbs *bid* and *speak*; the prenominal genitive NPs relate to the head nouns like subjects relate to verbs in a sentence:

(64) a   Rupert Murdoch will bid for Manchester United.
     b   Estelle Morris will speak at the conference.

(64c) contains an NP related to our test sentence (5a). Again, the subject NP of the original test sentence corresponds to the prenominal genitive NP:

(64) c   I am waiting for [$_{NP}$ [$_{NP}$ the customer in the corner's] order of the drinks].

Let us assume then that prenominal genitive NPs occupy the specifier position of the containing NP. Since possessive pronouns such as *his, her, their*, etc. replace prenominal genitives, we assume they also occupy the specifier of NP.

(65)

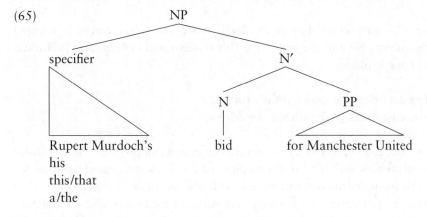

Recall also that the specifier position can be a locus for agreement relations. In English, genitive NPs or possessive pronouns do not agree with the head noun. French possessive pronouns agree with the head noun, as shown in (66):

---

[29]   For data that challenge this proposal see Exercise 20. See Haegeman and Guéron (1999: chapter 4) for introductory discussion; for advanced discussion see Abney (1987), Bernstein (2001), and the references cited there.

(66) a mon   résumé   du texte
        my (MASC-SG) summary (MASC-SG) of-the text
        'my summary of the text'

     b mes   résumés   du texte
        my (PL) summaries (PL) of-the text
        'my summaries of the text'

     c ma   description   du texte
        my (FEM-SG) description (FEM-SG) of-the text
        'my description of the text'

     d mes   descriptions   du texte
        my (PL) descriptions (PL) of-the text
        'my descriptions of the text'

We observe that the specifier of the NP unites two properties: agreement (3.1.2.1) and subjecthood (3.1.2.2). Both agreement and subject are concepts that we also operate with at the level of sentences. What we will try to do below is to elaborate an approach to the sentence in which agreement and subjecthood are tied to a specifier position.[30]

3.1.2.3 *Questions about the structure of sentences*
From the discussions above we conclude that the specifier position of the NP has some special properties: (i) it has agreement properties, and (ii) it has subject properties. In French, these two properties coincide in prenominal possessive pronouns.

   We have also mentioned that at the level of sentences, agreement is realized between the subject NP and the auxiliary. This is illustrated in (67a) and (67b): *has* is singular, *have* is plural.

(67) a The customer <u>has</u> ordered the drinks.
     b The customers <u>have</u> ordered the drinks.

It would be most economical to try to characterize agreement properties in a uniform way across sentences and NPs. If the specifier of NP is the privileged position for realizing agreement on the determiner, and if it also encodes "subjecthood," then ideally when the properties of agreement and subjecthood coincide at the sentence level, we would also like to associate them with a specifier position. Compare the structure of the NP as given in (65) with (68), the structure of the sentence elaborated so far.

---

[30] Exercises 1B, 11. See Chapter 4, section 3.2.2.1, and Exercise 6, for an illustration of different agreement patterns.

(68)

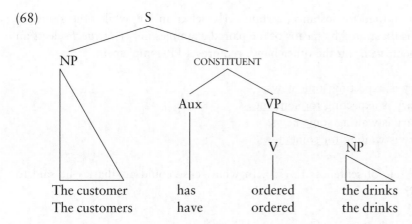

The customer	has	ordered	the drinks
The customers	have	ordered	the drinks

If agreement relations are established in specifier positions, then it would be an important move forward in our theory if we could say that the subject NP occupies a specifier position with respect to the auxiliary. This would amount to extending the projection schema for NPs to the sentence. How could this be done? We would need to identify a head, X, which takes a phrase as its complement, with which it combines to form X′, and whose specifier is the subject.

(69)

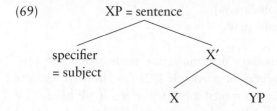

Try to superimpose the general format (69) on the sentence structure in (68). One way of aligning the two representations is to designate the auxiliary as the head of the sentence, and to identify the node which we had labeled provisionally as "CON-STITUENT" as the intermediate projection, dominating the auxiliary and the VP.

(70) a

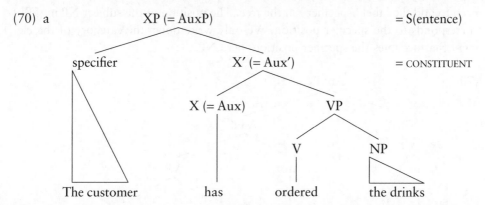

This representation means that we consider the VP as the complement of the auxiliary. Can we provide any motivation for this view? Recall that verbs select their complements, in that, for instance, certain verbs select an NP, while others select a PP, etc. This is illustrated by means of the paired examples in (71): *expect* selects an NP complement; *wait*, on the other hand, requires a PP complement.

(71) a   Mary is expecting <u>some news</u>.
          *Mary is expecting <u>for some news</u>.
      b   *Mary is waiting <u>some news</u>.
          Mary is waiting <u>for some news</u>.

Consider the sets of sentences in (72). In what sense could auxiliaries be said to select the VP?

(72) a   Mary is [_{VP} waiting for some news].
          *Mary is [_{VP} wait for some news].
          *Mary is [_{VP} waited for some news].
      b   Mary has [_{VP} waited for some news].
          *Mary has [_{VP} waiting for some news].
          *Mary has [_{VP} wait for some news].
      c   Mary will [_{VP} wait for some news].
          *Mary will [_{VP} waiting for some news].
          *Mary will [_{VP} waited for some news].

We might say that the choice of auxiliary determines the form of the VP: progressive *be* selects a VP headed by a present participle (72a), perfect *have* selects a VP headed by a past participle (72b), a modal auxiliary selects a VP headed by an infinitive (72c). In other words, the VP can be seen as being selected by, i.e. as being the complement of, the auxiliary.

For sentences with auxiliaries we could propose the structure in (70b). The constituent that combines with Aux′ is by definition a specifier: this constituent is inserted in a position defined as the specifier position. This means that we do not need to add the label "specifier" in the tree. The position of the subject NP in (70b) corresponds to the specifier position. We only write down the category of the element that occupies the specifier position, here NP.

(70) b

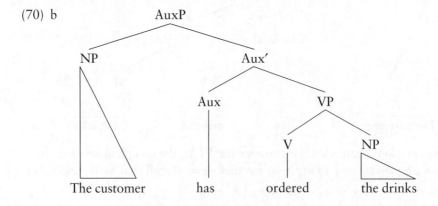

This raises the question as to how to deal with sentences without auxiliaries. We turn to this issue in the next chapter.[31]

3.2 Adjuncts and NPs

In addition to the core constituents of the VP, verb and complement, we proposed that we can also add modifiers such as, for instance, temporal PPs. Such modifiers are not selected by the verb, their categories are not determined by the verb heading the VP. For instance, a temporal specification can be expressed in a number of different ways:

(73)   a   The customer in the corner will order the drinks [$_{PP}$ before the meal].
  b   The customer in the corner will order the drinks [$_S$ when his guests arrive].
  c   The customer in the corner will order the drinks [$_{AdvP}$ later].
  d   The customer in the corner will order the drinks [$_{NP}$ this afternoon].

To integrate modifiers into the structure, we have introduced the concept of (left- or right-) adjunction, creating the augmented VP. If adjunction is available for building a VP, then the question arises if it is also available for an NP. Consider the underlined constituent in the following passage. What is its head? What is its category? Motivate your answer.

(74)   a   Marks and Sparks advice to its customers, as printed on <u>all their shopping bags</u>, is: To avoid suffocation, keep away from children. (Adapted from *Guardian*, 18.2.2002, p. 13, letter to the editor from Dick Brown, Arnside, Lancs)

The relevant string is an NP. To show that this is the case you can try using the NP as subject or object of a sentence. You can also replace the NP by a pronoun:

(74)   b   Marks and Sparks are reprinting <u>all their shopping bags</u>.
   Marks and Sparks are reprinting <u>them</u>.
  c   <u>All their shopping bags</u> have disappeared.
   <u>They</u> have disappeared.

Based on the data in (75), what is the category of *their shopping bags*?

(75)   a   Marks and Sparks advice to its customers, as printed on <u>their shopping bags</u>, is: "To avoid suffocation, keep away from children."

---

[31] Another question is how to deal with sentences containing more than one auxiliary. See Exercises 12 and 13, and Chapter 3, section 4. If adjunction is generally available as a way of augmenting a constituent we would expect to be able to adjoin constituents to a sentence (= AuxP). See Exercise 15.

b   Marks and Sparks are reprinting <u>their shopping bags</u>.
    Marks and Sparks are reprinting <u>them</u>.
c   <u>Their shopping bags</u> have disappeared.
    <u>They</u> have disappeared.

We conclude that both *all their shopping bags* and *their shopping bags* are NPs. *All* is not essential to form an NP, it provides additional information. We could add it onto the NP structure by left-adjoining it to the "core NP."[32]

(76)

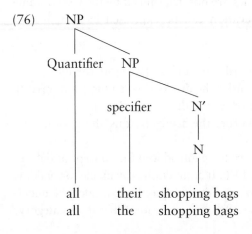

all	their	shopping bags	$[_{NP} [_Q$ all$]$ $[_{NP}$ their shopping bags$]]$
all	the	shopping bags	$[_{NP} [_Q$ all$]$ $[_{NP}$ the shopping bags$]]$

3.3 *Questions about the verb phrase*

Recall that an essential ingredient of scientific work is doubt.[33] We must always remain aware that our analyses are hypotheses. New insights or new developments in research may well mean that we must go back on what we think we know and revise earlier proposals. Having elaborated a hypothesis for the structure of the NP and applied it to the sentence, we have to reconsider our earlier hypothesis about the VP.

So far we have elaborated representations for the structure of (i) the VP, (ii) the NP, (iii) the sentence. We have used our findings for the structure of one of these constituents as a guideline to examine another constituent, but in the discussion we have left some areas unattended. In this section we reconsider the NP and VP and we will try to see to what extent, if at all, the structures are similar or different. Recall that we are interested in reducing the differences between the structures to a minimum. This approach will lead to a simpler theory.[34] Our theory is going to be simpler if we can say that NPs and VPs have the same structure. If they don't, we have to introduce two different structures, giving rise to a more permissive theory

[32] Exercise 13. For a more careful analysis see Shlonsky (1991).
[33] Chapter 1, section 1.2.4.
[34] For the role of simplicity see Chapter 1, section 1.2.3, and this chapter, section 2.4.2.

and also a more complex theory. In addition, the differences in structure that we have to postulate have to be explained by relating them to some other principle(s).

In the discussion of the structure of the NP, we identified four components of structure: the head, the complement, the specifier, and the adjunct. Generalizing this format for all syntactic structures, a syntactic constituent would be organized according to the format in (77):[35] a head, X, combines with a complement to form a partial constituent, X′, and this combines with the specifier to form the complete constituent (XP). In the literature, the term **intermediate projection** is used to refer to what we called a partial constituent, and the term **maximal projection** is used for the complete constituent, including the specifier. Adjoined constituents are satellites to the maximal projection; they are themselves maximal projections. For example, in our example (5a) the adjunct *before the meal* is a full PP.

(77) a

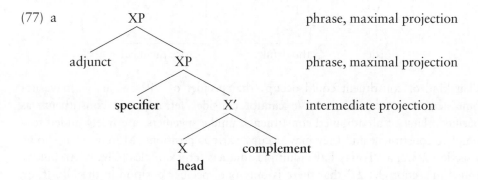

phrase, maximal projection

phrase, maximal projection

intermediate projection

However, the structure we arrived at for the VP was different in that we did not have the level of specifier:

(77) b

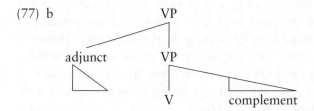

This difference in structure is not really satisfying. A number of questions arise. (i) Why is the combination of V + complement represented as a maximal projection (VP), while that of N + complement is represented as an intermediate projection (N′)? The answer to this question could be that this is because the VP lacks a specifier. This leads to the next question. (ii) Why does the representation for NP include a specifier, while that for VP does not?

Because we had empirical grounds to postulate representation (77a) for the NP, it seems natural to maintain it and to assume that, in principle, constituents CAN have

---

[35] (77a) replaces the earlier (41). How do the structures differ?

a specifier. It would then be desirable to generalize this format to the VP (and indeed to other categories). What would the structure of the VP be like if we assumed that it also had a specifier? Based on the structure of the NP in (77a), we could replace (77b) by (77c), which we apply to our example sentence:

(77) c

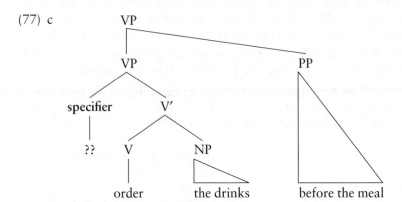

What kind of constituent could occupy the specifier of VP? So far, we have not come across any candidates. We cannot consider left-adjoined constituents as specifiers. First of all adjoined constituents, unlike specifiers, are freely added to a complete constituent and they may occupy various positions. Moreover, as shown in section 2.3.2, a VP may have multiple adjuncts (cf. examples (43g, h, i)), but we argued in section 3.1.2.2 that there is only one specifier position in the NP. If, on the other hand, we decided that there is no specifier in the VP, then we would have to explain why the VP lacks a specifier.

Recall also from section 3.1.2.2 that the specifier position of the NP could be occupied by a prenominal genitive NP or by a possessive pronoun, both of which have a subject-like relation to the head N. Let us explore this observation: by analogy with the NP, the specifier of the VP ought to be the subject NP. However, in assuming that the specifier of the VP is the subject we create a conflict with the structure of the sentences elaborated above, in which the subject is located outside the VP. Let us examine why we had concluded that the subject was located outside the VP. One argument for assuming that the subject is outside the VP was that the subject was seen to precede the auxiliary, which we considered as a separate unit that forms a constituent with the VP. Secondly, we have also seen that the subject precedes any adjuncts that are left-adjoined to the VP.[36] The examples in (78) illustrate both these points:

(78) a   [NP The customer in the corner] <u>will</u> [VP order the drinks before the meal].
       b   [NP The customer in the corner] will [VP <u>definitely</u> [VP order the drinks before the meal]].

---

[36]   Cf. section 2.2.1.

We will return to the relation between the subject and the VP in Chapter 4, but before doing so we will complete the representation of the structure of the sentence in Chapter 3.

Another problem that came out of the discussion at the end of sections 2.2 and 3.2 is the question how to deal with sentences without auxiliaries such as (39c), repeated here as (79). We will tackle this question in the next chapter.

(79)   The customer in the corner ordered the drinks before the meal.

4   Summary

In this chapter we have first elaborated a number of diagnostic tests for discovering sentence structure. Units of structure, or constituents, can be detected by manipulating the sentences in which they occur. We can try to replace strings of words by a smaller unit (substitution), we can make them the target of a question (question formation), we can move them around (movement), we can delete them (ellipsis), we can make them the informational focus of the sentence (clefting and pseudo-clefting), and finally, constituents can be co-ordinated. By means of these tools, we have decomposed English sentences and demarcated their core constituents.

The constituents of a sentence are formed around a core constituent, their head. For instance, an NP has a noun as its head. We have examined two competing hypotheses about the structure of the VP. According to one hypothesis, the VP contains the verb and the auxiliary (or the auxiliaries) of the sentence; according to the second, the VP contains the verb, its complements, and its adjuncts. The second hypothesis is both empirically and theoretically preferable. Further examination of the VP reveals that we need to postulate a more articulated structure in which we distinguish two hierarchical levels. This allows us to distinguish a core VP, the combination of the verb with its complement, from the augmented VP, a larger constituent which combines the core VP with adjuncts.

While discussing the structure of the VP we elaborated the binary branching hypothesis. This is a theoretical proposal to the effect that all syntactic constituents are the result of combining or merging two constituents, and that constituents are hierarchically organized around a head. The head first combines with its complement. The resulting constituent then combines with adjuncts.

In our examination of the structure of the NP we have revealed the need to identify an additional level of representation to allow for the creation of a specifier position. A noun head first combines with its complement to form N′, an intermediate projection of an NP. This intermediate projection combines with a prenominal element in the specifier position to form the fully completed NP, the maximal projection.

The specifier of the NP hosts a determiner element, a prenominal possessive pronoun, or a prenominal genitive NP. We assume that each syntactic position can contain only one constituent. We also assume that there is only one specifier position per NP. This means that an NP will contain either a determiner, or a possessive pronoun, or a prenominal genitive NP.

The specifier position of the NP is set apart by two distinctive properties: the constituent contained in it sometimes agrees with the head noun, and it sometimes seems to have subject-like properties. This observation has led us to the hypothesis that the subject of the sentence occupies a specifier position. In order to implement this hypothesis, we have elaborated a representation for sentences with auxiliaries. According to the proposal, sentences are built around auxiliaries: the auxiliary is the head of the sentence. The auxiliary takes a VP as its complement, forming an intermediate projection. This intermediate projection combines with the specifier position to form the maximal projection. The subject occupies the specifier position.

Given the observation that both the NP and sentence have a specifier position, we will have to address the question whether the VP also has a specifier position. In addition, given that not all sentences have an auxiliary, we will have to examine how to apply the structure elaborated for sentences with auxiliaries to sentences lacking auxiliaries.

Exercises

Contents

Exercise 1   Constituent structure in the NP (T, E)

A   Constituency tests (T)

Do the underlined strings in the following examples form a constituent? For each string, provide at least one argument to motivate your answer.

(1)   Have you read <u>our dean's</u> report of the meeting?

(2)   Our <u>new dean's wife</u> has been invited to give a lecture.

(3)   These <u>new students of English</u> are planning a trip to London and those are going to Paris.

(4) We all expected that they would <u>wait for us after the lecture</u>.

(5) I will meet <u>all the students of semantics next week</u>.

COMMENTS

In (1) the string *our dean's* is a constituent: it can be replaced by a pronoun (*his*), and we can also question it by means of *whose*. *Our dean's* is the genitive of the NP, *our dean*. Inside that NP, the possessive pronoun *our* specifies the reference of the genitive NP. The structure of the NP in (1) would be as in (6). The NP *our dean* occupies the specifier position inside the NP. We use the labels NP1 and NP2 to distinguish the two NPs: NP1 is the containing NP, NP2 is the prenominal genitive NP in its specifier. We attach the genitive ending *'s* to the N *dean*.

(6)

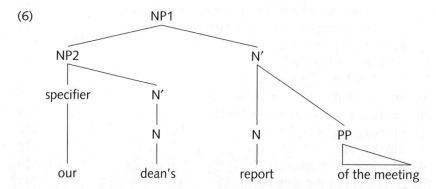

Observe that there are two NPs here: we have two nouns (*report*, *dean*), each of which has its own projection (NP1, NP2).

B   *Determiners and specifiers (E)*

In section 3.1.2.2 we accounted for the unacceptability of the examples in (63), some of which are repeated here as (7), by postulating (i) that a position can be occupied by only one constituent and (ii) that there is one specifier position in the NP.[1] The unique specifier position in the NP will then be occupied either by a determiner or by a prenominal genitive NP.

(7) a   *the Rupert Murdoch's bid for Manchester United Football Club
     b   *Rupert Murdoch's the bid for Manchester United Football Club

How would this be compatible with the observation that the examples in (8) are acceptable?

---

[1] For data that complicate this hypothesis see Exercise 20 below. For an introduction to complications see Haegeman and Guéron (1999: chapter 4). For a theoretical (but more advanced) discussion see Bernstein (2001).

(8) a   the teacher's books
     b   that teacher's books

Representation (6) above can help to clarify the issue of the occurrence of determiners and genitives in (8). In (8a), the determiner *the* is related to the noun *teacher*: we can replace the string *the teacher's* by the pronoun *his*. We can question the string *the teacher's* by means of *whose*. (9a) provides a structure:

(9) a

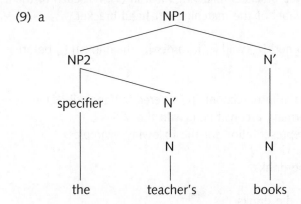

In (8b), similarly, the demonstrative *that* specifies the reference of *teacher*: *that teacher's books* roughly corresponds to *the books of that teacher*. We have seen that English demonstratives agree with the head noun. Consider representation (9b). According to the structure in (9b), do we predict that the demonstrative *that* will agree with the N *teacher* or will it agree with the N *books*? Is this prediction correct?

(9) b

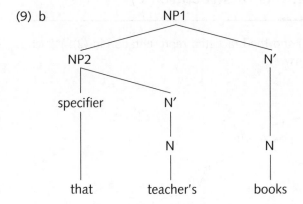

In (9b), the demonstrative *that* is the specifier of NP2, whose head is the N *teacher*. Thus we correctly predict that the demonstrative agrees with the head N of NP2: *that* is singular and so is *teacher*. The demonstrative in the specifier position of NP2 does not agree with the head of NP1: in our example the head of NP1, *books*, is plural.

   If we replace the singular N *teacher's* in NP2 by its plural counterpart *teachers'*, then the demonstrative will also have to be plural.

(10) a   those teachers' books
     b   *that teachers' books

Exercise 2   Bracketing representations (T)

Discuss why there are exactly three brackets following *meal* in (1). For each of the right-hand brackets identify the label of the matching left-hand bracket.

(1)   [$_S$ [$_{NP}$ The customer in the corner] [$_{Aux}$ will] [$_{VP}$ [$_{VP}$ order [$_{NP}$ the drinks]] [$_{PP}$ before the meal]]].

Does the representation in (1) take into account the layered VP analysis? Does it represent the auxiliary *will* as forming a constituent with the VP?
   Provide a labeled bracketing representation for the following examples:

(2)   The customers will order the drinks.

(3)   All the customers will order the drinks.

(4)   My analysis of this issue will quite probably surprise all the representatives of the media.

Exercise 3   Representations of structure (T)

Compare the tree diagram in (1) and the bracketed representation in (2). Which is more detailed? Motivate your answer.

(1)

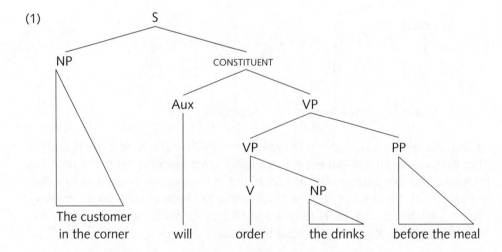

(2)   [_NP_ The customer in the corner] [_AUX_ will] [_VP_ order the drinks before the meal].

By adding the necessary brackets and labels, modify (2) so that it contains all the information contained in (1).

Exercise 4   Evidence for constituent structure (T)

Consider the underlined strings of words in the extracts below. The extracts themselves contain a clue to support an analysis according to which the underlined strings form a constituent. Try to find that clue. For each underlined constituent, identify the grammatical category (NP, VP, etc.). There is no need to draw the tree; you should merely explain on what basis the sequences could be argued to form a constituent.

Example
The news, when it comes, he seems to take —— well enough. (*Guardian*, G2, 26.7.2002, p. 2, col. 1)

- In this example, movement has affected the string *the news*. *The news* is the direct object of *take*. Its canonical position is to the immediate right of the verb. In the example it has been moved to the beginning of the sentence. The fact that it has been moved suggests that the string of words is a constituent. Moreover, the string *the news* is substituted for by the pronoun *it*.
- *The news* is an NP.

---

(1)   Is there anything that can prevent Hurricanes? To date, science and technology have not given us the ability to do so. (*Chicago Tribune*, 3.1.2004, section 1, p. 28, col. 1)

(2)   There are hardly any small movies that people go to, and some of the more interesting ones they won't go to. (*Guardian*, 1.11.2002, Review, p. v, col. 4)

(3)   I think we could adapt to being poor again if we had to. (*Guardian*, G2, 28.8.2002, p. 4, col. 2)

(4)   *Great Expectations*, I've read three times. (*Guardian*, G2, 1.4.2003, p. 12, col. 2)

(5)   The Bears are not a talented team and have not been in years, not even in 2001. (*Chicago Tribune*, 3.1.2004, S3, p. 2, col. 5)

(6) But what we do is <u>go to shopping centers and corporate parties downtown</u>. (Based on *Chicago Tribune*, 22.12.2002, section 1, p. 16, col. 6)

(7) The towns Paula Radcliffe has lived in (Nantwich, Bedford and Loughborough) are <u>the epitome of Middle England</u>. And so is she. (*Guardian*, 17.12.2002, p. 13, col. 1)

(8) If they must use <u>children's stories</u> in a vain attempt to make their speech sparkier, why can't they choose new ones? (*Guardian*, 12.2.2003, p. 2, col. 4)

(9) They are eyeing retirement and <u>just entering the work force</u>. (*Atlanta Journal-Constitution*, 23.11.2003, p. F5, col. 1)

(10) It's unbelievable how unlucky he's been, but he's certainly proved he's got tenacity. <u>Whether he'll get out of this difficult situation or not</u>, only time will tell. (*Guardian*, 8.2.2003, p. 2, col. 8)

Exercise 5 Focalizing a constituent by rightward movement (T, E)

We propose that a direct object is merged directly with the verb to form V'. The canonical object position is to the immediate right of the verb. In the following examples some direct object NPs are not found in their canonical positions. Identify the displaced objects, identify the verb that selects them, and try to restore the displaced objects to their canonical positions.

(1) "The Independent" is publishing daily each of the 30 Articles of the Universal Declaration of Human Rights, illustrated by Ralph Steadman, to mark its 50th anniversary on 10 December. (*Independent*, 13.11.1998, p. 13, cols 1–2)

(2) The government has delayed until the New Year the introduction of the controversial Bill to strip the 750 hereditaries of their right to speak and vote in the second chamber. (*Guardian*, 25.22.1998, p. 1, col. 1)

(3) We look forward to the opportunity to defend before the Supreme Court Maryland's historic ownership and regulation of this important natural resource. (*Washington Post*, 29.4.2003, p. A7, col. 1)

(4) Few if any authors on the region have so successfully compressed into 280 pages the basic outlines of Antarctic life and our relationship to its pristine abundance. (*Guardian*, Review, 22.11.2003, p. 11, col. 2)

(5) The argument has been that members of Congress get paid by the taxpayer their normal salary while they're running for office. (*Los Angeles Times*, 26.11.2002, p. A32, col. 3)

In the above examples the objects of the verbs *publishing* (1), *delayed* (2), *defend* (3), *compressed* (4), and *paid* (5), have apparently been shifted rightward. The effect of shifting the object to a rightward position is that it becomes the focus of the sentence, it is focalized.

(1′) "The Independent" is <u>publishing</u> —— daily [NP each of the 30 Articles of the Universal Declaration of Human Rights, illustrated by Ralph Steadman] to mark its 50th anniversary on 10 December.

(2′) The government has <u>delayed</u> —— until the new year [NP the introduction of the controversial Bill to strip the 750 hereditaries of their right to speak and vote in the second chamber].

(3′) We look forward to the opportunity to <u>defend</u> —— before the Supreme Court [NP Maryland's historic ownership and regulation of this important natural resource].

(4′) Few if any authors on the region have so successfully <u>compressed</u> —— into 280 pages [NP the basic outlines of Antarctic life and our relationship to its pristine abundance].

(5′) The argument has been that members of Congress get <u>paid</u> —— by the taxpayer [NP their normal salary while they're running for office].

Experiment: Replace each of the shifted objects in (1)–(5) by a personal pronoun. Are the resulting sentences acceptable? As suggested by the sharp degradation in acceptability of the examples below, we conclude that not all direct objects can freely be moved rightward away from the selecting verb.

(6) *The Independent' is publishing daily <u>them</u>.

(7) *The government has delayed until the New Year <u>it</u>.

(8) *We look forward to the opportunity to defend before the Supreme Court <u>them</u>.

(9) *Few if any authors on the region have so successfully compressed into 280 pages <u>them</u>.

(10) *The argument has been that members of Congress get paid by the taxpayer <u>it</u>.

The degradations in (6)–(10) can be related to the focalizing role of the rightward shift. Direct object NPs which are moved rightward tend to be focused. If some information is worth focusing then probably it will contain something new. Pronouns typically represent old information and therefore are not good candidates for focusing.

Consider the test sentence (11). Can we shift the object rightward?

(11)   The customer in the corner will order the drinks before dinner.

And what about (12)?

(12)   The customer in the corner will order all the drinks to go with the entire meal and the dessert before dinner.

Finally consider (13). How is the complement of the verb *argued* realized? Does the complement occupy its base position?

(13)   This week proved wrong the doomsayers who <u>argued</u> after the failures in Seattle in 1996 and The Hague in 1999 that the pace of globalisation had outstripped the international institutions' ability to respond, let alone to manage it. (Adapted from *Guardian*, 17.11.2001, p. 9, col. 2)

In (13) the complement of *argued* is a clause: *that the pace of globalisation had outstripped the international institutions' ability to respond, let alone to manage it*. For other examples in which the complement of the verb is a clause see Exercise 10.

Exercise 6   Structural ambiguity and co-ordination (T)

In the following extracts co-ordination with *and* may give rise to two interpretations. Discuss the two readings and identify how they have come about. How could you rephrase the sentences, changing as little as possible, to eliminate the ambiguity?

(1)   He added that the looting, though continuing, is much reduced. "You will see a guy or two carrying a table or chairs. We tell them to put it down <u>and</u> go home." (*Guardian*, 7.5.2003, p. 5, col. 14)

(2)   If you feel threatened in a mini cab, firmly ask the driver to stop <u>and</u> get out. (Adapted from *Guardian*, G2, 7.3.2003, p. 7, col. 2)

Exercise 7   Representing co-ordination (T, E)

Identify the co-ordinated constituents in the following examples. What is their category? How can we show that co-ordinating two constituents itself creates a constituent? What is the category of the co-ordinated constituent as a whole?

(1) a   The customer in the corner and his wife will order the drinks.

KEY AND COMMENTS

In (1a) we co-ordinate two NPs.

(1) b   [$_{NP}$ the customer in the corner]
     and
     [$_{NP}$ his wife]

We can cleft the resulting co-ordinated string, suggesting that it is a constituent.

(1) c   It is [[$_{NP}$ the customer in the corner] and [$_{NP}$ his wife]] who will order the drinks.

We can also question the string by means of *who*.

(1) d   Who will order the drinks?

In (1a/b) the co-ordinated string *the customer in the corner and his wife* is the subject of the sentence. It can be replaced by a pronoun.

(1) e   They will order the drinks.

Typically, pronouns like *they* replace NPs. So we conclude that the constituent consisting of two co-ordinated NPs in (1c) is an NP. (1f) is a provisional structure, in which we label *and* as a co-ordinator ("co-ord").

(1) f

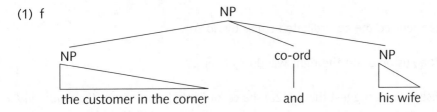

Based on the discussion above, how could we represent the structure of the underlined co-ordinated constituent in (2)?

(2)   The customer in the corner will <u>order the drinks and pay for the meal</u>.

NOTE

With respect to the discussion in section 2.4, observe that the representation of co-ordinated structures raises a problem for the binary branching hypothesis. We will not go into this issue here.[2]

Exercise 8   Structural ambiguity (T, E)

In section 1.8 of the chapter we discussed co-ordination of VPs and we introduced example (34b), repeated here as (1):

(1)   The customer in the corner will order the drinks and choose the dessert before the meal.

In the text, this example was used to illustrate the co-ordination of the VPs *order the drinks* and *choose the dessert*. First, use bracketing to represent the co-ordination as intended in the text. What does the temporal specification *before the meal* modify?

   The bracketing intended in the text discussion is that represented in (2a). The VP *order the drinks* and the VP *choose the dessert* are co-ordinated. The PP *before the meal* is added to the result of the co-ordination:

(2) a   The customer in the corner will
           [[$_{VP}$ order the drinks] and [$_{VP}$ choose the dessert]] before the meal.

The unit consisting of the co-ordinated VPs has the same distribution as a simple VP: in our example it follows the auxiliary *will*. We can pseudo-cleft the unit consisting of the co-ordinated VPs, as shown in (2b):

(2) b   What the customer in the corner will do before the meal is [order the drinks and choose the dessert].

Or we can replace the co-ordinated string by *do so*:

(2) c   The customer on the right will <u>do so</u> later.

These observations suggest that in (2a) the co-ordinated string *order the drinks and choose the dessert* is a VP. In tree format the co-ordinated VP could be represented by (2d). We complete the bracketing notation in (2e).

---

[2]   For discussion see Camacho (2003), Goodall (1987), van Oirsouw (1987), and the papers in Blakemore and Carston (2005).

(2) d

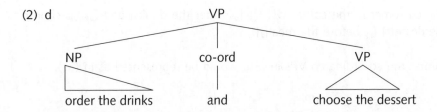

e The customer in the corner will
[VP [VP order the drinks] and [VP choose the dessert]] before the meal.

To complete the representation of the VP of (2a) we need to integrate the PP *before the meal*. We add the PP *before the meal* as a temporal adjunct of the co-ordinated VP in (2d/e). This representation means that the PP will bear on both components of the co-ordinated constituent:

(2) f

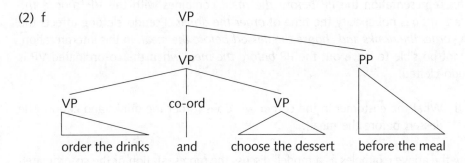

g The customer in the corner will
[VP [VP [VP order the drinks] and [VP choose the dessert]] before the meal].

According to representation (2f/g), both actions of 'ordering the drinks' and 'choosing the dessert' will take place before the meal.

Observe that there is a second interpretation possible for (1) and one that was not intended in the text discussion. The second interpretation is due to the fact that we can assign the temporal specification to a different domain. Can you see the second interpretation of (1)? In the second reading, (1) can be paraphrased as in (3a). How would we bracket example (1) to bring out this reading?

(3) a The customer in the corner will choose the dessert before the meal and order the drinks.

The alternative bracketing for text example (1), which was not intended in the discussion in the main body of the chapter, is shown in (3b). In this representation the PP *before the meal* is adjoined directly to the VP *choose the dessert*. The PP is not intended to modify the VP *order the drinks*. The co-ordinated VPs are *order the drinks* and *choose the dessert before the meal*.

(3) b   The customer in the corner will [$_{VP}$ [$_{VP}$ order the drinks] and [$_{VP}$ [$_{VP}$ choose the dessert] [$_{PP}$ before the meal]]].

In tree format the co-ordinated VPs in (3b) would be represented as in (3c).

(3) c

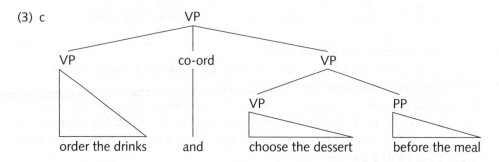

In this representation the PP *before the meal* combines with the VP *choose the dessert*. It does not specify the time of *order the drinks*. Pseudo-clefting affects the string *order the drinks and choose the dessert before the meal*. In this interpretation, it is not possible to leave out the PP *before the meal* when the co-ordinated VP is pseudo-clefted.

(3) d   What the customer in the corner will do is [order the drinks and choose the dessert before the meal].

Using the above examples as a model, discuss the representation of the co-ordinated VP in (3a).

NOTE

With respect to the discussion in section 2.4 you will conclude that the representation of co-ordinated structures raises a problem for the binary branching hypothesis. We will not go into this issue here.

Exercise 9   Co-ordination (T, E)

On the basis of the examples below, discuss whether the following generalization is valid:

> The co-ordinating conjunction *and* always links constituents of the same category.

(1)   Now that women are totally independent and earning their own money they are less likely to put up with a bad marriage. (*Guardian*, G2, 16.10.2002, p. 11, col. 2)

(2) We have expressed our disappointment to the Philippine government very clearly and at high levels. (*New York Times*, 1.8.2004, p. 3, section 4, col. 4)

(3) Which is true? Thompson demanded, folding his arms and glowering down at the witness. (*Wall Street Journal*, 26.3.2004, p. A6, col. 4)

(4) Winners included a day laborer in Florida who had recently been homeless and sleeping on cardboard boxes. (*New York Times*, 8.3.2004, p. C6, col. 4)

(5) Two men who survived the attack were being tended by marine medics and being prepared for evacuation to hospital. (Based on *Guardian*, 28.3.2003, p. 3, col. 1)

(6) I can understand that Jack Straw is a busy man, and unlikely to be able to afford the time for mathematics. (*Guardian*, 15.3.2003, p. 11, col. 8, letter to the editor from Greg Callus, University of York)

(7) His black shirt was soggy and hanging out of his pants. (*New York Times*, 8.3.2004, p. D1, col. 2)

(8) Fifty minutes later Sarah arrived at the hospital, unconscious and in a fit. At her home near Whitchurch in Cheshire, her mother, Pauline Campbell, was preparing to go out, having heard nothing from the prison and unaware that her only daughter was fighting for her life. (*Guardian*, 5.5.2003, p. 7, col. 1)

(9) If sound comes on both sides at exactly the same time and with the same amplitude, the mechanism doesn't move. (*Chicago Tribune*, 3.1.2004, p. 4, section 2, col. 6)

(10) We wanted justice and for the truth to be known. (*Guardian*, 12.11.2002, p. 6, col. 7)

Some of the examples above show that co-ordinated constituents do not always have identical categories. Discuss the problems raised by these examples for the representation of co-ordinate structures elaborated in Exercise 7.[3]

Exercise 10   Realization of subject and object (T, E)

In the discussion in this chapter we have systematically been using examples in which both subject and object are realized as NPs. This might give the impression that only NPs can function as subjects or as objects. Similarly, our examples of

---

[3]   For a proposal on how to handle such types of co-ordinations see Bowers (1993, 2001, 2002).

prepositional phrases always consisted of a preposition with an NP complement. Based on the examples below and using the concepts elaborated in the chapter, evaluate statements A, B, and C.

You should first read the statements carefully, and for each statement examine whether the examples are relevant and if so, in what way they confirm/disconfirm the statement.[4]

A   The subject of a sentence is always realized by a noun phrase.
B   The object of a verb is always realized by a noun phrase.
C   The complement of a preposition is always realized by a noun phrase.

(1)   Just because the US administration says that it has "no interest" in imple-menting the Kyoto protocol to control climate change doesn't mean it's dead. (*Guardian*, 31.3.2001, p. 9, col. 8, letter to the editor from Ritu Kumar)

(2)   She couldn't stop asking questions about whether they would be OK. (*Guardian*, Travel, 9.8.2003, p. xi, col. 1)

(3)   The skirt is also available in black, so now might be just the time to go for it. (*Guardian*, 24.11.2000, p. 8, col. 8)

(4)   That 85% of children spelt Hogwarts correctly is no surprise. (*Guardian*, 4.9.2002, p. 5, col. 2)

(5)   It's the curve of those thighs that has, surely, guaranteed that she's sent to Islamabad, even though above the waist is all we ever get to see on the television. (*Guardian*, G2, 25.10.2001, p. 10, col. 2)

(6)   She knew how many novels she would write. (Based on *Guardian*, Review, 2.8.2003, p. 14, col. 4)

(7)   I told Simon Kelner I wouldn't want to do the job on a long-term basis, and after a general election seems a natural departure time. (*Guardian*, G2, 16.4.2001, p. 13, col. 4)

(8)   Before 11 September seems like an innocent lost paradise. (*Guardian*, G2, 13.11.2001, p. 11, col. 5)

(9)   Many league members accept that some money is better than no money at all. (*Guardian*, 29.3.2002, p. 16, col. 1)

---

[4]   For PP subjects see Jaworska (1986). For clausal subjects see Koster (1978), Davies and Dubinsky (1999, 2001a), Miller (2001).

(10) You realise he hates for you to call him "Ollie", don't you? (Marcia Muller,
      Edwin of the Iron Shoes, 1993: 42)

Exercise 11   Constituent structure in the NP (T)

We might provide the structure in (1) for the NP *all those students of English*.
Discuss theoretical and empirical problems that arise.

(1)

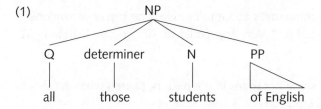

Exercise 12   Auxiliary strings (T, L)

In our discussion so far we have concentrated on sentences containing just one
auxiliary. This is only one of a number of patterns in which auxiliaries can be found.
Identify all the auxiliaries in the following examples. Which of the auxiliaries are finite?[5]

(1)   He would have stolen her fame.

(2)   You should have become an accountant.

(3)   He'll be staying at the local inn.

COMMENTS

As you can see, each example contains more than one auxiliary: (1a) contains a
modal auxiliary *would* and a perfect auxiliary *have*. The modal auxiliary is tensed:
past tense *would* contrasts with present tense *will*. The auxiliary *have* is not tensed,
it is an infinitive form and this is not affected by tense modifications; *would* is a
finite auxiliary and *have* is **non-finite**. Which are the finite/non-finite auxiliaries in
(2) and in (3)? We note that in each example there is just one finite auxiliary and
that this precedes the non-finite auxiliary. Could there be more than one finite
auxiliary in the string? Could the finite auxiliary be second or third in the sequence?
Experiment with examples (1)–(3) to answer these questions.

---

5   See Chapter 1, sections 2.2.2 and 2.4 for the concept "finite."

Exercise 13   Auxiliary strings (T, L)

In the following examples the symbol Ø signals that material has been omitted. Identify the omitted material. What is the category of the omitted constituent (VP, etc.)?

(1)   He drove her hard, he stole her fame or would have Ø if he could have Ø. (*Guardian*, Review, 24.5.2003, p. 5, col. 3)

(2)   "The Hershey chocolate company is about to be sold!" he says, eyes widening. "Who could have imagined it?" Very few could Ø. (Based on *Guardian*, G2, 26.8.2002, p. 2, col. 1)

(3)   Michael Jackson has, on some occasions in the past, not eaten when he should Ø. (*Guardian*, Review, 28.5.2003, p. 3, col. 1)

COMMENT

In (1) the omitted material is a VP: *stolen her fame*. The auxiliary *have* is retained. In (2) and (3) the omitted material combines a VP with an auxiliary: *have imagined it, have eaten*. We will tentatively conclude that because they can be subject to ellipsis such strings are constituents. Hence, the non-finite auxiliary (here *have*) and the VP together form a constituent. How do the following examples bear on this hypothesis?

(4)   Some 24% agreed top-up fees would not have mattered, while 35% would have considered other universities but probably still have chosen the same university. (Based on *Guardian*, 20.1.2003, p. 5, col. 2)

(5)   But we have been saying for 15 to 20 years that there are too many games in the top division and done nothing about it. (*Guardian*, 15.2.2003, *Sport*, p. 11, col. 5)

We return to the structure of sentences with multiple auxiliaries in Chapter 3, section 4.

Exercise 14   Attachments of adjuncts (T, L)

In this exercise we speculate about the application of adjunction. The exercise is longer and more discursive than some of the other exercises. The idea is that we carry further the type of argumentation elaborated in the chapter and see where that would lead us.

We will examine the consequences of the hypothesis that syntactic structure determines interpretation. Consider sentence (1a). Where would we locate the adjuncts *still* and *actively*?

(1) a   I am still actively monitoring the reporting of the press coverage of the trial.
         (*Guardian*, 29.11.2003, p. 7, col. 2)

COMMENT

The two adjuncts can both be adjoined to the VP headed by *monitoring*:

(1) b

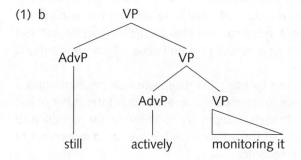

The different adjunction sites mirror the interpretation: according to (1b) 'it is still the case that we are actively monitoring it'. Or to use the technical term: the adverb *still* takes **scope** over the VP *actively monitoring it*; the adverb *actively* takes scope over the VP *monitoring it*. The structure in (1b) represents the **relative scope** of the adjuncts: an adjunct that is adjoined higher in the structure takes scope over one that is adjoined lower.

Consider sentence (2a), which was also given in Chapter 1, Exercise 4.

(2) a   Tony Blair was admitting that he had run into "tough times" <u>in recent months yesterday</u>. (Adapted from *Independent*, 5.9.2003, p. 2, col. 1)

We find two temporal specifications, the PP *in recent months* and the NP *yesterday*, one after the other. Can we adjoin them both to the VP headed by *run*? Obviously, if we did that, then we would create some redundancy. Since the stretch of time denoted by *in recent months* comprises the time specified by *yesterday*, the latter specification would be sufficient. On the other hand, if the time stretch referred to by *yesterday* had been intended to be distinct from that referred to by *in recent months*, and if both adjuncts were associated with the VP headed by *run*, then the two adjuncts would locate one and the same event ('running into tough times') at two different times, and we would end up with a contradiction. Adjoining both adjuncts to the VP headed by *run* is thus probably not the correct way to go about it if we think of the intended interpretation of the sentence.

Let us first pick out the main ingredients of (2a). Identify all the verbs in (2a). Which are lexical verbs? Which are auxiliaries? Which lexical verbs or auxiliaries are finite? Which are non-finite? What is the subject of *admitting*? What is the object of *admitting*? What is the subject of *had run into tough times*?

(2a) contains two lexical verbs *admitting* and *run*, and it also contains two finite auxiliaries, *was* and *had*. (2a) is a **complex** sentence: the complement of the verb *admitting* is itself realized by a sentence introduced by the **subordinating conjunction** *that*: *that he had run into tough times in recent months*. When a sentence functions inside another sentence we say it is **embedded**. We often use the term **embedded clause**.[6]

If you think about the intended interpretation of the temporal specifications *in recent months* and *yesterday*, you will conclude that *in recent months* modifies the VP *had run into tough times*, while *yesterday* modifies *admitting that he had run into tough times*. *In recent times* is an adjunct in the embedded clause; *yesterday* is an adjunct in the main clause.

Try to isolate the embedded clause by using the diagnostics we have introduced to identify constituents. For instance, (i) formulate a question that targets the object of *admitting*. (ii) Using the pseudo-cleft pattern, try to rephrase the sentence to bring out the different attachments of the adjuncts. (iii) Move the direct object of *admitting* to the beginning of the sentence.

(3) a What was Tony Blair admitting yesterday?
     That he had run into tough times in recent months.
   b What Tony Blair was admitting yesterday was that he had run into tough times in recent months.
   c That he had run into tough times in recent months, Tony Blair was admitting yesterday.

Finally, you can also shift the complement of *admitting* to the right, across *yesterday*.[7]

(3) d Tony Blair was admitting yesterday —— that he had run into tough times in recent months.

These various diagnostics lead us to propose that the adjunct *in recent months* is adjoined to the VP headed by *run*, and that the adjunct *yesterday* is adjoined to the VP headed by *admitting*. (2b) is a representation modeled on representation (70b) in the discussion section. In (2b) we have added *that* to the structure with the label C. We come back to the position of conjunctions like *that* in Chapter 5.

---

[6] We discuss embedded clauses in more detail in Chapter 5, section 2.3.
[7] For rightward shifting of objects see Exercise 5 above.

(2) b

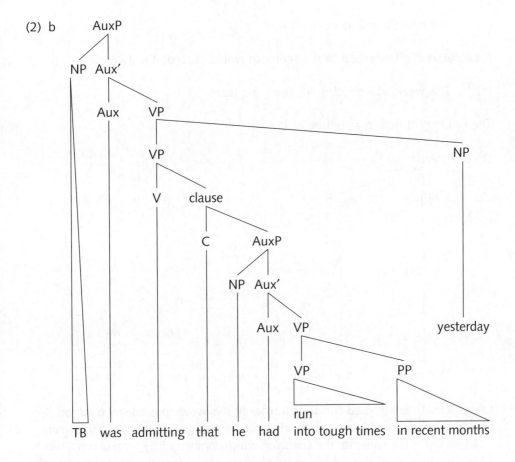

Exercise 15   Adjunction to the sentence (L, E)

In this exercise we speculate about the application of adjunction. The exercise is more discursive than some of the other exercises. The idea is that we pursue the argumentation elaborated in the chapter and see where that would lead us.

In representation (70b) in the chapter, we analyze sentences containing a finite auxiliary as projections of that auxiliary: the auxiliary heads the sentence, the sentence is an AuxP. In the representation we showed how the head of the sentence, Aux, takes a VP as its complement and has a subject NP as its specifier.

We did not discuss the possibility of adjunction to the sentence. However, if adjunction exists as a general option available to any structure formed according to the format elaborated in the chapter, then sentences ought also to be able to have constituents adjoined to them. Once again, if we were to conclude that adjunction to sentences is not possible then we would ideally have to explain this ban.

Consider (1a). If we were to left-adjoin the NP *this week* to the sentence, what would the resulting sentence be? Using (70b) as a model, draw a tree diagram for the sentence with the adjunct integrated into it.

(1) a   The director will meet the team.

A constituent left-adjoined to the sentence would precede the subject:

(1) b   This week, the director will meet the team.

The resulting structure would be as in (1c):

(1) c

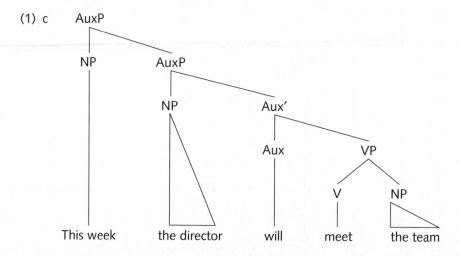

Observe that the adjoined constituent, the NP *this week*, precedes the subject. We have a structure in which a core AuxP is augmented with an additional element.

Adjunction is the name for the operation which combines fully formed constituents. So far, we have used this operation to integrate non-essential components into the structure. For instance, we used adjunction to add specifications of time or manner to the VP. These adjoined constituents were optional and they were peripheral to the VP. Could obligatory components of the sentence be found in an adjoined position?

Consider example (4) in Exercise 4, repeated here as (2a). The subject *I* is preceded by a constituent. What type of constituent is it? What would be the unmarked position for this constituent?

(2) a   *Great Expectations*, I've read three times. (*Guardian*, G2, 1.4.2003, p. 12, col. 2)

In this example *Great Expectations* is an NP. It is the name of a book. It is the object of the verb *read*. It can be replaced by a pronoun; we can question it with *what*. If we restore it to its base position we have (2b).

(2) b   I've read [NP *Great Expectations*] three times.

Before turning the page, try to draw a tree diagram for (2b), using diagram (70b) in the chapter as a model. You can spell out the contracted auxiliary *'ve* as *have*. The tree should look as follows:

(2) c

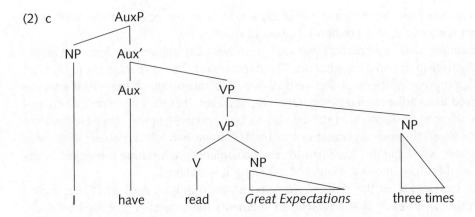

In (2b) the NP *Great Expectations* is the object of the verb *read*, and it occupies its base position in the core VP. In (2a) the NP *Great Expectations* precedes the subject, the NP *I*. However, *Great Expectations* is still the direct object of *read*. For instance, in (2a) we could not add a new object to the sentence:

(2) d **Great Expectations*, I've read *War and Peace* three times.

Sentences (2a) and (2b) are paraphrases: if (2a) is true, then inevitably (2b) is also true and vice versa. (2b) is the neutral pattern, in which the object occupies its canonical position and follows the verb; in (2a) the object has been fronted to achieve some presentational effect. Let us take this movement metaphor literally. Let us assume that in (2a) the object is first merged with the verb, but that it is subsequently moved to occupy a position to the left of the subject. What could the position to the left of the subject be? One option that comes to mind is that the NP *Great Expectations* is adjoined to the sentence. We use an arrow to indicate the movement.[8]

(2) e

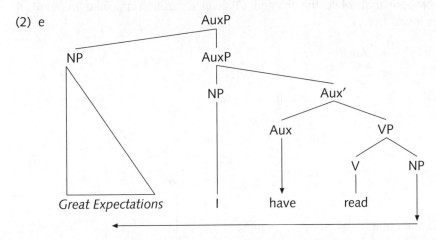

<hr />

8 In Chapter 4 we will introduce another notation to signal movement. We discuss the mechanisms of movement also in Chapter 5.

In (2e) we have first inserted *Great Expectations* as the object of the verb *read*. Then we move it to a position adjoined to AuxP.

Example (2a) is important because it shows that adjunction does not apply exclusively to optional constituents. The direct object *Great Expectations* in (2) is an obligatory complement of the verb. When it is taken out of the VP, it may be moved to an adjunction position. Observe, however, that the operation that creates the adjoined position could still be said to be "optional" in the sense that we are not obliged to move an object out of the VP. If we had left the object in its base position, we would not have had to resort to adjunction. Inserting the object in the VP is obligatory, moving it out and adjoining it is optional.

In section 1.4. in the chapter we came across examples such as (13) repeated here in (3). In each of the underlined segments the subject is preceded by a VP. How could we represent the structure of the underlined segments?

(3) a "They must talk about it, and [vp talk about it] they must", he said. Food for thought, there! It's a phrase that could add a measure of gravity to any press conference. "We must do this, and [vp do this] we must." (Simon Hoggart, *Guardian*, 29.1.2003, p. 2, col. 5)

   b But I was still a long way from figuring out what my goal was. I told the governor [of the prison] that I wasn't sure how I was going to manage it – but [vp manage it] I would. (*Guardian*, G2, 15.5.2003, p. 7, col. 4)

Assuming that the structure of the sentence is as in (70b), we would have to provide accommodation for a VP that precedes the subject. Among the tools available in our structure we have a possibility of adjunction. We might propose to adjoin the sentence-initial VP to the sentence as a whole, in the same way that we adjoined the temporal NP *this week* to AuxP in (1) and the object NP *Great Expectations* to AuxP in (2). According to (70b) the VP is the complement of the auxiliary. Again, we can propose that while the fronted VP is in a position adjoined to AuxP, it originates inside the VP.

(3) c

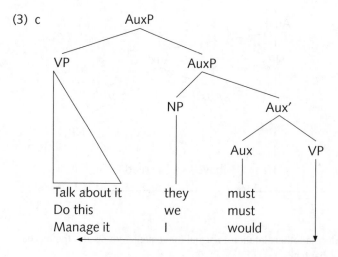

Exercise 16   Creating new words (T)

Comment on the internal make-up of the underlined words in the following extracts.

(1)   The Navy hopes the change will make a difference in its rigorous nine-week <u>sailorization</u> process. (*Chicago Tribune*, 30.11.2002, section 1, p. 18, col. 6)

(2)   The brigades have already taken part in exercises in preparation for Iraq, and the process of "<u>desertification</u>" – fitting special air filters, to painting the camouflage in desert colours and other changes – is under way. (*Guardian*, 7.1.2003. p. 1, cols 4–5)

(3)   Options are being investigated for the <u>desertisation</u> of the UK's CR2s (Challenger 2s). The army has bought 386 Challenger2 tanks – adapting all of them for desert conditions would cost more than £50m. (*Guardian*, 8.4.2002, p. 7, col. 8)

(4)   In a <u>lawyerly</u> way, she worked with her sister to lay down ground rules. (*New York Times*, 2.1.2003, p. F8, col. 1)

(5)   He gives me his best <u>schoolteacherly</u> look. (*Guardian*, G2, 20.1.2003, p. 7, cols 3–7)

Exercise 17   The internal structure of deverbal
nouns (E)

This exercise explores the internal structure of nouns.[9] Consider the underlined nouns in the examples below. Several of them can be related in form to a verb. Identify these nouns and for each noun give the related verb. Nouns with a clear morphological relation to a verb are called **deverbal** nouns.

(1)   Kim's <u>explanation</u> of the events did not satisfy me.

(2)   Kim's <u>accident</u> changed everything.

(3)   His <u>transformation</u> into a werewolf was unnerving.

(4)   Kim's <u>version</u> of the events was not satisfactory.

(5)   The <u>occurrence</u> of the accident changed everything.

(6)   Sue's <u>exploration</u> of Easter Island was uneventful.

[9]   This exercise is based on Fu, Roeper, and Borer (2001).

Table 1 Deverbal nouns and the related verbs

	Noun	Verb
(1)	*explanation*	*explain*
(3)	*transformation*	*transform*
(5)	*occurrence*	*occur*
(6)	*exploration*	*explore*

KEY AND COMMENTS

The nouns in Table 1 are deverbal. There is a debate among syntacticians whether the internal structure of deverbal nouns should contain a verb, i.e. whether representation (7a) or (7b) is preferable:

(7) a

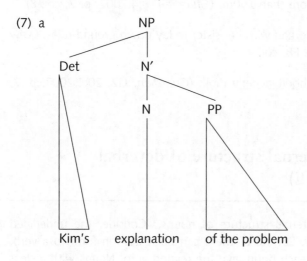

b

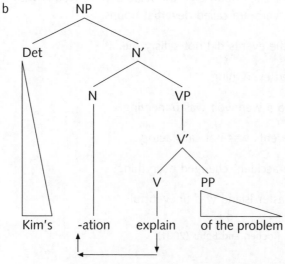

(7a) does not contain any indications that the noun *explanation* is related to a verb. According to (7b), the noun *explanation* is formed on the basis of the verb *explain*. According to this representation, the verb *explain* unites with the bound morpheme *-ation*, which is dominated by N, to form the deverbal N *explanation.* To what extent would the data in (8) be relevant for the choice between the two representations?

(8) a Kim's explanation of the problem to the tenants <u>thoroughly</u> did not prevent a riot.
 b The occurrence of the accident <u>suddenly</u> disqualified her.
 c His transformation into a werewolf <u>so rapidly</u> was unnerving.

Nouns for which there is no related verb stem (*version, accident*) would be taken to have a representation not containing a verb stem (7a). To what extent would the following data support this analysis?

(9) a *Kim's version of the accident thoroughly was not a big help.
 b *Kim's accident suddenly on the track disqualified her.

KEY AND COMMENTS

In (8), the deverbal nouns co-occur with an adverbial modifier (*thoroughly, suddenly, so rapidly*), which we normally expect to be adjoined to a VP. Structure (7b), with an NP dominating a VP, would allow the adverbial to be an adjunct to the VP. No such modifier is available for the nouns that are not related to a V-root (9), so representation (7b) would not be appropriate for these and we would opt for (7a).

 Example (10) is provided by Fu, Roeper, and Borer (2001). Discuss whether this example would be compatible with the hypothesis that deverbal nouns have the internal structure in (7b).

(10) Sue's <u>exploration</u> of Easter Island was impressive, but Amy's <u>doing so</u> was a real surprise.

In (10) *doing so* relates to *exploration of Easter Island*. If we assume that *do so* substitutes for a VP (see section 1.3), then the relevant VP could be based on the verbal root (*explore*) of the N *exploration* in (10). Representation (7b) will allow us to account for *do so* substitution. The substitutions with *do so* in (11) again relate to deverbal nouns.[10] Identify these deverbal nouns. What are the related verbs?

(11) a The defection of the seven moderates, who knew they were incurring the wrath of many colleagues in <u>doing so</u>, signaled that it may be harder to sell the GOP message on the crime bill than it was thought previously. (*Washington Post*)

---

[10] (11a, b, c) are also from Fu et al. (2001).

b   Even though an Israeli response is justified, I don't think it was in their best interest to <u>do so</u> right now.

c   His removal of the garbage in the morning and Sam's <u>doing so</u> in the afternoon were surprising.

d   Canon Michael Hunter, rector of St James parish church in Grimsby, said it was a sad day for natural justice and added that her return to the town would have caused problems but she should have been allowed to <u>do so</u>. (*Guardian*, 13.2.2004, pp. 1 and 2, cols 4, 5)

Observe that the empirical data are complex. Not all native speakers accept examples like (10) and those in (11). But speakers do agree on the compatibility of adverbials with deverbal nouns in (8) and the contrast with (9).

Exercise 18   Comparative linguistics: Deriving OV orders (T, E)

In this exercise we speculate about cross-linguistic word order variation. The exercise is longer and more discursive than some of the other exercises. The idea is that we carry further the type of argumentation elaborated in the chapter and see where that leads us.

In section 2.3.3 of the chapter we saw that in English the canonical position of the object is to the immediate right of V. Though the object can move away from that position (as shown by Exercises 4 and 15), it cannot occupy a position to the immediate left of V.

Consider the Old English examples in (1). What conclusions could we draw concerning the position of the direct object?

(1) a   Hwi sceole we <u>oþres mannes </u>niman?
        why should we another man's take
        'Why should we take something belonging to someone else?'
        (Ælfric, *Lives of Saints*, 24, 188) (from Fischer et al. 2000: 49)

    b   Hwi wolde God <u>swa lytles þinges him forwyrnan?</u>
        why would God so small thing him deny
        'Why would God deny him such a small thing?'
        (ÆCHom I, 1.14.2) (from Fischer et al. 2000: 49)

In these examples the complement precedes the verb. This is the unmarked order for Old English. Old English is referred to as an **OV** language, this in contrast to languages such as Modern English which are **VO** languages.

Recall from Chapter 1, section 3.2, that with respect to question formation, Old English seemed to behave like Modern Dutch and German. Consider the Dutch sentences below, paying attention to the position of the underlined object and the verb. Is Dutch an OV language or is it a VO language?

(2) a Ik denk dat Jan [NP dat boek] kent.
I think that John that book knows
'I think that John knows that book.'

   b *Ik denk dat Jan kent [NP dat boek].

(3) a Marie wil vanavond [NP een boek] lezen.
Mary wants tonight a book read
'Mary wants to read a book tonight.'

   b *Marie wil vanavond lezen [NP een boek].

Would the structure of the VP as elaborated in the discussion in the chapter allow us to represent the structure of the Old English sentences in (1) and of the Dutch examples in (2) and (3)? How could we enrich our theory in order to allow for these data?

   There are at least two ways of ensuring that we can also derive OV orders. One option to derive the Dutch sentences in (2a) and (3a) is to assume that in Dutch the base position of the complement position is to the left of V.

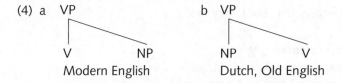

(4) a VP   b VP

We would then have to propose that languages differ with respect to their assembly techniques. While a verb will select an object to its right in English, it would have to select an object to its left in Old English and in Dutch.

   A second possibility would be to assume that the complement position of the verb in Old English and in Dutch is the same as that in Modern English, but that in Old English and in Dutch the direct object cannot remain in its base position in the VP and that it must move to a position inside the sentence but to the left of the verb. We could refer to the sentence-internal leftward shifting of the object as **object shift** (Holmberg 1986).

(5) a VP   b   VP

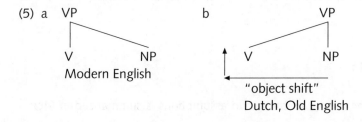

To complete representation (5b), we would have to specify which position the object NP moves to. Following on the discussion in Exercise 15 we might think, for instance, of adjoining the object to the VP.

(5) c

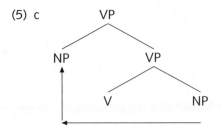

Whichever analysis we choose, we would have to explain why Modern English differs from Old English and Dutch. This means that either we explain why there is variation in the base position of the object (4) or we explain why Old English and Dutch require a displacement of the object (5) and why this displacement is not even available in Modern English.

Consider the Dutch examples in (6). Do they bear on the choice between (4) and (5)?

(6) a   Ik denk dat Marie [$_{NP}$ <u>dat boek</u>] erg goed kent.
        I think that Mary that book very well knows
        'I think that Mary knows that book very well.'

    b   Jan wil [$_{NP}$ <u>die tekst</u>] helemaal begrijpen.
        John wants that text completely understand
        'John wants to understand that text completely.'

According to the hypothesis in (4), the base position of the object in Dutch is left adjacent to the verb, that in English is right adjacent to the verb. In the Dutch examples in (6), the direct object NPs *dat boek* ('that book') and *die tekst* ('that text') precede the verb. However, these objects are separated from the verb by the adjuncts *erg goed* ('very well') and *helemaal* ('completely'). This means that even if we were to adopt (4b) to account for the OV order in Dutch, we would have to further supplement hypothesis (4) with an operation that moves the object to the left across the VP-adjoined constituent. In other words, even if we adopt (4) we need something like object shift. So to represent the sentences in (6) we would need:

(i)   Hypothesis (4b)
(ii) + Object shift (5b)

The combination of the output of these two assumptions is summarized in (4c):

(4) c

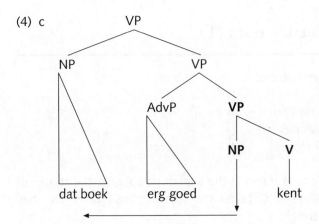

Hypothesis (5) expresses the cross-linguistic variation between VO languages and OV languages by means of the operation of object shift, which allows us to move the object leftward. According to (5) we do not also assume that the internal order of verb and complements varies. By simply using object shift we can derive the Dutch word order (6a) as in (5c):

(5) c

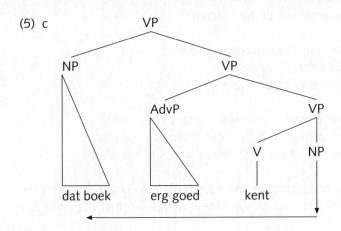

Both hypothesis (4) and hypothesis (5) allow us to derive the sentences in which the verb follows the object in (2), (3), and (6). Both hypotheses need object shift to derive the examples in (6), in which the object is non-adjacent to V. But hypothesis (4) also postulates there is variation in the base position of object and verb. Which hypothesis is theoretically preferred?[11]

---

[11] For the relevance of economy in theory building see also Chapter 1, section 1.2.3. Exercise 16 in Chapter 3 offers another illustration of the application of object shift. For an accessible discussion of the structure of Germanic SOV languages see Zwart (1997).

Exercise 19   Constituency tests (T)

The following sentence is from Hebrew:[12]

(1) a   Kol ha-yeladim zarku ?avanim.
        all the children threw stones
        'All the children threw stones.'

We may propose that like *all the children* in the English paraphrase, the string *kol ha-yeladim* in (1a) is a constituent. Consider the sentences in (1b–e). Do they provide evidence for constituency?

(1) b   Ze hayu kol ha-yeladim še-zarku ?avanim.
        it was all the children that-threw stones
        'It was all the children who threw stones.'

    c   Mi- še zorek ?avanim ze kol ha-yeladim.
        who-that throws stones it all the children
        'Those that throw stones are all the children.'

    d   Kol ha-yeladim, ?ani batu?ax še-zorkim ?avanim.
        all the-children, I sure that throw stones
        'All the children, I am sure throw stones.'

    e   ?etmol zarku štei banot ve-kol ha-banim ?avanim ?al ha-mora.
        yesterday threw two girls and all the boys stones on the teacher
        'Yesterday two girls and all the boys threw stones at the teacher.'

Now consider (2). In the first sentence the subject is *ha-yeladim kul-am* ('the children all'). On the basis of the examples in (2b–e) decide whether this string is a constituent:

(2) a   Ha-yeladim kul-am zarku ?avanim.
        the children all-3MPL threw stones
        'The children all threw stones.'

    b   Ze hayu ha-yeladim kul-am še-zarku ?avanim.
        it was the children all-3MPL that-threw stones
        'It was all the children who threw stones.'

---

12   The data in this exercise are based on Shlonsky (1991: 163–4). Thanks to Ur Shlonsky for help with (1a) and (2a). Exercises 12 and 21 in Chapter 4 pick up the variation between (1a) and (2a).

c Mi- še zorek ?avanim ze ha-yeladim kul-am.
   who-that throws stones it the children all-3MPL
   'Those that throw stones are all the children.'

d Ha-yeladim kul-am, ?ani batu?ax še-zorkim ?avanim.
   the children all-3MPL, I sure that throw stones
   'All the children, I am sure throw stones.'

e ?etmol zarku štei banot ve- ha-banim kul-am ?avanim ?al ha-mora.
   yesterday threw two girls and the boys all-3MPL stones on the teacher
   'Yesterday two girls and all the boys threw stones at the teacher.'

We conclude that both the sequence *kol ha-yeladim* ('all the children') and the sequence *ha-yeladim kul-am* ('the children all') are constituents in Hebrew. Discuss the relevance of (3) for this conclusion.

(3) ?Ra?iti ?et kol ha-banot ve-?et ha-banim kul-am.
     saw-1SG ACC all the-girls and-ACC the-boys all-3MPL
     'I saw all the girls and all the boys.'

Exercise 20   The specifier of NP (E)

In the discussion we assumed that each NP has one specifier and that articles, demonstratives, possessive pronouns, and prenominal genitives occupy the specifier of NP. This leads to the correct prediction for English that articles, demonstratives, possessive pronouns, and prenominal genitives are in complementary distribution:

(1) a *the this book
    b *the his book
    c *the Jane's book

Discuss the problems raised for this proposal by the following data:[13]

(2) a afto to vivlio
       this the book
       'this book' (Modern Greek: Horrocks & Stavrou 1987: 86)

---

[13] For introductory discussion see Haegeman and Guéron (1999, chapter 4). For general discussion of the structure of the noun phrase see also Bernstein (2001). For discussion based on Greek see Horrocks and Stavrou (1987: 86); on Hungarian see Szabolcsi (1983, 1994). For a discussion of possessives see also Giorgi and Longobardi (1991), Longobardi (1996), Alexiadou (2004a).

(3) a la   mia   amica
       the (FSG) my (FSG) friend (FSG)
       'my girlfriend' (Italian)

    b la   meva   casa
       the (FSG) my-(FSG) home (FSG)
       'my house'
       (Catalan, example from Longobardi 1996: 29, his (72a))

(4) a tu Chomsky   to vivlio
       of-the Chomsky the book
       'Chomsky's book' (Modern Greek, Horrocks & Stavrou 1987: 86)

    b tu vivliu   i kritiki
       of the book the criticism
       'the criticism of the book' (Modern Greek, Horrocks & Stavrou 1987: 86)

    c a   Mari   kalap-ja
       the Mary-NOMINATIVE hat-3SG
       'Mary's hat' (Hungarian, Szabolcsi 1994: 186)

    d Mari-nak   a   kalap-ja
       Mary-DATIVE the hat-3SG
       'Mary's hat' (Hungarian, Szabolcsi 1983)

(5) a The papers report on every move of the actress.
    b *The papers report on the every move of the actress.
    c The papers report on the actress's every move.
    d The papers report on her every move.

3 Lexical Projections and Functional Projections

Discussion

Contents

0 Introduction: Scope of the Chapter

In Chapter 2 we first established a set of diagnostic tools for identifying constituents in the sentence. Using these tools we then elaborated a representation of the structure of sentences with auxiliaries. The analysis led to the proposal that in sentences with auxiliaries the auxiliary is a pivotal element that creates the link between subject and VP.

In this chapter we complete the representation of the structure of the sentence. In particular we address the question whether sentences without auxiliaries can be argued to be formed along the lines developed in the preceding chapter. One point that will emerge is that in sentences without auxiliaries the inflectional ending of the verb is the pivotal element to relate subject and verb phrase. Based on this observation we will propose an analysis that covers both sentences with auxiliaries and those without. The structure we elaborate is one in which VP, the projection of the verb, is dominated by IP, a projection of the inflection. While the verb is a lexical head, the inflection is a functional head. VP is a lexical projection, IP is a functional projection.

We will see that the format for sentence structure elaborated for English can be extended to other languages, and we will provide an account for the difference between the position of the verb in French and in English.

Having identified the components of the sentence, our next step will be to take the sentence apart and examine how the components are put together. That is, we will examine how we form or "generate" sentences by putting together smaller units of structure. We will see that when putting together words to form a sentence, we make use of two basic operations: the operation Merge, which combines two units, and the operation Move, which selects a constituent in an existing structure and moves it to another position. When building the sentence we start with a verb and we progressively add constituents to build a more elaborate structure. Because of its central role in the make-up of the sentence, we will briefly consider the semantic relation of the verb to the remainder of the sentence. For instance, when a verb denotes an action, this will imply that there will be one or more participants to the action. We will look at how such participants are realized in the sentence. After having discussed the structure of sentences with no auxiliary as well as those with one auxiliary, we will finally examine sentences that contain more than one auxiliary.

The chapter is organized as follows: section 1 elaborates a proposal for the representation of sentences without auxiliaries. Section 2 is an inventory of the components of the system elaborated so far. Section 3 concerns the semantic relation between the verb and some of the components of the sentence. Section 4 deals with sentences with multiple auxiliaries. Section 5 is a summary.

1   The Structure of the Sentence

1.1   *The head of the sentence*

Diagram (1a) reproduces the general format for syntactic structure that we elaborated by looking at the noun phrase. In diagram (70b) of Chapter 2, repeated here as (1b) we molded our previous findings for the structure of the sentence according to the format in (1a).[1] We tentatively proposed that the head of the sentence is the finite auxiliary. Aux selects a VP as its complement and it takes the subject as its specifier.

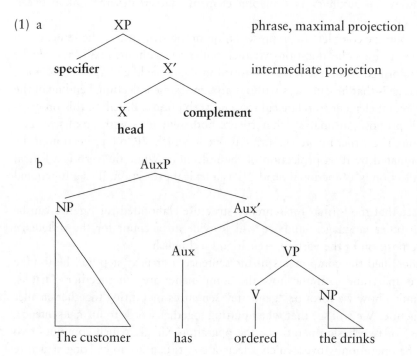

(1) a   XP   phrase, maximal projection

specifier   X′   intermediate projection

X   complement
head

b   AuxP

NP   Aux′

Aux   VP

V   NP

The customer   has   ordered   the drinks

According to representation (1b), a sentence is a projection of an auxiliary. The auxiliary is the pivotal element of the sentence: it first combines with its complement, a VP, which denotes some action/situation. The combination of an auxiliary and a VP is not yet a sentence. Following the schema in (1a) we label it Aux′. This newly formed constituent [auxiliary + VP] combines with the subject. The auxiliary is represented as a linking device that brings together a situation (an activity, a state of affairs) and the entity to which the situation applies. In addition, the auxiliary qualifies the validation of the link in terms of time and modality, that is, it indicates whether the link is valid in the present, in the past, in the future, or whether the link is probable, possible, etc.

---

[1]   See section 3.1.2.3 of Chapter 2.

If we define the auxiliary as a linker between the VP and the subject we can also account for the observation that sentences must have subjects. A sentence lacking a subject would be "unbalanced" in that the auxiliary could no longer function as a linker between its VP complement and another constituent. Metaphorically speaking, we could say that the absence of a subject creates an "imbalance," which would cause the sentence to "topple over" and crash. Another way of looking at this idea is to say that the subject serves to anchor the content of the sentence. Very often the information provided by the subject determines what the sentence is about. If a sentence lacked a subject, the information in the sentence would be unanchored and drift along without being able to be linked to other informational units.

However, in our account one immediate problem remains. If sentences with auxiliaries are projections of Aux, then how do we deal with sentences lacking an auxiliary? Are these fundamentally different? We turn to this issue now.

1.2 *Sentences without auxiliaries*

1.2.1 THE LINK BETWEEN SUBJECT AND VP

Let us compare a variant of the test sentence used in the previous chapter, (2a), with a variant without an auxiliary, (2b). Bracket (2a) in order to show its structure, using the hypothesis that sentences are projections of Aux. The result is (2c).

(2) a The customer in the corner will order the drinks.
    b The customer in the corner ordered the drinks.

One might assume that the structure of (2b) is as in (2d): a sentence (S) combines an NP and a VP.

(2) c [$_{AUXP}$ [$_{NP}$ The customer in the corner] [$_{AUX'}$ [$_{AUX}$ will] [$_{VP}$ order the drinks]]].
    d [$_{S??}$ [$_{NP}$ The customer in the corner] [$_{VP}$ ordered the drinks]].

If, as postulated in this book, the structure of the sentence determines its interpretation, (2d) suggests that sentences without auxiliaries are different in interpretation from those with auxiliaries. For sentences with auxiliaries, such as (2a), representation (2c) shows that the contribution of the auxiliary is to link the VP and the subject. The auxiliary also qualifies the validation of that link. For instance the auxiliary may specify that the link is validated in the future (*will*), or that is situated in the past (*has*), etc. According to (2d), when there is no auxiliary, a sentence would simply be a juxtaposition of an NP and a VP. Crucially, there is no linker to encode the relation between the two elements. This means in turn that the relation between subject and VP cannot be modified with respect to factors such as time or modality. Compare (2a) and (2b). Do you see a way in which the relation between the subject and the VP can be said to be modified in (2b)? At first sight, (2b) is not unlike a sentence such as (2e), in which the auxiliary *have* serves to locate the event in the past:

(2) e   [_{AUXP} [_{NP} The customer in the corner] [_{AUX'} [_{AUX} has] [_{VP} ordered the drinks]]].

The perfect auxiliary *have* and the past tense in English have a similar (though not identical) role to play: both place the event expressed in the sentence in the past time sphere. But this is not what representation (2d) shows: in this representation the expression of past time, the past tense ending *-ed*, is fully integrated as a part of the VP. To represent the linking role of the past tense, we could adopt a representation such as (2f) with a past time linker.

(2) f   [_S [_{NP} The customer in the corner] [PAST] [_{VP} order the drinks]].

Observe also that what is expressed by an auxiliary in one language may be rendered by an inflection in another and vice versa. For instance, French uses an inflectional ending to create a future tense (3a), while English uses the auxiliary *will* to express future time:

(3) a   Pierre achètera le journal demain.
         Pierre buy-FUT-3SG the newspaper tomorrow
         'Pierre will buy the paper tomorrow.'

     b   Peter will buy the paper tomorrow.

Similarly, the present perfect is expressed by means of an auxiliary in English but by an affix in Latin (3c). In both cases, English is the language using auxiliaries where another language uses inflection.

(3) c   ama-vi
         love-PF-1SG
         'I have loved'

Recall that our representations reflect how meaning is conveyed through structure. We would perhaps be missing something if we were to treat the inflectional endings of the verb as quite distinct from auxiliaries, since they convey similar interpretations.

1.2.2   THE SUBJECT REQUIREMENT

We suggested relating the fact that every sentence has a subject to the hypothesis that the auxiliary is the head of the sentence combined with the assumption that the auxiliary functions as a link between a VP and a subject. Sentences without auxiliaries and with tensed verbs also have to have subjects. However, if such sentences are not constructed around a linker, then, as things stand, we do not have any means to predict that these sentences too have to have subjects. We could of course devise a second explanation to account for the fact that sentences without auxiliaries have to have a subject. This would mean that we end up with two different explanations for the same pattern, namely that all finite sentences need subjects. It would not seem to be in the spirit of the scientific enterprise to come up with two explanations for what seems to be one pattern. One comprehensive explanation that covers both sentences with auxiliaries and those without would be preferable for reasons of theoretical economy.[2]

1.2.3   THE RELATION BETWEEN VP AND INFLECTION

1.2.3.1   *INFL as the head of the sentence*
In this discussion we are concerned with **finite** sentences; that is, sentences containing a lexical verb or an auxiliary in the present or past tense.[3] Let us examine representation (2d) in more detail, focusing on the content of the VP constituent. A tree representation for (2d) is (2g). This representation suggests that in sentences without an auxiliary and with a tensed verb we simply merge an NP with a tensed VP. What predictions do we make with respect to operations such as movement, or ellipsis, of the VP? Specifically, how do we expect such operations to affect the inflection *-ed* on the verb?

(2) g

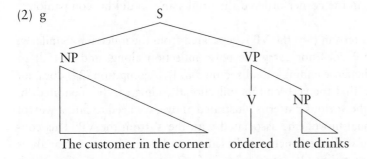

In (2d/g) the *-ed* ending of the verb is solidly fused with the V, hence it is part of the VP. We predict that whatever operation affects the VP should therefore also affect the ending on the verb, as this is fully integrated in the V and the VP. Let us see if this prediction is borne out.[4] Consider the underlined sentences in (4) paying particular attention to the location of the tense inflection in relation to the verb that it modifies.

(4) a   "But I couldn't rewind time, I just had to get over it." <u>And get over it she did</u>. (*Guardian*, 6.9.2001, p. 15, col. 8)

---

[2]   See also the discussion in Chapter 1, section 1.2.3.
[3]   Finiteness was discussed briefly in Chapter 1, section 2.2.2.
[4]   Exercise 1 is a revision of constituency tests.

  b We were told journalism is a science. It didn't make sense then <u>nor does it
     now</u>. (Adapted from the *Washington Post*, 29.4.2003, p. A22, col. 4).
  c Many astronauts have a ham radio license; <u>so does she</u>. (*Washington Post*,
     29.4.2003, p. A10, col. 3)

In (4a) the VP *get over it* is moved to an initial position.[5] Observe that the VP is not
fronted with an inflectional ending; we do not front the string *got over it*, but rather
we front the string *get over it*. Where is the tense marker whose interpretation
would have to be associated with *get (over it)*? The tense ending is seen to be detached
from the verb *get* itself and it is realized on *did*, an auxiliary that remains unaffected
by the movement. In (4b) the VP has been omitted. But the third person inflection
survives on the auxiliary *do*. In (4c) *so* replaces the VP, the third person inflection is
realized on *do*.

   The possible separation of the verb and its inflection can also be demonstrated on
the basis of (5a), the variant of our test sentence without an auxiliary.

(5) a The customer in the corner ordered the drinks.
     b What the customer in the corner did was [VP order the drinks].
     c Everyone expected that Bill would order the drinks. And [VP order the drinks],
        he did.
     d The customer in the corner ordered the drinks and so did his companion.

In the pseudo-cleft pattern in (5b) the VP is separated from the inflection. Similarly,
in (5c) the fronted VP does not carry the tense inflection along, and in (5d) *so*
replaces the VP but the tense ending is realized on *did*. Representation (2g) does not
lead to the prediction that the verb and its inflectional ending can be separated. In
order to account for the various patterns illustrated above, we need to find a way of
isolating the inflectional morpheme associated with the V from the VP. This conclusion is fully in line with the conclusion based on an informal semantic analysis
of the sentence represented in (2f), repeated here for convenience as (5e), in which
the past tense was isolated as a constituent separate from the VP.

(5) e [S [NP The customer in the corner] [PAST] [VP order the drinks]].

In a present tense sentence we can similarly set apart the third person singular
inflection:

(6) a The customer in the corner orders the drinks before the meal.
     b What the customer in the corner does is [VP order the drinks before the
        meal].

---

[5] If you would like to know which position the moved VP occupies, turn to Exercise 14 of
     Chapter 2 and to Exercise 3 of this chapter.

c   Everyone always expects that Bill will order the drinks before the meal. And [vp order the drinks before the meal], he invariably does.
d   The customer in the corner orders the drinks before the meal and so does his companion.
e   [s [NP The customer in the corner] [PRESENT] [vp [vp order the drinks] before the meal]].

(7a) offers a representation covering both (5e) and (6e): INFL stands for the inflection of the verb.

(7) a   [s [NP The customer in the corner] [INFL] [vp [vp order the drinks] before the meal]].⁶

For sentences with an auxiliary, we have proposed representation (7b):

(7) b   [AUXP [NP The customer in the corner] [AUX' [AUX will] [vp [vp order the drinks] before the meal]]].

The two representations suggest that there is still a considerable difference between the two sentence types, that with and that without an auxiliary, which seems unwarranted by the observations above. Crucially, in representation (7a) the sentence splits into three immediate constituents, the subject NP, INFL, and the VP. (7a) has not been adapted to the binary branching format. Let us try to reduce the two representations to just one. Observe that in finite sentences with auxiliaries, the auxiliary is itself inflected for tense. In other words, the auxiliary carries finite inflection. The following examples illustrate this point:

(8) a   The customer in the corner <u>is</u> ordering the drinks now.
b   The customer in the corner <u>was</u> ordering the drinks later.
c   The customer in the corner <u>has</u> ordered the drinks already.
d   The customer in the corner <u>had</u> ordered the drinks already.

All finite sentences contain some form of inflection, but not all finite sentences contain an auxiliary. Pursuing this path and taking into account that in the head position labeled Aux we insert an inflected auxiliary, we can combine (7a) and (7b). Rather than labeling the head position of the sentence Aux, we could label it INFL (or I). The head position INFL will host either the inflected auxiliary or just the inflectional ending of the verb. Based on this hypothesis, the structure for the sentence is then relabeled as in (7c):

---

⁶   An alternative would be to use tense as a cover label.

(i)   [NP The customer in the corner] [TENSE] [vp order the drinks before the meal].

(7) c

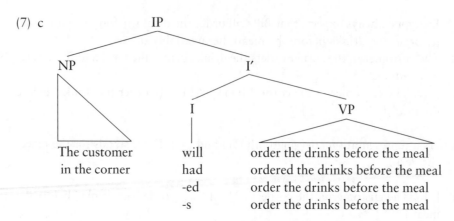

The head of the structure is I. I combines with VP to form I′; the intermediate projection. I′ combines with the subject to form IP.[7] The label IP stands for Inflection Projection or, in other words, a phrase headed by the inflection. We have managed to isolate both the auxiliary and the tense inflection from the verb and give them the same pivotal linking role. The resulting representation shows that:[8]

(i)   Sentences are centered around I.
(ii) I is a linker: it links a VP and a subject, both components are obligatory.
(iii) The content of I qualifies the linking, locating it in time and/or assigning some modal value to the relation.

1.2.3.2   Inserting *do* in I

As it stands, the structure in (7c) above does not yet allow us to form a sentence without an auxiliary. An inflectional ending of a verb cannot stand all by itself because it is a bound morpheme; it is an affix that must be hosted by a free morpheme. The past tense inflectional ending, *-ed*, must be attached to a verb. One way of saving an unattached *-ed* ending is by associating it with its own auxiliary. This is what happens when the auxiliary *do* is inserted. If we insert *do* under a head I with a past tense ending we derive (9):

(9) a   [IP [NP The customer in the corner] [I′ [I do + ed] [VP order the drinks before the meal]]].
    b   [IP [NP The customer in the corner] [I′ [I did] [VP order the drinks before the meal]]].

---

[7]   In the alternative representation (note 6) in which we represent the core constituent of the sentences as Tense, a sentence is a projection of T: TP.

(i)   [TP [NP The customer in the corner] [T′ [TENSE] [VP [VP order the drinks] before the meal]]].

[8]   Exercise 2.

In (9) *do* is not essential.[9] We can dispense with it if we attach the tense ending to V:

(9) c The customer in the corner <u>ordered</u> the drinks before the meal.

In (10a) *do* cannot be eliminated, as shown by (10b):

(10) a And [_{VP} get over it] she did. (cf. (4a))
      b *And [_{VP} got over it] she.

In (10a) *did* combines the past tense inflection with *do*. This sentence illustrates a leftward movement of the VP, *get over it*. As a result of this movement, the VP no longer occupies its canonical position to the right of the auxiliary. Apparently, when we move the VP, insertion of *do* becomes essential in the sentence. There is no way that we can realize the tense on the verb itself (10b). If we restore the VP to its original position, though, we can dispense with *do*:

(10) c And she did [_{VP} get over it].
      d And she got over it.

In our constructed example (9), *do* is also not essential. If language is guided by a principle of economy though,[10] the insertion of *do* should have some effect. If *do* were completely superfluous, by the principle of economy we should not insert it. To assess the possible impact of inserting *do* in a context where it could be omitted, let us look at some attested examples in which *do* could also have been absent.[11]

(11) a I don't remember much of anything she said in the church foyer or what I uttered back. She had that dazzling effect on me . . . What I <u>do</u> recall is that she invited me to a holiday party two nights later at the mutual friend's place. (*Chicago Tribune*, 22.12.2003, section 13, p. 9, col. 1)
      b Coleman, who describes himself as a "semi-professional punter", gave evidence at a trial in Southampton in October 2001 and his statements to the court then will form the basis of the case against him. It is still not clear if he will turn up for the 10 a.m. hearing at the club's headquarters in London, but the feeling at Portman Square yesterday was that he would indeed appear to defend himself. . . . If Coleman <u>does</u> appear this morning, the Jockey Club may also wish to inquire about another part of the evidence. (*Guardian*, 22.1.2003, p. 14, cols 1 + 2)
      c On Tuesday Clarett disputed the contention of university officials that he had failed to file the proper paperwork that would have allowed him to attend the funeral . . . Each side is right, Clarett <u>did</u> fill out the papers but

---

[9] See Chapter 1, section 2.2.3 for this use of *do*.
[10] As discussed in Chapter 1, section 2.2.3.
[11] For more examples of this use of *do* see Chapter 1, Exercise 7.

filled them out too late to receive tickets to fly home. (*New York Times*, 2.1.2003, p. D1, col. 1)

d   Jackson is hardly a virgin forest. Like most of the state's redwood land, it has been logged intermittently since about the middle of the 19th century ... But the forest <u>does</u> have thousands of acres of 80- to 100-year old redwoods. (*San Francisco Chronicle*, 28.11.2002, p. A34, col. 1)

If we eliminate the underlined occurrences of *do* in (11) we have to associate the inflectional ending of *do* with the verb itself. In (12) we reproduce the crucial parts of the contexts in which the sentences with *do* are used. Can you identify a common contextual factor for all these examples?

(12) a   I <u>don't remember</u> much of anything she said.
      b   It <u>is still not clear if he will turn</u> up for the 10 a.m. hearing at the club's headquarters in London.
      c   the contention of university officials <u>that he had failed to file the proper paperwork</u>
      d   <u>Jackson is hardly a virgin forest</u>.

By inserting *do*, the writer/speaker forcefully asserts the validity of the linking of the subject and the related event in a context in which this linking is not obvious. The contextual elements in (12) provide indications that the linking of the subject and the VP, which is emphasized by the insertion of *do*, is not self-evident and that it merits being highlighted. Inserting *do* highlights that link. This interpretation of the role of inserting *do* is in line with our proposal that the inflectional position of the sentence (I) encodes the linking between the subject and the VP. By inserting *do* in that position, we highlight the validation of that link.

1.2.3.3   *Associating V and I*
In (13a) identify the subject NP, the VP, the verb, and any VP-adjunct(s). Rephrase the sentence (i) by replacing the past tense form of the verb first by a combination of the auxiliary *have* + past participle, then (ii) by reorienting the sentence toward the future, using the auxiliary *will* with the infinitive.

(13) a   The department later modified the advice.

In the variants of (13a) that you will have created, the adjunct *later* remains to the left of the lexical verb, and the auxiliary is adjacent to the subject.

(13) b   The department has later modified the advice.
      c   The department will later modify the advice.

Adopting the format displayed above, the tree diagram for (13) will be as in (14), with alternative fillers for I.

(14)

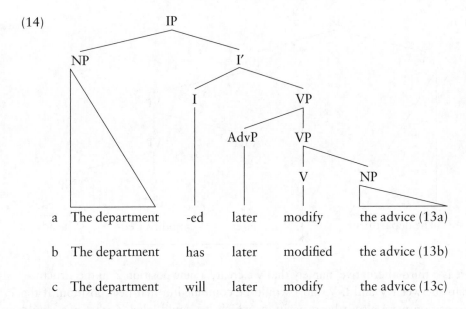

a	The department	-ed	later	modify	the advice (13a)
b	The department	has	later	modified	the advice (13b)
c	The department	will	later	modify	the advice (13c)

In example (13a) the tense ending *-ed* is located on the verb *modify*. So in representation (14a) we need to combine tense and verb. Let us examine how this is achieved. V and I are head positions. They contain heads, i.e. elements that form the nucleus of a projection. In (14a), the content of the head I is the inflectional ending *-ed*; the content of V is the lexical verb *modify*. These two heads need to be combined because *-ed* is a bound morpheme that has to attach to a verb. Presumably, looking at the tree, there are three options. One is that the verb *modify* is moved from its position V to the position I, where it combines with *-ed* (15a).

(15) a

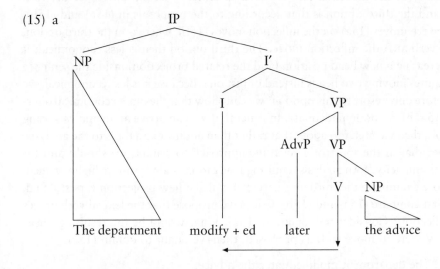

A second one is that the ending *-ed* is moved onto the verb (15b).

(15) b

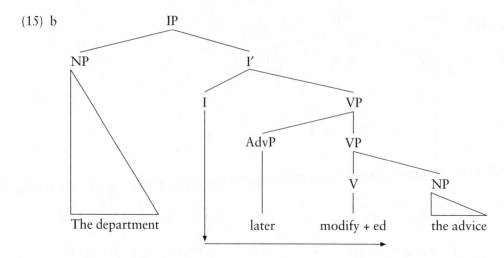

There is a third alternative, namely that we create a new position Z in the structure, perhaps between V and I. V and I would be combined in that new position. If the new position were also a head position, which we could label Z, then we would actually have to deduce that there is a complete new projection ZP in the structure. Should we actually pursue this third proposal?

We have postulated the head positions I and V. In the two options laid out above (15a, b), we need only those two positions plus a mechanism that moves one of the constituents from its own position to the position of the other. In the third option outlined above, we also have to move the inflection and the verb. Therefore, we still need this additional mechanism for moving a constituent from one position to another. But in addition to that, we also need to create a totally new position inside the structure for the inflection and the verb to unite. A second difference between (15a, b) and the third option is that according to the proposals in (15a) and (15b), either the verb moves (15a) OR the inflection moves (15b), whereas in the third option, both the verb AND the inflection move. The third option then is less economical: it requires creating a new head position (and the related projection) inside the sentence and it requires moving two heads instead of just one. Because it is less economical, we will therefore only resort to this option if we can show that the more economical alternatives (15a, b) are both inadequate. In general, if we can arrive at an analysis using fewer tools, then we prefer to adopt that rather than adding extra tools to the analysis. Remember that in the spirit of a scientific approach to syntax, we should aim for theoretical simplicity.[12] An analysis requiring fewer tools is always more highly valued.

So before examining the third alternative in which a new projection is postulated, we will first compare (15a) and (15b). Could we propose that the lexical verb moves to the inflection? Consider tree diagram (15a). What would be the resulting linear order? If V were to move to I, as proposed, then we ought to obtain (15c):

(15) c   *The department modified later the advice.

---

[12]   See Chapter 1, section 1.2.3.

But (15c) is not acceptable. The verb must follow the adjunct *later*, which we assume is adjoined to VP.

Could the inflection move onto the verb? What would be the resulting word order? If I moves to V, then we obtain (15d):

(15) d   The department later modified the advice.

(15d) is acceptable. The verb follows the adjunct *later*, which we assume is adjoined to VP.

Let us look at the geometry of the tree and in particular, let us look at the relative positions of the heads V and I in the tree diagram representation. From a geometrical point of view, which is higher, V or I?

(15) e

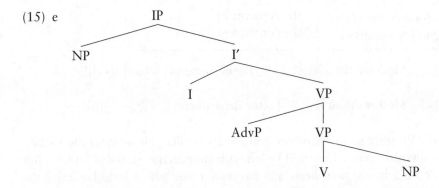

I combines with VP. I and the projection VP are on equal footing, both are immediate constituents of I′.[13] V is buried inside VP. V is an immediate constituent of the core VP, so V hierarchically is ranked lower than the augmented VP. This means that the head V is lower than the head I. When I joins V it "goes down" into VP. We say that in English I **lowers** onto V. Conversely, I is higher than V. If the verb were to move to I, then it would have to leave VP and go up in the tree. In that case, we would say that it **raises** to I.[14] As shown above, in English I lowers onto the verb and the verb cannot raise to I.

1.2.3.4   *When the inflection cannot lower onto V*

Suppose that we pick the VP in representation (15e) and move it to a position to the left of the subject. Leftward movement of the VP should not affect the content of the head I, which is inserted independently of the content of the VP. In (16a, b), the VP is moved to the left of the subject. The subject is the specifier of IP, the maximal projection of I. VP is also a maximal projection. Not every English sentence

---

[13]   For immediate constituents see Chapter 2, section 2.4.2.

[14]   We will discuss instances of V raising to I in sections 1.2.4 and 4.3 below. It is possible to rephrase the theory in a way that avoids lowering. See Chomsky (1995) and Adger (2003) for an introduction. We will not go into this issue here.

contains such a fronted VP. VP-fronting (or VP-preposing) is an optional operation that combines a VP with a clause. To represent the resulting structure, we propose that the fronted VP adjoins to IP. (16a) is a tree diagram representation, (16b, c) translate (16a) in the equivalent labeled bracketing representation.[15]

(16) a

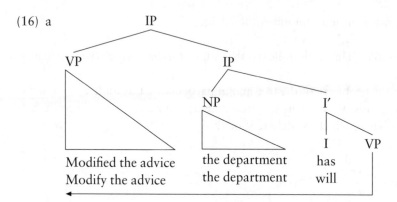

b   [IP [VP Modified the advice], [IP [NP the department] [I′ has [──]]]].

c   [IP [VP Modify the advice], [IP [NP the department] [I′ will [──]]]].

Let us apply VP-fronting to a sentence without an auxiliary. If we front the VP and there is no auxiliary under I, we will be left with an inflection stranded under I. But the inflection is a bound morpheme and has to combine with a verb. Lowering the inflection onto V, as we did before, now raises a problem. After movement of the VP, there will actually be no verb to lower the inflection onto (16d). Left alone, the inflection is also unable to survive in I because it is a bound morpheme. In such cases, we have to "rescue" the sentence by enabling the inflection to survive independently of the lexical verb in the verb phrase, and we insert the auxiliary *do* (16e).

(16) d   e

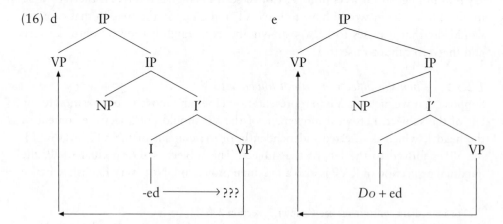

<hr />

[15]   For some discussion of this issue see also Exercise 15 in Chapter 2. In Chapters 4 and 5 we will return to the operation that moves constituents from one position to another position in the sentence.

In (16a) VP movement does not give rise to *do*-insertion. Can you explain why this should be? The answer is that in these examples, insertion of *do* is not required to rescue the sentence because the problem of the stranded inflection does not arise. The auxiliary is a free morpheme. The inflection is associated with the auxiliary, *will* is a present tense form (as opposed to *would*, which would be the past tense form). Since there is no need for inserting *do* we do not insert it. In VP-fronting contexts, *do* is inserted to rescue a pattern which would otherwise not survive. We can say that these patterns illustrate the effect of economy on the structure.[16] We only insert *do* if we cannot manage without it.

Recall that we examined the formation of questions in Chapter 1, section 2, and we observed that direct questions involve subject-auxiliary inversion, abbreviated as SAI. We also saw that we insert *do* and invert it with the subject whenever the relevant sentence lacks an auxiliary. Identify SAI patterns in (17):

(17) a   What are my borrowing options? How much can I afford? Where do I
         begin? (*New York Times*, 28.4.2003, p. A22, advertisement Fleet)
     b   The key question is: what do we know about the 96 new cases of SARS,
         who are the 96, when did they start, where did they live? (Based on *Wash-
         ington Post*, 29.4.2003, p. 18, col. 1)

We should again ask ourselves why *do* is inserted in some of the examples, and if possible we should try to relate the answer to the preceding discussion of the insertion of *do*. We saw in Chapter 1 that SAI is related to question formation. For sentences without an auxiliary, we would again want to end up saying that *do* is inserted as a last resort to rescue the structure. We have assumed that the auxiliaries are inserted in I and move to the left across the subject in cases of subject-auxiliary inversion. The position they arrive at, or their **landing site,** will be examined in Chapter 5. We should ask ourselves, though, which component is crucially targeted by SAI: is it the auxiliary itself or is it the inflectional element that is part of the auxiliary? In order to answer this question we will first extend our database and look at question formation in French.

1.2.4   VERB POSITIONS AND COMPARATIVE SYNTAX

1.2.4.1   French questions
In Chapter 1 we saw that French also displays SAI:

(18) a   A-t-elle toujours acheté le journal?
         has she always bought the paper
         'Has she always bought the paper?'

     b   A-t-elle toujours écrit des romans?
         has she always written novels
         'Has she always been a novelist?'

---

[16]   See Chapter 1, section 2.2.3.

But in contrast with the English pattern, when there is no auxiliary, direct questions in French can simply be formed by inversion of a tensed lexical verb and the subject.[17] We labeled this pattern subject-verb inversion or SVI. Why is there a difference between French and English?

   In order to understand the difference, we need to compare English sentences with their French counterparts. Unless we are proven wrong, considerations of economy lead us to assume that French sentences essentially have the same structure as English sentences, and, in particular, that French verbs also project a VP. The verb would be merged in the position V. We call the position in which the verb is inserted its **base** position.

(19)

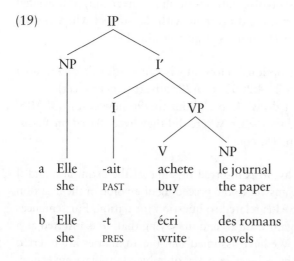

	a	Elle	-ait	achete	le journal
		she	PAST	buy	the paper
	b	Elle	-t	écri	des romans
		she	PRES	write	novels

Consider the examples in (20):

(20) a   Achetait-elle toujours le journal?
     a′ *Bought she always the paper?
     b   Ecrit-elle encore des romans?
     b′ *Writes she still novels?

In (20a) the verb *achetait* ('bought') cannot be occupying its base position, the head position of VP. If the verb were in its base position, it should be adjacent to its direct object *le journal* ('the paper'). Similarly, in its base position the verb *écrit* ('writes') would be adjacent to the direct object *des romans* ('novels') in (20b). In (21a) and in (21b), which are the acceptable counterparts to (20a′) and (20b′), the English verbs *buy* and *write* occupy their base positions.

(21) a   Did she always <u>buy</u> the paper?
     b   Does she still <u>write</u> novels?

---

[17]   See Chapter 1, section 3.1.1.

Why does English need *do* insertion in (21) and why does French not need a similar device in (20)? The difference cannot be due to the fact that SAI itself is restricted to English questions given the French data in (18), which also display subject-auxiliary inversion.

A further question arises for the French examples in (20), in which the verb inverts with the subject. Recall that we proposed as a working hypothesis that language is driven by economy: we do not insert elements unless they are needed. In the examples discussed so far, English *do*-insertion was motivated either by the need to highlight the link between subject and VP (in I), or, alternatively, because VP fronting had made the verb inaccessible to the inflection in I. In the latter case, there exists no alternative without *do*. Given the French data above, though, we can ask ourselves why English doesn't simply use the French strategy of inverting the verb with the subject, SVI, to form questions. Or, conversely, why does French use SVI? Formulating things in yet another way, how come French can use SVI at all and English cannot?

It could be that the contrast between English and French is to be directly related to the process of question formation as such, and that therefore we have to explain the phenomena in relation to questions. But it could also be that the observed contrast is due to a more general difference with respect to the behavior of the verbs in the two languages considered. In the latter scenario, we would expect to find other patterns in which English and French differ with respect to the position of the verb. In English, the verb occupies its base position next to the object in direct questions while in French the verb moves away from that position. Are there other situations in which the two languages differ in a parallel way, that is, in which the English verb remains in its base position while a French verb moves away? In the next section we will look at some such patterns.

The goal of the current discussion is to arrive at an explanation for the observed difference between English and French question formation. Ideally, we want to provide an account for this difference which relates it to some other property of the languages. We need to ask ourselves: "Could things have been different?" For instance, could English question formation have been more similar to French question formation? As we saw in Chapter 1,[18] the answer to both these questions is positive. English used to be different, and question formation in Old English used to be similar to question formation in present-day French:

(22) a Hwæt sægest þu, yrðling?
        what say you, peasant
        'What do you say, farmer?'
        (*Acoll*, 22, Van Kemenade 1987: 138)

     b Hu begæst þu work þin?
        how beget you work your
        'How do you carry out your work?'
        (*Acoll*, 22, Van Kemenade 1987: 138)

---

[18] Section 3.2.

c Hu lomp eow on lade?
   how happened you on journey
   'How did you fare on the journey?'
   (*Beowulf* 1987–1988, Pintzuk 1991: 138)

We do not want an account that implies that English could not have been different
from what it is today. We do not want to postulate that there is an absolute divide
between languages such as French, which can form questions by moving a verb
across the subject, and languages like English, which cannot. Whatever explanation
we propose in order to differentiate French and Modern English should ideally also
account for the difference between Modern English and Old English and it should
explain why English has changed.

1.2.4.2   *Verb positions in French and English*

Recall that we propose that in an English sentence the lexical verb remains under V.
The inflected auxiliary sits under I. The verbal inflection is inserted under I and
lowers onto V. This proposal correctly derives the observed patterns:

(i)   Subject – inflected auxiliary – adjunct –   V.
(ii) Subject –   adjunct –   inflected V.

Diagram (23) shows the structure.

(23)

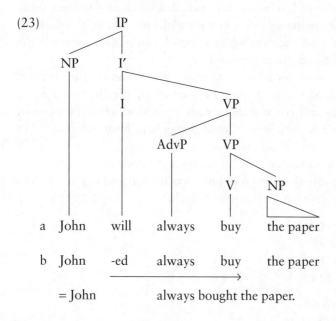

a John   will   always   buy   the paper

b John   -ed   always   buy   the paper

= John   always bought the paper.

Now consider the French equivalents of *John always bought the paper*. The French
verb is also the semantic nucleus of the VP; it is also first merged with its complement to create a core VP. Identify subject, verb, object, and adjunct in (24a), using
the English glosses provided. We assume that the adjunct *toujours* ('always') is like

its English counterpart and that it is VP-adjoined. This seems to be a reasonable assumption since *toujours* modifies the sentence in a similar way to the English adverb *always*. What conclusions do we reach concerning the position of the verb *achetait* ('bought') in (24a)? Could it be in V?

(24) a Jean achetait toujours le journal.
　　　　John bought always the paper
　　　　'John always bought the paper.'

If the French object NP *le journal* ('the paper') is in its base position, then the verb *achetait* ('bought') cannot be claimed to occupy its base position, V. Let us try to plot the position of the verb. We assume that the underlying structure of French is as in English, as shown in (24b). How could we derive the French word order in (24a)?

(24) b

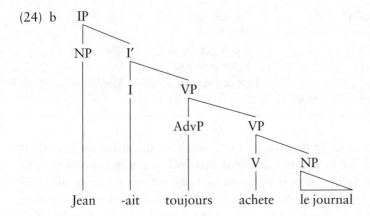

If English I and V unite by I-lowering onto V, giving the order adjunct-verb, then the simplest way to account for the observed French order verb-adjunct is to have V raise to I:

(24) c

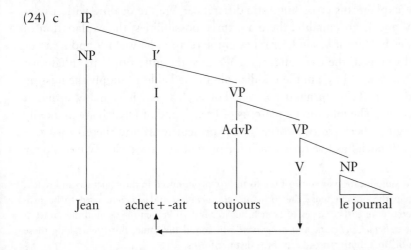

Table 1   Present and past tense paradigms for French and English

	French	English
Present tense	*acheter*	*buy*
First person singular	*J'achète*	*I*
Second person singular	*Tu achètes*	*You*
Third person singular	*Il achète*	*He*
First person plural	*Nous achetons*	*We*
Second person plural	*Vous achetez*	*You*
Third person plural	*Ils achètent*	*They*
Number of different verb forms:	. . .	. . .
Past tense		
First person singular	*J'achetais*	*I*
Second person singular	*Tu achetais*	*You*
Third person singular	*Il achetait*	*He*
First person plural	*Nous achetions*	*We*
Second person plural	*Vous achetiez*	*You*
Third person plural	*Ils achetaient*	*They*
Number of different verb forms:	. . .	. . .

This derivation corresponds to derivation (15a), which we discarded for English; it gives us the correct order for French. But of course, this is not the end of the discussion. The next question we need to address is why the inflection lowers onto V in English and why the verb raises to I in French. In both languages, the reverse pattern is not available. V cannot move to I in English (24d) and I cannot lower to V in French (24e):

(24) d   *John bought always the paper.
     e   *Jean toujours achetait le journal.

How could we explain this cross-linguistic difference? We are dealing with a relation between V and I. Presumably, there are three possibilities: the explanation of the difference lies in V, or it lies in I, or it lies in the relation between V and I. Let us look at the inflections in the two languages. We give the inflectional paradigm for the French verb *acheter* ('buy') in the middle column of Table 1. Supply the missing forms for English in the right-hand column. For each tense, how many different forms do you count? The inflectional patterns of French and of English are markedly different. In English there are two forms in the present tense and there is just one past tense form. French has five forms each for present and for past.[19] We could try

---

[19]   This is a slight simplification as some of the forms are pronounced in the same way in French. For instance, in the present tense the forms *achète*, *achètes*, and *achètent* used to be pronounced differently in earlier stages of French but in Modern French they sound the same; in the past tense *achetais*, *achetait*, and *achetaient* will sound the same. But even taking these forms as non-distinct, both tenses keep three distinct forms.

to account for the different behavior of the verb in English and in French by building a hypothesis that takes into account the differences between the inflections. Let us propose first that the different surface forms of the inflection signal the relative **strength** of the inflections: the more distinct forms there are in the paradigm, the stronger the paradigm is.[20] Pursuing this concept of strength, we could say that the inflection in French is strong and, that, by virtue of being strong, it can attract the verb, while the inflection in English is weak and that, because of its weakness, it cannot attract the verb. Because I cannot attract V in English, I will move down to unite with V.[21]

1.2.4.3 *Inversion*
Consider now the form of direct questions in French and in English:

(25) a   A-t-elle acheté le journal?
          has-she bought the paper
          'Has she bought the paper?'

      b   Achetait-elle le journal?
          bought-she   the paper
          'Did she buy the paper?'

      c   *Bought she the paper?

      d   Did she buy the paper?

      e   Has she bought the paper?

As we have seen before, in French the finite auxiliary inverts with the subject (25a). If there is no auxiliary, the finite verb inverts with the subject (25b). We conclude that it cannot be the case that in order to form a question we actually have to invert an auxiliary. There is, for instance, no inverted auxiliary in (25b); in this example, inversion affects the inflected verb. On the other hand, it also cannot be the case that question formation depends on the inversion of a lexical verb, since, for instance, in (25a) only the auxiliary inverts with the subject. So even though inversion is definitely related to the formation of questions, neither lexical verbs nor auxiliaries are necessary ingredients.

We have formulated the hypothesis that the French verb is attracted to I. In (25b) the verb moves up to a position to the left of the subject. In (25a) the inflected auxiliary moves to the left of the subject. What is the common factor between the inverted constituents in (25a) and (25b)? What is common between these inverted constituents is the inflection itself. In both cases, the content of the inflectional node I ends up to the left of the subject: in French the content of I is either a verb or

---

[20]   See Pollock (1989, 1997), Vikner (1997), and Rohrbacher (1999). For a critical view see Bobaljik (2002), Alexiadou and Anagnostopoulou (1998).
[21]   Exercises 6 and 7, also Exercise 18.

an auxiliary. We can speculate that this common factor, inflection, is essential in question formation. In order to signal interrogative force, we move the content of I to the left of the subject. Whenever French I contains a lexical verb, moving I will take along the lexical verb (25b). In English, I never contains a lexical verb, so we cannot derive (25c). If I contains an auxiliary, moving I to the left will invert the auxiliary with the subject (25e).

If English I fails to contain an auxiliary and if we were to move just I to the left of the subject we would end up with (25f):

(25) f   [$_I$ -ed] [$_{IP}$ she —— [$_{VP}$ buy the paper]]?
         *-ed she —— buy the paper?

Why does derivation (25f) not yield a possible sentence? The problem is once again that the inflectional morpheme *-ed* is a bound morpheme and that it cannot stand unattached. But if we were to lower it into VP and insert it onto V, then we would no longer signal interrogative force. In the case of VP fronting, we saw that an unattached inflectional ending in I was rescued by *do* insertion.[22] By applying *do* insertion to (25f) we derive the acceptable (25d).

The reason why lexical verbs can precede subjects in French questions is related to the fact that French lexical verbs can move to I. This in turn can be explained by our hypothesis concerning the relative strength of the inflection of the verb.

Recall that we have seen that Old English[23] lexical verbs inverted with subjects in questions. What would be your predictions concerning the inflectional paradigms of Old English: how would they compare to the patterns in Modern English? According to our hypothesis, the movement of lexical verbs is made possible by strong inflection. Thus we predict that Old English had a strong inflection. If you turn to any grammar of Old English you will find that the paradigms of the verb had indeed more different forms than is the case in current English. For instance, the verb *singan* ('sing') had the inflection in Table 2.

Table 2   Present tense inflectional paradigm for Old English *singan* ('sing')

Person	Singular	Plural
1	*sing-e*	*sing-en*
2	*sing-est*	*sing-en*
3	*sing-eþ*	*sing-en*

---

22   See section 1.2.3.4.
23   See section 1.2.4.1.

1.2.4.4 *Negative sentences*

Consider (26):

(26) a Jean ne mangeait pas de chocolat.
        John *ne* eat-PAST-3SG not chocolate.
    b *Jean ne pas mangeait de chocolat.
    c *John eats not chocolate.
    d *John not eats chocolate.
    e John does not eat chocolate.

In French, negation is expressed by means of two elements, *ne* and *pas*. Roughly, *pas* corresponds to English *not*. The element *ne* is not always realized. We will not discuss *ne* here and we will provisionally locate it in I. Let us assume that *pas* is like any adverbial and may be VP-adjoined.[24] Draw the tree diagrams for (26a).

(27)

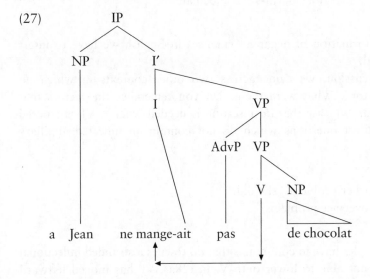

The verb *mange* is attracted to I *-ait* and will hence cross the VP-adjoined negation marker *pas*.

If English *not* is also VP-adjoined, we can account for the unacceptability of (26c). To obtain (26c), *eat* would have to have moved out of VP but we have seen that English lexical verbs do not leave VP. But (26d), in which V would remain in the VP and the ending *-s* would have lowered onto V, is also ungrammatical (27c):

[24] This is a rough approximation. For an introductory discussion see Haegeman and Guéron (1999). For more careful analysis see Pollock (1989), Haegeman (1995), Rowlett (1998), Zanuttini (1997a, b), and the references cited there. For discussion of negation in English see among others Klima (1964), Pollock (1989), Baker (1991), Ernst (1992), Haegeman (1995), Cormack and Smith (2002), and the references cited there.

(27)

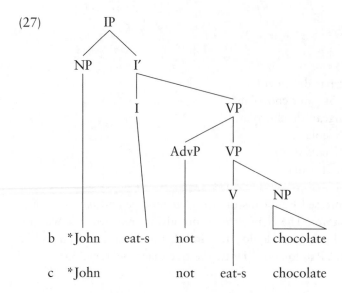

b   *John   eat-s   not   chocolate

c   *John   not   eat-s   chocolate

Apparently, for the formation of negative sentences in English we have to insert the auxiliary *do* (26e).

In our earlier discussion, we came across two other contexts in which *do* insertion was obligatory. What were these? Do you remember the factors that triggered *do*-insertion? We saw that *do* insertion is needed when a VP is fronted (28a) and also in direct questions which do not contain an inflected auxiliary (28b).

(28) a   And get over her problems, she did.
     b   Did she get over her problems?

What these two examples have in common is that *do* rescues a stranded inflectional morpheme which is not able to lower onto V. In (28a), VP has moved leftward and the morpheme in I cannot lower onto V inside VP any more. In (28b) I has to move to a position to the left of the subject to encode interrogative force and it cannot lower onto V. If I did lower onto V, the resulting sentence would not be interrogative.

(28) a′   Get over her problems she -ed.
          Get over her problems she do + ed.
     b′   -ed she get over her problems?
          Do + ed she get over her problems?

Extrapolating from these examples we could conclude that in negative sentences too *do* is inserted because the inflection would otherwise be stranded:

(27)

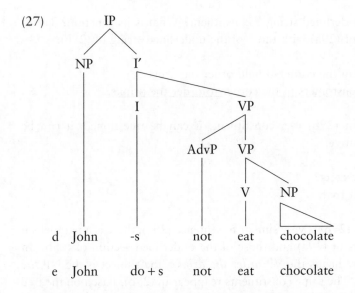

d John   -s   not   eat   chocolate

e John   do + s   not   eat   chocolate

If this is on the right track, then we conclude that in (26d) -*s* is not allowed to lower onto the verb *eat*, even though the VP has not moved and -*s* is in I. The reason why -*s* cannot lower onto V presumably has to do with the sentence being negative. What is the semantic contribution of negation to a sentence? Sentence negation crucially bears on the relation between the subject and the VP: a negated sentence signals that the link subject-VP does not obtain. Indeed, recall that in French the element *ne* is associated with the inflected verb in I. Let us assume that when *not* negates a sentence, the position I must remain filled because it is precisely the link between subject and predicate that is targeted by the negation. Let us assume that when I must be filled, its content cannot lower onto V. The inflection will remain in I and *do* will be inserted precisely to allow the stranded inflection to remain in I.[25]

1.3 Non-finite clauses with to

1.3.1 A FIRST HYPOTHESIS

In this section we turn briefly to sentences which lack a tensed verb or auxiliary. Such sentences are **non-finite**.[26] Here, we will only be looking at infinitival strings such as that underlined in (29b). In preparation for the analysis, draw the tree diagram representation for the structure of (29a). Then consider the underlined

---

[25] For problems with this proposal see Exercise 5.

[26] Since a non-finite sentence is typically embedded, the term non-finite clause would be more accurate. In practice, though, the terms clause and sentence are often used interchangeably in current syntactic discussions.

string in (29b). Is the underlined string a constituent? What is its function? Try to match the constituents of (29a) with those of the underlined string of (29b).

(29) a   The customers in the corner should order the drinks.
     b   I expected <u>the customers in the corner to order the drinks</u>.

The underlined string in (29b) is a constituent: it can be questioned; it can be replaced by a demonstrative.

(29) c   What did you expect?
     d   I did not expect that.

The underlined string in (29b) is very similar to sentence (29a): there is a parallelism between the constituents of (29a) and those of the underlined section of (29b). In (29a) the lexical V *order* heads the VP *order the drinks*; the subject is the NP *the customers in the corner*. The same constituents reappear in (29b). Based on the tree diagram that you have drawn for (29a), try to fit the constituents of the underlined string in (29b) into a tree. When doing this, the only problem that arises is the location of *to*. What would be the simplest way to insert *to* into a tree representation?

(29) e

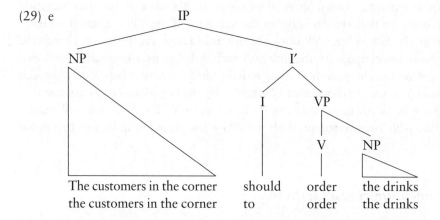

In (29e) *to* is inserted under I, suggesting it is a filler for the inflection of the verb.[27] Is *to* on a par with auxiliaries or is it more like the inflectional endings of the verb? In other words, does *to* have to attach to V? Is *to* a bound morpheme or a prefix?

---

[27]   If we had used Tense rather than I to denote the head of the sentence (footnotes 6, 7), we could distinguish finite clauses from non-finite ones by means of a system of features. Finite clauses would have a positive value for tense [+TENSE], non-finite clauses would have a negative value [−TENSE].

(i)   [TP [NP The customer in the corner] [T' [±TENSE] [VP order the drinks before the meal]]].

Discuss how the following examples provide evidence that *to* should not be treated as a bound morpheme:

(30) a   But Vita could not write the last act, because she did not know how to. (Victoria Glendinning, *Vita*, 1984: 118)
     b   He never asked for his attorneys. If he'd wanted to, he could have. (*Washington Post*, 29.4.2003, p. B1, col. 6)

In the examples above, a VP has been ellipted. The ellipsis does not affect *to*:

(31) a   because she did not know how to ~~write the last act~~.
     b   If he'd wanted to ~~ask for his attorneys~~.

In (32a) co-ordination affects two VPs, and *to* is outside the co-ordinated constituents.

(32) a   After the discovery of a £200m budget shortfall the BBC is being forced to cut costs and lay off staff. (Based on *Guardian*, 7.10.2002, p. 1, col. 1)
     b   After the discovery of a £200m budget shortfall the BBC is being forced to [[$_{VP}$ cut costs] and [$_{VP}$ lay off staff]].

The data above suggest that *to* is neither inseparable from V nor is it an integral part of the projection of V, VP. In order to confirm the hypothesis that *to* is not an inseparable part of a verb and of the related VP, complete the answer to (33a) using VP ellipsis. Apply VP-co-ordination to (33b).

(33) a   Do you expect the customers in the corner to order their drinks?
         No, actually I don't expect . . .
     b   We expect the customers in the corner to order their drinks and we expect them to proceed to their tables.

The resulting sentences show that *to* is not a prefix on the verb. Rather, *to* is a free morpheme that seems to occupy the same position as finite auxiliaries and as the verb inflection. We will adopt the hypothesis that *to* fills the inflection node I of infinitival clauses.[28]

(34) a   Do you expect the customers in the corner to order their drinks?
         No, actually I don't expect them to [$_{VP}$ ~~order their drinks~~].
     b   We expect the customers in the corner to [[$_{VP}$ order their drinks] and [$_{VP}$ proceed to their tables]].

1.3.2   CLAUSE TYPES: FINITE CLAUSES VS. NON-FINITE CLAUSES

If infinitival *to* is the filler for I, this means that *to* fills the head of the infinitival clause. As a consequence, the properties of *to* should determine the properties of the

---

[28]   Exercise 4.

complete clause. This is indeed the case: the filler of I signals the contrast between two types of clauses, namely "finite clauses" and "non-finite clauses."

Replace the subject NP *the customers in the corner* of the examples in (29) by a pronoun. You will find that the subject of the finite clause (29a) is replaced by a pronoun in the **nominative** form *they* (35a), that of a non-finite clause in (29b) by a pronoun in the **accusative** form *them* (35b):

(35) a   <u>They</u> should order the drinks.
      b   I expected <u>them</u> to order the drinks.

Recall that the specifier of a constituent has a special relation with the head of that constituent.[29] For instance, the subject of the sentence is located in the specifier position of I and the subject of a finite clause agrees with I. (35) shows how the nature of the head of the clause (finite/non-finite) correlates with the **case form** of its subject. A finite I takes a subject with a nominative form (*I, you, he, she*, etc.); a non-finite I takes a subject with an accusative form (*me, you, him, her*, etc.).

Some verbs select as their complements a specific type of clause. For instance, English *want* requires an infinitival clause and does not select a finite clause:

(36) a   I want [the customers in the corner to order their drinks now].
      b   *I want [that the customers in the corner order their drinks now].

The choice of the filler for I, *to* as opposed to a finite auxiliary or a finite inflection, determines the distribution of the whole clause. This is as expected if I is the head of the clause: the properties of the head INFL percolate up to its projection, IP, and are visible for an outside selector (e.g., a verb). A finite clause is a clause whose head is a finite inflection; a non-finite clause is a clause whose head is non-finite.

1.3.3 SOME PREDICTIONS

We have examined an embedded non-finite clause containing *to* and we have proposed that *to* is inserted in I. Let us now examine the **empirical coverage** of our hypothesis. The hypothesis leads to a number of predictions. Below we examine two of them.

1.3.3.1 *Co-ordination with* to

We have already examined VP co-ordination and its relation to the morpheme *to*. We have noted that VP co-ordination need not affect *to*. Which types of constituents are co-ordinated in the finite clauses in (37)?

(37) a   The customers should order their drinks and they can proceed to their tables.
      b   The customers should order their drinks and can proceed to their tables.

(37a) co-ordinates two constituents of the type IP; (37b) co-ordinates two constituents of the type I', i.e. consisting of strings modal auxiliary + VP.

---

[29]   See the discussion in Chapter 2, section 3.

(38) a   [IP The customers should order their drinks]

       +   [IP they can proceed to their tables]

    b   [IP The customers [I' should order their drinks]

       +   [I' will proceed to their tables]]

Let us try to apply I' co-ordination to a non-finite clause with *to* as the filler of I. Reduce the following co-ordinated clauses by co-ordinating (non-finite) I':

(39) a   We want the customers to order their drinks and we want them to proceed to their tables.

If we co-ordinate I' units this means that we co-ordinate two sequences *to* + VP. This is what we see in (39b, c):

(39) b   We want

       [IP the customers [I' to order their drinks]

               and [I' to proceed to their tables]]

    c   = We want the customers to order their drinks and to proceed to their tables.

Our proposal that *to* occupies I allows us to co-ordinate two infinitival VPs introduced by *to*.

1.3.3.2   The split infinitive

In the following examples we illustrate finite clauses with a modal auxiliary. Draw a tree diagram for the examples:

(40) a   The jury will unanimously condemn the doctor.

    b   The sisters should only play those tournaments.

We have proposed that in non-finite clauses the infinitive marker *to* occupies the inflectional head, I, and that, similarly to finite auxiliaries, *to* is not a bound morpheme. Hence, *to* will not need to lower onto V. Like the finite auxiliaries, *to* can remain under I. Following this reasoning, we would expect that *to* can be separated from V by material that is left-adjoined to VP:

(40) c

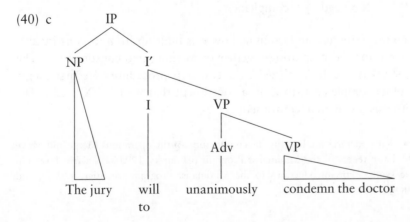

Is this prediction correct? Do we find sentences that display the sequence *to* + adjunct + V? We do indeed: the relevant sentences will exemplify the so-called **split infinitive** pattern. Though sometimes frowned upon by prescriptive authors and grammarians, the split infinitive is a well-attested phenomenon in English. Identify the relevant pattern in the following examples:

(41) a   The jury of seven men and five women took 33 hours and 55 minutes to unanimously find the doctor guilty of all the murder charges and forging the £386.000 will of his final victim. (*Guardian*, 1.2.2000, p. 1, col. 1)

   b   No one here is in a position to accurately assess the prior investigation. (*Chicago Tribune*, 30.11.2002, section 1, p. 20, col. 5)

   c   In the past few years, Web-sites allowing students to anonymously review their professors on their teaching have also been popular. (*San Francisco Chronicle*, 28.11.2002, p. A28, col. 2)

2   Building Structure by Merge and Move

2.1   *Summary so far*

In the preceding discussion we have described sentence structure: we have identified the constituents of the sentence and we have described how they are related to each other. So far we have mainly worked on completed sentences, whose components we have identified. In this section we take a sentence apart and we examine how we can put it back together. (42) is a schematic presentation of our general hypothesis about linguistic structure:

(42) a

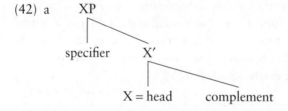

Let us break up this structure and examine how it is built up from its constituents. Syntactic units are formed by putting together or **merging** two constituents.[30] The construction of (42a) can be analyzed as a two-step procedure. We first merge the head X and its complement, to form a constituent that we label X' (42b). The complement itself is a complete constituent.

---

[30]   The proposal that structures are built by the combination of the operations Merge and Move is one of the basic tenets of the Minimalist Program (Chomsky 1995), the current version of generative syntax. For introductions to the Minimalist Program see Adger (2003), and Radford (2004).

(42) b

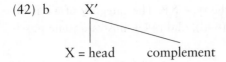

Then we merge the resulting constituent X′ with a specifier to form XP.

(42) c

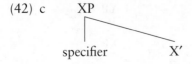

The two applications of Merge lead to the formation of a complete constituent, XP. Both specifier and complement are core ingredients of a structure.

Once we have completed a constituent such as that labeled XP in (42a) this finished product can be selected by another head, say Y. The selecting head Y will merge with the constituent and XP becomes the complement of the head it combines with:

(43) a

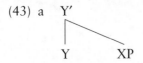

When a head merges with a completed constituent, the latter serves to "complete" the structure of the head, it satisfies some selectional requirement of the head. We call it the complement.

Alternatively, an already completed constituent may serve as the specifier of a structure, in which case it serves to delimit the application of that constituent: in (43b) XP is the specifier of a constituent headed by Z.

(43) b

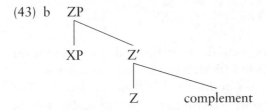

Another way of extending a structure is by adjunction. A completed constituent YP may be **adjoined** to another completed constituent, say XP. Adjunction is the merger of one fully formed constituent with another fully formed constituent. In the case of adjunction, there is an asymmetric relation between the adjunct and the constituent to which it adjoins. When an adjunct YP adjoins to a constituent of type XP, the resulting structure is an augmented XP. (44a) illustrates **left-adjunction** of YP to XP; (44b) illustrates **right-adjunction** of YP to XP. Observe that in both cases the output of the adjunction is a constituent of the type XP. The category of YP is no longer represented at the higher level. (44c), (44d), and (44e) illustrate some possible cases of multiple adjunction.[31]

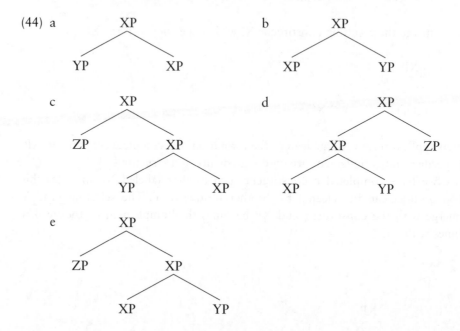

In (44a) and in (44b) XP merges with the adjunct YP to form an augmented XP. In (44c, d, e) there are two adjoined constituents, YP and ZP. The adjoined constituents are like peripheral satellites of the constituent XP.

In (45) it is the constituent XP that is the satellite to the constituent YP.

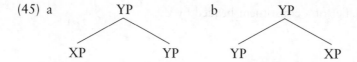

Recall that adjoined constituents do not complete the structure they associate with: a constituent is structurally complete even without any adjoined constituents.

So far we have come across the specifier position in NPs[32] and in clauses.[33] The question has already been raised[34] whether VP also has a specifier and if it does, how its specifier is realized. This issue will be tackled in Chapter 4.

[31] For example of multiple adjunction see Exercise 14 in Chapter 2 and Exercise 3 in this chapter.
[32] See Chapter 2, section 3.1.2.
[33] See section 1 of this chapter.
[34] Cf. Chapter 2, section 3.3.

2.2   Merge

Let us look at an invented sentence and think about how it is put together:

(46) a   The student will probably very carefully examine the data.

The semantic core of the sentence is the verb *examine*: the verb denotes the kind of situation that we are dealing with, and it determines which components will be obligatorily present. If we want to build a sentence containing the verb *examine*, we start off with the verb ((46b), step (i)). We add its complement, the direct object NP ((46b, step (ii)). The object is an essential ingredient, it serves to narrow down the action, telling us what is the entity that is the target of the examining. The verb selects the category of its complement; some verbs select NPs, others select PPs, etc. At the next stage ((46b), step (iii)), we add the adjunct of manner *very carefully*. This adverbial phrase "fine-tunes" the action expressed by VP: we specify how the action is carried out. Observe that the resulting constituent is labeled VP. We add another adjunct *probably* ((46b), step (iv)). The resulting VP is then selected by the auxiliary *will*: *will* sets the event in the future ((46b), step (v)) and it serves to link the VP to the subject: *the student* ((46b), step (vi)). One additional remark is in order here: when we add constituents such as NP, AdvP, etc. to the structure, these constituents have themselves been formed by the same Merge operation. We ignore these operations here, since they use the same mechanisms as those shown in (46b).

(46) b   (i)   V = *examine*

(ii)

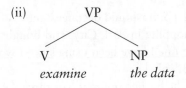

(iii)

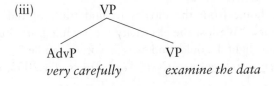

(iv)

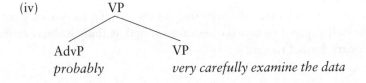

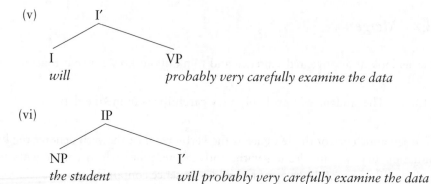

(v)   I′

I   VP
will   *probably very carefully examine the data*

(vi)   IP

NP   I′
the student   *will probably very carefully examine the data*

We build up the structure starting from V and by using the procedure **Merge** by which we combine two constituents to form a new constituent.

In section 2.3 below we elaborate in some more detail the idea that the verb is the semantic core of the sentence.

2.3   The operation "Move"

Once we have built up a certain amount of structure, we can also move around constituents from within the already existing structure. We call the position in which a constituent is merged in the structure its base position. The base position of the object, for instance, is that shown in (46b(ii)). It is right-adjacent to the lexical verb. The underlined segments of (47) are examples in which a constituent has been moved away from its base position. Identify the displaced constituent in the underlined sentences.

(47) a   Baxter said that he had been using a *Sinex* liquid decongestant . . . but then spotted the *Vicks* inhaler when shopping in Park City, and bought it since he preferred to use it. "<u>The British one I have been using since I was about nine</u>." (*Guardian*, 22.3.2002, p. 3, col. 1)

  b   <u>Everything I did right for 20 years, he burned up in two or three</u>. (*Washington Post*, 29.4.2003, p. C1, col. 1)

  c   That night, I came home from the movies to find trails of red candle wax all over the floors. "We lost the electricity for a while," my husband explained. "The only light I could find was a votive candle." <u>The red votive candle I haven't replaced yet</u>. (*New York Times*, 2.1.2003, p. G4, cols 1–4)

  d   Letter writer:
      [The cat] will rummage through our closets looking for socks, drag them to the hallway and then make a strange sound as though she is calling her imaginary kittens to eat.

Animal Doctor's Reply:
<u>Bringing such portable items home, or going through the house to find things to "gift" to you,</u> I interpret as a cat's way of showing affection. (Animal Doctor, *Washington Post*, 29.4.2003, p. C9, cols 1–2)

e   Our dustmen arrive too early for me to check, but our fishmonger and his staff in Petersfield all wear ties (Letters, October 22) and <u>very smart they look too</u>. (*Guardian*, 23.10.2002, p. 9, col. 5, letters to the editor from David Dew, Horndean, Hants)

f   "They must talk about it, and <u>talk about it they must</u>," he said. Food for thought, there! It's a phrase that could add a measure of gravity to any press conference. "We must do this, and <u>do this we must</u>." (*Guardian*, 29.1.2003, p. 2, col. 5)

The role of movement to create sentence structure will be the central theme of Chapter 5.[35]

3   Meaning Relations and Structure

3.1   *Thematic roles*

We have proposed that constituents of a sentence are to some extent determined by the choice of the lexical verb. For instance, if you are going to build a sentence around the transitive verb *examine*, you expect to merge the verb with an object. On the other hand, when using the intransitive verb *yawn*, you will not need such a complement. Some verbs select a complement of a certain type; other verbs don't require a complement. The selectional requirements of verbs – whether they require a complement and if so, what kind – are related to their meanings. The verb *examine*, for instance, refers to a situation involving two participants: the one who examines something or someone and the entity that is being examined. It is hard to think of a situation of 'examining' without also thinking of these two entities. For instance, if you were asked to draw a picture of the activity of 'examining', it is likely that your drawing would represent an examiner and the element that is being examined. On the other hand, the verb *yawn* does not express a situation involving two entities. A picture of the activity 'yawn' might well be restricted to a drawing of a yawning individual.

Some constituents of the sentence are inherently required by the meaning of the verb. It is as if each verb sets the scene for some kind of situation: the verb requires

---

[35]   For some suggestions as to what position the sentence initial constituents in the underlined sentences occupy we refer to Chapter 2, Exercise 15 and to Chapter 5. Exercise 8 of this chapter leads on to the discussion in Chapter 5.

a number of entities that will be involved in the situation. The participants in the situation are called the **arguments** of the verb. We say that a verb has an **argument structure**. When a verb is introduced as the nucleus of a VP, its argument structure is activated. *Examine*, for instance, is a verb with two **arguments**. The first argument is the AGENT of the activity. It is realized by the subject in (48a). The second argument refers to the entity that undergoes the activity, what we will call the THEME. In (48a) the second argument of *examine* is realized by the **direct object** NP. The distinct participant roles attributed to the arguments of the clause are also often referred to as **thematic roles**. A verb such as *give* in (48c) has three arguments: the AGENT, the BENEFICIARY, and the entity that is being transferred, the THEME.

(48) a   The student examined the project.
     b   The student yawned.
     c   The student gave the book to her friend.

(49) is a list of the labels that have been used in the literature to refer to the thematic roles that are associated with the arguments of a verb.[36]

(49) a   AGENT/ACTOR: the one who intentionally initiates the action.[37]
     b   THEME (1): the entity undergoing a change of state (location, possession).
     c   PATIENT: the entity undergoing the action. The PATIENT undergoes a change in its internal state (rather than terms of location or possession, both of which would be external states).
     d   EXPERIENCER: the entity experiencing some (psychological) state.
     e   BENEFACTIVE/BENEFICIARY: the entity benefiting from the action.
     f   GOAL: the entity toward which the THEME is displaced.
     g   SOURCE: the place/entity from which the THEME is moved as a result of the activity, the place/entity from which the action originates.
     h   LOCATION: the place in which the action or state is situated.
     i   CAUSE: the entity that unintentionally initiates the event.
     j   INSTRUMENT: the means by which an action is performed.
     k   POSSESSOR: the entity that owns something.

Sometimes the roles of PATIENT and THEME (1) are grouped into a single role THEME:

(49) l   THEME (2): the entity affected by the action.

---

[36]   For discussion of the relation between thematic roles and syntactic structure see, among others, Jackendoff (1987), Wilkins (1988), Grimshaw (1990), Levin and Rappaport-Hovav (1995), Reinhart (2000).
[37]   Exercises 9, 10, 11.

The following sentences illustrate the realization of thematic roles:

(50) a <u>Thelma</u> ate   <u>the apple</u>.
         AGENT   PATIENT/THEME (2)
      b <u>Thelma</u> handed <u>Louise</u>   <u>the text</u>.
         AGENT   BENEFICIARY THEME
      c <u>Thelma</u> liked   <u>the text</u>.
         EXPERIENCER   CAUSE[38]
      d <u>The wind</u> broke <u>the fence</u>.
         CAUSE   THEME

3.2   *Linking thematic roles and syntactic positions*

The argument structure of the verb determines to some extent the composition of a sentence. All the thematic roles associated with an active verb must be realized in the sentence; i.e. the verb must have a sufficient number of arguments to be able to **assign** all its thematic roles. It is often assumed that there is a one-to-one relation between thematic roles and arguments.[39] For instance, a verb cannot assign one thematic role to two different arguments. In (51a) the verb *examine* will either assign a thematic role to the NP *the project* or to the NP *the book*. But it cannot assign the same role twice. This means that one of the two NPs remains without a thematic role and hence cannot be related to the verb.

(51) a   *[$_{NP}$ <u>Thelma</u>] examined [$_{NP}$ <u>the project</u>] [$_{NP}$ <u>the book</u>].

We can make (51a) grammatical by creating a single argument out of the two noun phrases. In (51b) the constituent *the project and the book* co-ordinates the noun phrases *the project* and *the book*. The resulting constituent is itself also a noun phrase; it functions as one argument which realizes the second thematic role of the verb *examine*:[40]

(51) b   [$_{NP}$ <u>Thelma</u>] examined [$_{NP}$ [$_{NP}$ <u>the project</u>] and [$_{NP}$ <u>the book</u>]].

One single argument cannot normally be assigned two thematic roles. The verb *invite* takes two arguments in (52a). We infer that it assigns two thematic roles (52b).

---

[38]   For a discussion of the argument structure of psychological verbs such as *like, fear, frighten*, etc., see Belletti and Rizzi (1988). Though this paper is essentially on Italian, its findings extend to English. The paper is advanced and should be tackled only after Chapter 5.

[39]   See also Baker (1997), Newmeyer (2001).

[40]   For the structure of co-ordinated constituents see Chapter 2, Exercise 7. For problems with the label of co-ordinated constituents see Chapter 2, Exercise 9.

(52) a   <u>Thelma</u> invites <u>Louise</u>.
    b   *invite* thematic role 1: *Thelma*
                thematic role 2: *Louise*

(52c) is ungrammatical. In this example, both thematic roles associated with *invite* are meant to be assigned to the same argument, *Thelma*:

(52) c   *<u>Thelma</u> invites.
    d   *invite thematic role 1: *Thelma*
                thematic role 2: *Thelma*

If the AGENT of the invitation and the THEME both happen to be associated with the person referred to as Thelma, the object (though not the subject!) can be expressed by means of a reflexive (*herself* in (52e)).

(52) e   <u>Thelma</u> invites <u>herself</u>.
    f   *invite* thematic role 1: *Thelma*
                thematic role 2: *herself*

We have proposed that I is an inherent linker (see section 1.1): it links a VP to a specifier. Given the two-faced nature of I, a sentence always has a subject position available, the specifier of IP. This means that one argument of a verb can always be realized as the subject of the sentence. In the case of *examine*, the AGENT of *examine* is realized as the subject and the PATIENT is realized as the direct object, the NP that is first merged with the verb; *examine* selects one NP complement.

3.3   Relating the subject to the verb

When discussing the internal structure of the VP we proposed that adjuncts were more peripheral to the VP than complements (such as direct objects). Our motivation for this proposal was the observation that adjuncts are less central to the meaning of the VP than complements. Complements are selected by V. We can relate this intuition in terms of the concepts of argument and thematic role by saying that because complements are arguments of the verb, they receive a thematic role from the verb. Hence complements must be close to V and they are part of the core VP. VP-adjoined elements are outside the core VP: they do not receive a thematic role from the verb. Adjuncts need not be as close to the verb precisely because they do not receive a thematic relation from the V.

    However, now an internal contradiction arises in the way we have set up the structure of the sentence. The problem is that the subject NP will usually also receive a thematic role from the verb. Now in the tree diagrams elaborated so far, the subject NP occupies the specifier of IP.[41] Hence, in the structure we have elaborated, the

---

[41]   See Exercise 17 of this chapter, though, for complications.

subject is radically outside the VP and it is definitely not as close to V as any of the VP-adjoined constituents. How is it possible for the subject to receive a thematic role from V while it is located outside the VP and while it is further away from V than adjuncts? This state of affairs makes it hard to motivate the distinction between complements and adjuncts on semantic grounds. Our present representation makes it appear as if the subject had a weaker semantic relationship to V than VP-adjoined constituents, even though the subject is thematically related to V and adjuncts are not. If the tree structure is intended to reflect closeness of semantic relations, then we would expect all constituents that are thematically related to V to occupy a position inside the core VP. This would imply that the subject must be part of the core VP.

In order to relate the subject to the verb and to the VP we would need to create a position for the subject inside the VP. Recall that in our representation of the structure of the VP we have not yet made use of the specifier position. If we were to introduce a specifier to the VP that position could become the VP-internal position for the subject. Note that if we do integrate a subject position in the VP we end up with two subject positions.

In preceding discussions we have seen that to motivate a certain structure we might use either empirical arguments or theoretical arguments. If you go over the discussion above, do you think that our motivation for a VP-internal subject position at this point is mainly empirical or theoretical? In order to answer this question you should examine the reasoning that we adopt. Is it based on empirical data or is it based on the way our theory is conceived? Probably, your conclusion will be that our motivation has been essentially theoretical. Postulating a VP-internal subject position is based on two strands of reasoning. On the one hand, we want to create a closer structural relation between the subject and the verb because we want to have a fit between syntactic structure and interpretation. But this fit is one that we have set up as a goal of our theory, and which we use as a guideline for postulating structure. In addition, when elaborating our structures we had come up with the hypothesis that a projection could have a specifier. We have identified the filler for the specifier of NP and for the specifier of the clause. We have not yet identified any element that could qualify as the specifier of VP. The absence of a VP specifier would be a problem for our approach. We can generalize the specifier position to VP if we relate the subject NP to that position: the resulting VP will then also have a specifier and will therefore be fully in line with the structures proposed for the NP and for the clause. We will return to this point in detail in Chapter 4, where we will see that there also exist a number of empirical motivations for postulating that there is a position for the subject in the VP.[42]

3.4 Auxiliaries vs. lexical verbs

We have already come across a number of patterns in which auxiliaries and lexical verbs pattern differently. Before reading on, try to make a list of the differences

---

[42] See Exercises 17 and 18 for some empirical evidence supporting this idea.

between auxiliaries and lexical verbs. You will probably recall that sentences with auxiliaries do not require *do*-insertion in questions or in negative sentences with *not*. We can explain this if we assume that English auxiliaries can be inserted in I, while English lexical verbs do not move to I. Consider the sentences in (53). How many thematic roles would we associate with the verb *neglect*? How are these thematic roles realized in (53)? Assuming that each constituent can only carry one thematic role, do you think it is plausible that auxiliaries can assign thematic roles?

(53) a   The student neglected his studies.
      b   The student had neglected his studies.
      c   The student will neglect his studies.
      d   The student is neglecting his studies.

We deduce from the examples in (53) that auxiliaries cannot assign thematic roles. If they did, then we would expect that, compared to (53a), (53b–d) should contain at least one additional argument to realize the thematic role associated with the auxiliary, contrary to fact. So we conclude that auxiliaries, though by their nature verbs, do not assign any thematic roles. Lexical verbs are potential thematic role assigners.[43]

3.5   Lexical head vs. functional head

If we compare (54a) in the present tense and (54b) in the past tense, there is no difference in their thematic structure. Inflectional morphemes are not thematic role assigners. Their function is to place the event expressed by the verb with respect to time. This means then that the prototypical filler of I, inflection, is not a thematic role assigner. While V is a **lexical** head, a head such as I, which itself does not assign thematic roles, is said to be a **functional** head.[44] The lexical verb heads a **lexical projection**; I heads a **functional projection**.[45]

(54) a   John always eats chocolate.
      b   John always ate chocolate.

Note that this does not mean that I can never contain a lexical head that assigns thematic roles. We have seen that in French (54c), the lexical verb raises to I. As a

---

[43]   The fact that lexical verbs do and auxiliaries do not assign thematic roles could explain why the former are sometimes called "full verbs." (See Chapter 1, section 2.4.)

[44]   See also Chapter 1, section 2.4 for the concept "lexical."

[45]   Exercise 13 raises the question if projections of the N also are integrated into a functional projection.

result I will contain V, a thematic role assigner. But crucially, the verb is not directly merged in I. The verb is merged as the head of VP, and it has only ended up in I because it has been attracted there by the content of I, inflection (here the ending *-ait*). And once again the inflection itself is not a thematic role assigner.

(54) c   [$_{IP}$ Jean [$_{I'}$ [$_I$ aim-ait] [$_{VP}$ —— [$_{NP}$ du chocolat]]]].

4   Multiple Auxiliaries

4.1   *A first hypothesis: Clustering auxiliaries*

Identify the auxiliaries in the sentences in (55). Which is the finite auxiliary? How do you know? Form a direct question on the basis of these examples. Using the concepts developed so far, describe the processes used to form a question.

(55) a   The inspector will be staying at the pub.
      b   The press have been writing terrible things about him.
      c   Without this concession, he would have pulled the trigger.
      d   He could have been staying at the pub.

Each of the examples in (55) contains more than one auxiliary. In each of them, the first auxiliary is finite, witness the fact that it is tensed (present vs. past tense), and the finite auxiliary inverts with the subject to form a direct question. Below we have underlined the auxiliaries, we have indicated the tense form of the finite auxiliary, and we also illustrate SAI in direct questions:

(56) a   The inspector <u>will</u> (present, vs. *would*) <u>be</u> staying at the pub.
          <u>Will</u> the inspector be staying at the pub?
      b   The press <u>have</u> (present, vs. *had*) <u>been</u> writing terrible things about him.
          <u>Have</u> the press been writing terrible things about him?
      c   Without this concession, he <u>would</u> (past, vs. *will*) <u>have</u> pulled the trigger.
          <u>Would</u> he have pulled the trigger?
      d   He <u>could</u> (past, vs. *can*) <u>have been</u> staying at the pub.
          <u>Could</u> he have been staying at the pub?

The question arises how multiple auxiliaries get inserted into the structure of a sentence. In our earlier discussions, we inserted the inflected auxiliary under I. When we have more than one auxiliary we might think that we should insert all the auxiliaries as a kind of auxiliary cluster under I. This is illustrated in (57a), for example (56d). Let us evaluate this proposal.

(57) a

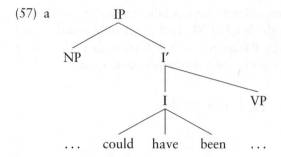

The first question that arises is whether (57a) is compatible with the theory we have
been elaborating. If you look at the tree diagrams with which we have been operating so far, and if you recall our proposals for structure,[46] you will decide that (57a)
is not compatible with our theory of structure. (57a) violates the binary branching
hypothesis. In (57a) I is ternary branching: there are three auxiliaries hanging directly
from I.

Needless to say, this particular problem can only arise with sentences with more
than two auxiliaries, such as (56d). When there are only two auxiliaries, the head I
would obviously be binary branching even if the auxiliaries formed a cluster.

We might decide that the binary branching hypothesis is wrong and that it should
be discarded, and we might re-introduce multiple branching into our theory. However, this rather rash step would increase the tools of our theory dramatically.[47] To
maintain that auxiliaries form a cluster, while at the same time preserving the binary
branching hypothesis, we could introduce binary branching inside I. (57b) and
(57c) are two ways of achieving this.[48] The labels Perfect and Prog(ressive) identify
which auxiliary is going to be inserted in the relevant position.

(57) b   c

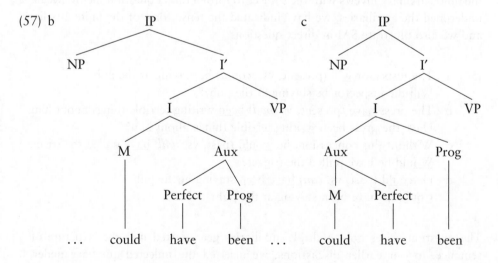

---

[46] From Chapter 2, section 2.4.2.
[47] Recall the discussion of the concept of economy in Chapter 1, section 1.2.3.
[48] A version of (57b) was proposed at one time (Chomsky (1975, 1972)).

Having solved a theoretical objection to (57a), let us now try to think of empirical evidence that could be invoked to support one of the structures in (57b, c). Alternatively, what kind of empirical evidence could be invoked to challenge one or the other?

Do the sentences with SAI in (56) bear on (that is confirm or challenge) the structures in (57b, c)? In fact, these examples are neutral with respect to the structures in (57b, c). SAI moves the finite auxiliary to the initial position, which means that the finite auxiliary is a constituent. This is the case in each of the representations in (57), in which the finite auxiliary forms the node I in combination with other auxiliaries. It is in principle possible to move a constituent from a larger constituent: for instance we can move an object NP out of a VP. In French, we have seen that V can leave VP and move to I.

To show that either (57b) or (57c) is appropriate we would have to find a construction pattern in which we move not just the finite auxiliary but, for instance, a cluster of two or three auxiliaries. This would provide empirical evidence for the clustering of the auxiliaries in I. Try moving a cluster of auxiliaries in the examples above. Are the resulting sentences grammatical? Clearly not, as shown in (58):

(58) a *Would be the inspector staying at the pub?
    b *Had been the press saying that things were wrong?
    c *Will have he pulled the trigger?
    d *Could have been he staying at the pub?
      *Could have he been staying at the pub?

That the examples in (58) are unacceptable could be due to the fact that the auxiliaries do not in fact form a cluster. But this explanation is only one possibility. It is conceivable that the unacceptability of (58) might also be due to some other factor(s). Perhaps SAI can only move the finite auxiliary. We do conclude, though, that SAI does not at the moment provide any direct support in favor of either (57b) or (57c).

Let us examine another prediction of the structures in (57b, c). Assuming (57b, c), any syntactic operation affecting auxiliaries should always target one individual auxiliary, or it should target a cluster of auxiliaries. Any operation should affect all the auxiliaries in I, or it should affect the two auxiliaries under Aux in (57b) or (57c). A syntactic operation could also target the VP. According to these representations, no operation should be able to affect, for instance, the rightmost auxiliary in the cluster under I as well as the VP. If we did find evidence that there is such an operation then that would mean that the auxiliaries do not form a cluster and we would have to devise an alternative structure. If possible, we would also try to offer empirical support for the new structure. This is what we will do in the next sections.

4.2   A second hypothesis: Auxiliaries as heads of VP

The attested sentences in (59) contain multiple auxiliaries. Read the sentences carefully, identify finite and non-finite auxiliaries, and decide to what extent, if at all, these data can be made to bear on the question raised in the preceding section concerning the structure of sentences containing multiple auxiliaries.

(59) a   He drove her hard, he stole her fame or would have if he could have. (*Guardian*, Review, 24.5.2003, p. 5, col. 3)
  b   You should have been an accountant and made some money so you could take care of your parents. (*Washington Post*, 29.4.2003, p. A23, col. 4)
  c   I should have gone on the stage or been a diplomat's wife or an international spy. (Mary McCarthy, *The Company She Keeps*, 1989: 3)
  d   I asked him where this Detective Inspector Thomas Lynley was from . . . He's from New Scotland Yard! Staying right here at the inn, he'll be. He booked a room hisself not three hours past. (Elizabeth George, *Missing Joseph*, 1993/1996: 144)

(59a) illustrates ellipsis: the VP associated with *have* has been omitted.

(59) a′   (he) would have ~~stolen her fame~~ if he could have ~~stolen her fame~~.

The application of ellipsis in (59a) is compatible with the representations in (57b, c) in that it shows that the VP must be able to be treated as a constituent. Once again, this example does not provide any support for the clustering of the auxiliaries (*would have*). Similarly, in (59b) and in (59c), VPs are co-ordinated:

(59) b′   You should have [vp been an accountant] and [vp made some money].
  c′   I should have [vp gone on the stage] or [vp been a diplomat's wife or an international spy].

Again, these examples simply confirm the constituent status attributed to the verb and its complements, the VP, but they do not bear on the grouping of the auxiliaries (*should have*). In (59d) the VP is fronted. Again this example confirms that VP is a constituent but does not bear on the clustering of auxiliaries (*'ll be*).

(59) d′   <u>Staying right here at the inn</u>, he'll be.

Now examine the examples in (60), which also contain multiple auxiliaries. Do these provide any arguments for determining the structural relations between auxiliaries? Where possible, try to group related examples.

(60) a   "The Hershey chocolate company is about to be sold!" he says, eyes widening. "Who could have imagined it?" Very few could. (Based on *Guardian*, G2, 26.8.2002, p. 2, col. 1)
  b   Some 24% agreed top-up fees would not have mattered, while 35% would have considered other universities but probably still have chosen the same university. (Based on *Guardian*, 20.1.2003, p. 5, col. 2)

    c   Michael Jackson has, on some occasions in the past, not eaten when he
        should. (*Guardian*, Review, 28.5.2003, p. 3, col. 1)

    d   But we have been saying for 15 to 20 years that there are too many games
        in the top division and done nothing about it. (*Guardian*, 15.2.2003, *Sport*,
        p. 11, col. 5)

The examples above do bear on the structures in (57b, c). Indeed, they illustrate the
patterns that the structures in (57b, c) are predicted to exclude. In (60) an operation
(movement, ellipsis, co-ordination) applies to a combination of one auxiliary of the
cluster and the VP, excluding the other auxiliaries in the cluster from the operation.
That such an operation should be possible is not predicted by either variant (57b) or
(57c). Let us examine some of the examples in (60) in detail.

   (60b) and (60d) illustrate co-ordination. In (60b) co-ordination affects two strings
consisting of a non-finite auxiliary *have* and a VP (61a). In (60d) co-ordination
affects a constituent containing the auxiliary *been* and the VP on the one hand, and
a VP on the other hand, (61b).

(61) a   35% would   [have considered other universities]
               but   [probably still have chosen the same university].
     b   we have   [been saying for 15 to 20 years that . . . in the top division]
            and   [done nothing about it].

If co-ordination affects constituents (as we have been assuming so far),[49] it is hard
to see how the auxiliaries could form a cluster of the type proposed in (57b, c). If
auxiliaries did indeed form a cluster, one would not expect that one particular
auxiliary could be affected by a syntactic operation which also affects the VP, while
the other auxiliaries of the cluster remain unaffected. The data suggest that we need
a structure in which we can operate on a (non-finite) auxiliary and the VP to its
right without at the same time affecting the finite auxiliary. In schematic terms we
need to be able to isolate AUX2 and the VP without affecting AUX1:

(62) a   subject   AUX1   <u>AUX2</u>   <u>VP</u>

Put differently, AUX2 and VP should be able to form a constituent. (62b) gives a
partial bracketing representation:

(62) b [_{IP} subject AUX1 [_{CONSTITUENT} AUX2 [_{VP} VP]]]

If you try to translate this representation into a binary branching tree diagram structure, you end up with something like (62c) as a first approximation. The provisional
label CONSTITUENT simply means that the auxiliary and the VP are grouped as one
entity.

---

[49] See Chapter 2, section 1.8.

(62) c

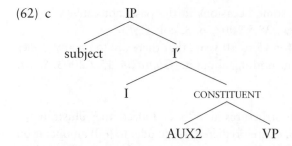

IP
subject   I′
I   CONSTITUENT
AUX2   VP

In (60a) and in (60c) ellipsis affects a combination of one auxiliary (*have*) and the VP. These patterns are compatible with the structure proposed in (62c): ellipsis applies to the newly identified unit, provisionally labeled CONSTITUENT.

(61) c   Very few could [CONSTITUENT ~~have imagined it~~].
      d   when he should [CONSTITUENT ~~have eaten~~].

On the basis of the argumentation above, we need to enrich our structure so that we can insert all the auxiliaries, both finite and non-finite. We have postulated that there is a unit formed of an auxiliary and the VP. The auxiliary is a head, the VP can be seen as its complement. Various questions come to mind: What are the heads in which the auxiliaries are merged? If auxiliaries are heads, they will give rise to a full projection of their own. What kind of a projection is headed by the auxiliary? Assuming the projection headed by the auxiliary also has a specifier, the question arises what, if anything, do we merge in that specifier position? Before answering this question let us first look at another issue concerning finite auxiliaries.

4.3   Finite auxiliaries

Throughout the discussion, we have inserted the finite auxiliary directly under I. Tree diagram (63) is based on the discussion in section 1 of this chapter.

(63)

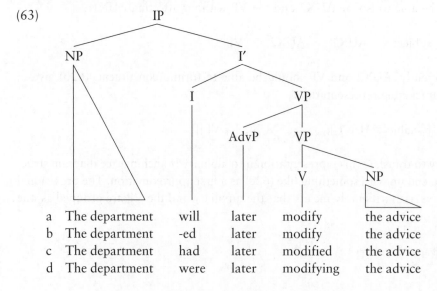

		NP	I	AdvP	VP (V)	NP
a	The department	will	later	modify	the advice
b	The department	-ed	later	modify	the advice
c	The department	had	later	modified	the advice
d	The department	were	later	modifying	the advice

Under I we find the present tense form of the modal auxiliary *will* (a), the past tense ending of the verb *-ed* (b), the past tense form of the auxiliary *have* (c), and the past tense form of the auxiliary *be* (d).

There is an inconsistency in our treatment of the tense inflection. In the case of an inflected lexical verb like *modify* we split up the verb and its tense or agreement inflection, inserting the latter in I. In the case of the modal auxiliary *will* and the auxiliaries *have* or *be*, we don't apply a split. In other words, we treat inflectional endings differently depending on the type of verb they associate with. We have not motivated this differential treatment. It would be simpler (and hence preferable) if all inflectional endings of the verb could be treated in the same way.[50] Would this be possible?

Let us first look at the auxiliaries *have* and *be*. First of all, we note that though these elements are often followed by a VP, they need not be. *Have* and *be* can be the only verb element in the sentence.

(64) a　John had lunch at the club.
　　 b　John is the captain.

So, without going into the details of the structures in (64), it seems reasonable to allow ourselves to treat *be* and *have* as verbs in their own right. In their independent uses, illustrated in (64), *have* and *be* are not necessarily finite: they need not be associated with a tense form; they may also be non-finite:

(64) c　John has <u>had</u> lunch at the club.
　　　　John is <u>having</u> lunch at the club.
　　　　John wants to <u>have</u> lunch at the club.
　　 d　John has <u>been</u> the captain.
　　　　John is <u>being</u> difficult.
　　　　John seems to <u>be</u> hungry.

We conclude that *have* and *be* are verbs with finite and non-finite forms.

In examples with multiple auxiliaries, we also find the auxiliaries *have* and *be* in their non-finite forms. This means rather uncontroversially that in their auxiliary use too, these verbs are not inherently finite. In the following examples we pair non-finite *be* and the non-finite lexical verb *keep*.

(65) a　The committee will probably <u>be</u> modifying the advice.
　　　　The committee will probably <u>keep</u> modifying the advice.
　　 b　The committee have probably <u>been</u> modifying the advice.
　　　　The committee have probably <u>kept</u> modifying the advice.

---

[50]　A further inconsistency is that we insert participles as one element, disregarding that they too contain an inflectional morpheme. We do not dwell on participial morphology here, as this would lead us too far. See for discussion Belletti (1990) and Friedemann and Siloni (1993). See also Exercise 14 of this chapter.

Recall that we assume that a lexical verb is merged as the head of the VP and that it subsequently combines with the tense inflection. Concretely, we propose that in English the inflection lowers onto the verb.

(66) a

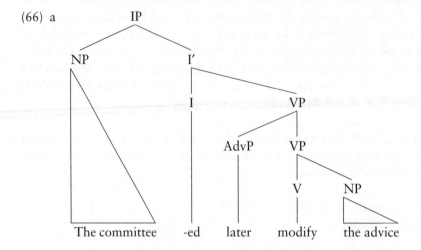

For the sake of internal consistency, ought we not to try to propose the same analysis for the auxiliaries *have* and *be*? We might propose that *have/be* are merged in the structure as verbs and that they subsequently combine with their inflection. In fact, if we did decide against this move, we would actually have to explain why we do not treat *have/be* as verbs here, since they seem to be able to act as a verb elsewhere.

Let us treat auxiliaries *be* and *have* as verbs. In their use as auxiliaries, *be* and *have* have the specific property of selecting a VP as their complement. The auxiliary *be* selects a VP complement with a present participle as its head; *have* selects a VP complement with a past participle as its head. The inflection of the auxiliary is inserted under I, just like any other verb inflection. Let us translate this in terms of the structure.

(66) b

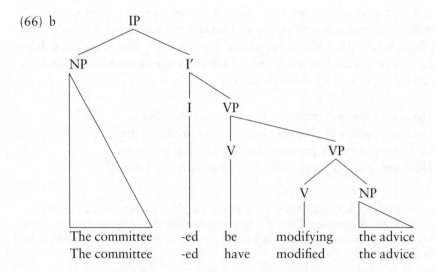

In other words, after having merged the components of VP (*modifying the advice, modified the advice*), we merge VP with the auxiliary (*be, have*) and we merge the resulting structure with the inflection. Hence, we no longer make any special provisions for the auxiliaries *be* and *have*, we treat them as verbs. Observe that in (66b) there are two VPs: one VP is headed by a lexical verb (*modifying/modified*), and one VP is headed by *be/have*.

We also need to make sure that auxiliaries and their inflectional endings are united. How can we do this? Given a structure like (66b), two procedures can be invoked.[51] We have discovered that English lexical verbs unite with their inflection as a result of the lowering of the inflection. On the other hand, French lexical verbs move up to the inflection. Since we initially provided evidence that the auxiliaries *be* and *have* occupy I, it seems reasonable to assume that they unite with their inflection by moving to I. This means that we preserve the essence of our hypothesis in Chapter 2 according to which a finite auxiliary occupies I. In addition, we align the auxiliaries *be* and *have* with other verbs by merging them as Vs taking a VP complement. When *be* and *have* take a VP complement we call them auxiliaries. As auxiliaries, *have* and *be* distinguish themselves from English lexical verbs in that they move to I.[52]

The fact that auxiliaries can move to I in English needs an explanation. Recall that auxiliaries such as *have* and *be* are members of a closed class.[53] They serve to signal temporal and aspectual relations. The perfective meaning signaled by English *have* would in fact be encoded by an inflection in Latin: 'I have loved' translates as *amavi*, the perfect form of the verb *amare*. *Amavi* consists of the verb *ama-* root with an inflectional ending *-vi*. We will not develop this point in detail. A full account for the movement of *have* and *be* to I could explore the semantic similarity to inflectional elements.[54]

In our previous discussions, modal auxiliaries were taken to be inserted directly under I. It is not obvious that we need to change that hypothesis. Consider the auxiliary *can*. It can be used to denote an ability, a capacity ascribed to the subject. However, the auxiliary can only be used in the forms *can* or *could*. In most varieties of English, we cannot, for instance, refer to a future capacity of the subject by using *can* in combination with the auxiliary of the future, *will*. Similarly, we cannot form a perfect tense with *can*:

(67) a   *He will can finish the book.
     b   *He has could finish the book.[55]

---

[51]   See section 1.2.3.3 of this chapter.

[52]   This also shows that the operation of a verb raising to I is not incompatible with the grammar of Modern English. What is not possible is for a lexical verb to move to I.

[53]   See Chapter 1, section 2.4.

[54]   For discussion see Emonds (1978), Pollock (1989), Chomsky (1995), and Roberts (1985). For an alternative approach which merges the auxiliaries in I-type heads see Cinque (1999).

[55]   There are English dialects, both in the United Kingdom and in the United States, which do allow double modals. For Scots see Brown (1992) and Miller (1993). For American varieties see for instance Battistella (1995). We leave these aside here. For the diachronic development of modals see Lightfoot (1979) and Roberts (1993).

Observe that it is not the intended meaning of (67) that causes the problem here. We may well want to refer to a future capacity of a person (67c), or we may want to refer to a past capacity with present relevance and use a perfect form (67d), but in order to do that we use a different construction.

(67) c He will be able to finish the book.
      d He has been able to finish the book.

Our conclusion is that modal auxiliaries never come without an associated tense. We can say that in standard Modern English, modal auxiliaries are inherently tensed; it is as if the tense and the base of the modal are welded together and can no longer be separated. So we will continue to insert them directly under I.[56]

(67) e

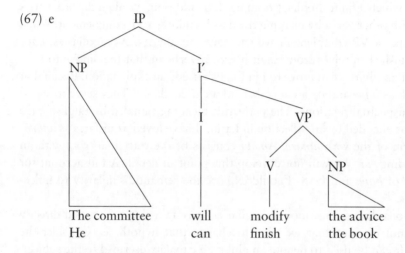

The committee	will	modify	the advice
He	can	finish	the book

4.4 The structure of auxiliary sequences

Having concluded that the auxiliaries *have* and *be* ought to be treated as verbs, with the particular property that they move to I to unite with their finite inflection, we can return to sentences with multiple auxiliaries and complete their structures. Consider for instance, (68a) and the partial structure in (68b), which we had arrived at in the preceding discussion. This structure has been improved by re-labelling the position "Aux" as V and by making this V the head of a VP. The revised representation (66b) is repeated in (68c):

---

[56] Of course in the dialects that allow double modals (note 55) the analysis will be different. In earlier stages of English modals did have non-finite forms (Lightfoot, 1979).

(68) a   These students would [have considered other universities].

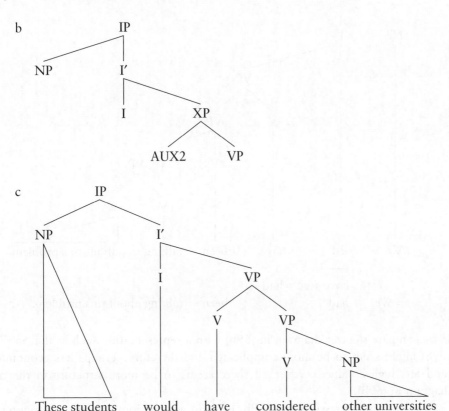

There are two projections of V: one is headed by the lexical verb *considered*, the other is headed by the auxiliary *have*.

What about (69a), in which I is occupied by the past tense auxiliary *had*?

(69) a   We had been talking about this problem.

To represent the structure we combine the proposals elaborated in this section. (i) On the one hand, *have* and *be* are treated as verbs, heading their own VP and selecting a VP complement. (ii) On the other hand, these auxiliaries are inserted independently of the finite inflection – *had* is decomposed into two morphemes: the verb root, which we represent as *have*, and the past tense inflection. The auxiliary is inserted in V and its past tense is inserted in I. (iii) *Have* moves to I to pick up the tense inflection.[57]

---

[57]   Exercise 12 shows that the same structure can be used for passive sentences. Exercise 15 introduces some empirical problems.

(69) b

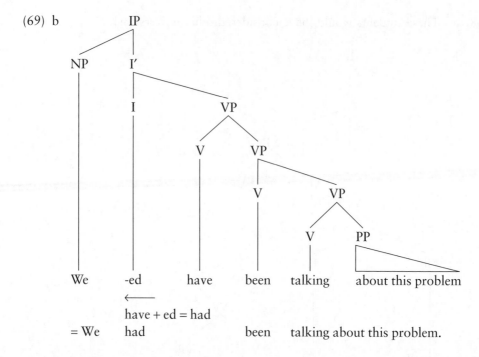

If we compare the tree diagram in (69b) with a representation such as that in (7c), (69b) might seem to be more complicated and therefore perhaps less economical (and less highly valued). After all there seems to be more structure in the tree diagram in (69b).

However the impression that (69b) leads to a more complex or less economical theory is deceptive. Let us examine the relevant components needed to form the tree in (7c) and that in (69b). We are concerned with sentences containing auxiliaries *have* or *be*. (7c) presents inflected auxiliaries like *had* and *was* as unanalyzable elements, they are inflected forms of the auxiliaries. In other words, (7c) has to assume the finite forms of the auxiliaries *have* and *be* are separate entities, and it also has to allow for the non-finite forms of *have* and *be*, which we have shown to be verbs and which project a VP. (69b), on the other hand, decomposes the finite forms of the auxiliaries *have* and *be* into more elementary units. It separates out the verbal root and the tense inflection. So according to (69b) auxiliaries are simply verbs that project a VP.

(69b) does require us to postulate that certain verbs in English, namely auxiliaries, raise to I, and that lexical verbs don't raise to I. However, that is not a complication to our theory since we need to allow for V-raising to I independently to account for the word order patterns in French. So once again, we do not require a new mechanism, we exploit an existing mechanism.[58]

We conclude that none of the elements required to replace representation (7c) by representation (69b) is new to the theory. We only make use of devices that are

---

[58] As mentioned in note 50, the assumption that participles are inserted with their inflection is not consistent with the current discussion and would have to be rethought. See also Exercise 14.

already needed independently. Hence assuming (69b) for sentences with finite auxiliaries is not more complex or less economical.[59]

5   Summary

The first part of this chapter completes the representation of the structure of the sentence. Pursuing the representation elaborated for sentences with auxiliaries in Chapter 2, we elaborate a representation that covers both sentences with auxiliaries and those without. The proposal starts from the observation that the inflection of the verb is a pivotal element in the sentence that links VP and subject. The sentence is seen as a projection of the inflection I. I selects a VP as its complement, and takes the subject as its specifier. I thus serves to relate the situation denoted by the VP to the entity denoted by the subject. I and V are united by a movement operation. French lexical verbs raise to the finite inflection in I; English I lowers onto lexical verbs. The difference between the two patterns is related to the strength of the inflection as reflected in the number of distinct forms in the verbal paradigm.

We conclude that our syntactic representations make use of two basic operations: the operation Merge which combines two units, and the operation Move which selects a constituent in an existing structure and moves it to another position. When building the sentence we start with a verb and we progressively add constituents to build a more elaborate structure.

The verb plays a central role in the semantic make-up of the sentence. Lexical verbs denote situations involving one or more participants, the arguments of the verb. These arguments have specific semantic relations with respect to the situation denoted by the sentence. The semantic relations between the verb and its arguments are referred to as thematic roles. Thematic roles are assigned to arguments on a one-to-one basis. In contrast with lexical verbs, auxiliaries do not assign thematic roles. Auxiliaries are functional elements.

In the final part of the chapter it is proposed that the auxiliaries *be* and *have* be treated as verbs selecting a VP complement. An auxiliary is inserted as a V head that merges with a VP complement. In finite clause, the auxiliaries *have* and *be* move to I to combine with the inflection. Modal auxiliaries, on the other hand, are inherently tensed, they lack non-finite forms and they are inserted directly under I.

Both the NP and the sentence have a specifier position. We still have to address the question whether VPs also have a specifier position. Because verbs have a thematic relation with their subjects we might wish to propose that the subject of the sentence should be seen as the specifier of the VP. However, so far we have been assuming that the **canonical** subject position is in the specifier of IP, in other words it is outside the VP. If there is a subject position inside the VP then we end up with two subject positions: the canonical subject position, the specifier of IP, and a VP-internal subject position.[60]

---

[59]   For some complications to the analysis, though, see Roberts (1990).

[60]   Exercise 17 introduces some empirical support for the hypothesis that there is more than one subject position.

Exercises

Contents

Exercise 1   Constituent structure (T)

Discuss how each of the examples below can be argued to contain some support for the hypothesis that the underlined strings of words are constituents:

Example

<u>The news</u>, when it comes, he seems to take —— well enough. (*Guardian*, G2, 26.7.2002, p. 2, col. 1)

- In this example, movement has affected the string *the news*. *The news* is the direct object of *take*. Its canonical position is to the immediate right of the verb. In the example it has been moved to the beginning of the sentence. The fact that it has been moved suggests the string of words is a constituent. Moreover, the string *the news* is substituted for by the pronoun *it*.
- *The news* is an NP.

---

(1)   Two decades of financial squeeze has eroded academic standards and <u>seriously damaged common-room morale</u>. (*Guardian*, 26.10.2002, p. 13, col. 1)

(2)   Lawyers who've <u>handled arbitration claims</u> for years . . . are getting very busy; lawyers who never have are joining the fray. (*Washington Post*, 29.4.2003, p. C2, col. 1)

(3)   Boyle testified that she told Malvo four times that he could be silent or <u>see an attorney</u> but that Malvo continued to talk about the shootings in a relaxed, almost convivial way. (*Washington Post*, 29.4.2003, p. B1, cols 3–4)

(4)   You could study this pattern for years and <u>still not wholly understand it</u>. (Ian Rankin, *The Falls*, 2001: 240)

Using the structural representation developed in this chapter, discuss the structural ambiguity of the following examples:[1]

(5)   He added that the looting, though continuing, is much reduced. "You will see a guy or two carrying a table or chairs. We tell them to put it down <u>and</u> go home." (*Guardian*, 7.5.2003, p. 5, col. 14)

(6)   If you feel threatened in a mini cab, firmly ask the driver to stop <u>and</u> get out. (*Guardian*, G2, 7.3.2003, p. 7, col. 2)

Exercise 2   The structure of the sentence (T)

Identify the category of the co-ordinated constituents in the attested example below. Is this co-ordination compatible with the structure we have elaborated for the sentence?

(1)   Mr Duncan Smith stepped out of central office into the autumn sunshine to declare angrily that he both welcomed the contest <u>and</u> would win it. (*Guardian*, 29.10.2003, p. 17, col. 1)

COMMENT

In this example the sequence *both . . . and* co-ordinates the units (i) [*welcomed the contest*] and (ii) [*would win it*]. In terms of our analysis these units can be taken to correspond to the constituent labeled I'. Observe, though, that co-ordination in

---

[1]   We already introduced these examples in Chapter 2, Exercise 6. Since we have made some progress in our discussion, it is a good idea to try to refine the answer you might have given when doing the exercise earlier on.

these examples affects only a partial projection, since the full projection would comprise the IP layer, that is, it would include the subject.

Exercise 3   Adjuncts, interpretation, and word order (T)

In this exercise we speculate about the application of adjunction. The exercise is longer and more discursive than some of the other exercises. The goal of the exercise is to further explore the consequences of the argumentation elaborated in the chapter and see where that would lead us.

Identify all the VP-adjuncts in the following examples. Represent adjunction by means of labeled bracketing.

(1)   The student will examine the text very carefully.

(2)   The students will very carefully examine the text.

(3)   One of the most controversial takeovers in British sporting history was last night awaiting a government decision. (Based on *Guardian*, 13.3.1999, p. 1, col. 1)

(4)   It is two-faced of the mayor to one day attack the private sector and the next day outbid them. (*Guardian*, 9.12.2000, p. 5, col. 7)

(5)   The new rule does not end judicial discretion but it <u>rightly seriously</u> curtails it. (based on *Guardian*, 27.3.2001, p. 9, col. 2)

You should end up with the following representations.

(1')   The student will [$_{VP}$ [$_{VP}$ examine the text] [$_{ADVP}$ very carefully]].

(2')   The student will [$_{VP}$ [$_{ADVP}$ very carefully] [$_{VP}$ examine the text]].

(3')   One of the most controversial takeovers in British sporting history was [$_{VP}$ [$_{NP}$ last night] [$_{VP}$ awaiting a government decision]].

(4')   It is two faced of the mayor to [$_{VP}$ [$_{NP}$ one day] [$_{VP}$ attack the private sector]] and [$_{VP}$ [$_{NP}$ the next day] [$_{VP}$ outbid them]].

(5')   The new rule does not end judicial discretion but it [$_{VP}$ [$_{ADVP}$ <u>rightly</u>] [$_{VP}$ [$_{ADVP}$ <u>seriously</u>] [$_{VP}$ curtails it]]].

Example (5') has two adverb phrases in mid position, *rightly* and *seriously*; we can replace each of the one-word adverbs by more elaborate constituents.

(6)   The new rule does not end judicial discretion but it [_{VP} quite rightly [_{VP} rather seriously [_{VP} curtails it]]].

The fact that we can replace adverbs that function as adjuncts on their own by a phrase of which these adverbs are the heads (*quite rightly, rather seriously*) confirms the proposal in section 2.1 that "adjunction is the merger of one fully formed constituent with another fully formed constituent": in general constituents adjoined to maximal projections are themselves maximal projections.

(i)   **Working hypothesis**
      Adjuncts to projections are themselves projections.

Could the adverbial adjuncts in (5) appear in a different order?

(7)   ??The new rule does not end judicial discretion but it [_{VP} seriously [_{VP} rightly [_{VP} curtails it]]]. (Based on *Guardian*, 27.3.2001, p. 9, col. 2)

Though (7) is perhaps not completely unacceptable, it is hard to give it an adequate reading. (5) can be paraphrased by (8):

(8)   It is right that the ruling seriously curtails it.

No such obvious paraphrase can be worked out for (7). The reordering of the adverbials has led to a serious degradation.
   The left to right **ordering restrictions** of the adjuncts seems to reflect the semantic contributions of the adjuncts. We paraphrase (5) as in (8), where the adjective phrase *right* modifies the seriousness of the degree of curtailment.
   For the interpretation of the structure in (5), the meaning of *seriously* is first added to the interpretation of the core VP *curtail it* to give the meaning of the augmented VP *seriously curtail it*. Then the resulting unit of meaning is further modified by *rightly*. Below are two representations for a VP with two adjuncts. In (9a) the adjuncts are both attached to one node; in (9b) they are stacked, with the lower adjunct_Y having a closer relation to VP than the higher adjunct_X. Which one of these structures would be preferable and why? When answering the question try to determine whether your answer addresses the theory as such or the empirical data that it purports to capture.

(9) a   b

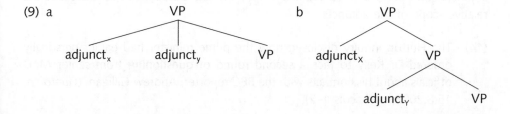

(9b) is preferable since it respects the binary branching hypothesis. Furthermore the build-up of the structure matches its interpretation in that (9b) suggests that a higher adjunct (to the left) is added to and modifies the constituent formed by the VP and the lower adjunct. We say that the higher adjunct$_x$ **takes scope** over the lower adjunct$_y$. Observe that in (9b) there is only a single VP, headed by the same verb. The VP consists of a core VP augmented by means of adjuncts. (Think of one house being extended by a veranda, a garage, a terrace, etc.)

Experiment: Could constituency tests be used to support representation (9b)? Try to front the VP containing just one adjunct. Also try to pseudo-cleft the VP with just one adjunct. You will create examples such as (10) and (11).

(10)   The new rule does not end judicial discretion but [$_{VP}$ seriously [$_{VP}$ curtail it]], it [$_{VP}$ rightly] does.

(11)   What it rightly does do is seriously curtail it.

Let us experiment with the data. Try inserting the adjunct *probably* in (1) and in (2) in a position between the modal auxiliary and the verb. Could *probably* be inserted to the right of *very carefully* in (2)?

(12) a   The student will probably examine the text very carefully.
     b   The student will probably very carefully examine the text.
     c   *The student will very carefully probably examine the text.

How would you represent the structure of (12a)?

As shown by (12b), the natural position for *probably* is to the left of *very carefully*. Draw a representation for (12b) modeled on the preceding discussion and using (9b) as your model. Do the following constructed sentences bear on the structure?

(13) a   Speaker A: The student will probably very carefully examine the text.
             Speaker B: He will indeed.
                          Will he really?
                          No he won't!
     b   What the student will probably do is very carefully examine the text.
     c   *What the student will very carefully do is probably examine the text.

Consider the examples below. Does the left-right sequencing of the underlined adjuncts correspond to their relative scope? Provide paraphrases to bring out the relative scope of the adjuncts.

(14)   The Hutton inquiry disclosed how the prime minister had earlier personally ordered Dr Kelly to face a second round of questioning from senior MoD officials about his contacts with the BBC reporter, Andrew Gilligan. (*Guardian*, 15.8.2003, p. 1, cols 1–2)

(15) Since the extended saga of the England captain's move from Manchester to Madrid bridged the seasons, it could be said that football <u>never really</u> went away. (*Guardian*, 9.8.2003, p. 19, col. 1)

(16) In Britain plant-based remedies have been largely ignored, especially since 1945 and the introduction of the NHS, which has <u>traditionally actively</u> discouraged herbal remedies. (*Guardian*, G2, 2.9.2003, p. 9, col. 2)

(17) The judges on the state's highest court <u>yesterday closely</u> questioned both sides over the constitutionality and legality of a recount. (*Guardian*, 8.12.2000, p. 2, col. 3)

(18) A study published last December found that only one of the top 10 medical schools in the US has clear regulations forbidding researchers from having a financial involvement in the companies they are <u>supposedly impartially</u> testing. (*Guardian*, 3.5.2001, p. 8, col. 6)

Recall that in the discussion of the structure of the VP,[2] we introduced two layers, which we kept relatively distinct. There was the core VP with the verb and its complement (for instance, the direct object) and then there was the augmented VP which introduced additional information, the adjuncts. This layering was meant to reflect the interpretative relation of the constituents to the verb: complements have a closer relation to the verb than adjuncts. For one thing, complements receive a thematic role. The hierarchical relation of adjoined adjuncts also reflects their semantic relation to the sentence: inner adjuncts are more closely connected to V than outer adjuncts. The analysis is in line with the hypothesis that syntactic structure maps into meaning.

Recall also from section 3.3 of the current chapter that this mapping hypothesis leads to a problem with respect to how we treat the subject since the subject has a closer semantic relation to V than, say, adjuncts. We turn to this in Chapter 4.

Exercise 4   Modals and *to* (T)

Consider the following examples in the light of the assumption that modal auxiliaries have the same distribution as the infinitival marker *to*.

(1) a Do you think John will object to your proposal?
    b I don't expect him to.

(2) a I expected that Mary would have understood the situation by now.
    b I expected Mary to have understood the situation by now.

---

2   Chapter 2, section 2.3.

(3) a   I will not give in to such pressure.
      b   To not give in to such pressure will be hard.

(4) a   *I not will give in to such pressure.
      b   Not to give in to such pressure will be hard.

Exercise 5   Sentential negation (E)

English sentences can be negated in a number of different ways. Identify the constituent that negates the sentence in the examples below:

(1)   I have not actually seen anyone at that shop.

(2)   I saw no one at that shop.

(3)   I have never actually seen anyone at that shop.

(4)   No English students attended the party.

Among the means of expressing negation we find two elements in mid position: *not* (1) and *never* (3). In the discussion we proposed that *not* is like an adverb and is adjoined to a maximal projection. This means that we should probably propose a similar analysis for *never*. Discuss the problems raised by the following examples for equating the status of *not* and *never*:

(5) a   He never liked this book.
      b   *He not liked this book.
      c   He didn't like this book.

(6) a   Never have I seen such horrible behavior.
      b   *Not have I seen such horrible behavior.

(7) a   I never will accept those conditions.
      b   *I not will accept those conditions.
      c   He asked me to accept those conditions but I never will.
      d   *He asked me to accept those conditions but I not will.
      e   *He asked me to accept those conditions but I would never.
      f   He asked me to accept those conditions but I wouldn't.

(8) a   Do you talk to him? Never.
      b   Do you talk to him? *Not.

COMMENTS

The data suggest that *not* and *never* should be differentiated. Consider the examples in (5). In the chapter we proposed that the finite inflection lowers onto the lexical verb in English. We also saw that this lowering is blocked by an intervening *not*.[3] Does the adjunct *never* also block the lowering of the inflection onto V? We must conclude that the syntactic properties of *not* and of *never* as the expressions of sentential negation are different. In particular, *not* is special in that it blocks the lowering of the inflection onto V.[4]

Exercise 6   Comparing languages (T, E)

In Table 1 we give the paradigms for the verb *hear* in Danish and in Icelandic (Vikner, 1997). Based on these paradigms and on the conditions we have elaborated for the movement of the finite verb to I, which of the sentences in (1) for Danish and in (2) for Icelandic would you predict to be grammatical?

(1) a   Da   at Johan ofte <u>spiser</u> tomater.
             that John often eats tomatoes
             'that John often eats tomatoes.'

    b   Da   at Johan <u>spiser</u> ofte tomater.

Table 1   Inflectional patterns in Danish and in Icelandic

	Danish		Icelandic	
	Present	**Past**	**Present**	**Past**
1sg	*hører*	*hørte*	*heyri*	*heyrði*
2sg	*hører*	*hørte*	*heyrir*	*heyrðir*
3sg	*hører*	*hørte*	*heyrir*	*heyrði*
1pl	*hører*	*hørte*	*heyrum*	*heyrðum*
2pl	*hører*	*hørte*	*heyrið*	*heyrðuð*
3pl	*hører*	*hørte*	*heyra*	*heyrðu*

---

[3]   Section 1.2.4.4.
[4]   For discussion of the status of *not* see also Klima (1964), Pollock (1989), Baker (1991), Ernst (1992), Haegeman (1995). For an accessible introduction see Haegeman and Guéron (1999).

(2) a Ic að Jón oft   <u>borðar</u> tómata.
          that Jón often eats   tomatoes
          'that John often eats tomatoes.'

   b Ic að Jón <u>borðar</u> oft tómata.

COMMENTS

Danish finite verbs are invariant, both in the present tense and in the past tense. The inflection is weak and the prediction is that the lexical verb ought not to move to I. (1a) ought to be grammatical and (1b) ought to be ungrammatical. These predictions are correct.

   In Icelandic the finite paradigms display a number of different forms, both in the present tense and in the past tense. So the inflection is strong and the prediction is that the lexical verb ought to move to I. (2a) ought to be ungrammatical and (2b) ought to be grammatical. These predictions are also correct.[5]

   For more detailed and sophisticated discussion of these data see Vikner (1997) and the references cited. Vikner provides a careful analysis of precisely what kinds of verb inflections are needed to trigger verb movement and he compares an array of Scandinavian languages. He also offers a good survey of the relevant literature.[6]

Exercise 7 Comparing languages (T, E)

We have observed that English grammar has undergone a change through its history. In Old English, paradigms of verb conjugation displayed a number of different forms and the lexical verb was mobile. For instance, the inflectional system was stronger in earlier stages of the language[7] and this allowed the lexical verb to invert with the subject. With the loss of its distinct inflectional endings, the English lexical verb has become less mobile.

   We might predict an analogous development for languages which today still have strong inflections if, for some reason, their inflections were to be eroded through time. Haitian Creole is a language whose lexicon is strongly based on French but whose word order is quite different from French, as illustrated in (1)–(4). The inflectional system is given in (5)–(6). Can we account for the difference in the positions of the finite verb in the Creole examples in (1)–(4) and their French counterparts in (7)–(10)?

(1) a Bouki deja   <u>pase</u> rad yo.
          Bouki already irons laundry their
          'Bouki has already ironed their laundry.'

   b *Bouki <u>pase</u> deja rad yo.

---

[5]   Exercise 16 is also concerned with the distribution of the verb in Icelandic.
[6]   For additional discussion of Germanic languages see also Rohrbacher (1999). For a critical view see Bobaljik (2002), Alexiadou and Anagnostopoulou (1998).
[7]   Cf. Chapter 1, section 3.2, and Chapter 3, section 1.2.4.

(2) a Mwen toujou <u>ekri</u>   manman mwen.
       I   always write mother my
       'I always write to my mother.'

    b *Mwen <u>ekri</u> toujou manman mwen.

(3) a Elèv la   byen <u>etidye</u> leson an.
       student the well study lesson the
       'The student has studied the lesson well.'

    b *Elèv la <u>etidye</u> byen/mal leson an.

(4) a Jak pa janm <u>di</u> bonjou.
       Jack NEG never says hello
       'Jack never says hello.'

    b *Jak <u>di</u> pa janm bonjou.

(5)   mwen /ou /li   /nou   /yo renmen Boukinèt
      I   /you /he/she /we/you /they 'love' Bouquinette

(6) a Boukinèt ta renmen Bouki (PAST)
    b Boukinèt ap renmen Bouki (FUTURE)

(7) a *Jeanne déjà   <u>repasse</u> le linge.
       Jeanne   already irons the laundry

    b Jeanne <u>repasse</u> déjà le linge.
       'Jeanne is already ironing the laundry.'

(8) a *Je toujours <u>écris</u> à maman.
       I always   write to mummy

    b J'<u>écris</u> toujours à maman.
       'I always write to mummy.'

(9) a *L'élève bien <u>étudie</u> la leçon.
       the pupil well studies the lesson

    b L'élève   <u>étudie</u> bien la leçon.
       'The pupil studies the lesson well.'

(10) a *Jacques ne jamais <u>dit</u>   bonjour.
        Jacques NEG never   says hello

     b Jacques ne <u>dit</u> jamais bonjour.
        'Jack never says hello.'

COMMENTS

When we consider the inflectional paradigm in (5) we see that there is no variation for person and number in Haitian Creole. Nor does the language have a distinct ending for past or for future, as shown by (6). Given an invariant verb form we deduce that the inflection is weak and hence we correctly predict the lexical verb to remain in V and to follow adjuncts. In French the finite inflection is strong and hence we expect the verb to move to I and to precede adjuncts. For more discussion of the syntax of the Haitian Creole verb see DeGraff (1997), which also contains a range of references. For an overview of the problems of Creole languages see also the discussion in DeGraff (1999) and the references cited there.

Exercise 8   Moved constituents (T, L)

We have elaborated a blueprint for the structure of the sentence in which we use two operations for assembling a sentence. These operations, discussed in section 2 of this chapter, are **Merge** and **Move**. So far we have concentrated mainly on the operation Merge, and we have only invoked the concept Move to account for the displacement of the verb. Consider the examples below. What is the category of the underlined constituents? Do you think these constituents occupy their base positions? If not, try to restore them to their base positions.

(1)   Our fishmonger and his staff in Petersfield all wear ties (Letters, October 22) and <u>very smart</u> they look too. (*Guardian*, 23.10.2002, p. 9, col. 5, letters to the editor from David Dew, Horndean, Hants)

(2)   <u>Everything I did right for 20 years</u>, he burned up in two or three. (*Washington Post*, 29.4.2003, p. C1, col. 1)

(3)   The payback burden varies according to earnings later in life, to about £60 a month, for example, for a civil servant, lower than that for a voluntary sector worker. <u>The paybacks</u> I don't think are unreasonable. (*Guardian*, 20.1.2003, p. 3, col. 3)

(4)   People retain a mystic faith in old exam results or in the snap judgements of school reports, dogged by lazy character assassinations for the rest of their days. That is why education should always try to praise a child's talents, not brand it with failure. <u>These things</u> she knew well, and it made her a humane politician and a good education minister. (*Guardian*, 25.10.2002, p. 7, col. 2)

(5)   There are hardly any small movies that people go to, and <u>some of the more interesting ones</u> they won't go to. (*Guardian*, Review, 1.11.2002, p. v, col. 4)

Examine the underlined sentence-initial constituents in the following examples. What is their base position? Why do you think that they are displaced?

(6) <u>How</u> can we stop this? (*Chicago Tribune*, 3.1.2004, S1, p. 33, col. 6)

(7) <u>What kind of delusional rock</u> is Smith living under? (*Chicago Tribune*, 3.1.2004, S3, p. 2, col. 6)

(8) I don't know <u>whom</u> I will be voting for then, but it won't be Bush. (*Chicago Tribune*, 3.1.2004, S1, p. 27, col. 3, letter to the editor)

(9) <u>How good</u> will he become? (*Chicago Tribune*, 3.1.2004, S3, p. 10, col. 5)

(10) <u>What</u> are they afraid of? (*New York Times*, 8.3.2004, p. C6, col. 5)

What examples (6)–(10) have in common is that the underlined constituent originates in a position to the right and has been fronted to a peripheral position in the sentence. The common factor shared by all these fronted elements is that the constituent is interrogative and encodes the scope of the question.

(6′) <u>How</u> can we stop this ——?

(7′) <u>What kind of delusional rock</u> is Smith living under ——?

(8′) I don't know <u>whom</u> I will be voting for —— then.

(9′) <u>How good</u> will he become ——?

(10′) <u>What</u> are they afraid of ——?

In (11)–(15) the underlined constituent has also been displaced. What is the motivation for the movement? Locate the base position of the moved constituent. Consider the distance between the moved constituent and its base position.

(11) <u>Who</u> do you think is the more moderate politician? (*Guardian*, 25.9.2003, p. 9, col. 6)

(12) <u>What</u> did they think they were making with those girls in there? Animated cartoons? (*Guardian*, 13.9.2003, p. 14, col. 2)

(13) At the end of the day everybody eats meat. <u>What</u> do you think your cat or dog eats? <u>Where</u> do you think that meat comes from? <u>Where</u> do you think Pedigree Chum comes from? (*Observer Magazine*, 7.9.2003, p. 41, col. 1)

(14)   What has the Chancellor been doing and <u>where</u> does he think the party is going? (*Guardian*, 27.9.2003, p. 4, headline)

(15)   Some are born great, some achieve greatness and some have greatness thrust upon them . . . <u>Which</u> do you think you were? (*Guardian*, G2, 27.10.2003, p. 6, col. 2)

COMMENT

In (11)–(15) again, the underlined interrogative constituent has been fronted to a peripheral position in the sentence. What distinguishes these examples from the earlier ones is that in (11)–(15) the fronted interrogative constituent has been lifted out of the clause in which it originates. We signal the clause from which the constituent has been extracted by square brackets in the simplified representations below. When a movement operation lifts a constituent out of a clause and into a higher clause we often talk about **long** movement. Examples (6)–(10) illustrate **short** movement.

(11′)   <u>Who</u> do you think [$_{IP}$ —— is the more moderate politician]?

(12′)   <u>What</u> did they think [$_{IP}$ they were making —— with those girls in there]?

(13′)   <u>What</u> do you think [$_{IP}$ your cat or dog eats ——]?
        <u>Where</u> do you think [$_{IP}$ that meat comes from ——]?
        <u>Where</u> do you think [$_{IP}$ Pedigree Chum comes from ——]?

(14′)   <u>Where</u> does he think [$_{IP}$ the party is going ——]?

(15′)   <u>Which</u> do you think [$_{IP}$ you were ——]?

Return to the examples (1)–(5). Identify the example in which the fronted constituent has undergone long movement.[8]

Exercise 9   Thematic roles: The expression of AGENT (T)

In (49) in section 3.1, we defined the thematic role AGENT as follows:

(1)   AGENT/ACTOR: the one who intentionally initiates the action.

---

[8]   The derivation of examples such as (6)–(15) will be discussed in Chapter 5, section 3.1.

Consider the generalizations (i) and (ii):

(i) The AGENT thematic role is always realized overtly, and it must be expressed by the subject of a sentence.
(ii) The subject of a sentence always realizes the AGENT thematic role.

On the basis of the three examples below discuss the validity of generalizations (i) and (ii).

(1) The news was <u>announced</u> by the director of the company.

(2) The thief was <u>arrested</u> later that night.

(3) John's analysis of the data surprised everyone.

COMMENT

(1) and (2) illustrate what are called **passive** sentences. The underlined verbs are the **passive** forms of the verbs; they are associated with the passive morpheme *-ed*. Typically a situation involving two participants can be presented either by means of an active sentence or by means of a passive one. Discuss how the thematic roles of the verb *announce* are realized in (1a). What about (1b)?

(1) a The director of the company announced the news.
    b The news was announced by the director of the company.

It appears that the passive morphology of the verb *announced* triggers a rearrangement in the arguments of the verb. Starting from the active verb, we build up the sentences in the way described in this chapter. Notably the AGENT of the action expressed by the active verb is realized by the subject NP, *the director of the company*, and as such it becomes the anchoring point for the information given in the sentence. (1a) gives information about the entity 'the director of the company'. In the passive version of the sentence, (1b), the AGENT of the activity is not expressed as a subject, rather it is made explicit by means of a PP introduced by the preposition *by*. The NP that denotes the entity affected by the activity, the THEME, now occupies the canonical subject position and has become the anchor of the information given in the sentence. (1b) is about the entity 'the news'.

(2) is also a passive sentence. Is the AGENT expressed? Can it be inferred? We conclude that in passive sentences the *by*-phrase expressing the AGENT need not be present. However, even when not overtly expressed, the AGENT of *arrest* can be inferred. For more discussion of such inferred AGENTS see Exercise 11.

In (3) the verb *surprise* does not take an AGENT argument: the full NP *John's analysis of the data* does not denote 'the one who intentionally initiates the action'. The subject denotes an event, events do not have intentions, so events cannot 'intentionally initiate the action'. The subject NP *John's analysis of the data* expresses a CAUSE. In the passive counterpart of (3) the CAUSE will also be expressed in a *by*-phrase:[9]

(4)   Everyone was surprised by John's analysis of the data.

Now let us turn to the NP *John's analysis of the data*. This NP contains as its head the noun *analysis*. In terms of its form, this noun is related to the verb *analyze*. A noun whose form is related to a verb is called a **deverbal** noun.[10] The verb *analyze* is associated with two thematic roles: the AGENT, the person doing the analysis, and the THEME, the entity that is being analyzed.

(5)   a   John analyzed the data.
      b   *analyze* thematic role 1: *John*
                   thematic role 2: *the data*

The thematic roles of the verb *analyze* are retained in the deverbal noun *analysis*. Turning to the NP *John's analysis of the data* we see that the AGENT of *analysis* is realized by the prenominal genitive NP *John's* and its THEME is realized by the NP *the data*, contained in a PP *of the data*.[11]

(6)   a   John's analysis of the data
      b   *analysis* thematic role 1: *John's*
                    thematic role 2: *(of) the data*

Exercise 10   Thematic roles: The expression of AGENT (T, E)

In (49), in section 3.1, we defined the thematic role AGENT as follows:

(1)   AGENT/ACTOR: the one who intentionally initiates the action.

Comment on the realization of the AGENT role associated with the underlined verbs in the following examples.

(2)   Dawson was <u>invited</u> by Sven-Goran Eriksson to the England get-together in November. (*Guardian*, 7.1.2003, p. 14, col. 2)

---

[9]   For the realization of arguments of such psychological verbs see also Belletti and Rizzi (1988). Though based on Italian data the conclusions of this paper are relevant for English.
[10] For some discussion of the formation of deverbal nouns see Chapter 2, Exercise 17.
[11] For a thorough discussion of the thematic structure of deverbal nouns see, among others, Williams (1981), Grimshaw (1990), Alexiadou (2001).

(3) The center is at a public facility, Huilongguan Hospital, and is being <u>funded</u> quite willingly by Beijing's city government. (*San Francisco Chronicle*, 28.11.2002, p. F6, col. 1)

(4) The *Which?* Web Trader scheme, which has been running since July 1999, is being <u>closed down</u> by the Consumers' Association because it is too expensive to maintain. (*Guardian*, 7.1.2003, p. 12, col. 5)

(5) A spokesman for Mr Bing said the money would be <u>paid</u> into a trust. (*Guardian*, 18.12.2002, p. 3, col. 4)

(6) The culture committee's motion was <u>drafted</u> by members of prime minister Silvio Berlusconi's Forza Italia party. (*Guardian*, 18.12.2002, p. 6, col. 3)

COMMENT

(2)–(6) illustrate what are called **passive** sentences. The underlined verbs are the **passive** forms of the verbs; they are associated with the passive morpheme -*ed*. Typically, a situation involving two participants can be presented either by means of an active sentence or by means of a passive one: (7) would be another illustration:

(7) a The director of the company announced the news.
    b The news was announced by the director of the company.

As we discussed in Exercise 9, the passive morphology of the verb gives rise to a rearrangement in the arguments of the verb. In an active sentence, the AGENT of the action denoted by the verb is realized by the subject NP, *the director of the company* in (7a), and it is the anchoring point for the information given in the sentence. (7a) gives information about the entity 'the director of the company'. In the passive version, (7b), the AGENT of the activity is not realized as a subject; rather it is made explicit by means of a PP introduced by the preposition *by*. The NP that denotes the entity affected by the activity, the THEME, now occupies the subject position and is the anchor of the information given in the sentence.

Consider the underlined passive verb in (8). Who is the AGENT? Is the AGENT expressed in the example?

(8) A student was <u>arrested</u> on suspicion of murdering special branch officer Stephen Oake in Manchester. (*Guardian*, 16.1.2003, p. 1, col. 4)

As already mentioned with respect to example (2) in Exercise 9, a passive verb does not require the presence of a *by* phrase. We propose that in the passive sentence, the *by* phrase, though it realizes a thematic role, is an adjunct. In (8) the *by* phrase is not realized because we can infer from the choice of verb, *arrest*, that the AGENT was the police.

Consider the underlined passive verbs in the following sentences. Is the AGENT of the action denoted by these verbs overtly expressed? Which component of the sentence do the bold faced parts of the sentence modify?

(9)   She was **deliberately** <u>killed</u>. (*Guardian*, 16.9.2003, p. 8, col. 7)

(10)   There is some technical study till mid-morning teabreak, then lunch at 1 p.m., which is <u>cooked</u> **together** but bought from a kitty to which all the men contribute. (*Guardian*, 7.9.2002, p. 7, col. 7)

(11)   The victims were <u>shot</u> **using a high powered rifle**. (*Guardian*, 10.10.2002, p. 2, col. 5)

(12)   **Using plastic gloves from the Harrods food hall**, the contents were then <u>inspected</u> and <u>shown</u> to Mr Fayed. (*Guardian*, 14.8.2002, p. 5, col. 7)

(13)   Mr. Mansfield said Blakely's behaviour was **intentionally** <u>directed</u> at Ellis, and given the history of the relationship it amounted to provocation. (*Guardian*, 17.9.2003, p. 6, col. 4)

Sentences (9)–(13) suggest that even when the AGENT of a passive verb is not expressed by a *by*-phrase, it still remains accessible for modifiers. In (9), for instance, the adverb *deliberately* modifies the attitude of the AGENT of *kill*, even though that AGENT is not overtly expressed. Similarly, in (10) the intended interpretation is that a number of people cook lunch together. Again *together* bears on the understood AGENT of *cook*. In (11) *using a high powered rifle* is a non-finite string which lacks an overt subject. The verb *using* is the present participle. *Using a high powered rifle* is a non-finite clause, in particular it is a participial clause. The subject of *using* is implicit. We interpret its subject as being identical to the implied AGENT of *shot*: those who shot the victims were using a high powered rifle.

We conclude that the understood AGENT in a passive sentence remains accessible to modification.

Exercise 11   Thematic roles: The implied AGENT (T, E, presupposes Exercise 10)

In Exercise 10, we discovered that even when implicit, the AGENT of an activity might be accessible for syntactic processes such as modification by an adverbial or by a participial clause. However, care must be taken when we state that an implicit element is syntactically accessible. In particular, not every element that we can infer from the meaning of a sentence is "accessible." Compare the expression of the AGENT role in the following examples.

(1) a We finally opened the door with the headmaster's key.

   b The door was finally opened by the junior staff member.

   c The headmaster's key finally opened the door.

In (1a) and in (1b) the AGENT of *open* is overtly expressed. In (1a) it is the subject of the sentence, *we*; in (1b) the AGENT is expressed by means of an adjunct *by* phrase; in (1c) the subject, *the headmaster's key*, realizes the INSTRUMENT role. From the fact that an INSTRUMENT is referred to we infer that an AGENT must be involved in the action. The AGENT is the one who uses the instrument. So we can say that in (1c) an AGENT can be inferred.

These data might lead us to expect that in the same way that the understood AGENT is accessible for modification in a passive sentence, the inferred AGENT in (1c), which contains a reference to an instrument, will be accessible for modification. Comment on this expectation using the following data.[12]

(2) a Expecting the worst, we finally opened the door with the headmaster's key.

   b Expecting the worst, the door was finally opened by the junior staff member.

   c *Expecting the worst, the headmaster's key finally opened the door.

COMMENT

There is a difference between the way an AGENT may be implicit in a passive sentence, in which it remains accessible for purposes of modification (1b), and the way the existence of an AGENT is inferred in a sentence such as (1c), in which the subject realizes an INSTRUMENT. Even under the assumption, which is possible though not necessary, that the headmaster is the AGENT in (1c), (1c) becomes unacceptable when we insert an adjunct modifying the AGENT (2c). Passivization has a way of preserving the AGENT in the sentence.[13]

Exercise 12   *Be* + passive VP (T)

Identify the constituents that are co-ordinated by the underlined conjunction *and* in the examples below.

(1) The scheme will start in London <u>and</u> be extended later to other parts of England. (*Guardian*, 3.10.2002, p. 3, col. 2)

(2) Mitrokhin has been interviewed on television <u>and</u> co-written a book with Professor Christopher Andrew. (*Observer*, Review, 16.9.2001, p. 15, col. 3)

(3) It is understood that one individual who sent an email containing footballers' names has been warned he could face a libel action <u>and</u> been asked to hand

---

[12] See also Reinhart (2000) for discussion of the relation between INSTRUMENT and AGENT.

[13] For a discussion of passivization see among others Baker, Johnson, and Roberts (1989).

over the names of the people he sent the message to. (*Guardian*, 2.10.2003, p. 3, col. 2)

KEY AND COMMENTS

The conjoined constituents are all VPs:

(1′) [$_{VP}$ start in London]
        + [$_{VP}$ be extended later to other parts of England]

(2′) [$_{VP}$ been interviewed on television]
        + [$_{VP}$ co-written a book with Professor Christopher Andrew]

(3′) [$_{VP}$ been warned he could face a libel action]
        + [$_{VP}$ been asked to hand over the names of the people he sent the message to]

Two of the VPs are simply projections of a lexical verb:

(4) a [$_{VP}$ start in London]
     b [$_{VP}$ co-written a book with Professor Christopher Andrew]

The other VPs contain the auxiliary *be* and a passive verb form.

(5) a [$_{VP}$ be extended later to other parts of England]
     b [$_{VP}$ been interviewed on television]
     c [$_{VP}$ been warned he could face a libel action]
     d [$_{VP}$ been asked to hand over the names of the people he sent the message to]

Following the discussion in the chapter, we assume that an auxiliary is a verb and heads its own VP. In (5) the auxiliary *be* selects a passivized VP, with which it forms a constituent:

(6)   VP

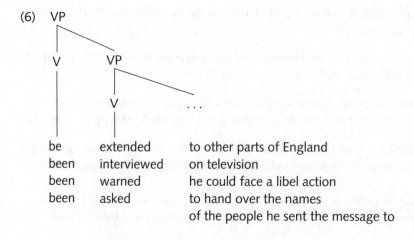

be	extended	to other parts of England
been	interviewed	on television
been	warned	he could face a libel action
been	asked	to hand over the names
		of the people he sent the message to

Discuss how VP ellipsis in the following extract provides further evidence for the hypothesis that passive *be* forms a constituent together with the lexical VP headed by the passive participle:

(7)   More than in any recent presidential election, the critical economic issue this year boils down to whether middle-income people think they are being squeezed. President Bush passionately argues they are not. (Adapted from *New York Times*, 1.8.2004, section 3, col. 2)

Exercise 13   Lexical heads and functional structure (E)

The merger operation that assembles the clause starts from a lexical element, a verb. A lexical head V projects a structure, VP, which is selected by a functional head. Merger of VP and I integrates the VP projection into a functional projection, IP. It would be interesting to examine if this pattern of a functional projection dominating a lexical projection is general. Do projections of other lexical elements also require a dominating functional projection? The noun is a case in point. The noun *analysis* in (1a) is the head of an NP. In (1b) we provide the type of structure proposed for the NP. Does the lexical projection NP merge with a functional structure? Try to rephrase the NP in (1a) by means of a sentence. To which sentential constituent would the genitive NP *the student's* correspond? And, in a sentence, which constituent would match the PP *of the problem*?

(1) a   the student's analysis of the problem
    b   NP

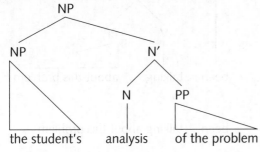

(1a) is closely similar in composition to the sentence (2a), whose structure is given in (2b):

(2) a   The student has analyzed the problem.
    b   [IP The student [I' [I has] [VP analyzed the problem]]].

We might try to generalize the hypothesis that a lexical projection is inserted as the complement of a functional head and also merge the NP with a functional head.

We could propose something along the lines of (1c), for instance, in which we associate the genitive marking with a functional head, which we label F. Draw the tree diagram that would correspond to (1c).

(1) c   [$_{FP}$ the student [$_{F'}$ [$_F$'s] [$_{NP}$ analysis of the problem]]]

Based on the discussion of the structure of the NP in the chapter, list the constituents that were shown to alternate with the genitive in (1a). Are these constituents all phrasal constituents?[14]

Exercise 14   Non-finite inflections (E)

Consider representation (69b) from the chapter, repeated here as (1):

(1)

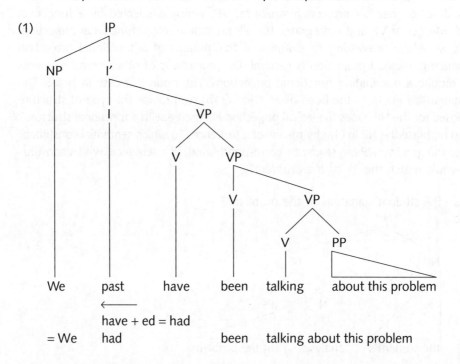

One point that emerges from the discussion in the chapter is that the finite inflection of the verb should be represented separately from V, and that this separation

---

[14]   The hypothesis that NPs must also be associated with functional structure was elaborated by Abney (1987). For introductory discussion of the structural build-up of the nominal projection see Haegeman and Guéron (1999) and Bernstein (2001). For more advanced discussion see, among others, Szabolcsi (1994), Giorgi and Longobardi (1991), Gavruseva (2000), and the references cited there.

applies both to lexical verbs and to auxiliaries. In sections 4.3. and 4.4 we made the point that if we represented inflectional endings separately for lexical verbs and if we failed to do so for inflections of auxiliaries, we would have to provide an account for this different treatment. The simpler theory is one in which all finite inflections are represented as separate. The one exception we did allow for is modal auxiliaries as these are inherently tensed and they lack non-finite forms.

However, careful readers will have detected another inconsistency. If finite inflections are to be represented separately from the associated verb stem, should the same not apply to non-finite inflections? Should we not treat all verbal inflections as separate from the stems they are associated with? What would the consequences be for the structure in (1)?[15]

Exercise 15   The structure of sentences: Extending the data (E)

Discuss the problems raised for the representation of sentence structure elaborated so far by the position of the underlined elements in the following examples:[16]

(1)   Michigan coach Lloyd Carr says sorry, but he <u>simply</u> can't go against the coaching association's policy and vote for Southern California as college football's No 1 team. (*Chicago Tribune*, 3.1.2004, S3, p. 1, col. 1)[17]

(2)   Jarvis <u>today</u> will wipe away some of the immediate gloom surrounding the support services group by announcing a £300 million contract to build 3,000 rooms for the University of Lancaster. (*Guardian*, 17.10.2003, p. 13, col. 1)

(3)   <u>A year ago</u>, these streets <u>at 4 a.m. of a Friday night</u> were raucous and reeling with drunks. (Based on *Atlanta Journal-Constitution*, 23.11.2003, p. F1, col. 5)[18]

(4)   I <u>never</u> could make out what those damned dots meant. (*Independent*, 14.4.2001, p. 20, col. 6)[19]

(5)   I expect house prices <u>over the year</u> to rise by 4 per cent. (*Times*, *Times 2*, 27.12.2000, p. 7, col. 1)

---

[15]   For some discussion see Belletti (1990) and Friedemann and Siloni (1993).
[16]   For some discussion see Pollock (1997). We return to some of the examples in Exercise 22 of Chapter 4.
[17]   Cf. Chapter 4, Exercise 22 (7).
[18]   For the position of *a year ago* see also Chapter 2, Exercise 15.
[19]   Cf. Chapter 4, Exercise 22 (8).

(6)   American officials <u>also</u> have cited a possible business dispute as a reason for
      the disappearance of the Angola jet. (*Chicago Tribune*, 3.1.2004, section 1,
      p. 6, cols 1–2)

(7)   We expect actors <u>in real life </u>to be like the characters they play, and of
      course, they're not. (Adapted from *Sunday Times*, News Review, 25.1.2001,
      p. 3, col. 6)

(8)   Today Gulliver <u>still</u> can barely stand to be among the Yahoos. (*Guardian*, G2,
      31.8.2004, p. 12, col. 1)[20]

(9)   The AP trophy <u>probably</u> will be presented to USC in Los Angeles, not New
      Orleans. (*Chicago Tribune*, 3.1.2004, S3, p. 2, col. 3)

(10) Parents and students <u>probably</u> wouldn't do that. (*New York Times, Educa-
      tion*, 1.8.2004, p. 16, col. 2)

Exercise 16   Object shift and verb movement in
Icelandic (E)

Consider the Icelandic example (1a). How could we explain the position of the verb
to the left of the negation marker *ekki* ('not')?

(1) a Jón las ekki bækurnar.
       John read not books
       'John didn't read the books.' (Collins and Thráinsson, 1993: 132, their (2b))

Draw a tree diagram for the sentence. Discuss how (1b) differs from (1a).

(1) b Jón las bækurnar ekki.
       John read books not
       'John didn't read the books.' (Collins and Thráinsson, 1993: 132, their (2a))

KEY AND COMMENTS

In (1a) the lexical verb *las* ('read') precedes the negation marker *ekki*. We saw
in Exercise 6 that Icelandic verbs have a strong inflection. We can assume that
the verb has moved out of the VP to I. In (2a) we use an arrow to show verb
movement.

---

[20]   Cf. Chapter 4, Exercise 22 (9).

(2) a

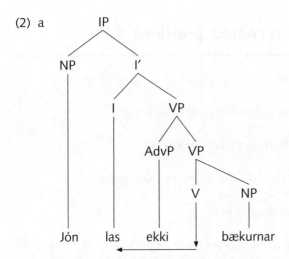

To derive the word order in (1b), we need an additional movement: we have to shift the object NP, *bækurnar* ('the books'), leftward to an IP-internal position. The operation which moves the object to the left within the IP domain is called **object shift**.[21] One possibility would be to propose that the object NP left-adjoins to the VP.[22] The movement of the verb and that of the object are both indicated by arrows in (2b).

(2) b $[_{IP}$ Jón $[_{I'}[_{I}$las] $[_{VP}$ $[_{NP}$ bækurnar] $[_{VP}$ ekki $[_{VP}$ $[_{V}$——] $[_{NP}$ ——]]]]]].

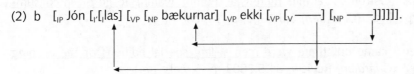

Consider the examples in (3). Has the lexical verb moved to I in (3a)? Has object shift taken place in (3a)? Consider (3b). Is object shift possible?

(3) a Jón hefur ekki lesið bækurnar.
John has not read the books
'John hasn't read the books.'

  b *Jón hefur bækurnar ekki lesið.
John has the books not read.

In (3) the participial form of the lexical verb *lesið* ('read') has not left the VP. In Icelandic there is a correlation between object shift to the left of the VP and movement of V to I. If there is no V-to-I movement, then object shift is not possible. This correlation is often referred to as **Holmberg's generalization** (Holmberg, 1986).

---

[21] For the discussion of the relevance of object shift in the derivation of the Germanic OV languages see Exercise 18 of Chapter 2.

[22] For alternative proposals see Holmberg (1986, 1999), Collins and Thráinsson (1993), Diesing (1997).

Exercise 17 Variations in subject positions (L)

Consider the following examples. Identify the subject of the underlined verbs.

(1) a Enough moralists were <u>objecting</u> to the theatre as it was.

(2) a A bomb is <u>waiting</u> to go off in consumers' pockets.

(3) a Some men were <u>selling</u> special editions of the evening paper.

(4) a A lot of things are <u>going</u> on around you.

Now consider the underlined strings in the (b)-sentences, which were the source for the (a)-sentences above. The (b)-sentences all contain a variant of the (a)-sentences. Describe the differences between the (a)-sentences and the (b)-sentences.

(1) b Putting a rogue on the stage as a hero was really daring, <u>there were enough moralists objecting to the theatre</u> as it was. (*Independent* 15.7.2004, p. 11, col. 2)

(2) b William Ostrom . . . admits <u>there is a "bomb" waiting to go off in consumers' pockets</u>. (*Guardian*, 6.5.2003, p. 14, col. 4)

(3) b When I came out <u>there were men selling special editions of the evening paper</u>. (*Guardian*, Review, 31.5.2003, p. 5, cols 3–4)

(4) b If you are staying with a family <u>there are a lot of things going on around you</u>. (*New York Times*, 1.8.2004, Travel section, p. 4, col. 5)

KEY AND COMMENTS

We will discuss example (1). In (1a) the subject is the NP *enough moralists*, and the lexical verb is *objecting*. The NP *enough moralists* occupies what we call the canonical subject position, the specifier of IP. When we form a direct question based on (1a), SAI affects the relative order of the NP *enough moralists* and the finite auxiliary *were*:[23]

(1) c Were enough moralists objecting to the theatre?

(1d) isolates the underlined section in (1b):

(1) d There were enough moralists objecting to the theatre.

---

[23] We turn to the position of the inverted auxiliary in Chapter 5.

In (1d), the NP *enough moralists* follows the finite auxiliary. This means that it does not occupy the specifier of IP, the canonical subject position. Rather, in the canonical subject position we find the word *there*. When applied to (1d), SAI changes the order of the auxiliary *were* and the element *there*.

(1) e Were there enough moralists objecting to the theatre?

On the other hand, in terms of its meaning, the NP *enough moralists* refers to the AGENT[24] of *objecting*, and it agrees with the auxiliary *were*, suggesting that it too is a subject. So we are faced with a sentence with two constituents that qualify as subjects. In turn, this means that we must provide two positions for these subjects in the structure of the sentence: the canonical subject position, which is the specifier of IP, and a second subject position which in (1b) is immediately next to the verb. We will examine such sentences in Chapter 4, section 3.2.2.[25]

Exercise 18 Modern Greek word order (T, L)

Consider the following examples in Modern Greek (Alexiadou, 1997). Does the Modern Greek verb move to I?

(1) O Petros   egrafe   panda megala grammata.
     the Peter-NOM write-IMP-3SG always long letters
     'Peter always wrote long letters.' (Alexiadou, 1997: 91 (17b))

(2) O Petros   etroge   sinithos sika.
     the Peter-NOM ate-IMP-3SG usually figs
     'Peter usually ate figs.' (Alexiadou, 1997: 93 (23a))

(3) O Janis   agorase   kthes   to aftokinito.
     the John-NOM bought-3SG yesterday the car
     'John bought the car yesterday.' (Alexiadou, 1997: 109 (62a))

(4) O sismos   katastrepse   entelos   to horjo.
     the earthquake destroyed-PERF-3SG completely the village
     'The earthquake destroyed the village completely.' (Alexiadou, 1997: 131 (14a))

Now discuss the word order displayed by the examples below. As shown by the English translations, these are to be interpreted as declarative sentences.

---

[24] Cf. section 3.2 for thematic roles.
[25] Exercise 18 also suggests that we need more than one subject position.

(5) Filise   o Petros   ti Maria.
     kissed-3sG the Peter-NOM the Mary -ACC
     'Peter kissed Mary.' (Alexiadou, 1997: 57 (15b))

(6) Ektise   i Maria   to spiti.
     built-3sG the Mary the house
     'Mary built the house.' (Alexiadou & Anagnostopoulou, 1998: 495 (7c))

(7) Diavaze sihna   o Janis   to vivlio.
     read-3sG usually the John-NOM the book-ACC
     'John was usually reading the book.' (Alexiadou, 1997: 62 (29))

(8) Efage   kala o Janis.
     ate-3sG well the John
     'John ate well.' (Alexiadou, 1997: 131 (13a))

KEY AND COMMENTS

Examples (1)–(4) suggest that the lexical verb moves to I in Modern Greek. As a result of the movement, the verb can be separated from its object by an intervening adverb. In (5) and in (6) the verb precedes the subject. Moreover, in (7) and in (8) the verb is separated from the subject by an adverb. If the verb moves from V to I and if the relevant adjuncts in (7) and (8) are VP-adjoined, then the position of the subject in these examples is unexpected. The discussion concerning the relation of the subject to the verb and the VP in section 3.3 bears on this.[26]

---

[26] The English data in Exercise 17 above also suggest the need for postulating more than one subject position. In Exercise 16 of Chapter 4 we return to the Modern Greek data discussed in the exercise. In Chapter 4 we will introduce the hypothesis that in addition to the canonical subject position, the specifier of IP, there is a second subject position, the specifier of VP. See also Exercises 6 and 7 in Chapter 4.

4 Refining Structures: From One Subject Position to Many

Contents

0   Introduction

This chapter returns to the representation we have elaborated for the structure of the sentence. We will try to refine the representation in order to capture the mapping of form to meaning. In a way this chapter is like a discovery trail through sentence structure. We start out from known territory and we go out into unknown territory. We will first look at some empirical and theoretical evidence to suggest that sentences must have more articulated structures than we had thought. In particular, we will take up the conclusion reached in Chapter 3, section 3.3. Up until that point we had been assuming that the subject occupies the specifier position of IP or SpecIP for short. As subjects typically occupy that position, SpecIP is the canonical subject position in English.

In the discussion in Chapter 3 we observed that while we had been identifying one position, SpecIP, as the subject position, it turns out that there are theoretical reasons for assuming that we need to also provide for a subject position in the VP. We will pursue this hypothesis here and take it to its consequences. While doing this, we will keep constant the basic principles of structure building that we have elaborated. Throughout the chapter, we will follow the same methodology: on the basis of the premises we start out with, and coupled with new empirical discoveries, we will formulate a hypothesis, test it, find problems with it, reformulate it, etc.

We will find arguments to introduce more subject positions. It is important to bear in mind, though, that our theory as such will remain unchanged. What changes is the implementation of the theory. This chapter provides an illustration of how linguistic theories develop through the interplay of two components: evidence from empirical data is one factor in the elaboration of a theory, but we also use conceptual arguments, that is, arguments driven by the kind of theory we have already developed.

We are trying to illustrate as precisely as possible the concrete process of elaborating a theoretical proposal. The hypotheses we will be elaborating are compatible with current thinking about syntax but they do not exhaustively represent the most recent developments of the theory. Our goal is to examine how a certain conclusion is arrived at using some specific analytic devices, but if we were to pursue the same strategy of thinking yet further we would see that what we propose here can again be challenged and must be modified. So even at the end of the discussion, there is still work to be done. This is an inevitable component of scientific research. Even if we were to present the results of the most recent work in syntax, we would still have to evaluate them and test them and we would discover that modifications are needed. Throughout all scientific work, an attitude of constructive criticism prevails. That is the nature of scientific research: it is never really "finished." We repeat the quotation given in the exercise section of Chapter 1:

In any branch of science there are only two possibilities. There is either nothing left to discover, in which case why work on it, or there are big discoveries yet to be made, in which case, what the scientists say now is likely to be false. (Nigel Calder, author of *Magic Universe: The Oxford Guide to Modern Science*. Cited in the *Guardian*, 3.6.2004, p. 6, col. 2)

This chapter will be different from the previous ones in that it is more of a "narrative." The idea is to trace step by step the reasoning that guides the construction of a theory. While doing this, we will point out the advantages and disadvantages of each modification as we go along.

The chapter is organized as follows: Section 1 is a recapitulation of the theory we have elaborated so far. Section 2 discusses the mapping of the form of the sentence to its meaning, that is, the fit between the structure elaborated and the interpretation associated with that structure. In particular, we raise the question why the subject, which is thematically related to the verb, is located strictly outside the VP. Section 3 provides a solution to the mapping problem and proposes that the subject is inserted in the specifier of the VP and that it is subsequently moved to the specifier of IP. Thus, the subject has a close link to V as well as being seen to occupy a VP-external position. Section 4 ties in the discussion in the preceding section with the discussion of sentences with multiple auxiliaries in Chapter 3, section 4. Section 5 is a summary.

1   Recapitulation

Discuss how the examples in (1) can be argued to offer support for the claim that the underlined strings of words are constituents:[1]

(1) a Two decades of financial squeeze has eroded academic standards and <u>seriously damaged common-room morale</u>. (*Guardian*, 26.10.2002, p. 13, col. 1)

 b You could study this pattern for years and <u>still not wholly understand it</u>. (Ian Rankin, *The Falls*, 2001: 240)

 c "They must talk about it, and <u>talk about it</u> they must," he said. Food for thought, there! It's a phrase that could add a measure of gravity to any press conference. "We must do this, and <u>do this</u> we must." (Simon Hoggart, *Guardian*, 29.1.2003, p. 2, col. 5)

 d Lawyers who've <u>handled arbitration claims</u> for years . . . are getting very busy; lawyers who never have are joining the fray. (*Washington Post*, 29.4.2003, p. C2, col. 1)

---

[1] For diagnostics of structure see Chapter 2, section 1.

In these examples, the underlined strings of words can be seen to be affected by a number of operations: in (1a–b), for instance, the relevant constituent is co-ordinated with another constituent, in (1c) VPs are fronted, and in (1d) the underlined string corresponds to the constituent omitted after the auxiliary *have* in the second sentence. The underlined constituents are all verb phrases: their head is a verb. On the basis of the data discussed in Chapter 3 we arrived at the conclusion that sentences are put together by merging pairs of constituents, according to the following schema:

(2) a

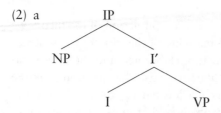

As illustrated by (1c), the structures formed according to the schema in (2a) can be modified by movement operations: in (1c) VPs are fronted, they are moved to a position to the left of the subject. We might provisionally say that such VPs are adjoined to IP.[2]

(2) b   [IP [VP Do this] [IP [NP we] [I′ must [VP ——]]]].

The position in which a constituent is merged is called its **base position**. The position that it attains after movement is called its **landing site**. In (2b) we show that originally the VP *do this* is the complement of the modal *must* by means of the arrow which links the base position [VP ——] with the landing site of the moved element, a position adjoined to IP. To represent the relation between the fronted VP and its base position, we could also use an alternative representation in which we actually show the VP in two positions: its base position, where it is merged as the complement of the modal auxiliary *must*, and the moved position adjoined to IP, in which it is pronounced or **spelt out**. To show that the VP is not pronounced in its base position we use the notational device of **strikethrough**: ~~do this~~.

(2) c   [IP [VP Do this] [IP [NP we] [I′ must [VP ~~do this~~]]]].

We might ask ourselves if it wouldn't be simpler to just use a representation in which all of the original VP in the base position disappears?

(2) d   [IP [VP Do this] [IP [NP we] [I′ must]]].

---

[2]   See discussion in Chapter 2, Exercise 15, and in Chapter 3, section 1.2.3.4.

(2d) suggests a radical change in the structure of the sentence. So far we had been assuming that the core of the sentence is the VP and that on top of this we construct a functional projection, IP. The original structure is fully preserved in representation (2c): notably, VP is still the starting point of the construction and it remains the complement of the modal. In representation (2d) the relationship between *must* and the VP has been irretrievably destroyed: according to (2d), the sentence is simply a projection of the modal in I, with the VP *do this* as an adjunct. (2d) does not preserve the format of the sentence before the movement; the strikethrough representation in (2c) does allow us to trace back the initial structure at the basis of the sentence. (2c) gives us the full information on the derivation of the sentence: how it has been built up by a combination of the operations Merge and Move. In this chapter and in Chapter 5 we will discuss a number of instances of movement and we will show the advantages of preserving the pre-movement structure.

2 Mapping Form onto Meaning: A Problem

2.1 Mapping form to meaning: Core constituent and periphery

Consider examples (1a) and (1b) above. The co-ordinated VPs in these examples are:

(3) a   [$_{VP}$ eroded academic standards]
    b + [$_{VP}$ seriously damaged common-room morale]

(4) a   [$_{VP}$ study this pattern for years]
    b + [$_{VP}$ still not wholly understand it]

In (3b) the adjunct *seriously* is part of the co-ordinated constituent, hence it is taken to be part of the VP. We assume that *seriously* is left-adjoined to the VP. Similarly, in (4b) the adjunct *still*, the negative marker *not*, and the degree adverb phrase *wholly* are left-adjoined to VP. We have been working on the assumption that adjoined constituents are less central to a phrase than the core constituents of that phrase, i.e. the head (here the verb) and its complement (here the direct object NP). A maximal projection is fully formed even if it lacks any adjuncts. The internal layering of the components of a projection is mapped onto the interpretation: the action described by the VP is defined by the verb and the complement, while the adjuncts provide additional fine-tuning.

(3) c

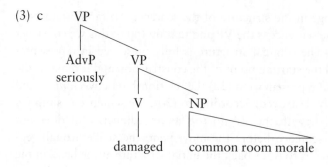

(4) c

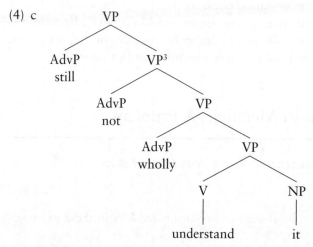

In (4c) the core VP *understand it* is "augmented" with three peripheral adjuncts, *still, not, wholly*. The interpretation of the VP can be read off from the tree: in (4c), the core meaning of the VP is encoded by the core VP, *understand it*, which denotes a psychological state. The adjunct *wholly* signifies that the state of the understanding covers the complete extent of the object *it*. The negation marker *not* is added to the unit *wholly understand it* and it denies that complete understanding. The adjunct *still* specifies a temporal interval. Observe that *not* negates the content of the VP *wholly understand it* and that *still* indicates the time interval of the content of the augmented VP *not wholly understand it*. We say that an adjoined constituent has **scope** over the constituent it adjoins to. *Still* has scope over the VP *not wholly understand it*; *not* has scope over the VP *wholly understand it*. If you compare the scope of the words *still* and *not*, the scope of *still* is **wider** than that of *not*. Or conversely, the scope of *not* is **narrower**. We can represent scope relations as in (4d):[4]

(4) d   *still > not*

---

[3] This representation of negation is a simplification. See Chapter 3, Exercise 5. For more careful analysis see Pollock (1989), Haegeman (1995), Rowlett (1998), Zanuttini (1997a, b).

[4] Exercise 3 of Chapter 3 also illustrates how structure expresses scope relations.

Similarly *not* takes scope over the VP *wholly understand it* while *wholly* only takes scope over the VP *understand it*. The scope of *not* is wider than that of *wholly*.

(4) e   *not > wholly*

We can combine (4d) and (4e) to show the relative scope of the stacked VP-adjuncts:

(4) f   *still > not > wholly*

The syntactic structure we have postulated can be seen as the input to the interpretive mechanisms that map linguistic forms into the corresponding interpretations. The structure allows us to assign scope to the adjuncts.[5]

2.2   Specifiers

Recall that in the preceding chapter[6] we came across a number of theoretical questions with respect to the representations of VP structures such as those in (3c) and (4c). In fact, when elaborating the structure for the NP in Chapter 2 we ended up with a structure in which, for instance, a prenominal genitive NP occupied a specifier position. We assumed that there is one such specifier position per NP, and that the same position also hosts the determiner, thus accounting for the complementary distribution of prenominal genitive and determiner. We abbreviate "specifier of NP" as **SpecNP**. As discussed in Chapter 3, the subject NP is the specifier of the sentence, IP. "Specifier of IP" is abbreviated as **SpecIP**. Again there is just one SpecIP: there is one subject per sentence. (5a) shows the position of the specifier in a maximal projection: the specifier is the constituent immediately dominated by the maximal projection, XP.[7] The specifier combines with the intermediate constituent X′.[8] (5b) is the representation of the structure of an NP, (5c) that of a sentence. The boldfaced NPs in (5b) and in (5c) occupy the specifier positions.

(5) a

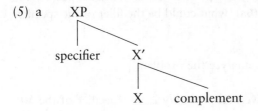

5   Exercise 22 concerns scope relations. However, the exercise is very speculative and it takes us well beyond the discussion. It should only be tackled at the end of the chapter.

6   Chapter 3, sections 2.1 and 3.3.

7   See the discussion of the format of the structure in Chapter 2, section 2.

8   The component of syntactic theory that sums up the format for syntactic structure is often referred to as X-bar theory.

b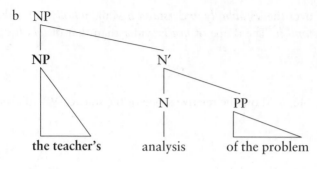

c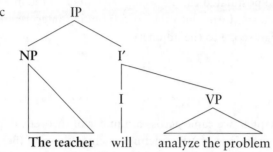

If both NPs and sentences ("IPs") have a specifier, the question arises whether the VP also has such a specifier position. In the discussion of the structure of the VP in Chapter 2,[9] we did not have any clear empirical reason for postulating a specifier for the VP. However, simply stating that the VP does not have a specifier because our data had not led us to postulate such a position is not sufficient. If the VP did indeed not have a specifier position at all, we would have to explain why this is. We would have to account for the asymmetry across categories: NPs have specifiers, IPs have specifiers, but VPs would not have them. Indeed, given the need to postulate specifiers in at least two constituents, the simplest theory will be the one in which no such additional stipulation is needed and in which all constituents, including VP, have a specifier. We have also seen that the simplest theory is preferred.[10] So let us examine whether the generalization of specifier positions to all maximal projections is workable. Taking a sentence such as (6a), what could be the filler of the specifier position of the VP?

(6) a   The teacher will [vp probably [vp analyze the problem]].

It is not plausible that the adjoined adverbial *probably* is the specifier of the VP. Recall that we assume that a maximal projection has just one specifier. But we have seen that adjunction is not restricted to just one constituent: a VP may have more than one adjunct (see (4c)). We also assume that adjoined elements are outside the core of the projection. The specifier, though, was taken to be part of the core of the

---

⁹   Chapter 2, sections 1 and 2.
¹⁰   Chapter 1, section 1.2.3.

NP and of the clause. Following this line of thinking, we would assume that the specifier of VP is not an adjunct. Based on the models in (5) for the projection of NP and IP, we would locate the specifier position in VP lower than left-adjoined VP-adjuncts, as shown in (6b):

(6) b

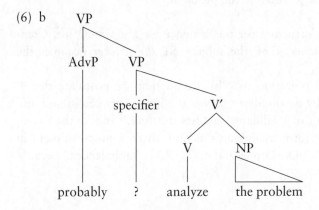

Specifier positions typically can host subjects. So we could make a bold move here and propose that the specifier of the VP is the subject. This move has some interesting consequences. In the preceding chapter,[11] we had come to the conclusion that we wanted to bring the subject closer to the verb because the subject usually receives a thematic role from the verb. If thematic relations are symptomatic of there being a close structural relationship between the assigner of the role (here the verb) and the receiver of the role (here the subject), then it would seem reasonable to expect the subject to be located somewhere in the VP. Suppose we merge the subject NP with V′. This means that the subject of a sentence occupies the specifier position of the VP, abbreviated as **SpecVP**. This is done in (7b). How would (7b) be spelt out or pronounced? Does (7b) provide the basis for the correct linearization of the sentence?

(7) a   The teacher will probably analyze the problem.
    b

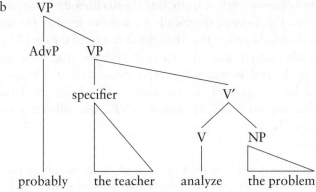

---

[11]   Chapter 3, section 3.3.

(7b) does not lead to the correct linear order or **spell out**: (7b) corresponds to the bracketing representation in (7c), which is spelt out as (7d).

(7) c   [$_{IP}$ [$_{I'}$ will [$_{VP}$ probably [$_{VP}$ the teacher analyze the problem]]]].
    d   *Will probably the teacher analyze the problem.

(7b/c) cannot be the ultimate structure for the sentence we are aiming for. Compared with the intended sentence, (7a), the subject NP *the teacher* occupies the wrong position.

    There is also a theoretical objection to (7b). Recall that we postulate that I, occupied by the inflection or by the auxiliary, serves as a linker between subject and predicate, and that the content of I validates/qualifies this link.[12] In (7c) the I position would not be able to perform its linking function: there is no constituent in the specifier of IP that could be linked up with the VP. (7c) is "unbalanced" because I does not have its anchor.[13]

2.3   Interpretation

The semantic organization of the structure in (7b) is quite appealing.[14] The VP is hierarchically organized and the complement, which has the closest semantic connection to V, is situated closer to V than adjoined elements, whose relation to V is looser. Similarly, as we have seen, adjoined elements themselves are stacked so that the closer the adjoined element is to the verb the closer its connection] to the VP.[15] For instance, in (4c) *wholly* encodes the degree of understanding; *not* denies the content of *wholly understand it* and *still* encodes a time span during which 'not wholly understanding it' holds. *Wholly* is more closely connected to *understand it* than *still*.

    The subject must be more closely connected to V than any of the adjoined constituents. After all, in (7a) the core information of the sentence is essentially 'who analyzes what', and the 'probability' of this event is in a sense secondary and additional to that core information. Before qualifying the likelihood of an event, we want to convey the nature of that event; specifically we want to identify the entities involved in the event. So we would expect that the subject is part of the core VP, that it is closer to V than an adjoined constituent such as *probably* in (6a). This relative closeness of the subject to the verb is encoded by representation (7b). The question is how to reconcile the linearization of the sentence in (7a), with the intuition expressed by (7b) that the subject is closely related to VP, and with the proposal that I links the subject and the VP.

---

[12]   Exercise 23 introduces sentences in which the predicate seems to precede the subject. However, this exercise should not be tackled until you have reached the end of the chapter.

[13]   See also Chapter 3, sections 1.2.1 and 1.2.2.

[14]   See the discussion in Chapter 3, section 3.3.

[15]   For illustrations see also Chapter 3, Exercise 3.

3 The VP-Internal Subject Hypothesis

3.1 *Displaced constituents: Movement and copies*

So far, when dealing with integrating the subject into the sentence we have only used the operation Merge. But recall[16] that we also need the operation Move, if only to allow for the fronting of constituents such as the VPs in our example (1c). Given that this operation must be independently available in our theory, let us apply it to the subject and at the same time refine the operation somewhat. We start from (7b), in which the subject has been merged VP-internally. We motivated this merger on a theoretical basis, namely by invoking the close semantic connection between subject and VP. We can now propose that in order to arrive at its position in (7a), the subject moves leftward and merges again with I', forming IP. Thus the subject becomes the specifier of IP as a result of movement:

(8) a   IP

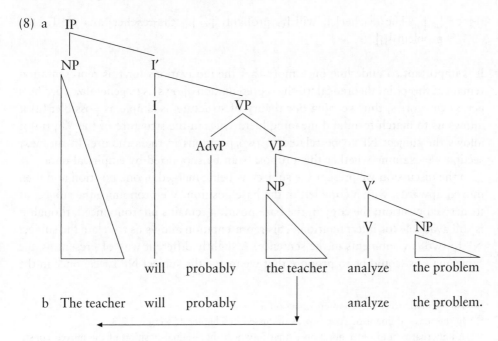

     will   probably   the teacher   analyze   the problem

   b   The teacher   will   probably   analyze   the problem.

Recall that we suggested in Chapter 3 that the subject in SpecIP functions as anchor for the information in the sentence. The subject satisfies the linking function of I: I validates the link between subject and predicate. The operation Move as proposed above enables us to achieve the correct linear order and enables the subject to anchor the sentence. It is important, however, that the movement should not undo the semantic relation we postulated between the subject *the teacher* and the verb *analyze*. In (8b) the subject NP continues to express the entity that carries out the

---

16   From Chapter 2, sections 1.4, 2.3.4, and also from Chapter 3, section 2.3.

activity. The subject realizes the thematic role AGENT, to use the technical term.[17] We conclude that the subject should somehow be represented twice in the sentence: it originates in the VP and it occupies the canonical subject position, SpecIP. To express the double affiliation of the subject in the sentence various technical devices are available.

One approach, the one we will adopt here, is to say that we merge the subject in the VP and that we move it to the specifier of IP. The result of the movement operation is that we leave a **copy** of the moved constituent in its original position. The original position at which a constituent is merged is also called the **base** position. The position that a constituent occupies after movement is called a **derived** position. As a result of the Move + Copy operation, the sentence contains two copies of the subject, one in the SpecVP and one in SpecIP. For reasons of economy,[18] when a sentence contains multiple copies of the same constituent, we pronounce ("spell out") only one such copy, in our example the one in the canonical position. We represent non-pronounced copies of a constituent by strikethrough: [$_{NP}$ *the teacher*].

(8) c   [$_{IP}$ [$_{NP}$ The teacher] [$_{I'}$ will [$_{VP}$ probably [$_{VP}$ [$_{NP}$ the teacher] analyze [$_{NP}$ the problem]]]]].[19]

It is important to underline once more that the motivations for this representation remain at this point theoretical: (i) the representation allows us to generalize specifiers across categories, thus keeping our theory of structure as simple as possible; (ii) it allows us to match form and meaning hierarchies in the structure of the VP; (iii) it allows the subject NP to be related to two positions in the structure. In the next section we examine whether this proposal can be supported by empirical data.

In the discussion we present the subject as being merged in one position and then moved upwards, with a copy left in the base position. We pronounce the subject at its derived position; the copy in the base position remains unpronounced, though it is still available for interpretation. This representation allows us to relate the subject NP to two environments in the sentence. A slightly different way of presenting the same analysis would be to propose that we merge the subject NP twice: once in the

---

[17]   For thematic roles see Chapter 3, section 3.

[18]   In the sense of linguistic economy as discussed in Chapter 1, section 2.2.3.

[19]   An alternative and older notation is that in which the original position of the moved constituent is marked with "t" for **trace** (ia). **Coindexation** (NP$_i$, t$_i$) is often used to link a trace to a moved constituent (ib).

(i) a   [$_{IP}$ [$_{NP}$ The teacher] [$_{I'}$ will [$_{VP}$ probably [$_{VP}$ [$_{NP}$ t] analyze [$_{NP}$ the problem]]]]].
    b   [$_{IP}$ [$_{NPi}$ The teacher] [$_{I'}$ will [$_{VP}$ probably [$_{VP}$ [$_{NP}$ t$_i$] analyze [$_{NP}$ the problem]]]]].

Instead of strikethrough, one can also use angled brackets < . . . > to surround non-pronounced copies:

(ii)   [$_{IP}$ [$_{NP}$ The teacher] [$_{I'}$ will [$_{VP}$ probably [$_{VP}$ [$_{NP}$ <the teacher>] analyze [$_{NP}$ the problem]]]]].

specifier of VP and once in the specifier of IP. In other words, the sentence could be argued to simply contain two identical **copies** of the subject, one merged in the VP specifier and one "re-merged" in the IP specifier. In the course of the derivation of the sentence, we first merge an NP VP-internally, which allows V to establish a thematic relation with the NP. (For instance, in (8) the NP *the teacher* is the AGENT of the verb *analyze*.) Then we insert a copy of that NP higher, in the specifier of IP, which allows I to accomplish its linking function between subject and VP. For reasons of economy, when a sentence contains multiple copies of the same constituent, we pronounce ("spell out") only one such copy, in our example that in the subject position. We can again represent non-pronounced copies of a constituent by strikethrough.

(8) d   [IP [NP The teacher] [I′ will [VP probably [VP [NP ~~the teacher~~] analyze [NP the problem]]]]].[20]

Representation (8d) is identical to (8c), except that we do not derive it by movement. What we do is merge the same NP twice; that is we insert one copy in SpecVP and one copy in SpecIP. This procedure is sometimes referred to as **multiple Merge**. The two proposals are very close, and it would probably be difficult to find empirical differences between them. Still, it is conceivable that one might propose that the multiple Merge proposal is "simpler" in that it invokes the application of an operation "Merge" without requiring movement. Both theories need to postulate copies. In what follows, we will continue to refer to "Move" operations because this gives us a way to track the sequencing of the various positions of a constituent. It is plausible though that whatever we say can be replaced by a theory that has multiple Merge.

A further point that comes out of our analysis is more general. So far we have been using the term "subject" as if it had a clear and unique reference. However, having proposed two subject positions in the sentence, the concept "subject" is now no longer a unitary phenomenon: whereas, before, we had postulated just one position for the subject in the sentence, now we postulate two positions. The VP-internal subject position encodes the semantic relation of the subject to the situation expressed by the VP; in the IP specifier position, the subject NP serves as the anchoring point for the sentence. The constituent that we label "subject" has a complex set of properties related to the semantics of the verb and to the informational structure of the clause. Our representation enables us to identify the different properties of the subject and associate them with different positions in the tree.[21]

---

[20] The "trace" notation illustrated in the preceding footnote appeals to an approach in terms of movement and copying. Strikethrough and angled brackets are neutral between a Move approach or an approach in terms of multiple Merge.

[21] See McCloskey (1997) for a comprehensive and thorough discussion of the concept of "subject" in linguistic theory. For discussion of subjects in Japanese and in English see Kuroda (1986) and Kitagawa (1994).

3.2 *Empirical support for the VP-internal subject hypothesis?*

We have now elaborated a theory in which a sentence contains two positions for the subject: SpecVP, in which the subject is merged, and SpecIP, into which the subject moves, leaving a copy in SpecVP. It is important to observe that our theory has not been made more complex: we need the operations Merge and Move independently.[22] We have simply made use of the same operations to refine the structure. The elaboration of the structure itself was motivated theoretically.

The question arises whether there are any indications in the language facts to corroborate the hypothesis that the subject is merged VP-internally. That the subject is in SpecIP is empirically founded: we literally "see" the subject in that position. SpecIP is the spell-out position of the subject. But do we have any evidence that the subject is merged in a lower position, i.e. in SpecVP? In this section we look at some data that bear on this issue.

3.2.1 FLOATING QUANTIFIERS

Compare the form and the interpretation of the sentences in (9). Identify the subject of each of the sentences. What is the category of the subject? Discuss how (9a) can be derived using the Merge and Move technique elaborated above.

(9) a   All astronauts don't speak the same language.
    b   Astronauts don't all speak the same language. (*Washington Post*, 29.4.2003, p. A10, col. 3)

The two sentences in (9) have a similar interpretation, but their form is different in that in (9a), *all* is part of the subject and in (9b), it appears somewhere to the right of the subject. Still, in (9b), the quantifier *all* bears on the subject NP, *astronauts*. There is what we could call a **discontinuous** constituent: the subject of (9b) is a quantified NP *all astronauts*, but the quantifier is not adjacent to the NP which it quantifies over. When a quantifier is not adjacent to the constituent which it quantifies over it is called a **floating** quantifier.[23]

The constituents in the canonical subject positions in the sentences in (9) are NPs: their most important element is the N *astronauts*. The quantifier *all* is NP-adjoined in (10a).

(10) a   [$_{NP}$ all [$_{NP}$ astronauts]]
     b   [$_{NP}$ astronauts]

Remember that there is no contradiction in calling *astronauts* an NP, even though it contains just one word. The unit *astronauts* is a constituent whose main (and only)

---

[22]   Recall that as an alternative to movement we could appeal to multiple Merge.
[23]   See also Sportiche (1988) and Koopman and Sportiche (1991). For an alternative view see also Doetjes (1992).

component is a noun. Both the NP *all astronauts* in (9a) and *astronauts* in (9b) can be substituted for by a pronoun:

(9) c <u>They</u> don't speak the same language.
   d <u>They</u> don't all speak the same language.

Along the lines sketched in the preceding section we derive (9a) as illustrated in (11):

(11) (i) V = *speak*

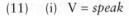

(ii)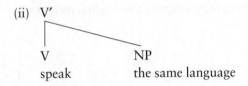

(iii)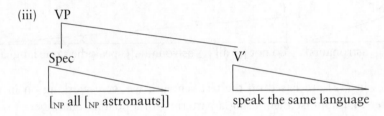

(iv)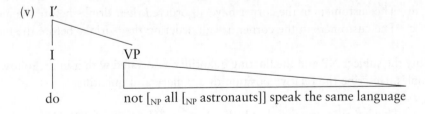

(v)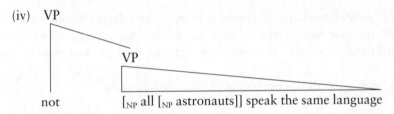

(vi)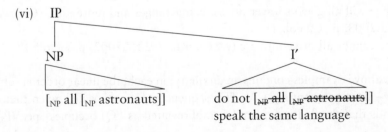

We assume that *don't* results from contracting *do* and the negative marker *not* into one word.

Consider step (vi): we merge the NP [$_{NP}$ *all* [$_{NP}$ *astronauts*]] first as SpecVP and then we move it to SpecIP, leaving a copy in SpecVP. This copy will be unpronounced. How could we derive the alternative pattern in (9b)? Starting from (11v): observe that in order to derive (11vi), we move the subject NP *all astronauts*. But *astronauts* itself is also an NP, so we could have decided not to move the outer NP but rather to move the inner NP, the core NP *astronauts*. As a result, we would leave the outer layer, containing *all*, behind in SpecVP. This derivation will yield the pattern in (9b). The quantifier *all* remains in the specifier of VP. It is sometimes said that the quantifier is **stranded**. The stranded quantifier signals the original merger site of the subject:

(11) (vi')

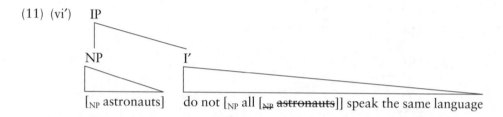

[$_{NP}$ astronauts]   do not [$_{NP}$ all [$_{NP}$ ~~astronauts~~]] speak the same language

The examples in (12) are based on the test sentence we were working on in the earlier chapters. Paraphrase them using a pattern with a floating quantifier.

(12) a   All the customers in the corner will order their drinks before the meal.
      b   All the customers in the corner have ordered their drinks before the meal.
      c   All the customers in the corner are ordering their drinks before the meal.

The result of floating the quantifiers in (12) is given in (12'):

(12') a   The customers in the corner will <u>all</u> order their drinks before the meal.
       b   The customers in the corner have <u>all</u> ordered their drinks before the meal.
       c   The customers in the corner are <u>all</u> ordering their drinks before the meal.

Identify the subject NP and the floating quantifier associated with it in the following examples. Describe the relative position of auxiliary and quantifier.

(13) a   They've all worked so hard. (Ian Rankin, *The Falls*, 2001: 418)
      b   They will all give us lower prices, better ranges and more jobs. (*Guardian*,
          1.5.2003, p. 12, col. 1)
      c   We cannot all drive into a city. (*Guardian*, 22.7.2002, p. 5, col. 3)

Each of the above examples contains an auxiliary; in each, the linear order is subject – auxiliary – floating quantifier – V. This sequencing is as expected given that our assumption is that the floating quantifier (abbreviated as FQ) occupies SpecVP.

(13′) a They   've   all worked so hard.
         subject   FQ
      b They   will   all give us lower prices, better ranges and more jobs.
         subject   FQ
      c We   cannot   all drive into a city.
         subject   FQ

We conclude that sentences with floating quantifiers related to their subjects offer empirical support for the proposal that the subject originates in the specifier of VP. The floating quantifier is like a residue in the base position of the subject.[24]

3.2.2 EXISTENTIAL SENTENCES

3.2.2.1 *Thematic subject and grammatical subject*
Identify the lexical verb in the following example. What is the subject NP?[25] Motivate your answer.

(14) a Three students are now working on this project.

The subject in (14a) is *three students*, and the lexical verb is *working*. When we form a direct question based on (14a), SAI affects the relative order of the NP *three students* and the finite auxiliary *are*:[26]

(14) b Are three students now working on this project?

The NP *three students* determines the agreement of the inflection of the auxiliary: *three students* is plural.

   Let us insert *are* in I and assume that the progressive form *working* is inserted as one word under V.[27] Using the Merge and Move technique, and assuming that the subject NP originates in the VP, show how we derive sentence (14a). What is the position of the unpronounced copy of the subject? Following the derivation outlined above we should proceed as in (15):

(15) a derivation of (14a)

      (i) V = *working*

---

[24] Exercises 3, 5, 8, and 9 are straight applications of the discussion. In Exercises 10, 11, and 12 we raise some problems. Exercise 21 looks at the agreement relation between a quantifier and the related NP in Hebrew.

[25] Exercise 17 of Chapter 3 introduced data similar to the data which we are dealing with here.

[26] We turn to the position of the inverted auxiliary in Chapter 5.

[27] Cf. Chapter 3, Exercise 14 for reservations concerning this proposal.

(ii) Merge V and its complement:

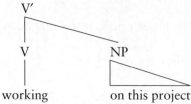

working   on this project

(iii) Merge V′ and the subject:

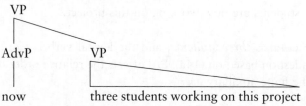

[NP three students]   working on this project

(iv) Adjoin *now* to the core VP:

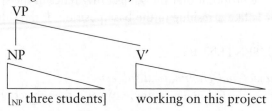

now   three students working on this project

(v) Merge VP and I:

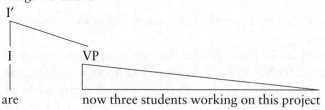

are   now three students working on this project

(vi) Provide anchor for I by merging subject NP and I′:

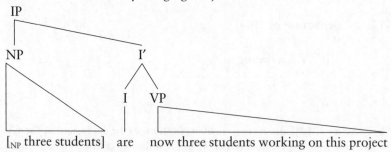

[NP three students] are   now three students working on this project

(15) b Spell out higher copy of subject NP:
[IP[NP Three students] [I′ are [VP now [VP three students working on this project]]]].

In derivation (15a) we merge the subject NP *three students* in SpecVP and subsequently we move it up to SpecIP, leaving a copy in the original position.

Arrived at stage (v) of derivation (15a), could we have proceeded differently?
Suppose we had not moved the subject up to SpecIP: what would happen? We
cannot just leave the specifier of IP empty, because the head I must link two components, the VP and what will be the specifier of IP, which, among other things,
we designated as the "informational" anchor of the sentence.[28]

(16) a   [IP —— [I' Are [VP now [VP three students working on this project]]]].
      b   *Are now three students working on this project.

Can we spell out (16a), but without moving the NP *three students* into SpecIP? To
maintain the linking function of I, we could try filling SpecIP with a different constituent. We insert the element *there* in SpecIP:

(17) a

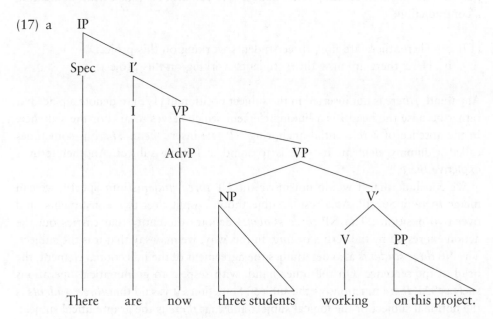

In (17a) *there* acts as a filler for the canonical subject position, SpecIP. The NP *three
students* remains in its base position, SpecVP. (17a) spells out as (17b).

(17) b   There are now three students working on this project.

Observe that the auxiliary *are* is plural. If the VP-internal subject had been singular,
we would have found singular agreement on the auxiliary. In these examples agreement is not realized in a specifier – head relation.

(17) c   There is now one student working on this project.

---

[28]   In Chapter 3, section 1.1.

Recall that in direct questions the auxiliary typically inverts with the subject. If *there* occupies the canonical subject position, then we predict that SAI will invert the auxiliary with *there*. This prediction is borne out:

(18)   Are there now three students working on this project?

In (17b) two properties normally associated with the unitary subject of a sentence are split over two constituents. The auxiliary inverts with *there* in a question (18); the auxiliary agrees with the NP *three students*.[29] In addition, the NP *three students* in (17b) refers to the entity engaged in the activity denoted by the verb *working, three students* denotes the AGENT. *There* does not denote an entity, it is mere a filler for SpecIP. Observe that the word *there* as used here is not the place indication used in opposition to *here*: to show this we may note that locative *there* can be added to this sentence without creating redundancy; *here* can also be added without creating a contradiction:

(19) a   There, there are now three students working on this project.
      b   Here, there are now three students working on this project.

Apparently, *there* is not inserted in the subject position in (17b) to denote a place but rather because the head I is a linking element which serves to anchor the sentence. In the absence of a referential anchoring NP, we insert *there*. *There* is sometimes called a **dummy** element. Its role is to stand in for the subject. Another term is **expletive** *there*.[30]

We conclude that if we do not move the NP *three students* into SpecIP, we can merge *there* in SpecIP. As a result, subjecthood is split over two constituents, and over two positions. The NP *three students* denotes the entity that carries out the action expressed by the verb *working*. In this way, we may say that it is the subject. The NP *three students* also determines the agreement of the inflectional element, the head of the sentence. On the other hand, with respect to grammatical operations such as SAI, *there* functions as the subject. Sometimes it is said that *three students* is the **notional subject** or the **logical subject** and that *there* is the **grammatical** subject, the **provisional** subject or the **expletive subject**. Using terminology elaborated in Chapter 3[31] we can add that *three students* is the **thematic** subject.

We may wonder whether *there*-sentences are associated with a specific interpretive effect. One effect of inserting *there* in the canonical subject position of the sentence is that the thematic subject does not move to the canonical subject position. We have postulated that the subject NP is inserted in SpecVP. This is its base position.

---

[29]   For some discussion of agreement patterns in *there* sentences see also Sobin (1997) and Schütze (1999). For a different pattern see also the examples in (6) of Exercise 2.

[30]   Exercise 2.

[31]   Section 3.

In sentences introduced by expletive *there*, the subject remains in its base position.[32] Hierarchically, the thematic subject remains "lower" in the structure. Linearly, the thematic subject remains in a position to the right of the canonical subject position. In a *there* sentence, the thematic subject is expressed later in the sentence than if it were to occupy the canonical subject position; when we hear or read such sentences the thematic subject comes later.

In general when communicating information we tend to organize that information in a particular way. We start on the basis of familiar information and we lead up to new information.[33] By locating a constituent toward the end of the sentence we signal it is relatively new information. In (17b) we present as new the information that three students work on the project. New information may also concern the very existence of an entity whose existence we did not know about, an entity that has recently come into existence, or at least of whose existence we have only recently been made aware. In (17b) we draw attention to the existence of the students and their participation in the action. Sentences with expletive *there* in the subject position and with a thematic subject in SpecVP are sometimes called **existential** sentences.

3.2.2.2 *A note on determiner choice*
Describe the difference in the realization of the subject NPs in the following sentences. When could we use such sentences? How could we describe the differences in the realizations of the subjects?

(20) a   A French student has arrived.
    b   The French student has arrived.

In (20a) the subject NP *a French student* is introduced by an indefinite determiner, the indefinite article *a*. In (20b) it is introduced by a definite article (*the*). The choice of the determiner is associated with a difference in meaning. In (20a) we signal that the entity denoted by the NP ('a French student') is new to the cognitive environment; we have not discussed this referent yet; we introduce the entity to be discussed by means of the sentence. In (20b) the entity denoted by the subject is presented as being already accessible somewhere in our cognitive environment: perhaps we have already mentioned the French student in the current discussion or perhaps we have a certain expectation given our knowledge of the situation. In English (as in fact in many languages), the definite article and the indefinite article are linguistic devices to indicate the discourse status of the entity referred to. When we wish to introduce a novel entity into the discourse we use the indefinite article for a singular NP. For plural NPs, we either do not find an article at all or we may use the quantifier *some* (unstressed and pronounced as [sm]).

---

[32]   For a complication see Exercise 14.
[33]   For instance, in this chapter we first recapitulate what we know already and then move on to new material. See Prince (1981).

(20) c   French students have arrived.
          Some French students have arrived.

If the existential sentence pattern serves to introduce the subject as novel then we predict that in existential patterns, subjects will typically be indefinite. If you go over the examples discussed so far once again, you will see that this prediction is borne out.[34]

3.2.2.3   *A note on verb choices and existential patterns*

In the derivation of the English existential sentences above we saw that we can leave a subject in its base position and insert *there* in the canonical subject position. However, the account might wrongly lead us to expect that we can simply leave every subject in the base position and insert the expletive *there*. We noted in the preceding section that the application of this strategy is restricted to sentences with indefinite subjects. If we were to assume that the existential strategy generalizes to all English sentences, however, we would wildly **overgenerate**: we would produce lots of unacceptable sentences. Consider (21). Using the step-by-step derivation discussed above to derive (17b), construct the sentences that would arise if we (i) left the subject in the base position, and (ii) merged *there* in the canonical subject position.[35]

(21) a   Three students have worked on this project.
      b   Three students worked on this project.

In (22) we outline the derivation of (21a):

(22) a   Derivation of (21a).

    (i)   V = *worked*

    (ii)   Merge V and its complement:

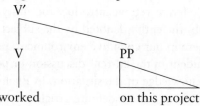

V'

V   PP

worked   on this project

---

[34]   That subjects of existential sentences are usually indefinite is referred to as the **definiteness effect**. For discussion of the existential pattern see also Milsark (1974, 1979), Safir (1985), Lumsden (1988), Belletti (1988), Law (1999).
[35]   You may insert inflected *have* under I and the past participle *worked* under V.

(iii)   Merge V′ and the subject NP:

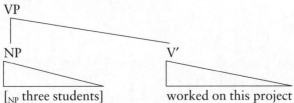

(iv)   Merge VP and I (see note 35):

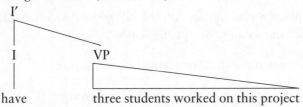

(v)   Provide anchor for I by merging subject NP and I′:

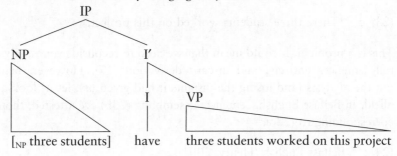

  b Spell out higher copy of subject NP:

[IP Three students [I′ have [VP ~~three students~~ worked on this project]]].

We have merged the subject NP *three students* in SpecVP and moved it up to SpecIP, leaving a lower (non-pronounced) copy.

Arrived at step (iii) of (22a), could we have proceeded differently? Suppose we had decided not to move the subject from SpecVP to SpecIP. As before, we cannot just leave the specifier of IP empty, because the head I must link two components, the VP and the specifier of IP, which serves as the anchor of the sentence. To spell out this sentence without moving the NP *three students*, we might once again try filling SpecIP with existential *there*:

(23) a   IP

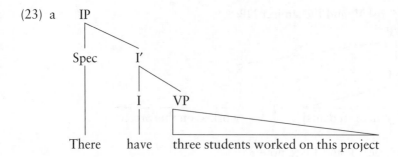

There   have   three students worked on this project

In (23a) *there* fills the position SpecIP, the NP *three students* remains in SpecVP. (23a) would spell out as an unacceptable sentence (23b):

(23) b   *There have three students worked on this project.

Though we have faithfully followed the steps of derivation (17a), the result is not acceptable. The same problem will arise if we try to create existential sentences on the basis of the second example in (21).

(23) c   *There three students worked on this project.

This is a problem. It could mean that we need to reconsider our analysis of existential sentences entirely, and discard derivation (17). However, before throwing out the analysis (and losing the insights it had given us), let us look a little further afield. In Belfast English, sentences resembling (23b) are attested, though not those corresponding to (23c).[36]

(24)   Belfast English (Henry, 2001):
    a   % There have hundreds of people phoned us.
    b   % There has something come in about this.

but

    c   % *There hundreds of people phoned us.
    d   % *There something came in about this.[37]

Belfast English allows the derivation of existential sentences with the auxiliary *have*, though it does not allow the pattern in the absence of an auxiliary. (24e) and (24f) give a partial representation of (24a) and (24b):

(24) e   % [$_{IP}$ There [$_{I'}$ have [$_{VP}$ hundreds of people phoned us]]].
    f   % [$_{IP}$ There [$_{I'}$ has [$_{VP}$ something come in about this]]].

---

[36]   The percentage symbol, %, indicates that only a subsection of speakers accept the example. When a percentage symbol is followed by an asterisk * this means that even for the relevant subsection of speakers the sentence is ungrammatical.
[37]   See also Henry (2001) and Cottell and Henry (2004).

In other languages, existential sentences can be fairly freely derived even in the absence of an auxiliary. Icelandic, for instance, allows sentences such as the following:[38]

(25) a að það hefur einhver borðað epli.
   that there has someone eaten (an) apple (Vikner, 1995: 189)
   'that someone has eaten an apple.'
   b að það borðaði einhver epli.
   that there ate someone (an) apple (Vikner, 1995: 219)
   'that someone ate an apple.'

In (25a) the canonical subject position is occupied by expletive *það*, and the AGENT of the action, the indefinite NP *einhver* ('someone'), follows the finite auxiliary *hefur* ('have'). Using our structures elaborated so far the sentence would have the partial structure in (25c):

(25) c að [$_{IP}$ það [$_{I'}$ hefur [$_{VP}$ einhver borðað epli]]].[39]

(25b) lacks an auxiliary but the existential pattern is possible. The finite lexical verb *borðaði* precedes the subject. Recall that depending on the strength of the inflection the lexical verb will either remain in the position V and I will lower onto V, or, alternatively, the lexical verb will raise to finite I.[40] If the subject *einhver* ('someone') occupies SpecVP then the position of the verb to its left suggests that V moves to I in Icelandic.

(25) d að [$_{IP}$ það [$_{I'}$ borðaði [$_{VP}$ einhver ~~borðaði~~ epli]]].

This would mean that the inflectional paradigm of Icelandic is strong, that is, that it contains many distinct forms. Table 1 contains the paradigms for the present tense and for the past tense of the verb *hear*.[41] For some reason, which we won't explore here,[42] Modern English does not allow the general application of the existential pattern. If you go over all the acceptable sentences in the preceding text you will find that they have in common the presence of *be*.[43] We assume then that there must be a special property in English that will mainly restrict the existential pattern to sentences with *be*.[44]

---

[38] Examples such as (25a) and (25b) in which a transitive sentence is used in the existential pattern are referred to as **transitive expletive constructions**. See Exercise 14 of this chapter for complications.

[39] For the position of the subordinating conjunction *að* ('that') see Chapter 5, section 2.3.

[40] See Chapter 3, sections 1.2.3.3 and 1.2.4. See also Chapter 3, Exercise 6.

[41] See Chapter 3, Exercise 6.

[42] See Bobaljik and Jonas (1996), Vikner (1995).

[43] This is a simplification. See Milsark (1974, 1979), Safir (1985), Belletti (1988), and for introductory discussion also Haegeman and Guéron (1999: chapter 2, section 3).

[44] Exercises 6, 7, 13, and 16 offer additional empirical support for the hypothesis that the subject originates in the VP. Exercises 14, 15, and 16 raise complications.

Table 1 Inflectional patterns in Icelandic

	PRESENT	PAST
1sg	*heyri*	*heyrði*
2sg	*heyrir*	*heyrðir*
3sg	*heyrir*	*heyrði*
1pl	*heyrum*	*heyrðum*
2pl	*heyrið*	*heyrðuð*
3pl	*heyra*	*heyrðu*

4 Subject Positions and Auxiliaries

4.1 *Auxiliaries and step-by-step movement of the subject*

When discussing the structural properties of sentences containing auxiliaries in Chapter 3,[45] we had not yet introduced the VP-internal subject hypothesis. In order to ensure that our theory remains internally coherent, we need to make sure that our different proposals for the structure of the sentence are consistent with each other. Recall from Chapter 1 that the knowledge acquired by scientists is cumulative and is part of a system. We cannot simply present unrelated insights, however interesting they may be. Let us return to the hypothesis that the subject originates in the specifier of VP and that it moves up to the canonical position, the specifier of IP, leaving a copy in the original position. Let us examine how this hypothesis ties in with the representations that we elaborated for sentences with multiple auxiliaries.

The auxiliaries *have* and *be* are verbs which head their own projection, VP. Following our theory about structure, these VPs can also have a specifier position. Consider a sentence containing an auxiliary that takes as its complement a VP headed by a lexical verb. The lexical verb assigns a thematic role to the subject; the auxiliary does not assign any thematic role.[46] By hypothesis, though, the VP headed by the auxiliary can have a specifier position.

Let us examine the movement of the subject from its VP-internal base position to the canonical subject position, SpecIP. What happens if the sentence contains more than one auxiliary? Sentences relevant for the discussion are (26a) and (26b).[47]

---

[45] Section 4.
[46] See discussion in Chapter 3, sections 3.3 and 3.4.
[47] These sentences are discussed as (68) and (69) in Chapter 3, section 4.4.

(26) a These students would have considered other universities.
   b We had been talking about this problem.

The question arises whether, starting from the specifier position of the lexical VP, the subject moves directly into SpecIP, or whether it transits via the intermediate specifier of the VP headed by the auxiliary. Consider the representations in (27), which we elaborated in Chapter 3.[48]

(27) a

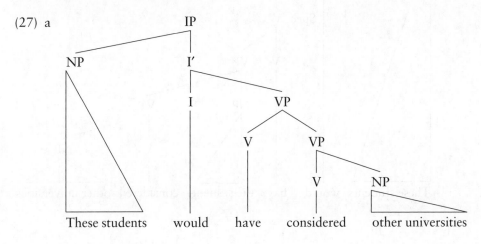

   b

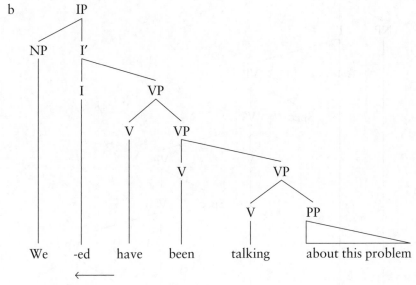

Revise representations (27a) and (27b), signaling the copy of the subject in its base position using the strikethrough notation. Also add in the specifier positions for the projections headed by the auxiliaries. Once you have done this, check the result with the representations below.

---

[48] (27a) and (27b) correspond to representations (68c) and (69b) in Chapter 3.

(28) a

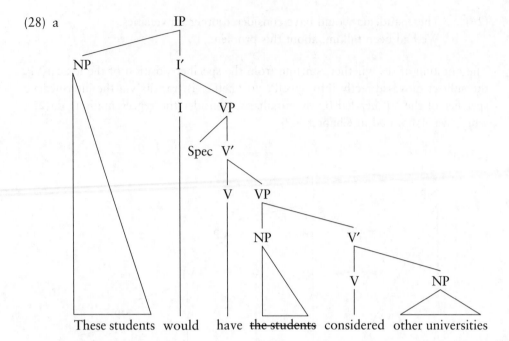

These students would   have ~~the students~~ considered other universities

b

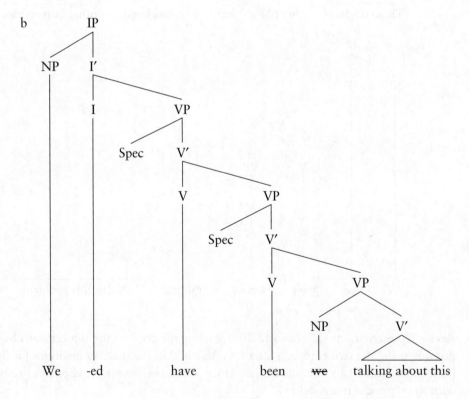

We   -ed   have   been   ~~we~~   talking about this

How does the subject NP move from the lower SpecVP to SpecIP? Does it move in one step? Or does it move step by step via the **intermediate** specifiers? In the latter case, we could assume that the subject leaves an unpronounced copy in the intermediate specifiers. This would mean that in a sense, the subject NP is the subject of the lexical VP but also of the VPs headed by the auxiliaries.

4.2 Empirical support for step-by-step movement

We cannot decide on the precise execution of the movement of the subject by simply looking at the tree diagram or at a random sentence. The relevant intermediate specifier positions, which are located between the auxiliaries and which would correspond to the specifiers of the VPs headed by auxiliaries, do not contain any overt elements, but this is also expected if the subject moves through them because the intermediate copies left by the subject would not be spelt out.

(29) a [$_{IP}$ These students would [$_{VP}$ ~~these students~~ have [$_{VP}$ ~~these students~~ considered other universities]]].
  = These students would have considered other universities.
 b [$_{IP}$ We [$_I$ -ed] [$_{VP}$ ~~we~~ have [$_{VP}$ ~~we~~ been [$_{VP}$ ~~we~~ talking about this]]]].
  = We had been talking about this.

What kind of evidence could we invoke in support of the step-by-step movement hypothesis? The evidence we are looking for has to show that in addition to SpecIP and SpecVP there are intermediate subject positions that contain unpronounced copies of the moved subject. Earlier sections in this chapter introduced empirical material to deal precisely with the issue of moved constituents and their residues. We postulated two subject positions in the sentence: SpecVP and SpecIP. The empirical support for the VP-internal subject position, SpecVP, was drawn from, among other things, the distribution of floating quantifiers (section 3.2.1). In this light, consider sentence (30a):[49]

(30) a All the students must have been sleeping.

In this example, the quantifier *all* has moved with the subject. Try stranding the quantifier in a lower position. McCawley (1988: 90) gives the following examples:[50]

(30) b The students must all have been sleeping.
  c The students must have all been sleeping.
  d The students must have been all sleeping.

---

[49] These data are from McCawley (1988: 92).
[50] Exercise 1.

In these examples, the quantifier *all* is stranded in intermediate positions. The positions occupied by the quantifier correspond exactly to the intermediate specifier position that we postulated above.[51]

(30) b′ [$_{IP}$ The students must [$_{VP}$ all ~~the students~~ have [$_{VP}$ ~~all the students~~ been [$_{VP}$ ~~all the students~~ sleeping]]]].

    c′ [$_{IP}$ The students must [$_{VP}$ ~~the students~~ have [$_{VP}$ all ~~the students~~ been [$_{VP}$ ~~all the students~~ sleeping]]]].

    d′ [$_{IP}$ The students must [$_{VP}$ ~~the students~~ have [$_{VP}$ ~~the students~~ been [$_{VP}$ all ~~the students~~ sleeping]]]].

The following attested examples illustrate the stranding of a quantifier in various positions:[52]

(31) a They would have <u>all</u> loved to come. (Mick Jagger, interview, BBC4, 12.12.2003, 7 o'clock news)

    b They'd <u>all</u> have gladly murdered Brooks. (Colin Dexter, *The Daughters of Cain*, 1995: 266).

    c Those leisured or flexi-working people who have the chance to go to the cinemas in the afternoon must <u>all</u> have wondered at some time if multiplexes are a front for something else. (*Guardian*, 24.5.2003, p. 17, col. 7)

5   Summary

This chapter reassesses the representation of the structure of the sentence in terms of the question of how well the structure we had elaborated so far can be mapped onto its interpretation. In English, SpecIP is the canonical subject position; subjects typically occupy that position. However, there are a number of theoretical reasons for assuming that we must also provide for a VP-internal subject position. These theoretical arguments are twofold. Firstly, there is an argument to be made for generalizing the specifier position to all maximal projections, thus eliminating the exceptional status of the VP (which lacks a specifier) as compared to NP and IP (which have a specifier). Secondly, there is a semantic argument that comes out of our attempt to have structure match meaning. In particular, if the subject were really located entirely outside the VP, it would come as a surprise that it can receive a thematic role from the verb, while VP-adjoined constituents, which are structurally closer to V, do not receive a thematic role.

In this chapter we elaborate the VP-internal subject hypothesis. We propose that the subject is first merged with V′. It is the specifier of VP. Then, when I′ has been

---

[51] Exercise 4.

[52] Exercises 17, 18, and 19 examine the structure of passive sentences.

built, the subject leaves the specifier of VP and moves to merge with I′, thus becoming the specifier of IP. The subject has a double affiliation in the sentence: it is both the subject of the sentence and that of the VP.[53]

The chapter provides empirical support for the hypothesis that the subject originates in the VP. That support comes from the distribution of floating quantifiers associated with the subject and from the distribution of the subject NP in existential sentences. Floating quantifiers associated with the subject can be seen to occupy a position adjacent to the lexical verb. We propose that such floating quantifiers are stranded in the base position of the subject, SpecVP. In existential sentences introduced by expletive *there*, the logical subject of the sentence is adjacent to the verb. Again we assume that it occupies its base position, SpecVP.[54]

If auxiliaries head independent VPs, their projections will also have a specifier position. Auxiliaries do not assign a thematic role, so there is no obvious filler for their specifier position. We assume that on its way from the specifier position of the lexical VP to the canonical subject position, SpecIP, the subject, which receives a thematic role from the lexical verb, moves through the intermediate specifier positions of the projections headed by the auxiliaries. Evidence for this step-by-step movement is provided by the fact that quantifiers associated with the subject may be found in the intermediate specifier positions.

---

[53] Exercise 23 introduces an additional word order pattern.

[54] For a general discussion of the traditional terms "subject" and "object" in relation to sentence structure see also the introduction and the papers in Davies and Dubinsky (2001b).

Exercises

Contents

Exercise 1   Floating quantifiers (T)

Consider the distribution of the floating quantifiers in the following examples (from Cottell and Henry, 2004). Does the discussion in the chapter allow us to derive the position of the quantifiers?

(1)   The students should have been all doing the exam at that time.

(2)   The students should have all been doing the exam at that time.

(3)   The students should all have been doing the exam at that time.

Exercise 2   Existential patterns (T, E)

Identify the existential sentences in the following examples. Discuss the derivation of the existential sentences.

(1)   There was nothing happening and the market just drifted. No business was going through. (*Guardian*, 22.6.2002, p. 4, col. 3)

(2)   William Ostrom admits there is a "bomb" waiting to go off in consumers' pockets. (*Guardian*, 6.5.2003, p. 14, col. 4)

(3)   There are probably fewer than a dozen major agencies in North America handling bookings for language schools world-wide. (*New York Times*, 1.8.2004, Travel section, p. 4, col. 4)

(4)   When I came out there were men selling special editions of the evening paper. (*Guardian*, Review, 31.5.2003, p. 5, cols 3–4)

(5)   If you are staying with a family there are a lot of things going on around you. (*New York Times*, 1.8.2004, Travel section, p. 4, col. 5)

Comment on the agreement patterns of *be* in the following examples:[1]

(6) a   There's no permanent jobs going, are there? (Josie Lloyd and Emlyn Rees, *Come Together*, 1999: 164)

---

[1]   For some discussion of agreement patterns in *there* sentences see also Sobin (1997) and Schütze (1999). See also Exercise 6 for comparative data on subject verb agreement.

b   A lot more people are going out, there's been a load of new clubs opening
     and the music scene has really come together. (*Observer Magazine*,
     21.11.2004, p. 35, col. 3)

Exercise 3   Floating quantifiers and *to* infinitives (T)

In Chapter 3[2] we briefly examined the structure of infinitival clauses. In which
position did we insert the infinitival marker *to*? Assuming that infinitival clauses also
allow quantifier floating, what should be the relative order of *to* and the floating
quantifier? Consider the underlined sequences in (1) and (2). Is the distribution of
the floating quantifier predicted by the analysis of *to* elaborated in Chapter 3?

(1)   It is not exceptional for experts to disagree among themselves. In fact, it would
      be exceptional if they were to all agree. (*Guardian*, 17.3.2004, p. 3, col. 4)

(2)   We believe it is crucial for communities to each have their own beat officer.
      (*Independent*, Review, 30.7.2004, p. 2, col. 2)

Exercise 4   Existential patterns in Belfast English (T)

Recall that in Belfast English the existential pattern generalizes to all types of sentences
with auxiliaries. In particular, transitive sentences with the auxiliary *have* also allow
the pattern:[3]

(1) a   Some students should have passed the tests.
    b   %There should have some students passed the tests. (Cottell and Henry,
        2004 (4))

Draw a tree diagram for (1b). Use the derivation in (15) in the text as your model
and remember that auxiliaries head independent V-projections.
    Consider example (2). Discuss how it provides empirical support for the step-by-
step movement of the subject:

(2)   %There should some students have passed the tests. (Cottell and Henry,
      2004 (4))

---

[2]   Section 1.3.
[3]   Section 3.2.2.3, example (24).

Exercise 5   Floating quantifiers (T)

Discuss the distribution of the underlined quantifiers in the following examples. How would we derive their positions? Do these examples give rise to any problems?

(1) We all want to take part but we don't necessarily all know how and where. (BBC radio 4, phone-in listener, 29.10.2002, 13.45)

(2) Four of the five – Andrew Acred, Richard Blues, James Munk and James Spooner – all celebrated as they picked up their results from the school yesterday. (*Independent*, 23.8.2002, p. 9, col. 1)

(3) But it has not all been easy. (*Guardian*, G2, 22.11.2002, p. 10, col. 3)

(4) We cannot all drive into a city. (*Guardian*, 22.7.2002, p. 5, col. 3)

(5) There is certainly a perception that it doesn't all filter through. (*Guardian*, G2, 2.10.2001, p. 13, col. 1)

Exercise 6   Verb-Subject-Object (VSO) languages (T, E)

Consider the following example, taken from Shlonsky (1997: 70). It illustrates the neutral word order of Standard Arabic:

(1) Katab-at Mona risaalat-an.
     wrote-3FS Mona a letter
     'Mona wrote a letter.'

As you can see, Standard Arabic displays VSO word order: the lexical verb *katabat* ('wrote') precedes the subject *Mona*. The canonical subject position is here postverbal. Assuming that an Arabic sentence is assembled in a way similar to an English sentence, how could we derive (1)?
   In Standard Arabic, VSO patterns alternate with SVO patterns, as illustrated in (2) and in (3). As the examples show, the alternation in word order is not free. Examine the glosses of the examples carefully. Discuss the correlation between verb morphology and its relative distribution with respect to the subject. (Examples from Ouhalla & Shlonsky, 2002: 13.)

(2) a Katab-a   l-ʔawlaad-u l-risaalat-a.
       write(PERF)-3MS the boys-NOM the letter-ACC
       'The boys wrote the letter.'

  b *L-ʔawlaad-u katab-a   l-risaalat-a.
     the boys-NOM write(PERF)-3MS the letter-ACC

(3) a L-ʔawlaad-u katab-uu   l-risaalat-a.
       the boys-NOM write(PERF)-3MPL the letter-ACC
       'The boys write the letter.'

  b *Katab-uu   l-ʔawlaad-u   l-risaalat-a.
     write(PERF)-3MPL the boys-NOM the letter-ACC

KEY AND COMMENTS

For reasons of economy, the simplest theory is one according to which, cross-linguistically, sentences are assembled in the same way, whether they be Arabic or English. If we assume that the Arabic sentence is derived in the same way that the English sentence is derived, then we start with the merger of the components of the VP. V (*katab* 'write') first combines with its complement (*risaalat-an*, 'a letter'), and then with its subject (*Mona*). Then the VP is merged with I. In order to derive the VSO order we can propose that the verb moves to I, while the subject remains in the specifier of the VP. As before, to preserve the semantic contribution of V in the VP and to preserve the structure of the sentence we use strikethrough to indicate the unpronounced copy of the verb.

(1) b

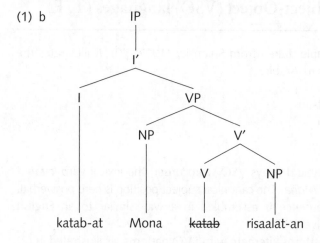

In (2) and (3) the subject is plural: *l-ʔawlaad-u* ('the boys'). In (2) the lexical verb does not agree in number with the subject: *katab-a* is singular and the subject *l-ʔawlaad-u* ('the boys') is plural. In this example, the lexical verb moves out of VP to I, but the subject remains in the specifier of the VP. We obtain the VSO order.[4]

---

[4] One point that remains unclear in this representation is why the specifier position of I is not filled. It could be the case that perhaps I is not universally a "linker" and that in some languages it does not require a specifier (see Goodall, 2001; McCloskey, 2001).

To preserve the semantic contribution of V in the VP and to preserve the structure of the sentence we use strikethrough to indicate the unpronounced copy of the verb.

(2) c   [$_{IP}$ [$_I$ katab-a][$_{VP}$ l-ʔawlaad-u ~~katab-~~ l-risaalat-a]].
     d

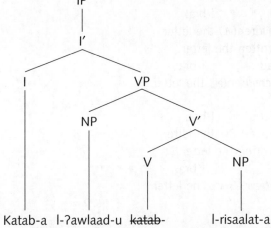

In (3) the lexical verb (*katab-uu*) is plural: it agrees in number with the subject (*l-ʔawlaad-u*, 'the boys'). In this case, the subject itself also has to leave the VP. We assume that it moves to the specifier of IP.

(3) c   [$_{IP}$ l-ʔawlaad-u [$_I$ katab-uu] [$_{VP}$ ~~l-ʔawlaad-u katab~~ l-risaalat-a]].
     d

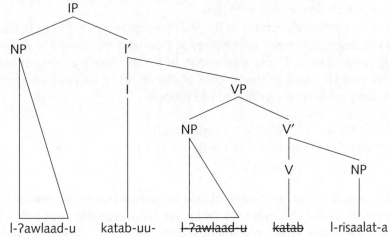

Recall that we had been proposing that the specifier – head relation in IP is the typical configuration for agreement. We can conclude from the data in (2) and (3) that for the verb in I to agree with the subject in Standard Arabic, the subject must occupy SpecIP. Or, putting it differently, moving the subject into the specifier of IP triggers agreement on the verb in I. The patterns in (2) and (3) confirm our hypothesis that agreement can be realized in a specifier – head relation.

Consider (4) and (5) from Moroccan Arabic (Ouhalla and Shlonsky, 2002: 13). Compare these data with the Standard Arabic data. What would you conclude concerning the correlation between subject agreement and subject movement in this language?

(4) a   Kətb-u   l-wlad   l-bra.
         write(PERF)-3PL the children(PL) the letter
         'The children have written the letter.'
    b *Kətb-   l-wlad   l-bra.
         write(PERF)-3MSG the children(PL) the letter

(5) a   L-wlad   kətb-u   l-bra.
         the children(PL) write(PERF)-3PL the letter
         'The children have written the letter.'
    b *L-wlad   kətb-   l-bra.
         the children(PL) write(PERF)-3MSG the letter

KEY AND COMMENTS

In Standard Arabic there is a correlation between movement of the subject to SpecIP and the realization of agreement morphology on the verb. For a verb to agree in number with its subject, the subject must move to specifier position of I. This pattern cannot be generalized to Moroccan Arabic. In Moroccan Arabic, the verb always agrees for number with the subject: with a plural subject *l-wlad* ('the children'), only plural *kətb-u* ('write') is possible. Subject movement to the specifier of IP is, however, not obligatory.

To allow for number agreement in the VSO pattern in (4a) we have to conclude that in some cases agreement morphology in I can also be realized in a matching relation between a head, I, and a lower NP. In our example the relevant head is I and the relevant NP occupies the specifier of the VP. We conclude that agreement does not always require a specifier – head relation.

(4) d [IP [I Kətb-**u**] [VP l-wlad   k̶ə̶t̶b̶ l-bra]].
         write(PERF)-3PL the children(PL) w̶r̶i̶t̶e̶ the letter

We came across a similar agreement relation between a higher inflectional element and a lower NP in our text examples (17b) and (17c), repeated here in (6). Could we say that the higher inflected element and the subject NP must be adjacent?

(6) a   There are now three students working on this project.

    b   There is now one student working on this project.

For proposals concerning the relation between agreement and movement see Chomsky (1995).

Exercise 7 VP ellipsis and Verb-Subject-Object (VSO) languages (E, presupposes Exercise 6)

Recall that the English VP can sometimes be omitted. Indicate VP ellipsis in the following examples by means of the symbol ∅. Reconstruct the deleted material.

(1) Only those who were in the room know the absolute truth of this story. No one else probably ever will. (*Washington Post*, 25.3.2004, p. D3, col. 5)

(2) If we could charge more money, we would. (*Wall Street Journal*, 29.3.2004, p. A6, col. 6)

(3) Everyone says you can't be scientific and fun, but we think you can. (*New York Times*, 8.3.2004, p. C5, col. 2)

VP ellipsis is typically used in answers to *yes/no* questions (4a). If the context supplies sufficient information we may even omit the VP both in the question and in the reply (4b).

(4) a Speaker A: Would you charge more money?
        Speaker B: We would [$_{VP}$ ∅].
    b Speaker A: Would you [$_{VP}$ ∅]?
        Speaker B: We would [$_{VP}$ ∅].

In (4b) both the lexical verb and its object have been omitted in the question and in the answer. Let us also represent VP ellipsis by means of strikethrough:

(4) c

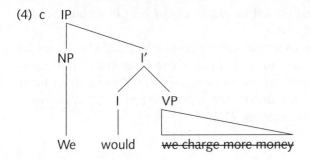

Consider the Irish examples in (5) (McCloskey, 2001: 161 his (4a), (5)). Using the English glosses provided, describe the position of the lexical verb in relation to the subject and the object.

(5) a Thóg sí   teach dófa ar   an Mhullach Dubh.
       raised she house for them on the Mullaghduff
       'She built a house for them in Mullaghduff.'

    b D'ól   sí   deaoch uische.
       PAST drink she drink water
       'She drank a drink of water.'

Using the discussion of Arabic in Exercise 6 as a model, how could we derive the
VSO pattern in Irish?

Discuss ellipsis in the Irish question answer pair (6b, c). How does the pattern in
(6) differ from VP ellipsis in English (4)? Can we account for this difference?

(6) a Thóg sí   teach.
       raised she house
       'She built a house.'

    b A-r   thóg?
       INTERROG-PAST raised
       'Did she?'

    c Creidim   gu-r thóg.
       believe-1SG that-PAST raised.
       'I believe she did.'

KEY AND COMMENTS

In English VP ellipsis deletes the content of VP. That is it affects V', the unpronounced
copy of the subject and VP adjuncts. VP ellipsis obviously leaves the subject in
SpecIP intact. In the Irish examples of ellipsis in (6), what seems to correspond to
English VP ellipsis paradoxically does not affect the verb while it does affect the
subject. In (6b) and in (6c) the verb *thóg* ('raised') is maintained; the subject
pronoun *sí* ('she') has been omitted. Let us examine how we can account for this
difference between English and Irish.

Irish is a VSO language. The canonical subject position is postverbal. If we try
to derive the VSO order in the way suggested in Exercise 6 for Arabic, this means
that in Irish the lexical verb evacuates the VP; it moves to I. On the other hand,
the subject remains in the specifier of VP. The representation in (7) is based on
representation (1b) for the Arabic example (1a):[5]

---

[5] As before, the question arises why the specifier position of I apparently need not be filled. It
     could be the case that I is not universally a "linker" and that in some languages it does not
     require a specifier (see Goodall, 2001; McCloskey, 2001).

(7)

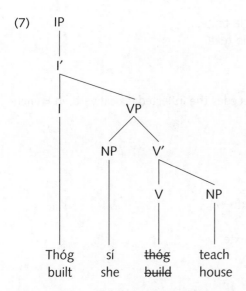

Thóg	sí	~~thóg~~	teach
built	she	~~build~~	house

Applied to (7), "VP ellipsis" will delete the content of VP. As the lexical verb *thóg* ('built') has "escaped" to I, VP deletion will not affect it. On the other hand, the subject *sí* ('she') remains in VP, there is no movement to SpecIP. Thus the subject will be affected by the ellipsis.[6]

Exercise 8 Verb positions, floating quantifiers, and comparative syntax (T)

In this chapter we assume that floating quantifiers are stranded in the specifier of the VP. We saw in Chapter 3, section 1.2.4.2, that languages vary with respect to the distribution of the lexical verb. In English the lexical verb remains in VP; in French it moves to I. Using these theoretical assumptions, which would you predict to be the acceptable word order in English: (1a) or (1b)? Is your prediction correct?

(1) a The students prepare all the text.
    b The students all prepare the text.

Which would you predict to be the acceptable word order in French: (2a) or (2b)?[7]

(2) a Les étudiants   préparent tous   le texte.
       the students-MPL prepare   all-MPL the text

---

[6] For complications see also Exercise 15.
[7] For some discussion of French see the comments section in Exercise 11.

b Les étudiants   tous   préparent le texte.
   the students MPL all MPL prepare the text.

KEY

While in English the floating quantifier precedes the inflected lexical verb, in French it follows it:

(3) a The students all prepare the text.
       *The students prepare all the text.

    b Les étudiants préparent tous le texte.
       the students prepare all the text
       *Les étudiants tous préparent le texte.

Exercise 9   Floating quantifiers and adjuncts (T, E)

Discuss the positions of the underlined quantifiers in the following examples. Discuss any problems that you encounter for our approach to the distribution of floating quantifiers.

(1) We should all not criminalise something, in ignorance of the facts. (*Independent*, 13.3.2001, p. 8, col. 3)

(2) We're all still waiting. (*Guardian*, 29.5.2002, p. 6, col. 8)

(3) We're all just scraping by. (*Guardian*, 15.9.2003, p. 14, col. 1)

(4) Brand managers are all now trying to establish an emotional connection with their target markets. (*Guardian*, 4.1.2001, p. 7, col. 1)

(5) Supermarket wines may all soon taste the same. (*Times*, 25.10.2001, p. 19, col. 8)

KEY AND COMMENTS

The data above are problematic if we assume that the quantifier must be stranded in the specifier of the VP and if the negation marker *not* and the adverbial adjuncts *still* (2), *just* (3), *now* (4), and *soon* (5) are left-adjoined to VP. The order which is predicted by our theory would be adjunct/*not* – floating quantifier – verb.[8]

[8] For discussion of the position of floating quantifiers see also Bobaljik (1995, 2003), Bowers (2001, 2002), and Boskovic (2004). See also Exercises 10, 11, and 12 for comparative data.

Exercise 10   Floating quantifiers and manner adjuncts
(T, E)

Provide the bracketed representation for the structure of sentence in (1), indicating unpronounced copies of moved constituents by strikethrough:

(1)   The girls will all wait for the teacher.

Now suppose we want to augment the VP in (1) with a left-adjoined manner adjunct *very patiently*. Based on your structure for (1) and on the discussion in the chapter, where would you predict that the manner adjunct will be located? Would you expect (2a) or (2b) to be the resulting word order? Is the prediction correct?

(2) a   The girls will all very patiently wait for the teacher.
     b   The girls will very patiently all wait for the teacher.

KEY AND COMMENTS

In (1) the subject is separated from the floating quantifier by the modal *will*. Following the discussion in the chapter we would represent the structure of (1) as in (3).

(3) a   [IP The girls [I' [I will] [VP all ~~the girls~~ [V wait] for the teacher]]].

In (3a) we signal the base position of the subject by strikethrough (~~the girls~~). In (3b) we show the position of left-adjoined VP adjuncts.

(3) b   [IP The girls [I' [I will] [VP _____ [VP all ~~the girls~~ [V wait] for the teacher]]]].

If we insert the adjunct *very patiently* in this position, we would expect that this adjunct would precede the floating quantifier.

(3) c   Inserting the adjunct:
         [IP The girls [I' [I will] [VP very patiently [VP all ~~the girls~~ [V wait] for the teacher]]]].

So we would predict that (2b) is the acceptable word order, contrary to fact: (2a) is acceptable, (2b) is not:

(4) a   The girls will all very patiently wait for the teacher.
     b   *The girls will very patiently all wait for the teacher.

These data are obviously problematic for our analysis.

Exercise 11   Floating quantifiers and adjuncts in French (T, E)

Using the glosses provided, represent the structure of the French sentence in (1) by means of labeled brackets, indicating unpronounced copies of moved constituents by strikethrough:

(1)   Les étudiants préparent tous le texte.
       the students prepare-3PL all the text
       'The students all prepare the text.'

Now suppose we want to augment the VP in (1a) with a left-adjoined manner adjunct *très soigneusement* ('very carefully'). Based on your structure for (1) and on the discussion in the chapter, where would you predict that the manner adjunct will be located? Would you expect (2a) or (2b) to be the acceptable word order? Is the prediction correct?

(2) a   Les étudiants préparent tous très soigneusement le texte.
         the students prepare all very carefully the text.

     b   Les étudiants préparent très soigneusement tous le texte.
         the students prepare very carefully all the text.

KEY AND COMMENTS

In (1) the subject is separated from the floating quantifier by the finite lexical verb *préparent* ('prepare'). The floating quantifier is stranded in the specifier position of the VP. We derive this order by assuming that the verb has raised leftward to I.[9] Following the discussion in the chapter we would represent the structure of (1) as in (3a).

(3) a   [$_{IP}$ Les étudiants [$_{I'}$ [$_{I}$ prépare-nt] [$_{VP}$ tous ~~les étudiants~~ [$_{V}$ ~~prépare~~] le texte]]].

In (3a) we signal the base position of the subject by strikethrough (~~les étudiants~~). Using (3a) as a starting point, we adjoin the adjunct *très soigneusement* to VP. In (3b) we show the position of left-adjoined VP adjuncts. We would predict that this adjunct will precede the floating quantifier.

(3) b   [$_{IP}$ Les étudiants [$_{I'}$ [$_{I}$ prépare-nt] [$_{VP}$ _____ [$_{VP}$ tous ~~les étudiants~~ [$_{V}$ ~~prépare~~] le texte]]]].

___

[9]   See Chapter 3, section 1.2.4.2.

If we insert the adjunct *very patiently* in this position, it will precede the floating quantifier.

(3) c Inserting the adjunct:
    [$_{IP}$ Les étudiants [$_{I'}$ [$_I$ prépare-nt] [$_{VP}$ très soigneusement [$_{VP}$ tous ~~les étudiants~~
    [$_V$ ~~prépare~~] le texte]]]].

So we would expect (2b) to be the word order of the sentence, contrary to fact: (2a) is acceptable, (2b) is not:

(4) a Les étudiants préparent tous très soigneusement le texte.
    the students prepare all very carefully the text
    'The students all prepare the text very carefully.'

   b *Les étudiants préparent très soigneusement tous le texte.

These data are obviously problematic for our analysis. Observe that we encountered exactly the same problem for English in Exercise 10.

Exercise 12 Floating quantifiers and adjuncts in Hebrew (T, E)

Consider the Hebrew examples in (1).[10] Using the English glosses provided as your guideline locate the subject, the floating quantifier associated with the subject, and the verb. Do you think that Hebrew has V-movement to I? Motivate your answer.

(1) a Ha-yeladim hiku kul-am ?et ha-mora.
    the-children hit all-3MPL the-teacher
    'The children all hit the teacher.'

   b Ha-banot hadfu kul-an ?et ha-kadur.
    the-girls hit-back all-3FPL the-ball
    'The girls all hit back the ball.'

Using labeled brackets, represent the structure of (1a) in order to show the position of the subject *ha-yeladim*, of the verb *hiku*, and of the floating quantifier *kul-am*. In our examples we note that the Hebrew quantifier shows overt agreement with the NP to its left.[11]

---

[10] All the Hebrew data in this exercise are from Shlonsky (1991: 172, his (21)).
[11] For related examples see Chapter 2, Exercise 19.

Now suppose we want to augment the VP in (1a) with a left-adjoined manner adjunct, be-ʔaxzariyut ('with cruelty'). Based on your structure for (1a) and on the discussion in the chapter, where would you predict that this adjunct will be found? Would you expect (2a) or (2b) to be the acceptable order?

(2) a   Ha-yeladim hiku <u>be-ʔaxzariyut</u> kul-am ʔet ha-mora.
         the-children hit   with cruelty   all-3MPL the-teacher

     b   Ha-yeladim hiku kul-am <u>be-ʔaxzariyut</u> ʔet ha-mora.
         the-children hit   all-3MPL with cruelty   the-teacher

KEY AND COMMENTS

In (1a) the subject is separated from the floating quantifier by the lexical verb *hiku* ('hit'). If the floating quantifier is stranded in the specifier position of VP, we conclude that the verb has raised leftward to I. Following the discussion in the chapter we would provisionally represent the structure of (1a) as in (3a).

(3) a   First hypothesis:
         [IP Ha-yeladim [I' [I hiku] [VP ~~ha-yeladim~~ kul-am [V ~~hiku~~] ʔet ha-mora]]].

In (3a) we signal the base position of the subject by strikethrough (*~~ha-yeladim~~*). As mentioned above, NPs precede the associated (inflected) quantifiers in Hebrew. We signal the base position of the verb by strikethrough (*~~hiku~~*). If we use the structure in (3a) as a starting point and we adjoin an adjunct to VP, we predict that this adjunct will occupy the slot indicated in (3b):

(3) b   [IP Ha-yeladim [I' [I hiku] [VP _____ [VP ~~ha-yeladim~~ kul-am [V ~~hiku~~] ʔet
         ha-mora]]]].

If we insert the adjunct *with cruelty* in this position, we predict that this adjunct will precede the floating quantifier:

(3) c   Inserting the adjunct:
         [IP Ha-yeladim [I' [I hiku] [VP <u>be-ʔaxzariyut</u> [VP ~~ha-yeladim~~ kul-am [V ~~hiku~~] ʔet
         ha-mora]]]].

So we would expect (2a), repeated as (4a), to be the acceptable word order of the sentence, contrary to fact: (4a) is ungrammatical. The adjunct should follow the floating quantifier as in (2b), repeated as (4b):

(4) a *Ha-yeladim hiku <u>be-ʔaxzariyut</u> kul-am ʔet ha-mora.
the-children hit   with cruelty   all-3MPL the-teacher

b Ha-yeladim hiku kul-am <u>be-ʔaxzariyut</u> ʔet ha-mora.
the-children hit   all-3MPL with cruelty   the-teacher
'The children all cruelly hit the teacher.'

These data are obviously problematic for our hypothesis. We were confronted with exactly the same problem for English in Exercise 10 and for French in Exercise 11.

Exercise 13   VSO patterns in Welsh (E)

In Exercise 7 we discussed word order in Irish, a Celtic VSO language. Based on the analysis for Irish, how could we account for the position of the verb and the subject in Welsh, another Celtic language?

(1) Darllen-ais i y   llyfr.
read   1SG I the book
'I read the book.' (Harlow, 1981: 219)

(2) Soni-ais i am y dyn.
talked 1SG I about the man.
'I talked about the man.' (Harlow, 1981: 219)

(3) a Gwelodd y plentyn ceffyl.
saw   the child horse
'The child saw a horse.'

b Gwnaeth y plentyn weld ceffyl.
did   the child see   horse
'The child did see a horse.' (Holmberg & Platzack, 1995: 57)

(4) a Ennill -odd John.
win-past   John
'John won.'

b Gwnaeth John ennill.
did   John win
'John won.' (Harlow, 1981: 223)

For complications see also Exercise 15. For a detailed discussion of Welsh see Roberts (2005).

Exercise 14   Subject position(s) in Icelandic transitive expletive constructions (T, E)

Exercises 9–12 have shown that the proposal according to which a floating quantifier related to the subject occupies SpecVP is not without its problems. In particular, the distribution of VP-adjoined adjuncts suggests that this hypothesis may have to be revised. The problem illustrated in the exercises was that while we would predict that the floating quantifiers follow VP-adjoined adjuncts, they actually precede them.

In section 3.2.2 of the chapter we discussed evidence for the hypothesis that there is a subject position in SpecVP based on so-called transitive expletive constructions. First try to reconstruct the argumentation on the basis of the Icelandic examples in (25) in the chapter, repeated here in (1).

(1) a   að það hefur einhver borðað epli.[12]
         that there has someone eaten (an) apple (Vikner, 1995: 189)
         'that someone has eaten an apple.'

    b   að það borðaði einhver epli.
         that there ate someone (an) apple (Vikner, 1995: 219)
         'that someone ate an apple.'

Using the discussion in the chapter as our basis, how would we analyze the Icelandic example (2)?

(2)   það klaruðu margar mýs ostinn.
      there finished many mice the cheese
      'Many mice finished the cheese.'
      (Alexiadou & Anagnastopoulou, 2001: 198, their (14b))

Now consider the following Icelandic examples. What problems do they raise for the analysis we elaborated?

(3) a   það klaruðu margar mýs alveg ostinn.
         there finished many mice completely the cheese
         'Many mice finished the cheese completely.'

    b   *það klaruðu alveg margar mýs ostinn
         there finished completely many mice the cheese
         (Alexiadou & Anagnastopoulou, 2001: 198, their (15))

---

[12]   For the position of the subordinating conjunction *að* ('that') see Chapter 5, section 2.3.

KEY AND COMMENTS

If the subject of the existential pattern is stranded in the specifier position of VP in the Icelandic examples above, we deduce that the verb *klaruðu* ('finished') in (2) has moved leftward. We can assume it has raised to I. We would represent the structure of (2) as in (4a). We signal the base position of the verb by strikethrough (~~klaruðu~~).

(4) a [$_{IP}$ það [$_{I'}$ [$_I$ klaruðu] [$_{VP}$ margar mýs [$_V$ ~~klaruðu~~] ostinn]]].

If we use (4a) as a starting point and we adjoin the adjunct *alveg* ('completely') to VP, we predict that this adjunct will precede the subject in SpecVP.

(4) b *[$_{IP}$ það [$_{I'}$ [$_I$ klaruðu] [$_{VP}$ *alveg* [$_{VP}$ margar mýs [$_V$ ~~klaruðu~~] ostinn]]]].

So we would expect (3b) to be the correct word order of the sentence, contrary to fact: (3b)/(4b) is ungrammatical. The VP-adjoined adjunct has to precede the preverbal subject as in (3a). Since (3b) is ungrammatical, the postverbal subject apparently does not remain in the specifier of VP after all: it must move leftward to a position which is itself lower than the position occupied by the verb. Since the subject is a full projection its landing site will either be an adjoined position or a specifier position.

(4) c [$_{IP}$ það [$_{I'}$ [$_I$ klaruðu] [$_{???}$ margar mýs [$_{VP}$ *alveg* [$_{VP}$ ~~margar mýs~~ [$_V$ ~~klaruðu~~] ostinn]]]]].

Obviously these data raise a problem for our analysis, and the problem raised is similar to that which we encountered in the preceding exercises.[13]

Exercise 15   VSO orders and subject positions
(E, presupposes Exercises 6, 7, and 13)

In Exercises 6 and 7 we discussed VSO languages. To account for Irish ellipsis data in Exercise 7, we proposed that, in the examples in (5), repeated here as (1), the postverbal subject occupies the specifier of VP.

(1) a Thóg sí   teach dófa ar   an Mhullach Dubh.
        raised she house for them on the Mullaghduff
        'She built a house for them in Mullaghduff.'

---

[13] For a first tentative analysis see Exercise 22 (10a) below. For discussion see Alexiadou and Anagnostopoulou (2001), Roberts (2005: 7–46), and the references cited there.

b   D'ól   sí   deaoch uische.
    PAST drink she drink water
    'She drank a drink of water.'

How would we represent the structure of (2)?

(2)   Chuala Róise an t-amhrán sin.
      heard   Róise that song
      'Rosie heard that song.'
      (Based on Alexiadou & Anagnastopoulou, 2001: 200, their (20))

Discuss the problems raised for the analysis by the Irish data in (3):

(3) a   Chuala Róise go mini roimhe   an t-amhrán sin.
        heard   Róise often   before it that song

    b   *Chuala go mini Róise an t-amhrán sin.
        heard   often   Róise that song
        (McCloskey, 1996; in Alexiadou & Anagnastopoulou, 2001: 200, their (20))

Discuss the consequences of these data for the analysis of the ellipsis pattern in Irish in Exercise 7.

KEY AND COMMENTS

If the postverbal subject is stranded in the specifier position of VP in the Irish examples in (1) and in (2), we infer that the verb *chuala* ('heard') in (2) has moved leftward. We can assume it has raised to I. Following the discussion in the chapter we would represent the structure of (2) as in (4a).

(4) a   [$_{IP}$ [$_{I'}$ [$_{I}$ Chuala] [$_{VP}$ Róise ~~chuala~~ an t-amhrán sin]]].

In (4a) we signal the base position of the verb by strikethrough (~~chuala~~). If we use the structure in (4a) as a starting point and we adjoin the adjunct *go mini roimhe* ('often before it') to VP, we predict that the adjuncts precede the postverbal subject in the specifier of VP.

(4) b   *[$_{IP}$ [$_{I'}$ [$_{I}$ Chuala] [$_{VP}$ go mini roimhe [$_{VP}$ Róise ~~chuala~~ an t-amhrán sin]]]].

So we expect (3b) to be the correct word order of the sentence, contrary to fact: (3b)/(4b) is ungrammatical. The adjuncts precede the subject as in (3a). Since (4b) is actually ungrammatical, we conclude that the subject cannot remain in SpecVP after all. Apparently, it must move leftward to a position which is lower than the position occupied by the verb. Since the subject is a full projection, its landing site will either be an adjoined position or a specifier position.

(4) c [IP [I' [I Chuala] [??? Róise [VP go mini roimhe [VP ~~Róise chuala~~ an t-amhrán sin]]]]].

This conclusion also raises a problem for the formulation of the ellipsis pattern in Exercise 7. If the postverbal subject in Irish occupied a higher VP-external specifier, then ellipsis would have to target a more comprehensive constituent. If on the other hand, the subject is adjoined to VP, then we can maintain the analysis proposed in Exercise 7.

Once again, the Irish data discussed here raise a problem for our analysis, and the problem raised is also similar to that which we encountered in the preceding exercises.[14]

Exercise 16   VSO orders and subjects in Modern Greek (E, presupposes Exercises 7, 13, 14, and 15)

In Exercise 18 of Chapter 3 we already introduced the examples in (1)–(2) below. We concluded there that the fact that the inflected verb is separated from its direct object by an adjunct suggests that V moves to I in Modern Greek.

(1)   O Petros   egrafe   panda megala grammata.
      the Peter-NOM write-IMP-3SG always long letters
      'Peter always wrote long letters.' (Alexiadou, 1997: 91 (17b))

(2)   O Peter   etroge   sinithos sika.
      the Peter-NOM ate-IMP-3SG usually figs
      'Peter usually ate figs.' (Alexiadou, 1997: 93 (23a))

In the light of the discussion of Exercises 6 and 7 above, can we account for the patterns in (3) and (4), given as (7) and (8) in Exercise 18 in Chapter 3?

(3)   Diavaze sihna   o Janis   to vivlio.
      read-3SG usually the John-NOM the book-ACC
      'John was usually reading the book.' (Alexiadou, 1997: 62 (29))

(4)   Efage   kala o Janis.
      ate-3SG well the John
      'John ate well.' (Alexiadou, 1997: 131 (13a))

Do these examples raise the problems for the VSO analysis that we were confronted with in Exercises 14 and 15 above?

---

[14]   For discussion see Alexiadou and Anagnostopoulou (2001) and the references cited there. For a first tentative analysis see Exercise 22 (10b) below.

KEY AND COMMENT

The postverbal subject in Modern Greek can be argued to occupy the specifier of VP. The Greek VSO patterns do not give rise to the problems encountered before. Unlike the transitive expletive patterns in Icelandic discussed in Exercise 14, or the VSO patterns in Irish discussed in Exercise 15, the postverbal subject in Greek follows VP-adjoined adjuncts:

(5) [IP [I Diavaze] [VP sihna [VP o Janis ~~diavaze~~ to vivlio]]].
          read   usually   the John-NOM the book-ACC
     'John was usually reading the book.' (Alexiadou, 1997: 62 (29))

(6) [IP [I Efage] [VP kala [VP o Janis ~~efagre~~]]].
          ate-3SG   well   the John
     'John ate well.' (Alexiadou, 1997: 131 (13a))

Exercise 17   Passivization and floating quantifiers (E)

Once again this exercise is longer and more discursive than the preceding exercises. Its purpose is to carry further the type of argumentation elaborated in the chapter and to see where that leads us. The exercise takes up the discussion of passivization in Exercises 9, 10, 11, and 12 of Chapter 3. These exercises are presupposed for the current exercise.

Describe the differences between sentences (1) and (2) below in terms of the realization of the arguments of the verb *arrest*. Specifically, identify the subject of each sentence.

(1)   The police officer will arrest the burglar.

(2)   The burglar will be arrested.

(1) is an active sentence; (2) is its passive counterpart. Informally put, the passive version in (2) is characterized by the fact that the AGENT role assigned by the verb *arrest* is not overtly realized, and that the argument which is assigned the THEME role is realized by the NP *the burglar* in the canonical subject position, SpecIP.

What sort of evidence could we invoke to say that in (1) the NP *the police officer* is the subject, while in (2) it is the NP *the burglar* that is the subject? For one thing, the NP *the police officer* agrees with the verb in (1). This is not easy to see in a sentence with a modal auxiliary because, typically, such auxiliaries do not show overt agreement, but if we replace the modal auxiliary by the auxiliary *have* to form the present perfect, then agreement is overt.

(3) a The police officer <u>has</u> arrested the burglar.

    b The police officers <u>have</u> arrested the burglar.

(4) a The burglar <u>has</u> been arrested.

    b The burglars <u>have</u> been arrested.

Intuitively, we want to say that the THEME argument of the passivized verb becomes the subject.

For the derivation of the active sentence, we assume that the THEME argument is realized by the NP *the burglar*. The verb *arrest* is merged with that NP to form V'. The meaning of a passive verb is closely similar to that of its active counterpart, and in particular, the verb assigns the same thematic roles. We might try to capture the semantic parallelism between an active verb and its passive counterpart by proposing that the thematic role THEME of a passive verb is also assigned in the complement position of the verb. In other words, the NP which realizes the THEME argument of a passive verb is merged with V to form V'.

If the THEME argument of a passive verb is first merged in V', we would have to conclude that it subsequently moves to the specifier of IP, the canonical subject position. In a passive sentence, the AGENT of the verb need not be overtly expressed (cf. (2)). Let us provisionally assume that in the passive sentence the NP that expresses the AGENT argument is not merged as the specifier of the VP. Consequently, the specifier of the VP is not filled.[15]

In the passive sentence, the NP which realizes the THEME argument ends up in the canonical subject position, SpecIP. If the specifier of the VP remains unfilled, the question arises whether the NP moves directly from the complement position dominated by V' to the canonical subject position, SpecIP, as shown in (5a), or whether it moves via the specifier of the VP, a position which, by hypothesis, has remained empty (5b).

(5) a [$_{IP}$ The burglar [$_I$ will] [$_{VP}$ be [$_{VP}$ arrested ~~the burglar~~]]].

    b [$_{IP}$ The burglar [$_I$ will] [$_{VP}$ be [$_{VP}$ ~~the burglar~~ arrested ~~the burglar~~]]].

Recall that, based on the discussion in Chapter 3, section 4, we assume that the passive auxiliary *be* projects its own VP. This raises an additional question. If the auxiliary *be* projects its own VP, this VP will also have a specifier position, through which the THEME NP *the burglar* might also transit on its way to SpecIP. This is shown in representation (5c):

---

[15] See Chapter 3, Exercises 10–13.

(5) c [$_{IP}$ The burglar [$_I$ will] [$_{VP}$ ~~the burglar~~ be [$_{VP}$ ~~the burglar~~ arrested ~~the burglar~~]]].

The spell-out of the representations in (5) will not differ, since the non-overt copies of the moved NP (~~the burglar~~) are not pronounced. All three representations spell out as (5d).

(5) d The burglar will be arrested.

What kind of arguments could we use to choose between (5a), (5b), and (5c)? What would a theoretical argument in favor of one of the representations be like? What type of empirical evidence could be invoked in support of one analysis or the other?

Consider the data in (6) and (7) from McCawley (1988: 90). Do they provide any arguments for choosing between (5a), (5b), and (5c). Why?

(6) a ?The children have been all vaccinated.
    b The children have all been vaccinated.

(7) a We have been all robbed many times.
    b We have all been robbed many times.

KEY AND COMMENTS

The sentences in (6) and in (7) provide empirical support for the hypothesis represented in (5c), namely that the subject of a passive sentence can move via the intermediate specifier positions. For (6), we could postulate that the floating quantifier *all* is stranded in one of the two intermediate landing sites. In representation (8), we assume that auxiliary *have* projects its own VP and moves to I.[16] Write out the sentences in their spell-out form:

(8) a ?[$_{IP}$ The children [$_I$ have] [$_{VP}$ ~~the children have~~ [$_{VP}$ ~~the children~~ been [$_{VP}$ all ~~the children~~ vaccinated ~~all the children~~]]]].
    b [$_{IP}$ The children [$_I$ have] [$_{VP}$ ~~the children have~~ [$_{VP}$ all ~~the children~~ been [$_{VP}$ ~~all the children~~ vaccinated ~~all the children~~]]]].
    c [$_{IP}$ The children [$_I$ have] [$_{VP}$ all ~~the children have~~ [$_{VP}$ ~~all the children~~ been [$_{VP}$ ~~all the children~~ vaccinated ~~all the children~~]]]].

As you can see: if you spell out (8b) and (8c), the resulting strings will be identical and correspond to (7b): this is because there is no overt element in the V position in which *have* is first merged: the auxiliary *have* moves to I. What kind of data

---

[16] For the position of auxiliaries see the discussion in Chapter 3, section 4.

might be able to distinguish between the pattern in (8b) and that in (8c)? What we would need is for *have* to occupy the V-position in which it is first merged, so that we can see whether the floating quantifier *all* is in the specifier of the VP headed by *all* or in that of the VP headed by *be*. How could we ensure that *have* remains in V? We could prevent *have* from moving to I if we inserted an element in I. Let us represent this element as X. In (9a) *all* will be found to the right of *have*, in (9b) it will be to the left of *have*:

(9) a [$_{IP}$ The children [$_I$ X] [$_{VP}$ ~~the children~~ have [$_{VP}$ all ~~the children~~ been [$_{VP}$ ~~all the~~
       ~~children~~ vaccinated ~~all the children~~]]]].
    = The children X have all been vaccinated.
   b [$_{IP}$ The children [$_I$ X] [$_{VP}$ all ~~the children~~ have [$_{VP}$ ~~all the children~~ been [$_{VP}$ ~~all~~
       ~~the children~~ vaccinated ~~all the children~~]]]].
    = The children X all have been vaccinated.

Which element could be inserted as X? If we were to insert a modal auxiliary under I, then *have* would remain in the position V and the floating quantifier appears either to its right or to its left:

(10) a [$_{IP}$ The children [$_I$ will] [$_{VP}$ ~~the children~~ have [$_{VP}$ all ~~the children~~ been [$_{VP}$ ~~all~~
        ~~the children~~ vaccinated ~~all the children~~]]]].
     = The children will have all been vaccinated.
    b [$_{IP}$ The children [$_I$ will] [$_{VP}$ all ~~the children~~ have [$_{VP}$ ~~all the children~~ been [$_{VP}$
        ~~all the children~~ vaccinated ~~all the children~~]]]].
     = The children will all have been vaccinated.

We tentatively conclude that there is some empirical support for postulating that passive sentences involve step-by-step movement of a constituent from the "complement position" in V' to the canonical subject position, SpecIP.

   The argumentation used here is analogous to that developed in section 4 of Chapter 4. In that discussion, we argued that in a sentence with multiple auxiliaries the subject NP moves from the specifier of the lexical verb via the intermediate specifiers of the VPs projected by the auxiliaries. Recall that in the discussion we used the data in (11) as evidence (McCawley, 1988: 90):

(11) a The students must all have been sleeping.
     b The students must have all been sleeping.
     c The students must have been all sleeping.

We might also address the choice between representations (5a), (5b), and (5c) from a theoretical point of view. Given that (11) offers evidence that the subject moves step by step from its base position to its landing site, we may propose a general hypothesis that movement always proceeds step by step.

Exercise 18   Passivization and floating quantifiers
(E, presupposes Exercise 17)

Discuss the relevance of the position of the underlined floating quantifier in the following examples for the derivation of passive sentences.

(1)   It's too bad they couldn't have <u>all</u> been tried together. (*Guardian*, 10.9.2002, p. 6, col. 2)

(2)   This is no doubt <u>all</u> being facilitated by what British ministers have hailed as the restrained behaviour of the Northern Alliance. (*Guardian*, 27.11.2001, p. 7, col. 1)

(3)   'Can they really <u>all</u> be so misled?' (*Guardian*, 6.2.2002, p. 4, col. 6)

(4)   These have now <u>both</u> been announced ahead of schedule and the company says this is why Sir Peter has called it a day. (*Guardian*, 1.11.2001, p. 3, col. 3)

(5)   The sums will only <u>all</u> be awarded if BT does better than its rivals over the next three years in a league table based on a financial metric known as total shareholder return (TSR). (based on *Guardian*, 1.11.2001, p. 3, col. 8)

Exercise 19   Floating quantifiers and the base
position of the subject in passive
sentences (T, presupposes Exercise 17)

This exercise is again more discursive than some of the preceding exercises. Our purpose is once again to carry further the type of argumentation elaborated in the chapter and see where that would lead us. The exercise presupposes Exercise 17.

   Return once more to the data in (6) discussed in Exercise 17, and the representations in (8). The examples and their representations are repeated here in (1) and (2):

(1)   a   ?The children have been all vaccinated. (McCawley, 1988: 90)
      b   The children have all been vaccinated. (McCawley, 1988: 90)

(2)   a   ?[$_{IP}$ The children [$_I$ have] [$_{VP}$ ~~the children~~ have [$_{VP}$ ~~the children~~ been [$_{VP}$ all ~~the children~~ vaccinated ~~all the children~~]]]].
      b   [$_{IP}$ The children [$_I$ have] [$_{VP}$ ~~the children~~ have [$_{VP}$ all ~~the children~~ been [$_{VP}$ ~~all the children~~ vaccinated ~~all the children~~]]]].

c [$_{IP}$ The children [$_I$ have] [$_{VP}$ all ~~the children have~~ [$_{VP}$ ~~all the children~~ been [$_{VP}$ ~~all the children~~ vaccinated ~~all the children~~]]]].

Though consistent with the hypothesis of stepwise movement, the sentences in (1) raise a problem. Throughout the discussion of passive sentences we have been assuming that the subject of a passive sentence originates as the complement of V: it first merges with V to form V'.

We also assume that floating quantifiers allow us to trace the route taken by the moved constituent. In the discussion of the two subject positions in Chapter 4, we proposed that the floating quantifier signals the base position of the subject, SpecVP. In the discussion of sentences with auxiliaries we concluded that a floating quantifier was to be found in each of the positions containing a non-pronounced copy of the subject.

In line with our analysis of the relation of a floating quantifier and the subject and using representations such as those in (2), which would you expect to be the lowest possible position of the quantifier associated with the subject of the passive sentence? If the floating quantifier could be found in literally all the positions that host a non-pronounced copy of the subject, we would also expect it to be available in the thematic position of the subject. In passive sentences, the thematic position of the subject is the complement position in V', that is a position to the right of the verb. Construct the appropriate sentence and check whether it is grammatical.

(2) d [$_{IP}$ The children [$_I$ have] [$_{VP}$ ~~all the children have~~ [$_{VP}$ ~~all the children~~ been [$_{VP}$ ~~all the children~~ vaccinated all ~~the children~~]]]].
    = *The children have been vaccinated all.

Surprisingly, a floating quantifier associated with the subject of a passive sentence can apparently never occur in the base position of that subject, that is, the position in which the NP is first merged with V and in which its thematic role is assigned. This obviously requires further investigation since we have been assuming that in active sentences a floating quantifier can signal the thematic position of the subject.[17]

Exercise 20 Passivization and existential patterns
(E, presupposes Exercises 17, 18, and 19)

Consider the underlined strings in (1a). Identify the lexical verbs. What is the subject of the first underlined string (i)? Motivate your answer. What is the subject of the second string (ii)? Using the concepts elaborated in Chapter 4, how could we relate the two patterns?

---

[17] For discussion see, for instance, Sportiche (1988) and Koopman and Sportiche (1991).

(1) There have been changes in trends and (i) <u>there's a lot less pesticide being</u>
     <u>used in the countryside these days than a decade ago</u>. The problem is that,
     although (ii) <u>a lot less is being used</u>, what is being used is a lot more effective
     – so there're less insects and seeds for birds to eat. (*Guardian*, 2.12.2003,
     p. 6, col. 6)

Clearly, it is tempting to relate the underlined patterns in (1) along the lines of the
discussion of existential structures in section 3.2.2 in this chapter. (1a) is a simplified
version of (i) and can be compared to (2a), (1b) is a simplified version of (ii) and can
be compared to (2b).[18]

(1) a   A lot less pesticide is being used.
(2) a   Three students are working on the project.

(1) b   There is a lot less pesticide being used.
(2) b   There are three students working on the project.

We could argue that (1b) supports the proposal that the subject of a passive
sentence originates in a lower position and moves to the specifier of IP. This
example would illustrate the pattern in which the NP *a lot less pesticide*, the THEME
argument of the verb *use*, has been moved to the specifier of the VP headed by the
passive auxiliary *be*, while the expletive *there* is inserted in SpecIP. In (1a), the THEME
is moved to SpecIP. In the representations below strikethrough shows the copies of
the moved NP *a lot less pesticide*. We insert *is* in I to simplify the representation.

(3) a   (= 1b) [$_{IP}$ There is [$_{VP}$ a lot less pesticide being [$_{VP}$ ~~a lot less pesticide~~ used ~~a~~
        ~~lot less pesticide~~]]].
     b (= 1a) [$_{IP}$ A lot less pesticide is [$_{VP}$ ~~a lot less pesticides~~ being [$_{VP}$ ~~a lot less~~
        ~~pesticide~~ used ~~a lot less pesticide~~]]].

Discuss the derivation of the passive sentences in (4).

(4) a   There has been some work presented in this workshop that really inspired
        me and made me perhaps rethink what I want to do in my own work, she
        said. (*New York Times*, 28.11.2002, p. B6, col. 1)
     b There have been nearly two dozen people kidnapped since Nicholas E. Berg,
        a radio-tower builder from Pennsylvania, was taken captive in Iraq in April
        and later beheaded. (*New York Times*, 1.8.2004, p. 1, section 4, col. 4)
     c There were already around 18,000 new titles a year being published in
        1960. (*Guardian*, Review, 13.3.2004, p. 10, col. 2)

---

[18]   See section 3.2.2.1.

See also Basilico (1998) for more careful discussion of passive and existential sentences, Caponigro and Schütze (2003) for extension to other sentence types and to Italian passivization. See Law (1999) for critical discussion.

Exercise 21   Floating quantifiers in Hebrew (E)

Consider the examples in (1),[19] which we discussed in Exercise 19 of Chapter 2. We showed in that exercise that both the string *kol ya-yeladim* ('all the children'), and the string *ha yeladim kul-am* ('the children all') are constituents. Using the glosses as a basis, describe the difference between the underlined NPs in (1a) and (1b).

(1) a   <u>Kol ha-yeladim</u> zarku ʔavanim.
         all the children threw stones
         'All the children threw stones.'

     b   <u>Ha-yeladim kul-am</u> zarku ʔavanim.
         the children all-3MPL threw stones
         'The children all threw stones.'

Exercise 12 of the current chapter showed that quantifiers can be floated in Hebrew. Consider the following examples: what restrictions on quantifier floating do these data reveal?

(2) a   Ha-yeladim hiku kul-am ʔet ha-mora.
         the-children hit   all-3MPL the-teacher
         'The children all hit the teacher.'

     a′ *Ha-yeladim hiku kol ʔet ha-mora.
         the-children hit   all the-teacher

     b   Ha-banot hadfu   kul-an ʔet ha-kadur.
         the-girls hit-back all-3FPL the-ball
         'The girls all hit back the ball.'

     b′ *Ha-banot hadfu   kol ʔet ha-kadur.
         the-girls   hit-back all the-ball

KEY AND COMMENTS

The quantifier *all* has two forms in Hebrew: it either precedes the NP and then it is invariant and takes the form *kol* or it follows the noun and then it is inflected for

---

[19]   The data in this exercise are based on Shlonsky (1991: 163–4). Thanks to Ur Shlonsky for help with (1).

person, gender, and number. Based on the primed examples in (2) we conclude that the invariant form of the quantifier, *kol*, cannot be stranded. Only the inflected postnominal quantifier can be stranded. This suggests that for an NP to be able to strand an associated quantifier it must appear to its left, the position at which it triggers the agreeing form.[20]

Exercise 22   Refining structures: From one functional head to many (T, E)

This is yet another long and discursive exercise. Its purpose is once again to explore one line of argumentation and see where that leads us. The goal of the discussion is not to provide a complete answer for the problem raised. Rather, the exercise tries to show how new hypotheses come about through the interplay of data and theory. The analysis elaborated in this exercise is not necessarily the definitive one. It is one way of handling the data in terms of the theory we have been elaborating.

In this exercise we explore the implications of the hypothesis that syntactic structure determines interpretation. We first examine the problems of interpretation raised by one example and try to provide an analysis. After the discussion further examples are given as an additional exercise. Consider example (1a).

(1) a   Turkey <u>could until very recently privately</u> congratulate itself on narrowly escaping a place in the front line. (*Guardian*, 21.11.2003, p. 16, col. 3)

We are interested in the underlined section of the example. Before we start the discussion, we will simplify the example by removing distracting elements that are not relevant to the point at issue. Such a modification of the data is not "cheating." Simplifying the data is a perfectly legitimate operation in scientific work: we are like the scientist who isolates the relevant data in the raw material he or she has collected, removing material that is not relevant for the enquiry. The simplified example we will be working on is (1b).

(1) b   Turkey <u>could until very recently privately</u> congratulate itself.

Draw a tree diagram for (1b). Represent the base position of the subject by means of the strikethrough notation. Consider the resulting structure in the light of the discussion of adjunct scope in section 2.1 of the chapter. Do the positions of the adjuncts correspond to their relative scope? What would be the scope domain of the modal *could*?

---

[20]   See Shlonsky (1991) for an account.

KEY AND COMMENTS

The structure of (1b) can be represented as in (2a):

(2) a

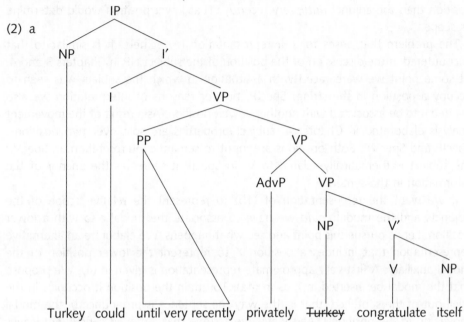

Turkey could until very recently privately ~~Turkey~~ congratulate itself

The positions of the adjuncts *until very recently* and *privately* reflect their relative scope. *Privately* modifies the VP domain; it specifies the manner in which 'Turkey congratulated itself'. As a first approximation we could say that the temporal PP *until very recently* delimits the period in which 'Turkey privately congratulated itself'. The PP *until very recently* has wider scope than the adverb phrase *privately*.

(2) b *until very recently > privately*

We can read off the scope of these two adjuncts directly from the structure.

While the adjuncts occupy positions that mirror their scope, this is not true for the modal auxiliary *could* in I. In this example the modal *could* expressed an ability. If we read the scope of an element off from the structure then the modal *could* would have to have scope over both adjuncts. However, we will naturally paraphrase (1) as in (3), where *until very recently* in fact modifies the period in which Turkey had the ability to congratulate itself in private. So *until very recently* should not just have scope over VP, it should also have scope over *could*.

(3) Until very recently it was the case that Turkey <u>was able to privately</u> congratu-
     late itself.
     until very recently > could > privately

This means that the scope relations of *until very recently* and *could* cannot be directly read off from the structure. The modal auxiliary *could* occupies the position in I. What we would really need is for *could* to be represented in a lower position than the adjunct *until very recently*. That lower position would determine its scope.

The problem that arises for our representation is not new. It is similar to that encountered in the discussion of the position of the subject NP in Chapters 3 and 4. At some point we were faced with a situation in which the subject was seen to occupy a position in the string, SpecIP, but for reasons of interpretation we also wanted it to be associated with another, lower, position. As a result of the movement analysis elaborated in Chapter 4, subject properties are split over two positions: SpecIP and SpecVP. Both positions are input to semantic interpretation: in SpecVP the subject is thematically related to V; in SpecIP it serves as the anchor of the information in the sentence.

If we want the representation of (1b) to represent the relative scope of the adjuncts and the modal *could* we have to associate the modal also with a lower position. Let us pursue this point and see what happens. We elaborate an alternative representation that includes a position X to represent the lower position of the modal auxiliary. A first very approximate representation is given in (4). We propose that the modal be inserted in X as in (4a). To attain the position it occupies in the spell-out of the sentence (that is, the way the sentence is pronounced), the modal moves up to the position I. As always, we assume that a moved constituent leaves an unpronounced copy in its base position (4b). We cannot yet detail the brackets here as we will first have to determine which constituents they are.

(4) Provisional representations:

  a [ᵢₚ Turkey [ᵢ] until very recently [ₓ could] [ᵥₚ privately [ᵥₚ ~~Turkey~~ congratulate itself]]].

  b [ᵢₚ Turkey [ᵢ could] until very recently [ₓ ~~could~~] [ᵥₚ privately [ᵥₚ ~~Turkey~~ congratulate itself]]].

In its lower position (X), *could* is in the scope of the PP *until very recently*. We propose that the modal moves from X to I, which is a head position. So far, we have been assuming that heads (auxiliaries, verbs in French) move to I. Let us generalize this idea and assume that the modal in X is a head and that X is a head position. If X is a head then we expect it to project a phrase, "XP."

In our earlier representation (2a) the PP *until very recently* was VP-adjoined. But in the new representation, the PP *until very recently* can no longer be left-adjoined to VP. The head X intervenes and it heads its own projection, XP. As a result, we propose that the adjunct *until very recently* is adjoined to the projection XP. (4c) completes the provisional representation above:

(4) c [ᵢₚ Turkey [ᵢ could] [ₓₚ until very recently [ₓₚ [ₓ ~~could~~] [ᵥₚ privately [ᵥₚ ~~Turkey~~ congratulate itself]]]]].

We have to determine the category of the new head X. Is X a head of the category V? This would mean that we treat the modal *could* as another auxiliary with its own VP-projection.[21] However, one objection to this is that English modals do not have any non-finite forms: *could* cannot be found as a participle, for instance:[22]

(5) a *He has so far could finish the book.
    b *Turkey has until very recently could privately congratulate itself.

Another proposal is to say that X is functional head in the IP domain. Recall that the content of I encodes the link between subject and VP in terms of tense, modality, etc. On the basis of the preceding discussion we could tentatively "decompose" I and postulate that there are two "inflectional heads" in the sentence: I1 and I2. We might, for example, specify that I2 encodes modality and that I1 encodes Tense, though we would obviously have to look at many more examples to substantiate this analysis.

(4) d

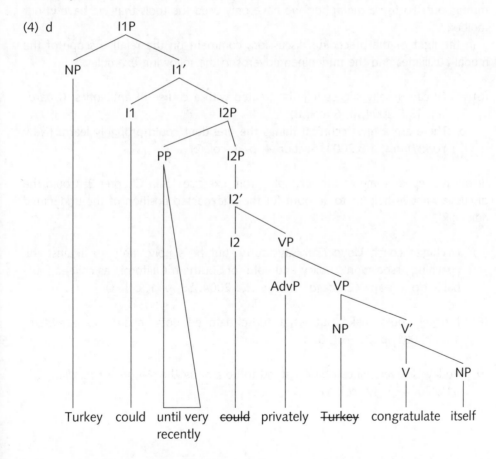

[21] See Chapter 3, section 4.3.
[22] See the discussion of (67) in section 4.3 of Chapter 3.

The PP *until very recently* is now adjoined to the projection of I2, meaning it delimits the duration of the 'ability'. *Privately* continues to have scope only over the VP *congratulate itself*. *Privately* does not restrict the ability. The relative scope of the two adjuncts as represented in (3) is retained in our new representation: *until very recently* has scope over a larger constituent (I2P) than *privately*.

That modals may be associated with a lower position is confirmed by those dialects of English that allow double modals:[23]

(5)   He'll can get you one. (Brown, 1992: 75)

We might object that our representations are becoming more and more complicated. This is not obviously the case, though. Though the structures we have are definitely more articulated, it is not necessarily true that the theory we are elaborating is itself becoming more complex. In order to arrive at the articulated structure above, we have merely implemented the argumentation that we had developed throughout. To use a metaphor: we have only used the tools that we have in our toolbox.

In the light of the preceding discussion, comment on the relative scope of the modal auxiliaries and the underlined adverbs in the following examples:

(6) a   TB can <u>usually successfully</u> be treated with a course of antibiotics. (*Guardian*, 13.8.2004, p. 6, col. 8)
     b   There are a few technical things the president could <u>probably</u> learn. (*New York Times*, 1.8.2004, Section 4, p. 4, col. 2)

Below we repeat some of the examples from Exercise 15 in Chapter 3. Could the discussion above help us to account for the unexpected position of the underlined adjunct?

(7)   Michigan coach Lloyd Carr says sorry, but he <u>simply</u> can't go against the coaching association's policy and vote for Southern California as college football's No 1 team. (*Chicago Tribune*, 3.1.2004, S3, p. 1, col. 1)

(8)   I <u>never</u> could make out what those damned dots meant. (*Independent*, 14.04.2001, p. 20, col. 6)

(9)   Today Gulliver <u>still</u> can barely stand to be among the Yahoos. (*Guardian*, G2, 31.8.2004, p. 12, col. 1)

---

[23]   For double modals in Scots see Brown (1992) and Miller (1993). For American varieties see for instance Battistella (1995). For modals in earlier stages of English see Lightfoot (1979) and Roberts (1985).

The hypothesis that a functional head such as I can be decomposed into a more articulated structure is due to Pollock (1989) and has become known as the **Split Infl Hypothesis.**[24]

The Split Infl hypothesis has further consequences. Recall that in previous exercises we discovered the need for an additional position for the subject. This was the case for instance, with respect to the transitive expletive construction in Exercise 14 and with respect to the Irish VSO patterns in Exercise 15. Pursuing the Split Infl hypothesis we might postulate that the lower subject positions identified in the earlier exercises correspond to the specifier positions of lower functional heads.

(10) a [$_{I1P}$ það [$_{I'}$ [$_{I}$ klaruðu] [$_{I2P}$ margar mýs [$_{VP}$ *alveg* [$_{VP}$ ~~margar mýs~~ [$_{V}$ ~~klaruðu~~] ostinn]]]]].

b [$_{I1P}$ [$_{I'}$ [$_{I}$ Chuala] [$_{I2P}$ Róise [$_{VP}$ go mini roimhe [$_{VP}$ ~~Róise chuala~~ an t-amhrán sin]]]]].

Exercise 23   Predicate inversion in English (E)

Consider the following examples:[25] they illustrate a construction type referred to as **predicate inversion** or "inversion around *be*" (Emonds, 1976; Birner, 1992, 1994; Birner & Ward, 1992).

(1) a Complicating matters is cost. (*Washington Post*, 10.12.2002, p. A16, col. 1)

b Helping to run the house were a cook, a housemaid and a manservant. (Carol Shields, *Jane Austin*, 2001: 123)

c (The thieves paid the £6 entrance fee and made their way to the staircase hall, where they overpowered the guide and took the painting from the wall.) Waiting for them outside were the Volkswagen and at least one other, but probably two, accomplices. (*Guardian*, G2, 28.8.2003, p. 6, col. 2)

These examples can be contrasted with the more neutral word order patterns in (2).[26]

(2) a Cost is complicating matters.

b A cook, a housemaid and a manservant were helping to run the house.

c The Volkswagen and at least one other, but probably two, accomplices were waiting for them outside.

---

[24]   Pollock's own analysis was based on other empirical material. See also Cormack and Smith (2002) for the scope of modals. See Svenonius (2002), Ernst (2002, 2004), Alexiadou (2004b), Cinque (1999, 2004a), and Nilsen (2004), among others for the distribution of adverbials. See Cinque (1999) for further decomposition of I.

[25]   Examples (1a) and (1b) were discussed in Exercise 12 of Chapter 1.

[26]   For the discourse function of the predicate inversion construction see Birner (1992, 1994), Birner and Ward (1992).

How do we derive the sentences in (2)? Assuming that the sentences in (1) have a similar underlying structure, how could we derive them?

KEY AND COMMENTS

Following the analysis elaborated we could assume that (2a) is derived in the by now familiar way, with the subject NP *cost* being merged as the specifier of the VP and moving out to the specifier position of IP. The auxiliary *was* is merged as the head of a VP and moves to I, the subject NP *cost* undergoes step-by-step movement to the specifier of IP:[27]

(3) a [$_{IP}$ [$_{NP}$ Cost] [$_I$ was] [$_{VP}$ ~~cost be~~ [$_{VP}$ ~~cost~~ [$_{V'}$ complicating matters]]]].

To derive the predicate inversion pattern in (1a), we might propose that the constituent containing the verb *complicating* and the object *matters* moves, while the subject NP *cost* is stranded in the specifier of the VP:

(3) b **Hypothesis**
        [$_{IP}$ [$_{V'}$ Complicating matters] [$_I$ was] [$_{VP}$ [$_{V'}$ ~~complicating matters~~] ~~be~~ [$_{VP}$ cost [$_{V'}$ ~~complicating matters~~]]]].

Observe that in this case we have to move an intermediate projection (V′). This is potentially worrying, as we have not really used such a projection for any movement operation yet.

TWO MORE COMPLICATIONS

Assuming the analysis in (3b), we would predict that there is relatively free variation between the two patterns discussed here, i.e., that, depending on the informational organization of the sentence we want to put forward, we can either front the subject to SpecIP (as in the examples in (2)) or we can front V′ (as in the examples in (1)). Is this prediction correct?

(4) a I wonder whether three students from Romania will be waiting in the corridor.
    b *I wonder whether waiting in the corridor will be three students from Romania.

(5) a I expect the candidates for the exam to be waiting in the corridor.
    b *I expect waiting in the corridor to be the candidates for the exam.

Discuss the problem raised for the analysis in (3b) by the application of predicate inversion in the following examples. Could we claim that V′ has been fronted, stranding the subject in the specifier of VP?

---

[27] See section 4 of this chapter.

(6)   Still peeking through the attitudes of Labour politicians high and low are glimpses of doubt about their right to be where they are. (*Guardian*, 9.4.2002, p. 8, col. 3)

(7)   Confidently riding the horse is the beautiful, dark-haired Tamsin. (*Observer*, 24.20.2004, *Review*, p. 5, col. 2)

(8)   A recent survey of senior-class presidents in high schools around the nation has shown that 73% approve of draft registration for 18-year-old men and 51% favor prayer in public schools. Sharply dividing the class presidents was the issue of abortion – 50% supported a woman's right to terminate an unwanted pregnancy; 32.5% opposed it. (*Philadelphia Inquirer*, 3.9.1983, from Birner & Ward, 1992: 9, their (21a))

(9)   Ashenden duly distributed the Welcome Trusthouse Forte forms, already completed for the sections dealing with Company, Next Destination, Settlement of Account, Arrival, Departure and Nationality. Only remaining for the tourists to fill in were the four sections headed Home Address, Telephone, Passport Number and Signature. (Colin Dexter, *The Jewel that was Ours*, 1992: 23)

(10)   Now living with the Morrises was Janey's sister, Bessie Burden, who had joined them in the last few months at Red House, after her father died. (Fiona MacCarthy, *William Morris*, 1995: 198)

Exercise 24   Language typology (T, E, presupposes Exercises 6, 7, 13, and 16)

In this chapter we have discussed a number of different languages. We have identified two properties that determine their word order:

(i)   The verb moves to I.
(ii)   The subject moves to SpecIP.

Based on the discussion in the chapter and on the data in the preceding exercises, complete Table 1, writing + if the language displays the property and – if it does not.

The combination of two variable properties leads to four possible combinations. In the blanks in Table 2 fill in the languages that display the corresponding combination. Are all combinations attested?[28]

---

[28]   For a discussion of the typology see Baker (2002).

Table 1   Language typology

Language	V to I	Subject to SpecIP
Arabic		
English		
French		
Irish		
Modern Greek		
Welsh		

Table 2   Inventory of languages

	V to I	V remains in V
Subject to SpecIP		
Subject does not move to SpecIP		

5   The Periphery of the Sentence

Discussion

Contents

0 Introduction

This final chapter completes the overview of the structure of the sentence. So far, we have mainly concentrated on sentences whose leftmost constituent is the subject. We did occasionally discuss examples in which the subject is preceded by some other constituent, but the discussion did not go into details. In this chapter, we explore how interrogative constituents and auxiliaries to the left of the canonical subject position are structurally integrated into the sentence. We will also examine how a fully formed sentence can be integrated into a larger structure as an embedded clause.

We continue to assume that structures are derived by means of the operations Merge ('assemble, put together') and Move. As before, we use the binary branching format for structure: a head merges with a complement, the resulting constituent merges with a specifier to complete the projection, and two fully formed projections can be combined by adjunction. The current chapter focuses on the importance of the operation Move. One of the issues that will be raised is how far a constituent can be moved and whether there are any obstacles to the Move operation, that is, whether there are factors that can stop a constituent from moving from one position to another.

The chapter returns to one of the empirical issues raised in Chapter 1, the derivation of questions. In English, question formation usually requires that there be some material to the left of the canonical position of the subject. So we will investigate how to integrate this area of the sentence into the structure we have been assuming. In addition, we briefly look at the derivation of relative clauses, which also implicate the area of the sentence to the left of the subject. The mechanisms elaborated for the derivation of questions will be extended to the derivation of relative clauses.

In the chapter we will put forward a number of constraints on the way a constituent is moved and this will lead to the prediction that sentences violating these constraints should be ungrammatical. That is to say, such sentences should not be generated by our grammar. The analysis of grammatical sentences exemplifying movement may confirm that their derivation obeys the constraints we have postulated. But the fact that all the sentences we come across obey the constraints is not sufficient to confirm the prediction that all sentences violating such constraints are ungrammatical. At various points in the chapter we will test the prediction made by our analysis by experiment: we will construct examples that contain precisely the patterns that violate the constraints. According to the prediction following from our hypothesis such sentences should be unacceptable.

The chapter is organized as follows. Section 1 recapitulates the main issues covered in the previous chapters. In section 2 we examine how finite interrogative sentences are derived in English. We will see that the operation Move can be used to account for the derivation of such sentences. In section 3 we examine some of the constraints on the operation Move. In section 4 we briefly look at non-finite interrogative clauses. Section 5 deals with relative clauses. Section 6 is a summary of the chapter.

1   Recapitulation

Throughout this book, we have elaborated a set of hypotheses for the structure of sentences. These hypotheses form a theory, a system of principles of syntax, which we take to be the instructions for the derivation of sentences. Ideally, the theory we elaborate must be powerful enough to allow us to derive all and only sentences that are acceptable. In other words, the theory should not be too powerful: it should not **overgenerate**, that is, it should not allow the derivation of unacceptable sentences.

At this point it may be important to underline that a scientific theory is not static, it is not like a painting, for instance, which is an entity that, once it is finished, is "fixed" and does not change any more though our perception of it may change. A scientific theory is dynamic. Confronted with new empirical data or with new theoretical hypotheses, scientists may well reconsider some of their earlier hypotheses. A scientific theory must continuously be evaluated and adapted. Evaluating a theory of syntax may be done with respect to two types of questions:

(i)   What is the internal organization of the theory? Are the principles that make up the theory internally consistent? Are there any redundant principles that we could eliminate, leading to a more economical theory?

(ii) What is the empirical coverage of the theory? Does the theory generate the right type of sentence? Does the theory generate any unacceptable sentences?

Try to summarize the various components of the theory that we have elaborated and illustrate how they account for the derivation of sentence (1a). Does the current version of our theory allow us to derive sentences (1b), (1c), and (1d)?

(1) a   The spy should destroy these instructions.
     b   Obviously, the spy should destroy these instructions.
     c   These instructions, the spy should destroy.
     d   Should the spy destroy these instructions?

In the discussion we have adopted a general hypothesis about linguistic structure summarized schematically in (2).[1] Our hypothesis is that all constituents are derived by **merging** (= putting together) two constituents. We can read the derivation of representation (2a) from the bottom to the top in the following way. We first merge the head of the constituent, X, with its complement, forming X′; then we merge X′

---

[1]   As mentioned in Chapter 4, note 8, the component of syntactic theory which sums up the format for syntactic structure is referred to as X-bar theory.

with another constituent, the specifier, to form XP. The complement and the specifier are closely related to the head X and together they form the core constituent.

(2) a X-bar theory: The blueprint for structure

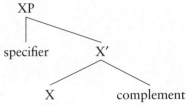

In addition, a fully formed constituent (which we could label YP, ZP, etc.) may be **adjoined** to another constituent. Adjunction is another application of Merge. Its specific property is that it merges constituents that are already complete in themselves. We assume that adjunction may apply both to the left and to the right. Adjunction is represented in (2b).

(2) b left-adjunction   right-adjunction

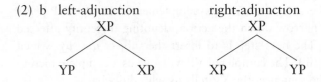

In addition to assembling a structure by the operation Merge, that is by merging two constituents, we can modify the structure obtained at some point by the operation Move. This operation removes a constituent from one position, and merges it in another position in the same structure. Move allows us to represent the fact that one constituent "belongs" to two positions in the structure. Continuing to work our way upward in the sentence, we take a constituent from a lower position and move it into a higher position. For instance, to account for the fact that the subject of a sentence has a close semantic relationship with the verb, we proposed in Chapter 4 that the subject is first merged in a VP-internal position. To explain how the subject ends up in its canonical position, the specifier of IP, we propose that it moves to that position. In order to represent that the moved constituent also "belongs" in the lower position we use the device of copies: a copy of the moved constituent remains in the base position, while the moved constituent is merged in the higher position. It is the higher "moved" copy that eventually is spelt out (pronounced). We use the strikethrough representation (~~subject~~) to signal the position of the non-pronounced copy.[2] Using the format in (2), we have elaborated a representation of the basic structure of the sentence. In the first stage of the analysis, we had arrived at the structure in (3) below. A projection of the lexical head (V) is dominated by a projection of a functional head that encodes inflectional features (see Chapter 3, section 1.2.3). VP is a lexical projection; IP is a functional projection.

---

[2] We also saw in Chapter 4, section 4, that movement proceeds stepwise. We will come back to this point in detail in section 3.2 below.

(3)   The structure of the sentence

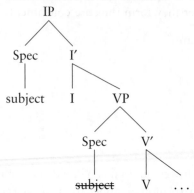

The system allows us to derive (1a). The semantic nucleus of (1a) is the verb *destroy*. The verb denotes the situation we are dealing with and it determines which constituents are obligatory in the sentence.[3] So, in order to build a sentence, we start off with the verb *destroy* (i). We merge it with its complement, here the NP *these instructions*, which serves to narrow down the action, denoting the entity affected by the act of destroying (ii). The next step is to insert the subject *the spy*, which denotes the AGENT of *destroy* (iii). The completed VP will give us a complete picture of the activity expressed in the sentence: the VP tells us who did what.

(4)   (i)   V = *destroy*

      (ii)

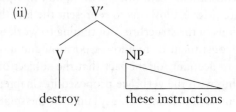

      (iii)

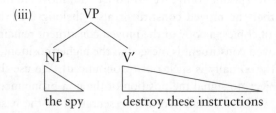

Next we build the dominating functional structure, the projection IP. I merges with VP. We insert the modal auxiliary *should* in I. *Should* locates the situation expressed in the sentence in the future and shows that the action expressed in the VP is

---

³   See Chapter 3, sections 3.1, 3.2, 3.3.

desirable to the speaker. I also determines a perspective, an anchor for the information given in the sentence. I projects and we create its specifier. The subject moves up to the specifier of I (iv).

(4) (iv)

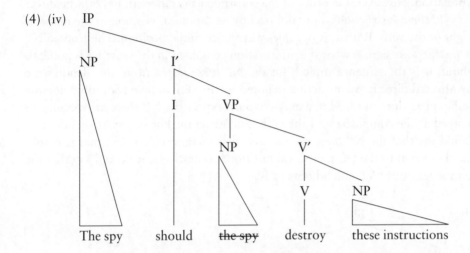

We build the structure starting from the semantic core, the verb, and by using the operation **Merge**, which combines two units, and the operation **Move**, which displaces units that are already part of the structure to a higher position.

Can we also derive the other examples in (1) using the above representations? With respect to (1b), the derivation can proceed as in (4), but there is an additional constituent in initial position, the adverbial phrase *obviously*.

(5) a   [$_{IP}$ the spy should destroy these instructions]
    b   + [$_{AdvP}$ obviously]

This additional constituent is optional; it does not receive a thematic role from the verb. The communicative function of *obviously* is to express the speaker's attitude to the content of the sentence. Recall that we can adjoin constituents to maximal projections. We could assemble (1b) by (left)-adjoining the AdvP to the projection IP.

(6)

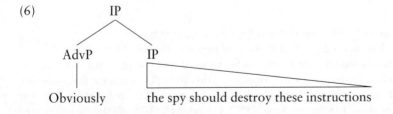

Compare (1a) and (1c), repeated here as (7a), in terms of their form and their meaning.

(7) a   These instructions, the spy should destroy.

(7a) has the same components as (1a) and the two sentences are very similar in interpretation. However, the order of the constituents is different. In (7a), the direct object NP, *these instructions*, does not occupy its canonical position to the immediate right of the verb. Rather, it occupies a sentence-initial position. The fronted NP *these instructions* signals what the information contained in the sentence is going to be about, it is the sentence **topic**.[4] But the NP *these instructions* also denotes the entity affected directly by the action denoted by the verb *destroy*. So, following the assembly procedure outlined above, we would expect the NP *these instructions* to be merged as the complement of the verb. Following the line of reasoning adopted, we could say that the NP *these instructions* first merges with V and that it is subsequently moved to the left-peripheral position.[5] Tentatively, we could say that the object moves out of VP and adjoins to IP:[6]

(7) b

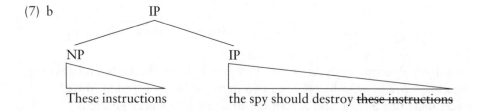

(1d) is familiar from the first chapter of the book; it illustrates a direct question. The subject NP *the spy* is preceded by the inverted modal auxiliary, *should*. Let us assume that, as before, the auxiliary *should* is first merged in I. The fronting of the auxiliary to the left of the subject signals the illocutionary force of the sentence, that is, it shows that the sentence is a question.[7] In Chapter 3[8] we concluded that in SAI the content of I inverts with the subject. In this chapter we will integrate the inverted constituent into the structure. We will do this using the format we have elaborated. As we will see, we will not need to invoke any novel mechanisms: we will be able to derive the word order of interrogative sentences by using a combination of the operations Merge and Move. As before, we elaborate a hypothesis and test it by examining its predictions.

---

[4]   For an early discussion of the concept "topic" see Reinhart (1981).

[5]   See also Chapter 3, section 1.2.3.4, and for more illustrations Exercise 15 in Chapter 2.

[6]   One question that arises is whether a fronted object should really be presented as having the same relation with IP as the adverbial *obviously* in (1b). We will not address this issue here as it would lead us to a lengthy discussion beyond the scope of an introductory text. For some discussion of object fronting see Rizzi (1997), Haegeman (2003), and the references cited there.

[7]   Recall from Chapter 1, section 2.3.2, that SAI does not always give rise to question interpretation.

[8]   Section 1.2.4.

2 Constructing the Periphery of the Sentence

2.1 Direct yes/no questions

In Chapter 3 we observed that to form a direct question in English we move the finite auxiliary from I to a position to the left of the subject (SAI). When a finite sentence lacks an auxiliary we move the content of I and we insert the auxiliary *do* as a supporting element to allow the inverted inflectional morpheme to survive in the position to the left of the subject. In French direct questions, the verb itself is able to move to a position to the left of the subject (SVI). This is compatible with our hypothesis that it is the content of I that moves leftward: we had seen that in French the lexical verb can move to I.

Let us assume that the inverted auxiliary in English and the inverted verb in French end up in the same position to the left of the subject.[9] SAI (or SVI in French) means that the content of I moves to the left of the subject. I is a head, so SAI/SVI is movement of a head. So far, we have been assuming that a head moves to a head position. For instance, we proposed in Chapter 3, section 4.3, that English auxiliaries are merged in V and move to I; French auxiliaries as well as French lexical verbs merge in a head position and move to I. If SAI/SVI is head movement, the landing site of SAI/SVI must be a head position to the left of the subject position. Let us provisionally label this head "X." The head X merges with IP. By the blueprint for structure outlined above, X and IP form a constituent X'.

(8) a

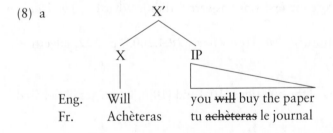

	X	IP
Eng.	Will	you ~~will~~ buy the paper
Fr.	Achèteras	tu ~~achèteras~~ le journal

Would it be possible to let the structure terminate here? Given the way we conceive the structure of constituents, is (8a) a legitimate representation? The answer is both "yes" and "no." (8a) does correspond to our blueprint (2a). However, once we have postulated a head, which combines with a complement, we would expect there to be a completed projection ("XP"). This would also make a specifier position available. The complement of the head X in (8a) is IP, that is, the sentence. (8b) is what we would expect to generate following the system we have set up.

---

[9] Exercise 23 in Chapter 4 shows that we should not derive all sentences in which an auxiliary precedes the subject by means of SAI. Exercise 15 in the current chapter shows that not all postverbal subjects in French necessarily occupy the same position.

(8) b

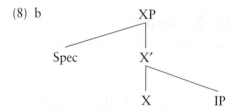

At this point, (8b) is only motivated on a theoretical basis. We have not provided any empirical support for projecting the XP level; nor have we discussed what kind of elements could fill the specifier position. A further question is to determine the nature of the head X. We turn to these issues immediately.

2.2   A filler for SpecXP?

What kinds of constituents could occupy specifier of X in (8b)? Or, putting it differently, is there any type of constituent that naturally tends to precede the inverted auxiliary in direct questions? We are looking for a constituent that "specifies" the question as expressed by the inversion of the auxiliary. The underlined examples in (9) suggest one answer. It is tempting to associate the interrogative constituent, or the *wh*-constituent, to the left of the auxiliary with the specifier position. Would this make sense in terms of the relation of this constituent to the question it introduces?

(9) a   "Which way are you going? Shall we walk a bit?" he began, putting the
          second question before the first was answered. (Edith Wharton, *The House
          of Mirth*, 1998: 201)
     b   How much can I afford? (*New York Times*, 28.4.2003, p. A22, advertise-
          ment Fleet)

Compare the interpretations of the questions (10a) and (10b), which are both based on (9a).

(10) a   Are you going to the park?
      b   Which way are you going?

Question (10a) could be said to be general: it is about whether or not a certain activity ('going to the park') will take place. (10a) is called a *yes/no* **question**: the expected answer is *yes* or *no*. (10b) is different: when asking (10b), we take it for granted (or we **presuppose**) that the activity of going somewhere will take place, but we don't yet know its GOAL. The initial *wh*-constituent *which way* specifies the **focus** or the **scope** of the question: it specifies the domain of application of the question, what the question is about. It is also an indication of the type of answer expected: as a reply to (10b) we expect to be provided with some constituent to match the interrogative constituent. Questions like (10b) are called **constituent**

questions. Because most interrogative constituents contain a word beginning with *wh-* such questions are also called ***wh*-questions.**

If we assume that the initial ***wh*-constituent** in a constituent question occupies the specifier position of XP in (8b), it has a specifier–head relation with the head X, which hosts the inverted auxiliary. The fronted *wh*-constituent interacts with the illocutionary force: its function is to specify the domain of the question. On the other hand, remember that the fronted *wh*-constituent also has a function within the IP domain. More precisely, the *wh*-constituent in our example has a semantic relationship with the verb. The NP *which way* indicates the GOAL argument of the verb *going*. So we also want to link the *wh*-constituent to a VP-internal thematic position. We can do this by first merging the NP *which way* VP-internally as a complement of the verb. *Which way* is merged with V to form V', and it then moves to the specifier position of XP, leaving a copy in the VP. As shown by (11), we can use the same analysis to derive example (9b).[10] The *wh*-constituent *how much* is both the complement of the verb *afford* and the element that marks the scope of the question. Again it first merges with V and then moves to SpecXP, leaving a copy.

(11) XP = CLAUSE/SENTENCE

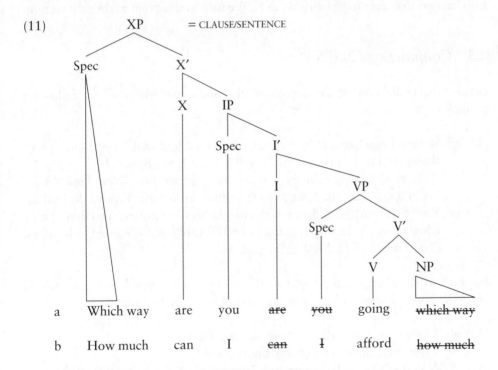

What label shall we use to designate the head X? The fillers for X we have come across so far are auxiliaries which have moved from the position I to X. Would it make sense to re-label X as "Aux"? What would be the problems with this label?

[10] For subject movement see Chapter 4.
  We will insert inflected auxiliaries under I to simplify the representations.

Though the label Aux might at first sight seem appropriate when we restrict the scope of our enquiry to English, it becomes less adequate once we take into consideration the fact that French lexical verbs can precede the subject as a result of inversion.[11] Recall that this was also possible in Old English.[12] Labeling the head position occupied by the inverted head Aux would mean that we only capture a subset of facts.[13]

To derive SAI/SVI the content of I moves to the left of the subject. Whether an auxiliary or a verb moves to the left of the subject depends on whether an auxiliary or a verb occupies I. However, the label I is also not suitable to designate the landing site X of the inverted head because I is already used as the label for the linking head that merges with VP and whose specifier is the subject. We do want to keep the two heads apart. For one thing, as can be seen in (11), the specifier of X need not be a subject.[14]

One problem for labeling X is due to the fact that so far, we have only been looking at heads that are moved to X but which themselves originate in another position. For the labeling of X it would be important to find out whether there are any elements that are merged directly in X. We turn to this point in the next section.

2.3 Conjunctions and SAI

Discuss the realization of the objects of the underlined verbs in the following examples.

(12) a What do you like and hate about your job? I <u>love</u> that I am talking about skiing all day. (*Independent*, Traveller, 25.9.1999, p. 8, col. 7)
   b Well, he said, I <u>like</u> that there are so many pretty girls. (*New York Times*, 2.1.2003, p. B2, col. 1, letter to the editor from Miles Fisher, 19, Dallas)
   c Your first brush with the capital is incredibly disorienting. You don't <u>know</u> whether one Tube stop is going to be 100 yards or if it's going to be miles. (*The Times*, 25.11.2000, p. 12, col. 1)

For each of the examples the object of the verb is itself realized by a sentence. In (12c) the object of *know* consists of the co-ordination of two sentences:

(12) a′ I <u>love</u> [that I am talking about skiing all day].
   b′ I <u>like</u> [that there are so many pretty girls].
   c′ You don't <u>know</u> [[whether one Tube stop is going to be 100 yards]
        or [if it's going to be miles]].

---

[11] Chapter 1, section 3.1 and Chapter 3, section 1.2.4.
[12] Chapter 1, section 3.2 and Chapter 3, section 1.2.4.
[13] We will discover a further objection to using the label Aux for X in section 2.3.
[14] On whether the specifier of XP actually can be a subject see the discussion in section 2.8.

When a sentence functions as a constituent inside another sentence it is often referred to by means of the term **clause**; it is a **subordinate clause** or an **embedded clause**. The bracketed subordinate clauses in the primed examples above function as complements of the verbs and are therefore also called **complement clauses**. As these clauses realize the direct objects of the verbs, another term that is used is **object clauses**. The subordinate clauses are introduced by the words *that*, *whether*, and *if*.

(13)   a   that I am talking about skiing all day
       b   that there are so many pretty girls
       c   whether one Tube stop is going to be 100 yards or
           if it's going to be miles

Traditionally, words such as *that*, *if*, *whether*, which introduce embedded clauses, are labeled (subordinating) **conjunctions**. In this book, we will use the more recent term **complementizer**. Complementizers serve to introduce subordinate or embedded clauses; they enable a clause to function inside another clause, for instance as a complement of a verb. Complementizers are **functional elements**.[15] The class of words that function as complementizers is **closed**:[16] any given language has a restricted set of words that have this "complementizing" function. Complementizers serve to encode illocutionary force. The complementizers *if* and *whether* signal that the subordinate clause is interrogative, while *that* indicates that the clause is declarative.[17]

As shown by (12c), a subordinate interrogative clause can be introduced either by *if* or by *whether*. Could we combine both conjunctions in one and the same clause? Try inserting *if* in the first embedded clause in (12c) and try adding *whether* to the second. This gives us (12c″):

(12)   c″   You don't <u>know</u>   *whether if one Tube stop is going to be 100 yards or
                                     *if whether it's going to be miles.

---

[15]   See Chapter 3, section 3.5 on the difference between lexical elements and functional elements.
[16]   See Chapter 1, section 2.4, and Chapter 3, section 4.3 on "closed classes."
[17]   In Chapter 1, note 10, we signaled that a more careful semantic analysis should make a distinction between the concepts "interrogative clause" and "question." For a good and accessible discussion see Huddleston (1994). For a more advanced semantic analysis see Ginzburg (1999). See McCloskey (forthcoming) for some syntactic consequences of the typology of interrogatives.

It is also not the case that all embedded clauses introduced by the complementizer *that* are assertions. Compare, for instance, (ia) and (ib):

(i)   a   John explained [that we cannot afford this car].
      b   John regrets [that they cannot afford this car].

While in (ia) the content of the embedded clause is asserted (by John), in (ib) it is presupposed. See Kiparsky and Kiparsky (1971) and Hooper and Thompson (1973) for early discussion of the syntactic consequences of the typology. See Hegarty (2003) for a recent discussion.

Apparently, the conjunctions *if* and *whether* are in complementary distribution.[18] To account for the fact that we cannot insert both *if* and *whether* to the left of a subject, we could propose that *if* and *whether* occupy the same position.

   Replace the two co-ordinated indirect questions in (12c) by two co-ordinated direct questions.

(14) a   <u>Is</u> one Tube stop going to be 100 yards
        b   or <u>is</u> it going to be miles?

In each of the co-ordinated direct *yes/no* questions in (14), the subject is preceded by the auxiliary; in indirect *yes/no* questions the subject is preceded by the interrogative complementizer *if* or *whether*. Can we combine SAI and the conjunction *if* or *whether*? To check whether this is possible, we could try to find relevant examples in which SAI coincides with the insertion of an interrogative complementizer. However, even if we do not find any examples, this would not ultimately prove that the combination of the conjunction *if/whether* with subject auxiliary inversion is impossible. We can also try to run an experiment in which we control the data, we construct the type of sentence we want to study, and we examine the result. We need a sentence in which subject-auxiliary inversion has taken place and which is at the same time introduced by a conjunction. Our experiment could consist of three stages. First we construct a direct question with SAI; then we turn that example into an embedded interrogative; finally, we insert a conjunction. Unfortunately, the second step of the experiment is not straightforward. We might start from the direct questions in (14), which display SAI. However, when we embed the sentences in (14) as complements of a verb the resulting sentences are unacceptable for most speakers of English:[19]

(14) a′   *You don't know <u>is</u> one Tube stop going to be 100 yards.
        b′   *You don't know <u>is</u> it going to be miles.

Inserting a complementizer does not improve the sentences (14a″, b″), but this does not mean that the combination of the complementizer and the inversion is the cause of the ungrammaticality. Even without the complementizer the examples were ungrammatical.

(14) a″   *You don't know if <u>is</u> one Tube stop going to be 100 yards.
        b″   *You don't know if <u>is</u> it going to be miles.

To test the compatibility of SAI with complementizers, we need to work with legitimate instances of embedded inversion and then we can check whether such

---

[18]   See Chapter 2, section 3.1.2.2 for another illustration of complementary distribution.
[19]   Hiberno English, the variant of English spoken in Ireland, does allow for this pattern. See Henry (1995). Exercise 5 illustrates this variant of English. The exercise can be tackled at the end of the present section.

examples allow insertion of the complementizers *if* or *whether*. Consider the following examples:[20]

(15) a <u>Had I known you were coming</u>, I would have baked a cake.
   b <u>Had the money not been returned</u>, the evidence would have pointed strongly to a conclusion that the NRCC "financed" the Forum. (*Washington Post*, 29.4.2003, p. A18, col. 3)

In (15a, b) SAI is found in conditional clauses. The examples can be paraphrased as in (16). The examples in (15) could be considered as the second step of the experiment: the sentences display embedded SAI. (16) shows that the conjunction *if* can also introduce a conditional clause.

(16) a <u>If I had known you were coming</u>, I would have baked a cake.
   b <u>If the money had not been returned</u>, the evidence would have pointed strongly to a conclusion that the NRCC "financed" the Forum.

We can now get on to the third step of the experiment, that is, we can insert the conjunction *if* in the conditional clauses in (15). Is the result acceptable?

(16) a′ *<u>If had I known you were coming</u>, I would have baked a cake.
   b′ *<u>If had the money not been returned</u>, the evidence would have pointed strongly to a conclusion that the NRCC "financed" the Forum.

The ungrammaticality of (16a′) and (16b′) suggests that the inverted auxiliary and the complementizer are in complementary distribution. Why would this be? One plausible account could be that there is a single head position to the left of the subject and that this position hosts either the inverted auxiliary or the conjunction.

Recall that in the preceding section we had already identified the head position X in representation (8). This head was argued to host the inverted auxiliary. The complementary distribution of the inverted auxiliary and the complementizer leads us to the hypothesis that X also hosts the complementizer. Whereas the auxiliary moves to X from I, the complementizer does not originate in another position. Let us propose that the complementizer is directly merged in the position X. Let us therefore re-label the position X as "C." C stands for complementizer. The position C is the position where complementizers are merged with the clause they introduce. The choice of C (*if, whether, that*) signals illocutionary force. In the absence of a conjunction, the position C may host the inverted auxiliary.[21]

If we re-label X in (8) as C, then we will also re-label X′ as C′, and XP as **CP**. The specifier of XP in (8b) becomes the specifier of CP (or **SpecCP**).

---

[20] We discussed them in Chapter 1, section 2.3.2, examples (32) and (33).
[21] Representation (17) is simplified in that we have not indicated the unpronounced copy of the subject in the specifier of VP. This is because the focus of the discussion is on the CP area.

(17)

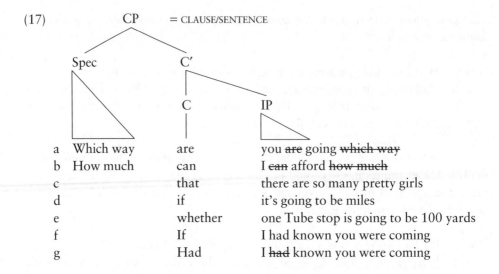

a	Which way	are	you ~~are~~ going ~~which way~~
b	How much	can	I ~~can~~ afford ~~how much~~
c		that	there are so many pretty girls
d		if	it's going to be miles
e		whether	one Tube stop is going to be 100 yards
f		If	I had known you were coming
g		Had	I ~~had~~ known you were coming

2.4   Some terminology

Sentences are derived by means of two operations: Merge and Move.[22] Merge assembles a structure of hierarchically organized constituents. Move displaces a constituent from the position in which it has been merged and merges it at some higher position in the structure. Moved constituents leave a copy.[23] Merge is used to insert a novel element into a structure, and also to (re)insert a moved element into the structure.[24]

2.5   Evidence for copies

In interrogative sentences, the sentence-initial *wh*-constituent is moved from a position inside the sentence. Moved constituents leave copies to ensure that the relations they have with various constituents in the sentence can remain encoded. For instance, when a direct object NP is moved to the sentence-initial position, its copy in the VP allows us to establish the thematic relation with the verb, while the pronounced copy in the initial position specifies the scope of the question. This motivation for copies is theoretical or conceptual. It follows from the way we set up our theory. We assume that the syntactic structure of a sentence maps onto its interpretation, that there is a direct correlation with the form of the sentence and its interpretation.

---

[22]   For a brief discussion of a system that only uses Merge (and "Multiple Merge") see Chapter 4, section 3.1.
[23]   Chapter 4, section 3.1.
[24]   Exercises 1, 3.

In the discussion of the movement of the subject[25] we provided some empirical evidence for our movement hypothesis. One type of evidence was provided by sentences in which (part of) the subject had been stranded in a lower position, giving rise to a discontinuous constituent. Would there be any similar empirical support for the hypothesis that moved interrogative constituents leave copies? Consider the two formulations of Mrs Pettigrew's question in the following extract. Identify the object of the verb *mean* in both formulations. In what way could such an example be relevant for the theory of movement that we have been elaborating here?

(18)   "What do you mean by that exactly?", said Mrs Pettigrew, "What exactly do you mean?" (Muriel Spark, *Memento Mori*, 1977: 81)

The two formulations of Mrs Pettigrew's question are very similar:

(19) a   What exactly do you mean?
      b   What   do you mean exactly?

In (19a), the object of *mean* is *what exactly*, an interrogative constituent or a *wh*-constituent. This *wh*-constituent occupies an initial position. We analyze (19a) as an instantiation of leftward movement: we have displaced the *wh*-constituent *what exactly* from the complement position of the verb *mean* to the specifier position of the projection CP. The fact that the string can be moved suggests that *what exactly* is a constituent.

(19) c   [$_{CP}$ What exactly [$_{C'}$ [$_C$ do] [$_{IP}$ you [~~PRESENT~~] [$_{VP}$ ~~you~~ mean ~~what exactly~~]]]]?[26]

In the alternative formulation of the question we find a discontinuous constituent *what . . . exactly*. The direct object NP of *mean* is split up: its interrogative component, *what*, is moved to SpecCP and is separated from *exactly*. The two variants of the sentence seem to have the same interpretation. We can relate the derivation of the two variants if we assume that in (19b) the moved interrogative pronoun *what* and the adverb *exactly* are first merged as one constituent and then movement of *what* strands the adverb *exactly*. In (19d) *exactly* is represented as a residue of the moved constituent.[27]

(19) d   [$_{CP}$ What [$_{C'}$ [$_C$ do] [$_{IP}$ you [~~PRESENT~~] [$_{VP}$ ~~you~~ mean [~~what~~ exactly]]]]]?

---

[25]   See Chapter 4, section 3.2.
[26]   For present tense inflection we use the symbol -*s* for the third person singular morpheme. We use the symbol PRESENT for other person and number combinations, because they lack overt manifestations. In (19d) and similar examples, *do* in C spells out the moved present tense ending. For more careful discussion of the inflection of "bare verbs" in English see Pollock (1994).
[27]   For more careful discussion of these patterns see also McCloskey (2000: 63–4, note 8 and the reference cited there).

McCloskey (2000) provides the West Ulster English examples in (20) (McCloskey, 2000: 58, his (2)). Identify the objects of the underlined verbs. How do we derive the word order in these questions? Represent the structure of the examples, using labeled bracketing and indicating non-pronounced copies of moved constituents by strikethrough:

(20) a What all did you <u>get</u> for Christmas?
     b Who all did you <u>meet</u> when you were in Derry?

Based on the discussion so far, we would provide the representations in (21):

(21) a [$_{CP}$ [$_{NP}$ What all] [$_{C'}$ [$_C$ did] [$_{IP}$ you [$_I$ -ed] [$_{VP}$ ~~you~~ get [$_{NP}$ ~~what all~~] for Christmas]]]]?
     b [$_{CP}$ [$_{NP}$ Who all] [$_{C'}$ [$_C$ did] [$_{IP}$ you [$_I$ -ed] [$_{VP}$ ~~you~~ meet [$_{NP}$ ~~who all~~] when you were in Derry]]]]?

McCloskey (2000: 58) reports that West Ulster English usage offers some interesting variants of the sentences above:

> In addition to [20], though, West Ulster English allows [22]:
>
> [22] a What did you get all for Christmas?
>   b Who did you meet all when you were in Derry?
>
> The quantifier *all* in [22ab] is construed with the interrogative pronoun . . . that is, the examples in [22] are synonymous (completely so, as far as I have been able to tell) with those in [20].

Using the examples in (20) as a starting point, how would you represent the alternative formulations for the questions as given in (22)? How do these examples bear on our current discussion?

Once again, it seems plausible that *what . . . all* in (22a) and *who . . . all* in (22b) are discontinuous constituents. While the interrogative pronouns *what* and *who* have moved to the specifier of CP, the associated quantifier *all* has been stranded in the base position. The floated quantifier would then signal the base position of the object.

(23) a [$_{CP}$ What [$_{C'}$ [$_C$ did] [$_{IP}$ you [$_I$ -ed] [$_{VP}$ ~~you~~ get [~~what~~ all] for Christmas]]]]?
     b [$_{CP}$ Who [$_{C'}$ [$_C$ did] [$_{IP}$ you [$_I$ -ed] [$_{VP}$ ~~you~~ meet [~~who~~ all] when you were in Derry]]]]?

2.6 Indirect constituent questions

We saw in our discussion of question formation[28] that indirect questions do not tend to give rise to SAI. Identify the indirect questions in (24):

---

[28] Chapter 1, especially section 2.3.

(24) a David S. Chu, under-secretary of defense for personnel and readiness, said last week the Pentagon needs a freer hand in determining who is hired, how much they are paid and what types of jobs they do in order to shape a department that is more agile in carrying out its mission of national defense. (*Washington Post*, 29.4.2003, p. Q21, col. 5)

   b You could rehash the night before, talk about what adjustments you need to make, whether it was great or whether you caved and did something you probably shouldn't have. (*Washington Post*, 10.12.2002, p. F4, col. 2)

   c Mrs Smegma showed me to a room, then gave me a tour of the facilities and outlined the many complicated rules for residing there – when breakfast was served ... which hours of the day I would have to vacate the premises and during which brief period a bath was permitted (these seemed, oddly, to coincide), how much notice I should give if I intended to receive a phone call or remain out after 10 p.m. (Adapted from Bill Bryson, *Notes from a Small Island*, 1996: 15–16)

   d She knew how many novels she would write and what they would be about. (*Guardian*, 2.8.2003, Review, p. 14, col. 4)

In the following examples, the embedded questions do display SAI, which is not the most usual order.[29] Rephrase the indirect questions in (25) to undo SAI:

(25) a All he wants to know is which boxes have I ticked on the forms he keeps giving me to fill in. (*Guardian*, G2, 15.3.2001, p. 9, col. 8)

   b People ask why was I not at Coniston when Bluebird was raised. (*Guardian*, 15.3.2001, p. 5, col. 8)

In this section, we make the derivation of indirect questions more precise. We continue to adopt the hypotheses elaborated already. We will first experiment on the basis of an invented example. This is because in such an example we control the material and we ensure that we are not distracted by complications that are perhaps not relevant for the point at issue.

Let us look at the underlined string in (26a). Is this string a constituent? What is its grammatical function? Consider the internal structure of the underlined string. Identify the lexical verb. What is the direct object? Identify the subject. Do subject and object occupy their canonical positions?

(26) a The students wondered <u>which analysis they should adopt</u>.

Among other things, the underlined string contains a lexical verb, *adopt*, and a subject NP, *they*. The subject occupies its canonical position: it precedes the modal auxiliary *should*, which occupies I. The NP *which analysis*, which functions as the

---

[29] For an (accessible) discussion of inversion in embedded questions in Hiberno English see Henry (1995).

object of *adopt*, does not occupy its canonical position in the VP headed by *adopt*, but it has moved leftward to a peripheral position. Could the object have remained in its canonical position to the right of the verb? If we simply return the interrogative object NP to its base position the result is not acceptable:

(26) b *The students wondered they should adopt <u>which analysis</u>.

Why should this be? What could be the reason why the NP *which analysis* has to move leftward? And where does it move? Replace the object in (26b) by a non-interrogative object. Is the resulting string acceptable?

(26) c *The students wondered they should adopt <u>this analysis</u>.

Can we now make (26c) grammatical by moving the object NP *this analysis* leftward?

(26) d *The students wondered <u>this analysis</u> they should adopt.

How can we rephrase (26c) to make it acceptable? One strategy is to insert the conjunction *if* or *whether* to the immediate left of the subject of the embedded clause:

(26) e The students wondered <u>if</u> they should adopt this analysis.
     f The students wondered <u>whether</u> they should adopt this analysis.

An alternative strategy is to replace the verb *wonder* by *believe*:

(26) g The students <u>believed</u> they should adopt this analysis.

The data suggest that there is a correlation between the presence of the verb *wonder* in the main clause and the internal make-up of the embedded clause. With *wonder* as a main verb, we either introduce the embedded clause by means of the conjunction *if/whether* or we move a *wh*-constituent to the left of the subject. These two manipulations are related: the verb *wonder* selects an interrogative clause as its complement. The conjunctions *if* and *whether* are one way of encoding illocutionary force, they signal that the embedded clause they introduce is interrogative. An alternative way of encoding interrogative illocutionary force is to shift a *wh*-constituent to the left in the embedded clause. In the latter case, the shifted *wh*-constituent will specify the scope of the question.

For direct interrogatives, we have already proposed that interrogative force is encoded in the part of the structure labeled CP. In keeping with this hypothesis, it would be simplest (and therefore it would be preferable) to use the structures that we have in place to account for the position of the fronted *wh*-constituent in indirect questions. The function of the fronted *wh*-constituent is to specify the scope of the question. We can propose that, as was the case in direct questions, the *wh*-constituent in indirect questions is moved to the specifier of the embedded CP.

In indirect questions in which we front a *wh*-constituent, the position C remains obligatorily empty in Modern English. However, we have to postulate a head C because, in the absence of the head C, we would no longer be able to project a constituent and create the relevant specifier position. In (27) below we give a schematic representation.[30]

(27)

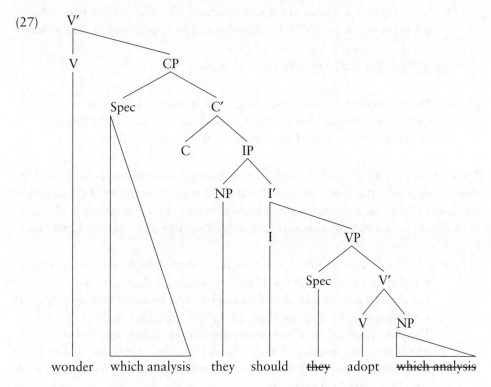

2.7 Uniqueness of specifiers and multiple questions

The canonical position of the subject is SpecIP: among other things, the subject specifies the domain of application of the VP, the subject says what the sentence is about. For instance in (28a), the property "run an Indian restaurant" is applied to the referent of the subject NP *John*:

(28) a John runs an Indian restaurant.

We know that IP has only one specifier (28b). If we want two NPs to function as subjects of a sentence, we co-ordinate them, thus turning them into one constituent (28c).

(28) b *[NP Mary] [NP John] will run an Indian restaurant.
     c [NP [NP Mary] and [NP John]] will run an Indian restaurant.

---

[30] Exercises 4, 5, 6, 7, 8.

Similarly, the specifier of CP encodes the scope of the question, the domain to which the question is applied. Identify the fronted interrogative constituents in embedded questions in the following examples.

(29) a   It has become a matter of dispute what John said to George.
      b   It has become a matter of dispute to whom John said that he had to leave.
      c   It has become a matter of dispute who said to George that he had to leave.

Consider (30). What is wrong with these examples?

(30) a   *It has become a matter of dispute what to whom John said.
      b   *It has become a matter of dispute to whom who said these things.
      c   *It has become a matter of dispute what who said to John.

The examples in (30) all contain two sentence-initial *wh*-constituents in the embedded clause. Apparently this is not possible. How could we account for this? Observe that we cannot claim that a question cannot bear on more than one constituent. (31) contains attested examples of questions with more than one interrogative constituent:

(31) a   I don't know who spotted who first, but within a couple of days The Bruiser was Jeffrey's minder and confidante. (*Guardian*, G2, 7.4.2003, p. 2, col. 2)
      b   For the past few months, KidsPost has had articles about who does what at a newspaper. (*Washington Post*, 29.4.2003, p. C13, col. 2)
      c   The chronological structure seems sensible in theory, but in fact is dull. As she marches doggedly forward from Praxitiles' *Aphrodite of Knidos* to Madonna, we can predict which names will occur in which order. (*Guardian*, 29.3.2003, p. 14, col. 5)
      d   There was still much confusion, and many yawns, about exactly who had said what when, and sent which emails to whom when. (*Guardian*, 2.3.2002, *The Editor*, p. 5, col. 2)
      e   I will be letting people know more about exactly who knew what and when. (*Independent*, 27.2.2000, p. 8, col. 4)
      f   The question of who gives how much is of intense interest to non-profit groups as they search for sources to make up for falling government, foundation and corporate funding. (*Washington Post*, 29.4.2003, p. A7, col. 3)

Using (31) as a model, let us try to rephrase the questions in (30) to make them acceptable while retaining the two interrogative constituents. One way of "repairing" the examples in (30) is illustrated in (32). Compare the two sets of examples.

(32) a   It has become a matter of dispute what John said to whom.
      b   It has become a matter of dispute who said these things to whom.
      c   It has become a matter of dispute who said what to John.

Both (30) and (32) contain sentences with more than one interrogative constituent. The difference between them is that in the acceptable examples in (32) there is only one sentence-initial interrogative constituent, while in the unacceptable examples in (30) there are two. One way of accounting for the unacceptability of the examples in (30) is to assume that each projection has a unique specifier position. If more than one constituent moves to the specifier of CP there will be a "collision" and, to use a term used in recent Minimalist approaches to syntax,[31] the derivation will **crash**. In the acceptable examples in (31) and (32), there is one such sentence-initial *wh*-constituent, *who*, and the other *wh*-constituents occupy their base position.

2.8 Subject interrogatives

2.8.1 INDIRECT QUESTIONS

In fact, on closer inspection (32b) and (32c) and the attested examples in (31) raise a question. In these examples, the sentence-initial interrogative constituent is the subject. We may wonder which position the sentence-initial subject *wh*-constituent occupies. Two hypotheses for the representation of (31a) are given in (33). Discuss the difference between the two representations in (33).

(33) a   I don't know [$_{CP}$ [$_{IP}$ who spotted who first]].
      b   I don't know [$_{CP}$ who [$_{IP}$ ~~who~~ spotted who first]].

Does a sentence-initial interrogative subject occupy its canonical position, SpecIP, as in (33a)? Or is it in SpecCP, as in (33b)? The same question arises in a sentence in which the only interrogative constituent is a subject. For (34a) too, we could propose either representation (34b) or (34c):

(34) a   I don't know who spotted the thief first.
      b   I don't know [$_{CP}$ [$_{IP}$ who spotted the thief first]].
      c   I don't know [$_{CP}$ who [$_{IP}$ ~~who~~ spotted the thief first]].

There is no direct evidence in the examples to help us decide. For instance, we cannot simply determine the structure by inspecting the word order derived by the representations above: both representations lead to a correct spell-out. There may be some theoretical arguments in favor of the hypothesis that the interrogative subject has moved to SpecCP (i.e. in favor of representations (33b) and (34c)). First, recall that we propose that illocutionary force is encoded in the CP domain. In a sentence that contains just an interrogative object NP, that NP has to be moved to the left periphery to signal illocutionary force in SpecCP (cf. (26a)). If we fail to move the interrogative constituent, the sentence is unacceptable (cf. (26b)). So,

---

[31] See Chomsky (1995).

on the assumption that interrogative force has to be signaled in the CP domain, representations (33b) or (34c) are preferable.

We proposed that each constituent has one specifier. This hypothesis ties in with the idea that the function of the specifier is to specify a unique domain of application. If the subject *who* has been fronted to SpecCP in (33b) or in (34c), we predict that no other interrogative constituents can move there; hence we correctly rule out (33c) in which the interrogative object is also fronted. Assuming representation (33b) there would be no room to front the object interrogative.

(33) c   *I don't know who who spotted first.

If we adopt (33a) or (34b), we have two problems: (i) we do not encode interrogative force in the CP domain, and (ii) we fail to explain why the object interrogative *who* cannot move to the periphery of the clause (33c). (33d) would be the representation based on (33a) with fronting of a second *wh*-constituent in (33a):

(33) d   *I don't know [CP who [IP who spotted ~~who~~ first]].

In (33b)/(34c) movement of *who* to SpecCP does not lead to any reorderings in the sentence. This type of movement is sometimes referred to as **string-vacuous** movement.

2.8.2   DIRECT SUBJECT INTERROGATIVES AND INVERSION

In the preceding section we discussed the question whether a subject *wh*-constituent undergoes movement to SpecCP. The examples discussed there were embedded interrogatives. The same question arises with respect to direct subject questions.

Consider direct question (35a) and compare the three (partial)[32] representations, (35b), (35c), and (35d). Each of the three representations makes a different claim. Discuss and compare these claims.

(35) a   Which candidate will finish first?
      b   [CP Which candidate [IP ~~which candidate~~ will finish first]]?
      c   [CP Which candidate will [IP ~~which candidate will~~ finish first]]?
      d   [CP [IP Which candidate will finish first]]?

In (35b) the claim is that the interrogative subject *which candidate* has moved to the specifier of CP. In that position it specifies the scope of the question. The auxiliary *will* remains under I. According to (35c), the interrogative subject *which candidate* has moved to SpecCP and the auxiliary *will* has also moved to C. The movement of the auxiliary from I to C would be a manifestation of a phenomenon that we have come across already: movement of an interrogative constituent to SpecCP coincides

---

[32]   We do not represent the VP-internal copy of the subject as this is not relevant here.

with SAI, movement of the content of I to C. According to (35c), the auxiliary inverts with the (non-pronounced) copy of the subject in SpecIP, ~~which candidate~~. According to (35d), finally, neither subject interrogative nor auxiliary move.

Which of these representations is preferable? Again, there is no direct evidence in the examples to help us decide. All three representations lead to the same word order.

Let us first address the question whether the auxiliary remains in I (35b) or moves to C (35c). In our discussion of direct questions in Chapter 1[33] we introduced SAI. SAI is represented in (35c). Suppose we do opt for (35c) as our representation of a direct question about the subject. In this example the auxiliary is first merged in I and moves to C. We can ask ourselves what the analysis represented by (35c) leads us to predict for direct questions with an interrogative subject and without auxiliaries.

In order to assess the issue, let us turn to direct questions lacking an auxiliary. Consider the derivation of the questions in (36).

(36) a Which candidate will they invite?
     b Which candidate did they invite?   (unstressed *did*)
     c Which candidate DID they invite?   (stressed *did*)

In (36a) the modal auxiliary *will* moves from I to C. In (36b), the content of I (here the past tense morpheme) inverts with the subject and in order to rescue the stranded past tense inflection we insert *do* as a "last resort." Observe that the auxiliary *do* can but need not be stressed in this example. The stressed variant of *do* would occur when we want to contrast the content of the question with an assumption or expectation in the context (36c).[34]

(36b) shows that when a direct question lacks an aspectual or a modal auxiliary, SAI gives rise to *do* insertion. This is because movement of I to C will lead to a stranded inflection. Because I-to-C movement in sentences without auxiliaries leads to *do* insertion, we can deduce that in direct questions where *do*-support is required I-to-C movement has taken place. Specifically, if sentences with interrogative subjects and without auxiliaries require *do* insertion we conclude that there has been I-to-C movement. Conversely, if sentences with interrogative subjects and without auxiliaries do not require *do* insertion we conclude that there has not been I-to-C movement.

Let us see what happens in the interrogative sentences introduced by a subject interrogative constituent and lacking an auxiliary. Based on (36) we create (37a). The acceptable version of (37a) lacks *do*; if we insert unstressed *do*, the sentence becomes unacceptable. Stressing *do* renders the sentence acceptable.

(37) a Which candidate invited them?
     b *Which candidate did invite them?   (with unstressed *did*)
     c Which candidate DID invite them?   (with stressed *did*)

---

[33] Section 2.3.
[34] Cf. Chapter 1, Exercise 7, and Chapter 3, section 1.2.3.2.

Suppose there were indeed movement of the content of I to C in direct questions such as (35a). In (37), an example lacking an auxiliary, the application of
I-to-C movement would move just the inflectional ending of the verb (here the
past tense morpheme -*ed*). This should lead to *do* insertion, where *do* can be
unstressed. This prediction is not borne out: unstressed *do* is not present in (37b).
Only stressed *do* is available (37c), but as we have seen, stressed *do* is inserted
for emphasis and is not a reflex of the movement of I to C. In other words, the
absence of *do*-insertion in subject interrogatives suggests that they are not affected
by I-to-C movement. This means in turn that there is no SAI. We conclude that
in (35) the auxiliary *will* does not move to C and that representation (35b) is
preferable to (35c) because the former does not display movement of I to C while
the latter does. Apparently then, if we assume that interrogative subjects move to
SpecCP we have to admit that this movement does not trigger movement of the
content of I to C.[35]

(35b) is preferred to (35c). What about (35d)? The difference between (35b) and
(35d) is like that between (34c) and (34b) discussed in the preceding section. In
(35d), which matches (34b), neither the subject nor the auxiliary undergo movement. What would be the predictions of this representation for a sentence without
an auxiliary? Are there any drawbacks to this analysis?

If we assume that the interrogative subject does not move, then the absence of
inversion and of *do*-insertion is as expected. But this alternative analysis also presents
a number of drawbacks, as we saw in the preceding section. First, there are some
theoretical questions. If the interrogative subject does not move to SpecCP, we
would have to explain (i) why it need not move there, unlike non-subject interrogative constituents, and (ii) how an interrogative subject *wh*-constituent in SpecIP
can specify the scope of the question. Normally, the scope of a constituent question
is encoded in the specifier position of C. Furthermore, assuming that the SpecCP
still remains available, we might expect that another interrogative constituent could
actually move there. If this movement triggers SAI, the result is (35e). This example
spells out as the ungrammatical (35f):

(35) e   *[$_{CP}$ Which books [$_C$ will] [$_{IP}$ who [$_I$ ~~will~~] [$_{VP}$ ~~who~~ buy ~~which books~~]]]?
       f   *Which books will who buy?

2.9   *A note on* that-*omission in English*

We saw that declarative subordinate clauses are introduced by the complementizer
that. Often, the complementizer *that* can be absent:

---

[35]   The question arises why subject interrogatives do not trigger movement of I to C. See Rizzi
       (1996) and for a recent account see Pesetsky and Torrego (2000).

(38) a Boyle testified <u>that</u> she told Malvo four times <u>that</u> he could be silent or see an attorney. (Based on *Washington Post*, 29.4.2003, p. B1, cols 3–4)

   b Boyle testified she told Malvo four times he could be silent or see an attorney.

Though there are no subordinating conjunctions in (38b), we will assume that the CP level of the subordinate clauses is projected. This is because the embedded clauses are declarative, and we assume that it is the CP layer that encodes illocutionary force.

(38) c Boyle testified [$_{CP}$ [$_C$] [she told Malvo four times [$_{CP}$ [$_C$] [he could be silent or see an attorney]]]].

When the C position of a finite embedded clause is not filled, it gets a "default" declarative reading.[36]

3 How Far Can You Move? And How Do You Get There?[37]

3.1 "Long" movement

Consider examples (39). Are they direct questions or indirect questions? How are the arguments of the verb *eat* realized in (39a)? Does the direct object of *eat* occupy its base position?

(39) a What does your cat eat?

   b What do you think your cat eats? (Based on *Observer Magazine*, 7.9.2003, p. 41, col. 1)

The object of *eat* in (39a) has been fronted because it is interrogative. The present tense inflection is also inverted with the subject (SAI) and *do* is inserted to allow the fronted inflection to survive. The resulting structure is as in (40a):

(40) a [$_{CP}$ What [$_C$ does] [$_{IP}$ your cat [$_I$ -s] [$_{VP}$ ~~your cat~~ [$_{V'}$ eat [$_{NP}$ ~~what~~]]]]]?

---

[36] See also section 3.2.3.1 and Exercise 14 for some constraints on the insertion of *that*. The exercise should be tackled after you've worked your way through the chapter.

[37] In this book we can tackle only a few of the many issues raised by movement of interrogative (and relative, see section 5 below) constituents. For a survey of a number of issues see Richards (2001) and the references cited there.

In (39b) the interrogative pronoun *what* continues to be interpreted as an argument of the verb *eat*, but it precedes *you*, the subject of the verb *think*. *Think* selects a clause as its complement: *that your cat eats*. Something is missing in this string: the object of *eat* has moved out of the embedded clause. In (39a) the object of *eat* moves to the SpecCP of the clause constructed around the verb *eat*. In (39b) the object of *eat* moves to the SpecCP of the clause constructed around the verb *think*. In (39b) the sentence constructed around *think* is a direct question: the speaker expects the interlocutor to provide an answer filling in the specification of *what*. *What*, the interrogative element that narrows down the scope of the question, originates inside the embedded clause as the object of *eat*. Observe that the embedded clause itself is NOT a question. Using the description above, insert CP, IP, and VP brackets in (39b), and represent the deleted copies of moved constituents by strikethrough.

(40) b   Provisional representation for (39b).[38]

[$_{CP}$ What [$_C$ do] [$_{IP}$ you [$_I$ PRESENT] [$_{VP}$ ~~you~~ think

[$_{CP}$ [$_C$] [$_{IP}$ your cat [$_I$ -s] [$_{VP}$ ~~your cat~~ [$_{V'}$ eat-s [$_{NP}$ ~~what~~]]]]]]]]?

(40b) represents the result of the derivation: *what* occupies the periphery of the higher clause, specifying the scope of the question. The *wh*-constituent *what* has undergone long distance movement, or **"long movement."**

Below are some more attested examples of long movement.[39] Identify the moved interrogative constituent. What is its base position? As you will see, interrogative constituents that have undergone long movement can have a range of grammatical functions:

(41) a   It baffles me as to who Tony Blair imagines will work in the universities of the future. (*Guardian*, 27.11.2002, p. 9, col. 8, letter to the editor from Hannah Cooke, Broadbottom, Cheshire)

  b   Who do you think is the more moderate politician? (*Guardian*, 25.9.2003, p. 9, col. 6)

  c   What do you think was the great appeal of the Tramp? (*Guardian*, Review, 1.11.2003, p. 12, col. 3)

  d   What did they think they were making with those girls in there? (*Guardian*, 13.9.2003, p. 14, col. 2)

  e   At the end of the day everybody eats meat . . . What do you think your cat or dog eats? Where do you think that meat comes from? Where do you think Pedigree Chum comes from? (*Observer Magazine*, 7.9.2003, p. 41, col. 1)

---

[38]   See section 2.9 for the hypothesis that even in the absence of the complementizer *that* the embedded CP is projected.

[39]   Some of these examples were introduced in Chapter 3, Exercise 8, examples (11)–(15).

f   Where does the Chancellor think the party is going? (Based on *Guardian*, 27.9.2003, p. 4, headline)

g   Who does he think he is? (*Guardian*, 8.10.2003, p. 14, col. 4)

h   Some are born great, some achieve greatness and some have greatness thrust upon them ... which do you think you were? (*Guardian*, G2, 27.10.2003, p. 6, col. 2)

i   Of Pam Teare ... Lord Hutton asked: "From what source or sources did you think the name would leak?" (*Guardian*, 21.8.2003, p. 8, col. 3)

j   Why do you think the Daily Mail and others have invested so much effort in discrediting me personally? (*Guardian*, 30.9.2003, G2, p. 11, col. 5)

k   Given current reserves and consumption, when is it predicted that the world's oil will run out? (*Guardian*, 14.1.2004, p. 15, col. 4, letter to the editor from Jeff Lewis, Exmouth, Devon)

The moved constituent is a subject in (41a–c); it is an object in (41d). In (41e) *what* is the object of the lower verb *eat*; *where* is the complement of the preposition *from* in the lower clause. In (41f) *where* is a directional complement of the verb *go*; in (41g) and (41h) an interrogative predicate is moved from the lower clause; in (41i–k) adjuncts undergo long movement. In the examples below we represent the position from which the underlined interrogative constituent has been moved by dashes:

(42) a   <u>who</u> Tony Blair imagines —— will work in the universities of the future

b   <u>Who</u> do you think —— is the more moderate politician?

c   <u>What</u> do you think —— was the great appeal of the Tramp?

d   <u>What</u> did they think they were making —— with those girls in there?

e   <u>What</u> do you think your cat or dog eats ——?
      <u>Where</u> do you think that meat comes from ——?
      <u>Where</u> do you think Pedigree Chum comes from ——?

f   <u>Where</u> does he think the party is going ——?

g   <u>Who</u> does he think he is ——?

h   <u>Which</u> do you think you were ——?

i   <u>From what source or sources</u> did you think the name would leak ——?

j   <u>Why</u> do you think the Daily Mail and others have invested so much effort in discrediting me personally ——?

k   <u>when</u> is it predicted that the world's oil will run out ——?

In the next section we will examine how long movement such as that illustrated above proceeds.[40]

---

[40]   Exercise 2.

3.2 *Intervention effects and step-by-step movement*

3.2.1 BLOCKING MOVEMENT

3.2.1.1 *A hypothesis*

An interrogative constituent undergoes leftward movement to the CP domain, where it determines the scope (i.e. the domain of application) of the question. As shown by the long movement examples (41), the interrogative constituent can cross clause boundaries on its way to its landing site, a SpecCP position. Recall also that we assume that the structure of the sentences is tripartite:

(43)   CP > IP > VP

We assume that each projection of a head makes available a specifier position.

To account for the **derivation** of interrogative sentences with long movement, we must address the question of how the moved constituent proceeds. Consider our provisional representation (40b). The arrows in the representation suggest that the moved constituent *what* moves directly from its base position in the embedded clause, in which it is the object of the verb *eat*, to the specifier position of a CP of the main clause, whose verb is *think*.

However, this is not the only derivation possible. Remember that even in the absence of *that* the embedded CP is available.[41] So, rather than going directly to the specifier of the CP constructed on the verb *think*, we could also imagine that movement goes stepwise. In a first step, *what* moves to the specifier of the embedded CP built around the verb *eat*. Then, in the second step, *what* could move to the higher clause. The second application of movement would leave a copy which, being a lower copy than that in the main clause SpecCP, will not be pronounced. (44) is a representation of this alternative step-by-step derivation:

(44)   [cp What [c do] [ip you [i PRESENT] [vp you think

         [cp what [c] [ip your cat [i -s] [vp your cat [v′ eats [np what]]]]]]]]?

What kind of data could be used as evidence that the interrogative constituent has transited through the intermediate SpecCP? Could we devise any experiments to help us decide? Recall that step-by-step movement leaves an unpronounced copy in the intermediate landing site. How could we determine if there is a copy of the moved constituent *what* in the lower SpecCP in (44)?

---

[41]   See section 2.9.

We postulate that a projection of a head has only one specifier. In Chapter 4,[42] we examined subject movement and we proposed that the subject moves step by step, via the available intermediate specifiers. If these two assumptions are generalized, then (i) there is one specifier position per CP,[43] and (ii) movement of interrogative constituents applies stepwise. From these two assumptions, we deduce that long movement proceeds via the specifier positions of intermediate CPs. The analogy with step-by-step subject movement would be a theoretical argument in favor of step-by-step movement of the interrogative constituent. If step-by-step movement applies to interrogative constituents then, once one constituent occupies a SpecCP position, we predict that this should block long movement of additional interrogative constituents out of the relevant CP.

(45) $[_{CP}$ $[_{CP}$ *wh-* $[_{CP}$
             ＊＊＊＊◀━━━━━━━

3.2.1.2 Testing the hypothesis

Our hypothesis is that movement of interrogative constituents proceeds stepwise. In other words, no movement can skip an intervening SpecCP. The analysis predicts that the grammar will not generate sentences in which movement of an interrogative constituent has crossed an interrogative constituent in a SpecCP of an intermediate sentence. Examples formed in this way should be ungrammatical and should not occur. The attested examples of long movement in (41) are all compatible with the hypothesis: there is no intervening interrogative constituent between the fronted interrogative constituent and its base position. However, these and similar acceptable examples of long movement do not prove conclusively that movement could not have crossed an intervening interrogative constituent. The observation that we do not find any examples in which long movement crosses an interrogative constituent is not conclusive evidence either. Perhaps their non-occurrence is a mere side-effect of the kind of material we have examined. Perhaps the construction is stylistically highly marked and therefore extremely rare though not impossible.[44] We must be sure that moving an interrogative constituent across a filled SpecCP (45) really leads to an unacceptable output. What we can do is construct examples that use the derivation in (45) and see if they are ungrammatical, as our hypothesis predicts.

Consider the grammatical (41d) repeated here as (46a):

(46) a <u>What</u> did they think they were making —— with those girls in there?

The interrogative constituent *what* has moved from the embedded clause to the main clause. In principle, it can transit via the embedded SpecCP, which is empty. In (46b) we provide only the labeled brackets relevant to our discussion.

---

[42] Sections 3 and 4.
[43] See also section 2.7 for motivation.
[44] Recall the discussion of the generalization "all swans are white" in Chapter 1, section 2.3.

(46) b [$_{CP}$ <u>What</u> did [$_{IP}$ they think

          [$_{CP}$ ~~what~~ [$_{IP}$ they were making ~~what~~ with those girls in there]]]]?

(46b) is compatible with the hypothesis that movement cannot skip an intervening SpecCP but it does not confirm its general validity. What we need to show is that if the constraint on stepwise movement is NOT respected the sentence is ungrammatical. In order to test the prediction implied by (45) we modify (46b). We fill the embedded SpecCP with an interrogative constituent. For instance, we can turn the place adjunct *in there* into the interrogative variant, *where*, and front it to the embedded SpecCP. This will turn the embedded clause into an interrogative complement clause. In (46b) the main verb, *think*, selects a declarative complement. To allow for an interrogative complement clause, we have to change the verb of the main clause. We replace *think* by *wonder*.

(46) c *[$_{CP}$ <u>What</u> did [$_{IP}$ they wonder [$_{CP}$ where [$_{IP}$ they were making ~~what~~ with those girls ~~where~~]]]]?

Though we can figure out what (46c) is intended to mean, it is not a grammatical sentence.

    Suppose that there is a "shortest step" constraint on movement: preferentially movement must apply step by step, landing the moved constituent in intermediate potential landing sites between its base position and its ultimate landing site. A moved constituent will first go to the nearest landing site and then move on to the next one. If a moved constituent is forced to cross a potential landing site, then it cannot proceed through the shortest steps possible and hence it is in violation of the shortest step constraint (cf. (45)). In (46c), the specifier of the CP in the embedded clause is filled by the interrogative constituent *where*. It will therefore be impossible for the interrogative object NP *what* to move from the embedded clause to the specifier of the CP of the main clause, because this movement would have to take a big leap and cross the intermediate position. In (46d) we label the lower clause CP2 and the higher clause CP1. This is to make it easier to read the representation.

(46) d

*[$_{CP1}$ <u>What</u> did [$_{IP}$ they wonder

         [$_{CP2}$ <u>where</u> [$_{IP}$ they were making ~~what~~ with those girls ~~where~~]]]]?

On the assumption that there is just one specifier per CP, we account for the degradation in (46c/d) by means of the hypothesis that *wh*-movement proceeds stepwise. If an intermediate specifier position is already filled, this will block movement of another constituent. In other words, the degraded status of (46c/d) offers indirect support for the hypothesis that all movement, including the long movement of interrogative constituents, proceeds step by step.

    The hypothesis that movement is done step by step can be seen as one implementation of a more general property of the language system. Recall that in Chapter 4 we proposed that the subject has its base position in the specifier of VP. This hypothesis enabled us to define thematic relations in terms of local relations: a head (here the verb) assigns its thematic roles in the domain that it controls, the VP. We could say that the **constraint** that all movement must go step by step is another instantiation of a general **locality** requirement on syntactic relations. Thematic role assignment is local: that is, a head assigns a thematic role "locally," within its projection. Movement is "local": that is, a constituent moves into a "local" SpecCP before moving into a remote SpecCP.

Assuming step-by-step movement for the fronting of *wh*-constituents allows us to account for the degradation of examples in which we try to extract an interrogative constituent from an interrogative clause (46c/d). This evidence is indirect and hinges on a number of theoretical assumptions. We have not provided any direct overt evidence for the step-by-step movement hypothesis. Using indirect evidence is a legitimate strategy in scientific research and it is used in other sciences. For instance astronomers use it to pinpoint the existence of planets and planetary systems:

> Until 1995, there was no evidence at all of planets orbiting other stars. Since the first dramatic discovery eight years ago, researchers have identified more than 100 planetary systems within 150 light years of Earth.
>
> No one has seen any of these planets: researchers infer the presence of an orbiting planet from a kind of wobble in the light from the parent star. (*Guardian*, 4.7.2003, p. 7, col. 1, Tim Radford, Science Editor)

With respect to movement of interrogative constituents, the **intervention** effect that arises when an interrogative constituent occupies an intermediate SpecCP and hinders or blocks movement of another interrogative constituent (46c/d) could be compared to the "wobble" created by a planet in the light of its parent star.

3.2.2   EMPIRICAL EVIDENCE FOR STEP-BY-STEP MOVEMENT

In addition to the indirect evidence for stepwise movement, there is also some direct evidence. In section 2.5 of this chapter we discussed examples like those in (47), in which movement of an interrogative constituent had stranded an element. (47a) shows the stranding of *exactly*; (47b) and (47c) from West Ulster English illustrate the stranding of the quantifier *all*.

(47) a   What do you mean <u>exactly</u>? (cf. (18))
     b   What did you get <u>all</u> for Christmas? (cf. (22a))
     c   Who did you meet <u>all</u> when you were in Derry? (cf. (22b))

The stranded elements, *exactly* and *all*, were taken to remain in the base positions of the moved direct objects. In his article on *wh*-movement in West Ulster English, McCloskey also discusses the examples in (48) (McCloskey, 2000: 63, note 8). Try to provide the bracketed representations of these three examples. Can you see why these examples bear on the current discussion?

(48) a   What exactly did he say that he wanted?
      b   What did he say that he wanted exactly?
      c   What did he say exactly that he wanted?

The data in (48) can be interpreted as offering empirical support for the hypothesis of step-by-step movement of the interrogative constituent. In (48a) *what exactly* moves to SpecCP. In (48b) we might propose that *exactly* is stranded in the base position of the object, and in (48c) we might propose that *exactly* is stranded in the intermediate specifier position:[45]

(49) a   [$_{CP}$ [$_{NP}$ What exactly] [$_{C}$ did] [$_{IP}$ he [$_{I}$ -~~ed~~] [$_{VP}$ ~~he~~ say
          [$_{CP}$ ~~what exactly~~ that [$_{IP}$ he [$_{I}$ -~~ed~~] [$_{VP}$ ~~he~~ want-ed ~~what exactly~~]]]]]]?
      b   [$_{CP}$ [$_{NP}$ What] [$_{C}$ did] [$_{IP}$ he [$_{I}$ -~~ed~~] [$_{VP}$ ~~he~~ say
          [$_{CP}$ ~~what~~ that [$_{IP}$ he [$_{I}$ -~~ed~~] [$_{VP}$ ~~he~~ want-ed [$_{NP}$ ~~what~~ exactly]]]]]]]?
      c   [$_{CP}$ [$_{NP}$ What] [$_{C}$ did] [$_{IP}$ he [$_{I}$ -~~ed~~] [$_{VP}$ ~~he~~ say
          [$_{CP}$ [~~what~~ exactly] that [$_{IP}$ he [$_{I}$ -~~ed~~] [$_{VP}$ ~~he~~ want-ed [$_{NP}$ ~~what exactly~~]]]]]]]?

Discuss the relevance of the West Ulster English sentences in (50) for the hypothesis of step-by-step movement (data from McCloskey, 2000: 61, his (8)).

(50) a   What all did he say (that) he wanted?
      b   What did he say (that) he wanted all?
      c   What did he say all (that) he wanted?

We can again interpret the data in (50) in line with our hypothesis. If we assume that the quantifier *all* is stranded after the movement of *what* in (50b) and in (50c), then it is reasonable to say that in (50b) *all* occupies the object position. In (50c) *all* could then be said to be stranded in the specifier of the intermediate CP:

(51) a   [$_{CP}$ [$_{NP}$ What all] [$_{C}$ did] [$_{IP}$ he [$_{I}$ -~~ed~~] [$_{VP}$ ~~he~~ say [$_{CP}$ [$_{NP}$ ~~what all~~] (that) [$_{IP}$ he
          [$_{I}$ -~~ed~~] [$_{VP}$ ~~he~~ want-ed [$_{NP}$ ~~what all~~]]]]]]]?
      b   [$_{CP}$ [$_{NP}$ What] [$_{C}$ did] [$_{IP}$ he [-~~ed~~] [$_{VP}$ ~~he~~ say [$_{CP}$ ~~what~~ (that) [$_{IP}$ he [$_{I}$ -~~ed~~] [$_{VP}$ ~~he~~
          want-ed [$_{NP}$ ~~what~~ all]]]]]]]?
      c   [$_{CP}$ [$_{NP}$ What] [$_{C}$ did] [$_{IP}$ he [$_{I}$ -~~ed~~] [$_{VP}$ ~~he~~ say [$_{CP}$ [$_{NP}$ ~~what~~ all] (that) [$_{IP}$ he
          [$_{I}$ -~~ed~~] [$_{VP}$ ~~he~~ want-ed [$_{NP}$ ~~what all~~]]]]]]]?

3.2.3   SUBJECTS AND OBJECTS

3.2.3.1   *The complementizer* that

We saw that subordinate declaratives are introduced by the complementizer *that*. Often, the complementizer *that* can be absent. We repeat the examples discussed in section 2.9 here.[46]

---

[45]   There are complications, though, which are discussed in McCloskey (2000: 64, note 8).
[46]   For an early discussion of the data dealt with here see Perlmutter (1971).

(52) a Boyle testified <u>that</u> she told Malvo four times <u>that</u> he could be silent or see
an attorney. (Based on *Washington Post*, 29.4.2003, p. B1, cols 3–4)
 b Boyle testified she told Malvo four times he could be silent or see an attorney.

In our earlier example of long extraction, the complementizer *that* can sometimes
be inserted in the embedded C:

(53) a What do you think your cat eats? (= (39b))
 b What do you think <u>that</u> your cat eats?
 c [CP What [C do] [IP you [I PRESENT] [VP ~~you~~ think

[CP ~~what~~ [C that] [IP your cat [I -s] [VP ~~your cat~~ [V' eats [NP ~~what~~]]]]]]]]?

In the attested examples of long movement in (41), the embedded CP does not contain an overt complementizer. In some of the examples, though, the complementizer
that can be inserted; in others, on the other hand, inserting *that* will lead to sharp
ungrammaticality. Try inserting *that* in the examples in (41). Try to identify the
factor that sets apart the examples in which inserting *that* leads to ungrammaticality.

(54) a *It baffles me as to who Tony Blair imagines <u>that</u> —— will work in the
universities of the future.
 b *Who do you think <u>that</u> —— is the more moderate politician?
 c *What do you think <u>that</u> —— was the great appeal of the Tramp?
 d What did they think <u>that</u> they were making —— with those girls in there?
 e What do you think <u>that</u> your cat or dog eats ——?
 Where do you think <u>that</u> that meat comes from ——?
 Where do you think <u>that</u> Pedigree Chum comes from ——?
 f Where does he think <u>that</u> the party is going ——?
 g Who does he think <u>that</u> he is ——?
 h Which do you think <u>that</u> you were ——?
 i From what source or sources did you think <u>that</u> the name would leak
 ——?
 j Why do you think <u>that</u> the Daily Mail and others have invested so much
effort in discrediting me personally ——?

Inserting *that* leads to ungrammaticality in those sentences in which a subject has
been extracted from the embedded clause. We have discovered a **subject/object
asymmetry**: while subjects cannot be extracted across the complementizer *that*
(54a, b, c), there is no problem for object extraction (54d, e). It would be important
to explain this constraint on subject extraction. One possibility would be to relate
the constraint on subject extraction to the fact that the subject is extracted from a
position adjacent to the complementizer while the object is not extracted from such
a position. Alternatively, we might wish to relate the observed asymmetry to the

fact that while the object is extracted from its VP-internal thematic position, the subject has first been moved from its base position, SpecVP, to SpecIP, a VP-external position. We will not pursue this issue here.[47]

3.2.3.2 *Blocking subject movement*

Recall that it is difficult to move an interrogative pronoun out of a CP whose specifier is already filled by a *wh*-constituent. Consider (55a), a constructed example. What is the function of the underlined interrogative constituent?

(55) a   *Which book did you wonder on which day they will publish?

Compare (55a) and (55b). Both examples in (55) are degraded, but (55b) is generally felt to be unacceptable, while some speakers may marginally tolerate (55a). Why should this be?

(55) b   **Which book did you wonder on which day will appear?

Let us represent the derivations of both examples, representing the unpronounced copies of the moved *wh*-constituents by strikethrough. In order not to overload the representation in (56), we do not represent the unpronounced copies of the subjects of *wonder* and of *publish* because these do not concern us here.

(56) a   *[$_{CP}$ Which book did [$_{IP}$ you wonder [$_{CP}$ on which day [$_{IP}$ they will publish ~~which book~~]]]]?
      b   **[$_{CP}$ Which book did [$_{IP}$ you wonder [$_{CP}$ on which day [$_{IP}$ ~~which book~~ will [$_{VP}$ ~~which book~~ appear]]]]]?

We discover a further subject/object asymmetry: moving an object out of a clause whose SpecCP contains an interrogative constituent (56a) leads to some degradation, but moving a subject out of such a clause leads to a worse degradation. Obviously, it would be important to provide an account for this asymmetry, and preferably one that ties in with the subject/object asymmetry that we discovered in relation to *that* insertion. However, such an account would go well beyond the scope of this introduction.

4   The Periphery of Non-Finite Clauses

So far we have only discussed the periphery of finite interrogative clauses. Let us look at the structure of non-finite interrogative clauses. We will examine to what

---

[47]   Exercise 11. For a discussion of adjacency and anti-adjacency see Culicover (1991, 1993), Rizzi (1997), Pesetsky and Torrego (2000). For the role of the extraction site see Rizzi (1990) and Richards (2001) and the references cited there.

extent we can fit non-finite interrogative clauses into the structures that we have already elaborated for finite clauses.

4.1   For *as a conjunction for non-finite clauses*

Provide arguments for considering the underlined strings in the following examples as constituents.

(57) a   You realise he hates <u>for you to call him "Ollie"</u>, don't you? (Marcia Muller, *Edwin of the Iron Shoes*, 1993: 42)
   b   He did intend <u>for Endrina to join him as a runner</u>. (*Guardian*, G2, 15.2.2001, p. 4, col. 2)

The underlined strings function as the objects of the verbs *hate* and *intend*. We can paraphrase them by means of a finite sentence:

(58) a   He hates it <u>that you call him "Ollie"</u>.
   b   He did intend <u>that Endrina should join him as a runner.</u>

In the underlined strings in (57), the inflection of the clauses is non-finite, it is realized by *to*.[48] The subject is realized by an NP (*you*, *Endrina*). While the finite counterparts of these clauses would be introduced by the conjunction *that*, the non-finite variants are introduced by *for*: *for* fills the C position in a non-finite clause.

(57) c   [~IP~ He [~I~ -s] [~VP~ ~~he~~ hate-s [~CP~ [~C~ for] [~IP~ you [~I~ to] [~VP~ ~~you~~ call him "Ollie"]]]]].

4.2   *Non-finite interrogative clauses*

4.2.1   *WHETHER*

Consider (59a), a constructed example whose form is familiar from the preceding discussion. The underlined embedded clause is interrogative, it is introduced by *whether*. Using labeled bracketing, represent the structure of the example. (59b) is an attested example. Compare the underlined segment of (59b) with that in (59a). Identify similarities and differences between these two segments. Try to fit the underlined segment of (59b) into the structure you have devised for (59a).

(59) a   The politicians are deciding <u>whether they should sever their ties with the arrested businessman</u>.
   b   The convictions are likely to have far reaching consequences, with a number of senior British politicians, including Lord Steel, having to decide <u>whether</u>

---

[48]   See Chapter 3, section 1.3.

to sever their ties with his extensive network of companies. (Based on *Guardian*, 15.11.2003, p. 8, col. 7)

(59a) and (59b) both contain an embedded interrogative clause. That in (59a) is finite, its lexical verb is *sever*, the subject is *they*, the inflection is realized by the modal auxiliary *should*, and the illocutionary force is signaled by *whether*. The verb *sever* assigns an AGENT thematic role to the subject *they*. We can represent the derivation of (59a) by (60a):

(60) a [$_{IP}$ The politicians [$_I$ are] [$_{VP}$ ~~the politicians be~~ [$_{VP}$ ~~the politicians~~ deciding [$_{CP}$ whether [$_{IP}$ they [$_I$ should] [$_{VP}$ ~~they~~ sever [$_{NP}$ their ties with the arrested businessman]]]]]]].[49]

In (59b) the embedded interrogative clause is also introduced by *whether*, but the clause is non-finite: the lexical verb is *sever* and the inflectional marking is realized by *to*. The non-finite variant of the embedded clause lacks an overt subject, but we interpret the embedded clause as if there were an implicit subject. Specifically, the verb *sever* will assign its AGENT thematic role to a non-overt NP that is interpreted as coreferential with the main clause subject *a number of senior British politicians, including Lord Steel*. We represent this non-overt NP as [$_{NP}$ Ø]. Let us assume that this subject, [$_{NP}$ Ø], also originates in the specifier of VP and moves to the specifier of the non-finite IP to allow I to fulfil its linking function.

(60) b [$_{CP}$ whether [$_{IP}$ [$_{NP}$ Ø] [$_I$ to] [$_{VP}$ [$_{NP}$ ~~Ø~~] sever [$_{NP}$ their ties with his extensive network of companies]]]].

The attested examples below illustrate non-finite interrogative clauses introduced by *whether*.

(61) a Each European country will be free to choose <u>whether</u> to include records of treatment received, photographs, and biometric data. (*Guardian*, 15.11.2003, p. 16, col. 4)

    b The RMT executive is to meet on Monday to decide <u>whether</u> to call underground-wide strikes. (*Guardian*, 21.11.2003, p. 6, col. 2)

    c Lieberman said he was already in the State Senate when he mused about <u>whether</u> to open the ice cream shop at a "perfect" site on the Yale campus

---

[49] We assume that *they* moves step by step from the SpecVP headed by *sever* to SpecIP. Similarly, the subject NP *the politicians* moves step by step from the SpecVP associated with *deciding* to the specifier of IP. There is an unpronounced copy of the moved subject in the specifier position associated with the projection of the auxiliary *be*. See Chapter 4, section 4 for discussion.

or continue to practice law. (*Atlanta Journal-Constitution*, 23.11.2003, p. A4, col. 5)

In non-finite interrogatives *whether* cannot be replaced by *if*.[50]

4.2.2 FRONTED INTERROGATIVE CONSTITUENTS

Consider (62a). In this example the embedded clause is interrogative and is introduced by the fronted interrogative pronoun *who*. *Who* originates in the complement position of the preposition *on*. Using labeled bracketing, represent the structure of this example. Indicate non-pronounced copies of moved constituents by strikethrough.

(62) a   They don't know who they should rely on.

(62b) is an attested example. How does it differ from (62a)? Try fitting the components of (62b) into your representation for (62a).

(62) b   They are panicking because they don't know who to rely on. (*Washington Post*, 29.4.2003, p. A18, col. 5)

For (62a) the representation will be as in (63a):

(63) a   [$_{IP}$ They [$_I$ don't] [$_{VP}$ ~~they~~ know [$_{CP}$ who [$_{IP}$ they [$_I$ should] [$_{VP}$ ~~they~~ rely [$_{PP}$ on [~~who~~]]]]]]].

If we try to fit (62b) into this structure we end up with the following partial representation:

(63) b   (First approximation)
     [$_{IP}$ They [$_I$ don't] [$_{VP}$ ~~they~~ know [$_{CP}$ who [$_{IP}$ —— [$_I$ to] [$_{VP}$ rely [$_{PP}$ on [~~who~~]]]]]]].

We can again fit the constituents of the non-finite clause in (62b) fairly easily into the representation designed for its finite counterpart (62a). The only problem is that the subject of the infinitival clause in (62b) is non-overt. Again, because the subject of the embedded clause in (62b) remains implicit, we represent it by the symbol [$_{NP}$ Ø]. Again, we assume that this non-overt subject starts out as the specifier of the verb and that it moves to the specifier of IP to provide a linking element for the I' constituent. The non-overt subject of the infinitive is interpreted as coreferential with the subject of the main clause, i.e. *they*.

(63) c   [$_{IP}$ They [$_I$ don't] [$_{VP}$ ~~they~~ know [$_{CP}$ who [$_{IP}$ [$_{NP}$ Ø] [$_I$ to] [$_{VP}$ [$_{NP}$ ~~Ø~~] rely [$_{PP}$ on [~~who~~]]]]]]].

---

[50] See also Exercise 3 for some problems with the syntax of *whether*.

5   Relative Clauses: An Introduction

5.1   *Movement of the relative pronoun*

Section 3 dealt, among other things, with constituent questions or *wh*-questions such as those in (64).[51]

(64)   a   Who had he met at the party?
      b   I wonder [CP who he had met at the party].

We postulated that these sentences are derived by moving an interrogative constituent to SpecCP in order to signal the scope of the question. In addition, the fronted *wh*-constituent has a grammatical function inside the clause. Both in the direct question (64a) and in the indirect question (64b), *who* is the direct object of *met*. Following the argumentation elaborated above the representation of the structure of the embedded interrogative clause in (64b) is as in (64c).

(64)   c   [CP who [IP he [I had] [VP ~~he have~~ [VP ~~he~~ met ~~who~~ at the party]]]][52]

Now consider (65a):

(65)   a   I interviewed [NP the man who he had met at the party].

The direct object of the verb *interviewed* is the NP *the man who he had met at the party*. We can replace this string by the pronoun *him*; the constituent can be the focus of a cleft sentence.

(65)   b   I interviewed <u>him</u>.
      c   It is <u>the man who he had met at the party</u> that I interviewed.

The head of the NP is a noun, *man*. This noun is preceded by a determiner (*the*) and it is followed by a string, *who he had met at the party*, whose function is to narrow down the reference of the noun phrase. The string *who he had met at the party* helps to identify which entity with the property 'man' we are talking about. The embedded clause tells us 'which man I interviewed'.

---

[51]   The aim of section 5 is to offer a first overview of the derivation of relative clauses. The section offers the "traditional" analysis. For a more comprehensive introductory discussion see Haegeman and Guéron (1999). For a more recent and very influential analysis see also Kayne (1994: chapter 8).

[52]   Recall that we assume that there is an unpronounced copy of the moved subject in the specifier position associated with the projection of the auxiliary *have*. See Chapter 4, section 4, for discussion.

The string *who he had met at the party* is itself a finite clause: it contains a subject (*he*), a finite lexical verb (*met*), and the I position is filled by the auxiliary *had*. The pronoun *who* precedes the subject and we will assume that once again it occupies the specifier of CP.

(65) d [$_{CP}$ who [$_{IP}$ he [$_I$ had] [$_{VP}$ ~~he have~~ [$_{VP}$ ~~he~~ met ~~who~~ at the party]]]].

There are a number of formal parallelisms between the embedded clause in (64b) and that in (65a). Both in (64b) and (65a) the embedded clause starts with a *wh*-constituent (*who*). In both examples, this *wh*-phrase precedes the subject NP of the embedded clause. In both clauses the *wh*-constituent is the direct object of the verb *met*. We assume that in both cases the *wh*-constituent occupies the specifier of CP. In our earlier example (64b), the embedded clause was interrogative. It was the complement of the V *wonder*, which selects an interrogative clause as its complement. The status of the embedded clause in (65a) is different: the clause is not the complement of a verb; rather it serves to modify a head N (here *man*). The embedded clause in (65a) is a **relative clause**. In (65a), the pronoun *who* narrows down the reference of the N *man*. When used to introduce a relative clause, *who* is called a **relative pronoun**. In its use as a relative pronoun, *who* indicates the type of the embedded clause (here relative), and it also has a grammatical function inside that clause. The noun phrase to which a relative pronoun refers is called its **antecedent**. For human antecedents we use the relative pronoun *who*, for non-human antecedents we use the relative pronoun *which*:

(66) a I like the book [$_{CP}$ which you gave me].   *which* = object
     b They reviewed the books [$_{CP}$ which arrived first].   *which* = subject

Observe that many *wh*-pronouns double up as relative pronouns and as interrogative pronouns, and the clauses they introduce will accordingly be either relative clauses or interrogative clauses. In (67) we give a few examples.[53]

(67) a I wonder [$_{CP}$ <u>who told him about Bill's departure</u>].   Interrogative
        This is [$_{NP}$ the person [$_{CP}$ <u>who told him about</u>   Relative
        <u>Bill's departure</u>]].
     b I wonder [$_{CP}$ <u>which I should buy him:</u>   Interrogative
        <u>the green sweater or the blue one</u>].
        He did not like [$_{NP}$ the sweater [$_{CP}$ <u>which I bought him</u>]].   Relative
     c I asked them [$_{CP}$ <u>whose car they had used</u>].   Interrogative
        [$_{NP}$ The woman [$_{CP}$ <u>whose car they had used</u>]] will be paid.   Relative

The moved constituent *whose car* in (67c) contains both the possessive pronoun *whose* and the noun *car*. *Whose* is the specifier of the NP *whose car*; it denotes the

---

[53] Exercise 9. For relative clauses introduced by *that* see Exercise 14. This exercise should be tackled after you have finished section 5.

possessor of the entity that the NP refers to. If we want to question a possessor of the entity referred to by an NP, we apparently cannot just move an interrogative possessor on its own (68a), but we have to move the containing NP along. We say that we move along or we **pied-pipe** the NP.

(68) a   *I asked them [$_{CP}$ whose they had used ~~whose~~ car].

Analogously, when forming a relative clause for which the antecedent corresponds to a possessive pronoun, we must pied-pipe the NP:

(68) b   *[$_{NP}$ The woman [$_{CP}$ whose they had used ~~whose~~ car]] will be paid.

In the same way that an interrogative pronoun can be moved out of its own clause and function as the marker of interrogative force in a higher clause, a relative pronoun can move out of its own clause. (69a) is a constructed example, (69b) is an attested example.

(69) a   I know the candidates [$_{CP}$ who [$_{IP}$ they said [$_{CP}$ that [$_{IP}$ they will nominate this year]]]].
     b   A Pakistani jeweler said today that his picture is among those of five men [$_{CP}$ who the F.B.I. says [$_{CP}$ [$_{IP}$ may have entered the United States on doctored passports]]]. (*New York Times*, 2.1.2003, p. A9, col. 2)

5.2   Constraints on movement: Some predictions

Our hypothesis is that relative clauses are derived essentially along the lines of interrogative clauses. In particular, we assume that relative pronouns undergo movement similar to the movement of interrogative pronouns. This hypothesis leads us to a number of predictions. Given that movement of an interrogative pronoun is made difficult by certain factors, the same factors should also lead to a degradation for the movement of a relative pronoun. In section 3.2.1 we introduced the shortest step constraint on movement. Long movement of an interrogative pronoun was shown to lead to ungrammaticality if the specifier of an intervening CP was already occupied by a *wh*-constituent. We predict that, in the same way, the movement of a relative pronoun will degrade if it crosses a filled specifier of an intervening CP.

In section 3.2.3, we saw that the presence of the complementizer *that* in the position C blocks the movement of an adjacent interrogative subject. We predict that the presence of *that* should also block extraction of an adjacent relative subject. We will examine these two predictions here.

5.2.1   INTERVENTION EFFECTS ON THE MOVEMENT OF THE RELATIVE PRONOUN

When we apply long movement in interrogative clauses, the moved *wh*-constituent moves step by step via the intermediate specifiers of CP. Coupled with the assumption that each CP has only one specifier, this allowed us to predict the degraded status of (55a) repeated here as (70):

(70)   *[CP Which book did [IP you wonder [CP on which day [IP they will publish]]]]?

If the derivation of relative clauses proceeds like that of interrogative clauses, a relative pronoun also moves stepwise. We predict that relative fronting out of an interrogative clause will lead to a degradation. Observe that once again attested examples which are compatible with a derivation using stepwise movement do not constitute conclusive evidence for our hypothesis. What we have to show is that examples in which movement cannot proceed stepwise are ungrammatical. For instance, relativization out of an interrogative clause should not be grammatical. Again, we cannot test our hypothesis by looking for examples to confirm this. By definition, being ungrammatical, the relevant examples should not occur. It is not because we don't find any examples of relativization out of an interrogative clause that we can conclude that such examples do not exist.[54]

To test our hypothesis we can run an experiment and create the very conditions that should lead to the degradation. We construct a relative clause in which the relative pronoun undergoes long movement. In other words, the pronoun starts from the embedded clause and moves up to a higher clause. If we then insert an interrogative constituent in the specifier of an intermediate CP, we should find a degradation. Starting from (69a) above, repeated here as (71a) let us test our prediction.

(71) a   I know the candidates [CP who [IP they said [CP that [IP they will nominate ~~who~~ this year]]]].

To construct the decisive kind of example, we have to modify the declarative embedded clause in (71a), and turn it into an interrogative clause. However, the verb *said* in (71a) does not select an interrogative complement clause. In order to allow for an interrogative complement clause, we have to replace the verb *said* by a verb selecting an interrogative clause. Let us replace *said* by *wondered*. Within the complement clause we replace the temporal specification *this year* by a *wh*-constituent, which we move to the specifier of the embedded CP. (71b) is a partial representation:

(71) b   *I know the candidates [CP who [IP they wondered [CP when [IP they will nominate ~~who~~]]]].

As predicted, (71b) is not acceptable: the interrogative constituent *when* in the specifier of lower CP blocks the passage of *who* to the higher specifier position. These data support the hypothesis that both relative pronouns and interrogative pronouns move step by step.[55]

---

[54]   See section 3.2.1.2.

[55]   Exercise 10A. Exercises 12 and 13 introduce another pattern which blocks movement.

5.2.2   SUBJECT MOVEMENT AND THE COMPLEMENTIZER *THAT*

We discovered[56] a subject-object asymmetry with respect to the filler of the C position in embedded clauses from which a constituent is moved. When we move an interrogative subject out of an embedded clause, we cannot insert the conjunction *that* in the C position adjacent to the non-pronounced copy of the subject. This was illustrated by examples (54a, b, c) repeated here as (72).

(72) a   *It baffles me as to who Tony Blair imagines <u>that</u> will work in the universities of the future.
  b   *Who do you think <u>that</u> is the more moderate politician?
  c   *What do you think <u>that</u> was the great appeal of the Tramp?

If relative pronouns move in a way similar to interrogative pronouns, then they ought to display a similar subject/object asymmetry. In (69a), repeated here for convenience as (73a) the object is extracted.

(73) a   I know the candidates [$_{CP}$ <u>who</u> [$_{IP}$ they said [$_{CP}$ <u>that</u> [$_{IP}$ they will nominate this year]]]].

The complementizer *that* is realized in the embedded clause, from which the direct object *who* has been extracted. The complementizer may also remain unexpressed:

(73) b   I know the candidates [<u>who</u> they said [they will nominate this year]].

(69b), repeated here for convenience as (74a), is an illustration of long movement of a subject relative pronoun. In the attested example, the complementizer *that* is not realized in the C position of the clause from which the subject *who* has been moved. Indeed, the complementizer *that* cannot be inserted in the lower clause (74b):

(74) a   A Pakistani jeweler said today that his picture is among those of five men [$_{CP}$ <u>who</u> the F.B.I. says [$_{CP}$ [$_{IP}$ may have entered the United States on doctored passports]]]. (*New York Times*, 2.1.2003, p. A9, col. 2)
  b   *A Pakistani jeweler said today that his picture is among those of five men [<u>who</u> the F.B.I. says [<u>that</u> may have entered the United States on doctored passports]].

The contrast between object extraction in (73) and subject extraction in (74) can be analyzed as another effect of the subject-object asymmetry in moving *wh*-constituents.

---

[56]   Section 3.2.3.1.

5.3 A non-overt relative pronoun

5.3.1 THE DATA: RELATIVE CLAUSES WITHOUT A RELATIVE PRONOUN?

Consider once again the derivation of the relative clause in (74a). What is the subject of *says*? What is the subject of *may have entered . . . passports*? As you can see, the relative pronoun *who* has undergone long movement. In representation (74c) we indicate all the unpronounced copies of the relative pronoun by strikethrough (~~who~~):[57]

(74) c   five men [CP who [IP the F.B.I. says [CP ~~who~~ [IP ~~who~~ may [VP ~~who~~ have [VP ~~who~~ entered the United States on doctored passports]]]]]]].

Compare the underlined string in (75a) with the relative clause in (74a). What is the subject of *believe*? What is the subject of *may have entered the United States illegally from Canada*?

(75) a   F.B.I. agents investigating falsified identity papers are expanding their drag-net for a growing list of foreign-born men <u>they believe may have entered the Unites States illegally from Canada</u>.

At first sight it looks as if the subject of *may have entered . . .* is missing. Using the constructed example (73a) as a model, we could insert a subject relative pronoun:

(75) b   F.B.I. agents investigating falsified identity papers are expanding their dragnet for a growing list of foreign-born men <u>who</u> they believe may have entered the Unites States illegally from Canada.

In (75c) we represent all the copies of the relative pronoun *who* in (75b):

(75) c   foreign-born men [CP <u>who</u> [IP they believe [CP ~~who~~ [IP ~~who~~ may [VP ~~who~~ have [VP ~~who~~ entered the Unites States illegally from Canada]]]]]]].

If the verb *enter* assigns a thematic role to *who* in (75b), then in (75a) *enter* will also have to assign this thematic role. It is proposed that in (75a) a relative pronoun has also moved to SpecCP but that this pronoun is itself not pronounced. In other words (75a) would have the representation in (75d):

(75) d   foreign-born men [CP ~~who~~ [IP they believe [CP ~~who~~ [IP ~~who~~ may [VP ~~who~~ have [VP ~~who~~ entered the Unites States illegally from Canada]]]]]]].

[57]   Recall that we assume that there is an unpronounced copy of the moved subject in the specifier position associated with the projection of the auxiliary *have*. See Chapter 4, section 4, for discussion.

When a relative pronoun is left unpronounced, we can refer to it as a non-overt or null pronoun. In (75d) the non-overt pronoun undergoes movement in the same way as its overt counterpart in (74c).[58]

5.3.2   EVIDENCE FOR MOVEMENT OF A NON-OVERT PRONOUN

We proposed that in (75a) the relative clause which modifies *foreign-born men* is introduced by a non-overt relative pronoun (~~who~~). As shown in (75d), we assume that the non-overt pronoun starts out as the subject of *entered* and undergoes step-by-step (long) movement to SpecCP. What kind of evidence could we provide to support this analysis?

Recall that movement of *wh*-constituents is subject to a number of constraints. In section 3.2.1 we introduced the shortest step constraint on movement: long movement of an interrogative pronoun is blocked if a specifier of an intervening CP is already occupied by a *wh*-constituent. In section 3.2.3, we saw that long movement of a subject *wh*-constituent is blocked if the adjacent C position is filled by *that*. If (75a) is derived by long movement of a non-overt relative pronoun, then we predict that both the effect of shortest step constraint on movement and that of the constraint on the extraction of the subject should be manifested here. Let us examine each of these points in turn.

5.3.2.1   *Step-by-step movement*
When we apply long movement in interrogative clauses, the moved *wh*-constituent moves stepwise via the specifier(s) of the intermediate CP(s). Coupled with the assumption that each CP has only one specifier, this allowed us to predict the ungrammaticality of (71b) repeated here as (76):

(76)   *I know the candidates [$_{CP}$ who [$_{IP}$ they wondered [$_{CP}$ when [$_{IP}$ they will nominate ~~who~~]]]].

(76) is not acceptable because the interrogative constituent *when* in the specifier of the lower CP blocks the transit of the relative pronoun *who* to the specifier position of the higher clause.

If relative clauses lacking a relative pronoun are derived by movement of a non-overt pronoun, we predict similar intervention effects. Non-overt pronouns should always move stepwise. In other words, there should not be any relative clauses in

---

[58]   In fact, there are two ways of looking at this. One option is to say that in examples without an overt relative pronoun the pronoun is an abstract entity: it is merged as a non-overt element. This is what is traditionally meant by a term such as "non-overt pronoun." We might, however, also say that in relative clauses without an overt pronoun, a genuine pronoun is merged and then moved but that all copies, including the highest one, end up not being pronounced. The difference between these two ways of thinking is subtle and relates to theoretical assumptions. It is not clear that the two analyses would make different empirical predictions.

which a lower SpecCP inside the relative clause is filled by an interrogative constituent. Our hypothesis predicts that certain patterns should not occur. As before,
the fact that we do not actually come across the relevant examples as such is not
conclusive.[59] However, we can test our prediction by means of an experiment. By
inserting a *wh*-constituent in the specifier position of an intermediate CP in (75a),
we will create a blockade for the movement of the non-overt pronoun ~~who~~. As in
earlier similar experiments,[60] we also must make sure that the embedded interrogative CP can be the complement of the verb it is merged with. (77a) is a constructed
example of this type. We have replaced *believe* by *wonder*, and we have moved the
manner adjunct *how* to the specifier of the CP embedded under *wonder*. If the
relative clause is indeed the result of movement of a non-overt pronoun, we predict
that there should be a degradation in grammaticality. Because we are moving a
subject we expect the degradation to be severe.[61] The prediction is correct:

(77) a *F.B.I. agents investigating falsified identity papers are expanding their
        dragnet for a growing list of foreign-born men they wonder <u>how</u> may have
        entered the Unites States from Canada.

In (77b) we indicate the path of the illicit movement of the non-overt relative
pronoun by the strikethrough notation:[62]

(77) b *foreign-born men [$_{CP}$ ~~who~~ [$_{IP}$ they wonder [$_{CP}$ <u>how</u> [$_{IP}$ ~~who~~ may [$_{VP}$ ~~who~~
        have [$_{VP}$ ~~who~~ entered the Unites States from Canada ~~how~~]]]]]].

5.3.2.2 *Subject movement and the complementizer* that

In sections 3.2.3 and 5.2.2 we discussed a subject-object asymmetry in relation to
the realization of the C position in embedded clauses from which a constituent is
extracted. When we move a subject interrogative pronoun or a subject relative
pronoun out of an embedded clause, we cannot insert *that* in the C position adjacent
to the non-pronounced copy of the moved subject. For interrogative pronouns this
was illustrated in examples (54a, b, c) repeated in (78). For relative pronouns this
was shown in (74b), repeated here as (78d).

(78) a *It baffles me as to who Tony Blair imagines <u>that</u> will work in the univer-
        sities of the future.
     b *Who do you think <u>that</u> is the more moderate politician?
     c *What do you think <u>that</u> was the great appeal of the Tramp?

---

[59] Again we encounter the "white swan problem." Chapter 1, section 2.3, and this chapter,
      section 3.2.1.2.
[60] Sections 3.2.1.2 and 5.2.1.
[61] See section 3.2.3.2.
[62] Exercise 10 (A and B).

d   *A Pakistani jeweler said today that his picture is among those of five men <u>who</u> the F.B.I. says <u>that</u> may have entered the United States on doctored passports.

If, as we claim, the underlined relative clause in (75a), repeated here as (79a), is derived by movement of a non-overt relative pronoun ~~who~~, itself the subject of an embedded clause, then we predict that insertion of the conjunction *that* should lead to ungrammaticality. As shown by (79b) this prediction is correct:

(79) a   F.B.I. agents investigating falsified identity papers are expanding their dragnet for a growing list of foreign-born men <u>they believe may have entered the Unites States illegally from Canada</u>. (*New York Times*, 2.1.2003, p. A9, col. 2)

   b   *F.B.I. agents investigating falsified identity papers are expanding their dragnet for a growing list of foreign-born men they believe <u>that</u> may have entered the Unites States illegally from Canada.

(79b) is degraded in the same way that (78d) is degraded, confirming the non-overt relative pronoun hypothesis.[63]

6   Summary

This chapter completes the overview of the structure of the sentence. We returned to the derivation of interrogative sentences discussed in Chapter 1, focusing on the functional domain of the sentence in which illocutionary force is encoded. We also examined how a fully formed sentence can be integrated into a larger structure and become an embedded clause. In our discussion of the sentence we have postulated another layer of functional structure, CP. We have also refined the application of Move.

The main body of the chapter focused on the derivation of interrogative clauses. We assumed that a functional head C encodes illocutionary force. In embedded clauses C hosts the conjunction (here called complementizer). In direct questions, C hosts the fronted auxiliary of SAI. The specifier of CP hosts the fronted interrogative constituent which serves to define the scope of a constituent question.

The operation Move plays an important role in the derivation of questions. A distinction is made between short movement, in which a constituent moves to the specifier position of the CP in whose VP it is merged, and long movement, in which a constituent moves out of the CP in which it has first been merged, and lands in the specifier of a higher CP. In the case of long movement, we have observed intervention

[63]   Exercise 14. For more extensive introductory discussion of the analysis of relative clauses see also Haegeman and Guéron (1999, chapter 2, section 1.2).

effects. A moved *wh*-constituent cannot cross a *wh*-constituent in the specifier of a SpecCP located between the base position of the moved constituent and its landing site. We have also discovered a subject-object asymmetry with respect to long movement. When a subject undergoes long movement, the C-position that is left-adjacent to its copy must not be filled by *that*. No such constraints hold for long movement of an object.

Like interrogative clauses, relative clauses implicate the CP area, the area of the sentence to the left of the subject. The mechanisms elaborated for the derivation of interrogative clauses can be extended to derive relative clauses. The constraints on movement of interrogative elements carry over to movement of relative elements.

We have also discovered that while the highest copy of a moved interrogative constituent is always overt, all copies of the relative pronoun, including the highest copy, may be non-pronounced. This can be interpreted to mean that a non-overt pronoun is moved. Evidence for postulating such a non-overt pronoun is the fact that relative clauses lacking an overt relative pronoun are subject to the same constraints on movement as relative clauses introduced by an overt relative pronoun.

In the course of the discussion we have repeatedly had to rely on constructed sentences to test our predictions. This was because the predictions that we wanted to test concerned negative generalizations. If all movement proceeds stepwise, for instance, then we predict that movement should never skip an intervening SpecCP. In order to test such a "negative prediction" we cannot simply base ourselves on the observation that the corresponding sentences do not actually occur. We have to construct the relevant sentences ourselves to examine their status.

Needless to say, although this is the final chapter of this introductory book, we have not provided an exhaustive and definitive theory of syntax. The aim of the book was to show how to think about syntax. The book tries to show how syntactic research is done. It also presents a survey of some of the results that have been formulated over the years using this methodology. Many points of syntax have not been discussed at all, and for many others, the discussion is very partial and tentative; this is also because there is still a lot of ongoing debate about the best way to analyze the constructions. However, even if it had been feasible to provide a full survey of current syntactic theory, we would still not have been able to claim that this book is the definitive version of a theory of syntax. Research into the structure of language continues and continuously brings with it novel discoveries and theoretical innovations. After all, this is what science is all about:

> In any branch of science there are only two possibilities. There is either nothing left to discover, in which case why work on it, or there are big discoveries yet to be made, in which case what the scientists say now is likely to be false. (Nigel Calder, author of *Magic Universe: The Oxford Guide to Modern Science*. Cited in *Guardian*, 3.6.2004, p. 6, col. 2)

Exercises

Contents

Exercise 1   SpecCP or C (T)

Consider the following sentences, focusing on the underlined embedded clause:

(1) a I wonder <u>what they will buy</u>.
    b I wonder <u>when they will come</u>.

At first glance, it might not be obvious whether the words *what* and *when* occupy the specifier position (c) or the head position (d) of the embedded CP.

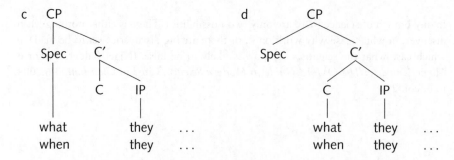

What do you think is the appropriate analysis? How could the following examples help us choose between representations (c) and (d)?

(2) a I wonder which book they will buy.
    b I wonder on which day they will come.

(3) a What will they buy?
    b When will they come?

(4) a %I wonder what will they buy.   (OK in Northern Hiberno English)
    b %I wonder when will they come.   (OK in Northern Hiberno English)

Draw the complete tree diagram representation for the underlined string in (1a) and describe the way the sentence is derived.

Exercise 2   Fronting operations (T)

In the following examples the underlined constituent has been fronted. Locate its base position. What is its function? Has it undergone short movement or long movement?

(1)   <u>While a probationary officer</u>, he said a more senior officer had asked him: "Is it in your religion to lie?" (*Guardian*, 29.10.2003, p. 8, col. 1)

(2)   I've had plenty of advice over what I should say in this speech. <u>Some of it</u> I have even asked for. (*Guardian*, 1.10.2003, p. 6, col. 5)

(3)   <u>A stunningly beautiful building</u>, La Fenice certainly is. (*Guardian*, 6.12.2003, p. 3, col. 1)

(4)   "They must talk about it, and <u>talk about it</u> they must," he said. Food for thought, there! It's a phrase that could add a measure of gravity to any press conference. "We must do this, and <u>do this</u> we must." (*Guardian*, 29.1.2003, p. 2, col. 5)

(5)   It's unbelievable <u>how unlucky</u> he's been, but he's certainly proved he's got tenacity. <u>Whether he'll get out of it or not</u>, only time will tell. (*Guardian*, 8.2.2003, p. 2, col. 8)

(6)   Mr Blair's point was that <u>everything the British had asked for in Greece</u> they had got. (*Guardian*, 7.7.2003, p. 2, col. 5)

(7)   <u>How long he spent there</u>, she couldn't say. (Ian Rankin, *The Falls*, 2001: 328)

(8)   If Tony Blair had listened to us, then I don't think he would have been in the
       mess he's found himself in and if he starts to listen now, he could lead us
       into a great third term. (Adapted from *Guardian*, 27.9.2003, p. 5, col. 6)

(9)   By the next election, I intend that we will offer a really fresh alternative to
       the other two parties. (*Guardian*, 24.9.2003, p. 16, col. 7)

(10) Kerry said he is running to "restore people's trust that what we say we
       mean." (*USA Today*, 26.3.2004, p. A4, col. 5)

Exercise 3   The status of *whether* (T)

We have been assuming that the words *that, if, whether,* and *for* are conjunctions.
Discuss the type of clause these conjunctions introduce. Which position do conjunctions occupy in our structures? Draw a tree diagram for the following sentences:

(1)   I wonder whether I should marry this man.

(2)   I wonder whom I should marry.

(3)   I wonder whether to marry this man.

(4)   I wonder whom to marry.

(5)   I wonder how I can establish a family.

(6)   I wonder how to establish a family.

COMMENT

In your representations, you will probably have inserted *whether* as a head under C
and you will have inserted the interrogative constituents *whom* and *how* under
SpecCP. Such a representation means that we assign *whether* to the class of heads,
while *whom* and *how* are maximal projections. What motivates treating *whom* and
how as maximal projections?[1] Discuss the problems raised for this analysis by the
following attested example:

(7)   Whether and whom to marry, how to express sexual intimacy, and whether
       and how to establish a family – these are among the most basic of every
       individual's liberty and due process rights. (*Guardian*, 19.11.2003, p. 2, col. 3)

---

[1]   See Exercise 1 for evidence.

Exercise 4   Exclamatives (T)

Consider the following examples. What is the function of the underlined constituent? What kind of clause does it introduce?

(1) <u>What a picture of doom and gloom</u> you paint. (*Guardian*, 26.4.2003, p. 10, col. 7)

(2) <u>What a player</u> Heskey would be if he had Rooney's confidence. (*Guardian*, 13.3.2003, p. 15, col. 4)

(3) <u>What a good memory</u> you've got. (Muriel Spark, *The Bachelors*, 1963: 170)

(4) He's shown <u>what a genius</u> he is again. Those flashes show <u>what a talent</u> he is. (based on *Guardian*, Sport, 7.4.2003, p. 3, col. 5)

(5) <u>How badly</u> money is wasted in education. (*Guardian*, 5.3.2002, p. 5, col. 6)

COMMENT

The fronted constituents in the above examples introduce exclamative clauses.[2]

Exercise 5   Complementizers and inversion (T, E)

Discuss the contrasts in grammaticality between the following sentences.

(1) a If your back-supporting muscles should tire, you will be at increased risk of lower-back pain. (based on *Independent on Sunday, Sports*, 14.10.2001, p. 29, col. 3)
   b Should your back-supporting muscles tire, you will be at increased risk of lower-back pain.
   c *If should your back-supporting muscles tire, you will be at increased risk of lower-back pain.
   d *Should if your back-supporting muscles tire, you will be at increased risk of lower-back pain.

In section 2.3 of the chapter we account for the complementary distribution of complementizers and inverted auxiliaries by assuming that they target the same position,

[2] For a detailed discussion of the syntax and semantics of exclamative sentences see Zanuttini and Portner (2003).

C. In that section we use conditional clauses rather than embedded interrogative clauses for the discussion. This is because on the one hand, we need embedded clauses to test the distribution of conjunctions and on the other hand, SAI is not possible in embedded interrogatives in Standard English.

Hiberno English does allow for embedded inversion. Consider the following data from Henry (1995: 107, her (25)). Do they corroborate our analysis?[3]

(2) a   They couldn't work out whether we had left.
    b   They couldn't work out if we had left.
    c   %They couldn't work out had we left.
    d   %*They couldn't work out whether had we left.
    e   %*They couldn't work out if had we left.

Exercise 6   Complementizers and negative inversion (T, E)

In Chapter 1, section 2.3.2, we discussed **negative inversion**. This is the phenomenon whereby SAI is triggered by a negative constituent. The following examples, correspond to (34) in Chapter 1. Identify the inverted auxiliary; identify the negative constituent which triggers inversion.

(1) a   Not one word of evidence have they brought to support that. (*Guardian*, 11.12.2001, p. 4, col. 7)
    b   Within a year of Hague becoming leader, the party had a ballot of its membership to say that not within the lifetime of this parliament would Britain enter the Euro. (*Guardian*, G2, 13.5.2002, p. 7, col. 2)

Consider the examples in (2): in (2a), the fronted constituent contains a negative NP *no account* and it leads to inversion, in (2b), the fronted constituent also contains a negative NP *no time* and yet there is no inversion. Can you see why there should be this difference?

(2) a   On no account should you talk to her.
    b   In no time she had finished her homework.

COMMENT

Though in both examples the fronted constituent is a PP containing a negative element, the negative component serves to negate the clause only in (2a). Sentential

---

[3]   Henry (1995) offers an accessible introduction to some of the properties of Hiberno English. See also Duffield (1993).

negation bears on the link subject–VP, hence on I. When the fronted negation has sentential scope it attracts I.

In (2b) the negation expressed by *no time* does not affect the clause as a whole: *in no time* does not negate the sentence. (2b) does not mean that she has not finished her homework. What (2b) means is that 'she had finished her homework', and that 'finishing her work took very little time'. Since negation does not have sentential scope it does not interact with I. A negation marker such as *no* in (2b) whose scope is restricted to the containing constituent is sometimes said to express **constituent negation**.

Compare the interpretation of the sentence-initial negative constituents in the following pairs:[4]

(3) a With no job, Mary would be happy.
    b With no job would Mary be happy.

(4) a With no clothes does Robin look attractive.
    b With no clothes, Robin looks attractive.

Exercise 7   Non-adjacent inversion: A problem (T, E)

Discuss the problems that the following examples raise for the structure of the CP that we have been postulating:

(1) Why for the first two years of government did they do absolutely nothing? (*Guardian*, G2, 23.1.2001, p. 13, col. 4)

(2) And why in Paris did the Americans modify the agreement at the last minute with the purpose of gaining the signature of the KLA and avoiding that of Yugoslavia? (*Guardian*, 13.4.1999, p. 4, col. 2)

(3) Why after the chaos on the railways and the near collapse of British Telecom does he believe that private management will improve the efficiency of the health service? (*Guardian*, 21.5.2001, p. 11, col. 7)

COMMENT

If we assume that a fronted interrogative constituent occupies a specifier position (i.e. SpecCP) and that an inverted auxiliary moves to the head associated with that position (i.e. C), we predict that the fronted constituent and the inverted head will be adjacent. Because there is no position in between the specifier and the head, there cannot be any intervening constituent. This prediction is contradicted by the

---

[4] For discussion see Haegeman (2000a) and the references cited there.

examples above in which the fronted *wh*-constituent is separated from the inverted auxiliary by an intervening constituent.[5]

Exercise 8   Problems in the left periphery (T, E)

Consider the following examples. Discuss which problems, if any, they pose for the clause structure we have been elaborating so far.

   You should discuss the examples individually and also try to discover more general patterns that are shared by several examples. For your answer, you should classify the examples according to the type of problem(s) they raise. Observe that the fact that problems arise does not mean that the theory is to be rejected, simply that improvements are needed.[6]

(1)   Doctors' leaders have opposed the proposal on the basis that in no other profession are employees restricted from using their free time as they wish. (*Independent*, 18.10.2000, p. 11, col. 1)

(2)   They feel that it's possible that not many months ago that anthrax – a small quantity of it – was handed over in Prague, Czechoslovakia, to Mohammed Atta, one of the pilots of one of the planes that flew into the World Trade Centre. (*Guardian*, 16.10.2001, p. 4, col. 2)

(3)   Even now, a senior editor points out that, if she really is such a simple soul, how did she wind up at a top literary agency, Peters, Fraser and Dunlop? (*Sunday Times*, 18.2.2001, p. 5, col. 1)

(4)   But I completely understand that once they found him that his daughter wanted a funeral. (*Guardian*, G2, 7.2.2002, p. 9, col. 2)

(5)   I feel very strongly that if women are experiencing domestic violence that they should tell their GP. (*Guardian*, 22.12.2003, p. 7, col. 7)

Exercise 9   *Wh*-movement (T)

Identify all the instances of movement of a *wh*-constituent in the following examples. Classify your examples depending on the type of clause that the moved constituent

---

[5]   For some discussion see Haegeman (2000b) and the references cited there.
      Notice that in (1)–(3) above the interrogative constituent is *why*. For discussion of *why* see Rizzi (2001).

[6]   For more detailed discussions of the structure of the CP domain see Rizzi (1997). For English and Hiberno English see McCloskey (forthcoming).

introduces (relative/interrogative; finite/non-finite). Locate the base position of the moved constituent and identify its function (subject, object, adjunct).

(1) Within 10 minutes you'll hit upon a television program designed to monitor the most intimate details of our lives in the hopes of finding something mildly amusing with which to capture the attention of fickle viewers. (*Chicago Tribune*, 22.12.2003, Section 13, p. 2, col. 2)

(2) Thrilled, he accepted the change and brought along several stuffed animal friends who he thought would like the fire-truck bed too. (*Washington Post*, 10.12.2002, p. F4, col. 4)

(3) A lot of designers come from the perspective of being inventors, which I think is so bogus. (*New York Times*, 28.11.2002, p. D5, col. 2)

(4) Amy and her mom are together in the kitchen one night. Her mom says she should learn how to cook. Amy seizes the moment: "What kind of husband do you see me with?" (*Washington Post*, 10.12.2002, p. A15, col. 1)

(5) The National Design Museum turned down the Boyms' proposal in 1994 to sell everyday items like light bulbs, graced with the museum's logo, as gift shop merchandise, which it told Mr Boym was uncommercial thinking. (*New York Times*, 28.11.2002, p. D4, col. 1)

(6) [Her mother] doesn't know that Amy has already fallen [for a boyfriend] . . . Amy spends hours talking to him on her cell phone, which she sleeps with under her pillow. (*Washington Post*, 10.12.2002, p. A15, col. 1)

(7) Inevitably, the changes have laid bare frictions – which all sides say were inevitable, and perhaps healthy – within Trinity Parish, which operates St. Paul's, and New York's Episcopal world. (*New York Times*, 28.11.2002, p. A28, col. 1)

(8) The SEC has no chief accountant and can't sensibly appoint one until it's clear whom this official would report to. (*Washington Post*, 10.12.2002, p. A28, col. 1)

(9) There are dozens of great new TVs out there. The critical question, even more than what to buy, is when to buy. (*Chicago Tribune*, 22.12.2002, Section 15, p. 3, col. 1)

(10) [Nawid's family] now have no land on which to build, even if they had the money. (*New York Times*, 2.1.2003, p. A8, col. 3)

Exercise 10   Constraints on extraction (T, E)

10A   Consider (1). Identify the antecedent of the relative pronoun *who*. Insert left-hand brackets labeled "[$_{IP}$" and "[$_{CP}$" in the representation of the underlined relative clause. Add the appropriate right-hand brackets. Represent the unpronounced copy of the relative pronoun by strikethrough (~~who~~). Signal the implicit subject of an infinitive by means of the symbol [$_{NP}$ Ø] in the SpecIP position. Discuss any problems that arise.

(1)   For decades now, the post of Arts minister has been a dumping ground for nice people <u>who political leaders of the day don't know where else to put</u>. (*Independent on Sunday*, 9.5.2004, p. 24 News, col. 1)

KEY AND COMMENTS

In (1) the relative pronoun *who* must have first merged with the verb *put*. This verb is found in a non-finite interrogative clause whose SpecCP is filled by a *wh*-constituent *where else*. The extraction of *who* is unexpected because we have seen that moving a *wh*-constituent across a filled specifier of an intervening CP leads to a degradation.

(1')   nice people [$_{CP}$ who [$_{IP}$ political leaders of the day don't know

[$_{CP}$ <u>where</u> else [$_{IP}$ [$_{NP}$ Ø] to [$_{VP}$ [$_{NP}$ Ø] put ~~who~~]]]]].

10B   In section 5.3 of the chapter we postulated that a relative pronoun may be non-overt. Consider the attested examples in (2). For each example insert left-hand brackets labeled "[$_{IP}$" and "[$_{CP}$" in the representation of the underlined relative clauses. Add the matching right-hand brackets. Represent unpronounced copies of the relative pronoun by strikethrough (~~which~~). Signal the implicit subject of infinitives by means of the symbol [$_{NP}$ Ø] in SpecIP. Discuss the problems raised by the examples. Would the examples in (2) offer any arguments against the hypothesis that relative clauses may be introduced by an unpronounced pronoun (~~which~~)?

(2)   a   These are things <u>experienced infielders know how to do</u>. (*USA Today*, 26.3.2004, p. 15C, cols 2–3)

b   There's only one thing <u>we don't know how to do properly</u>, and that's sing like the northern hemisphere sides. (*Guardian*, 13.11.2003, p. 21, col. 6)

c   These are struggles <u>the government decided how to conduct</u> before it came to power, and the case for its policy then remains as correct as ever. (*Guardian*, 26.11.2002, p. 8, col. 6)

d   Something <u>I know how to do</u> is close a deal. (*New York Times*, 1.8.2004, p. 7 (ST), col. 4)

e   We did everything <u>we knew how to do</u> to continue to pursue al Quaeda. (*Wall Street Journal*, 29.3.2004, p. A14, col. 5)

KEY AND COMMENTS

Assuming that the examples in (2) are derived by movement of a non-pronounced relative pronoun ~~which~~, they display the same unexpected pattern illustrated in (1) in section A:

(2)′ a things [CP ~~which~~ [IP experienced infielders know [CP how [IP [NP Ø] to do ~~which~~]]]]

 b one thing [CP ~~which~~ [IP we don't know [CP how [IP [NP Ø] to do properly ~~which~~]]]]

 c struggles [CP ~~which~~ [IP the government decided [CP how [IP [NP Ø] to conduct ~~which~~]]]]

 d something [CP ~~which~~ [IP I know [CP how [IP [NP Ø] to do ~~which~~]]]]

 e everything [CP ~~which~~ [IP we knew [CP how [IP [NP Ø] to do ~~which~~]]]]

Taken all by themselves the unexpected examples in (2) might at first sight be thought to constitute evidence against the non-overt relative pronoun hypothesis. After all, a non-overt pronoun would be moved across an interrogative constituent (*how*). However, example (1) in section A shows a similar unexpected pattern with an overt pronoun. This means that even with respect to the non-expected patterns, non-overt relative pronouns (represented as ~~which~~ in (2′)) behave in the same way as pronounced pronouns (*who* in (1)).[7]

Exercise 11   Relative clauses and resumptive pronouns (T, E)

While discussing the derivation of relative clauses and of interrogative clauses we have been assuming that a *wh*-constituent is moved from its base position, in which it leaves an unpronounced copy. For instance, for the embedded clauses for our discussion examples (64b) and (65a), repeated here as (1a) and (1b), we proposed representation (1c), in which ~~who~~ signals the unpronounced copy of the moved relative pronoun *who*.

(1) a I wonder who he had met at the party.
  b I interviewed the man who he had met at the party.
  c [CP who [IP he [I had] [VP ~~he have~~ [VP ~~he~~ met ~~who~~ at the party]]]][8]

---

[7] Observe that several of the unexpected examples in (2) concern the sequence *know how to*. It may well be that the pattern *know how to* has special properties. Cinque (2004b: 140) shows that the Italian analogue of *know how to* also displays special properties.

[8] Recall that we assume that there is an unpronounced copy of the moved subject in the specifier position associated with the projection of the auxiliary *have*. See Chapter 4, section 4, for discussion.

Discuss the problems raised for this analysis by the following attested example:

(2)   It was a background discussion which my understanding was that it would not appear anywhere. (*Guardian*, 21.8.2003, p. 9, col. 5)

COMMENTS

In this example, instead of having an unpronounced copy in a lower position of the relative pronoun *which* we find the pronoun *it*. When a pronoun occupies a position in which we would have expected an unpronounced copy of a *wh*-constituent we refer to it as a **resumptive** pronoun.

(2′)   It was a background discussion [CP which [IP my understanding was [CP that [IP it would not appear anywhere]]]].

Could we remove the resumptive pronoun and replace it by an unpronounced copy of the relative pronoun *which*? That is to say, would the spell-out of (3a) be acceptable?

(3) a   *It was a background discussion [CP which [IP my understanding was [CP ~~which~~ that [IP ~~which~~ would not [VP ~~which~~ appear anywhere]]]]].

Forming relative clauses such as that in (2) without using the **resumptive** pronoun strategy leads to an ungrammatical result, because such examples violate the constraint on subject extraction (see section 3.2.3.1).

(3) b   *It was a background discussion which my understanding was that would not appear anywhere.

Exercise 12   Extraction from adjunct clauses and resumptive pronouns (E)

In Exercise 11 we discovered that resumptive pronouns can be inserted to overcome constraints on movement. Consider the examples below, which also contain resumptive pronouns in a lower position of a relative pronoun. Locate the relative pronoun and the related resumptive pronoun. Can you remove the resumptive pronoun (that is, can you replace it by an unpronounced copy of the relative pronoun)?

(1)   Bernie is the type of man who when you shake hands with him, it's a deal. (*Guardian*, G2, 11.7.2001, p. 5, col. 3)

(2) They say he was a workaholic and that work was a drug which when he couldn't have it anymore he got depressed. (Jonathan Frantzen, *The Corrections*, 2001: 75).

KEY AND COMMENTS

The relative pronouns in examples (1) and (2) are related to a resumptive pronoun inside an adjunct clause. The relative pronoun is outside the adjunct clause while the resumptive pronoun is inside it.

(1′) Bernie is the type of man who [$_{CP}$ when you shake hands with him], it's a deal.

(2′) They say he was a workaholic and that work was a drug which [$_{CP}$ when he couldn't have it anymore] he got depressed.

For (1) and in (2) replacing the resumptive pronouns by an unpronounced copy of the relative pronoun would lead to a degradation. Representations (3a, b) would correspond to sentences (4a, b):

(3) a Bernie is the type of man who [when you shake hands with ~~who~~], it's a deal.
    b They say he was a workaholic and that work was a drug which [when he couldn't have ~~which~~ anymore] he got depressed.

(4) a *Bernie is the type of man who [when you shake hands with], it's a deal.
    b *They say he was a workaholic and that work was a drug which [when he couldn't have anymore] he got depressed.

These examples reveal a further constraint on movement of relative pronouns: extracting a relative pronoun from an adjunct clause also leads to a degradation.

Exercise 13   Movement from adjunct clauses (E)

In Exercise 12 we discovered that it is not possible to extract a relative pronoun from an adjunct clause. The relevant examples (4a, b) from Exercise 12 are repeated here in (1).

(1) a *Bernie is the type of man who when you shake hands with, it's a deal.
    b *They say he was a workaholic and that work was a drug which when he couldn't have anymore he got depressed.

In the discussion we have assumed that movement of the relative *wh*-pronoun is similar (or identical) to the movement of the interrogative pronoun. What predictions do we make for the status of the following interrogative examples? Are these predictions correct?

(2) a   Who would it be a deal when you simply shake hands with?
     b   Which drug did he get depressed when he couldn't have any more?

KEY AND COMMENTS

(2a) is unacceptable; (2b) is degraded and for many speakers it is also unacceptable.
The degradations are predicted by our hypothesis that movement of relative pronouns and movement of interrogative pronouns are two instantiations of the same
operation Move.

Exercise 14   *That* relatives (T, E)

(1a) corresponds to the text example (75a). Compare the underlined string in (1b)
with the relative clause in (1a):

(1) a   F.B.I. agents investigating falsified identity papers are expanding their drag-
         net for a growing list of foreign-born men <u>they believe may have entered
         the Unites States illegally from Canada</u>.
     b   F.B.I. agents investigating falsified identity papers are expanding their
         dragnet for a growing list of foreign-born men <u>that they believe may have
         entered the Unites States illegally from Canada</u>.

We have proposed that in (1a) a non-overt relative pronoun undergoes (long)
movement. In the literature it is often proposed that in (1b) a relative pronoun has
also moved to SpecCP, but again this pronoun is not pronounced. In other words
(1b) would have the partial representation in (1c).

(1) c   foreign-born men [$_{CP}$ ~~who~~ that [$_{IP}$ they believe [$_{CP}$ ~~who~~ [$_{IP}$ ~~who~~ may [$_{VP}$ ~~who~~
         have [$_{VP}$ ~~who~~ entered the Unites States illegally from Canada]]]]]][9]

Consider the examples below. Discuss how they provide support for the non-overt
pronoun hypothesis represented in (1c).

(2) a   *F.B.I. agents investigating falsified identity papers are expanding their
         dragnet for a growing list of foreign-born men that they wonder <u>how</u> may
         have entered the Unites States from Canada.
     b   *F.B.I. agents investigating falsified identity papers are expanding their
         dragnet for a growing list of foreign-born men that they believe <u>that</u> may
         have entered the Unites States illegally from Canada.

---

[9]   Recall that we assume that there is an unpronounced copy of the moved subject in the specifier
      position associated with the projection of the auxiliary *have*. See Chapter 4, section 4, for
      discussion.

KEY AND COMMENTS

In (2a) we have inserted the interrogative constituent *how* in the specifier position of an intermediate CP. This leads to a strong degradation in acceptability of the example. Similarly, inserting *that* in the position adjacent to the subject position from which the non-overt relative pronoun would have been moved leads to a strong degradation in (2b). These two effects are identical to those discussed in connection with movement of overt interrogative and relative pronouns in sections 3.2 and 5.2 of the chapter, and they also extend to movement of non-overt relative pronouns as discussed in section 5.3.

One point needs to be added here: in Modern English the complementizer *that* can only be used to introduce a relative clause if the constituent in SpecCP itself is non-overt. If both the constituent in SpecCP and the complementizer *that* in the adjacent C position are overt (representation (1d)), the resulting sentence is ungrammatical (1e):[10]

(1) d   *foreign-born men [$_{CP}$ who that [$_{IP}$ they believe [$_{CP}$ ~~who~~ [$_{IP}$ ~~who~~ may [$_{VP}$ ~~who~~ have [$_{VP}$ ~~who~~ entered the Unites States illegally from Canada]]]]]].

   e   *F.B.I. agents investigating falsified identity papers are expanding their drag-net for a growing list of foreign-born men <u>who that they believe may have entered the Unites States illegally from Canada</u>.

Discuss how the *that* relative in (3) could be derived:

(3)   These are precisely the kinds of things <u>that students and faculty members will find at the newly renovated Milbank Memorial library</u>. (*New York Times, Education*, 1.8.2004, p. 19, col. 1)

Exercise 15   Postverbal subjects and inversion in French (E)

Consider the French examples in (1). How could we represent the structure for (1a)? And for (1b)? On the basis of their English glosses you might be tempted to assign to (1b) the same structure as (1a). The only difference would be that while the subject in (1b) is a lexical NP *les étudiants* ('the students'), that in (1a) is a pronoun.

(1) a   Combien d'argent dépensent-ils?
        how much money spend-3PL they
        'How much money do they spend?'

---

[10]   There is a similar effect with interrogatives, cf. section 2.6.

b   Combien d'argent dépensent les étudiants?
    how much money spend-3PL the students
    'How much money do the students spend?'

On the basis of the data below, can we maintain that (1a) and (1b) have the same derivation?

(2) a   Combien d'argent ont-   ils   dépensé?
        how much money have-3PL -they spent-PART
        'How much money have they spent?'

    b   *Combien d'argent ont   les étudiants dépensé?
        how much money   have-3PL the students spent-PART

(3) a   *Combien d'argent ont   dépensé   ils?
        how much money   have-3PL spent-PART they

    b   Combien d'argent ont   dépensé   les étudiants?
        how much money have-3PL spent-PART the students
        'How much money have the students spent?'

(4) a   *Je me demande combien d'argent dépensent-ils.
        I wonder   how much money spend-3PL they

    b   Je me demande combien d'argent dépensent les étudiants.
        I wonder   how much money spend-3PL the students
        'I wonder how much money the students spend.'

    c   Je me demande combien d'argent ont   dépensé   les étudiants.
        I wonder   how much money have-3PL spent-PART the students
        'I wonder how much money the students have spent.'

(5) a   Dépensent-ils   beaucoup d'argent?
        spend-3PL they a lot of money
        'Do they spend a lot of money?'

    b   *Dépensent les étudiants beaucoup d'argent?
        spend-3PL   the students a lot of money

KEY AND COMMENTS

The derivation of (1a) is relatively straightforward: we assume that the inflected verb *dépensent* ('spend') has undergone inversion (SVI) and has moved to C. The fronted direct object *combien d'argent* ('how much money') is an interrogative constituent in SpecCP:

(1) c $[_{CP}$ $[_{NP}$ Combien d'argent] $[_C$ dépensent] $[_{IP}$ ils $[_I$ ~~dépensent~~] $[_{VP}$ ~~ils dépens-~~ $[_{NP}$ ~~combien d'argent~~]]]].

One might think that (1b) has the same derivation, with a lexical NP *les étudiants* ('the students') rather than a pronoun (*ils*, 'they') as the subject in SpecIP. But the additional data show that the distribution of pronominal subjects is different from that of full NP subjects.

In (2a) the inflected auxiliary *ont* ('have') has moved to C, the lexical VP is headed by a past participle *dépensé* ('spent').

(2) c $[_{CP}$ $[_{NP}$ Combien d'argent] $[_C$ ont] $[_{IP}$ ils $[_I$ ~~ont~~] $[_{VP}$ ~~ils av-~~[11] $[_{VP}$ ~~ils~~ dépensé $[_{NP}$ ~~combien d'argent~~]]]]]?

(2b/d) shows that the analogue of derivation (2a/c) with an NP subject is ungrammatical:

(2) d *$[_{CP}$ $[_{NP}$ Combien d'argent] $[_C$ ont] $[_{IP}$ les étudiants $[_I$ ~~ont~~] $[_{VP}$ ~~les étudiants av-~~ $[_{VP}$ ~~les étudiants~~ dépensé $[_{NP}$ ~~combien d'argent~~]]]]]?

Rather, as shown by (3b), a lexical subject must occupy a position to the right of the participle. This is a position in which the pronominal subject cannot occur (3a).

As shown by (4a), with pronominal subjects, SVI is restricted to main clauses. In contrast, the inverted position occupied by lexical subjects is also available in embedded interrogatives (4b), in which the lexical subject can also follow a participle (4c).

(5a) shows that with a pronominal subject, SVI is also found in *yes/no* questions. On the other hand, in *yes/no* questions lexical subjects cannot occupy the postverbal position.

We conclude that though both (1a) and (1b) contain postverbal subjects, we have to distinguish their structures.[12]

---

[11] In (2c) we represent the root of the verb *avoir* ('have') as *av-*. This is an approximation.

[12] For introductory discussions of these data see Battye, Hintze, and Rowlett (2000: 202–5) and Rowlett (2005). For advanced discussion see Kayne (1972), and Kayne and Pollock (1978, 2001).

   For examples in English in which a postverbal NP subject is not derived by SAI see Chapter 1, Exercises 11 and 12, and Chapter 4, Exercise 23.

Bibliography

Aarts, Bas and Liliane Haegeman (forthcoming) English word classes and phrases. In Bas Aarts and April McMahon (eds), *The Handbook of English Linguistics*, Oxford: Blackwell.

Abney, Steven (1987) The English Noun Phrase in its Sentential Aspect. PhD dissertation, MIT.

Abraham, Werner, Sam Epstein, Hoskuldur Thráinsson, and Jan Wouter Zwart (eds) (1996) *Minimal Ideas*, New York and Amsterdam: John Benjamins.

Adger, David (2003) *Core Syntax*, Oxford and New York: Oxford University Press.

Alexiadou, Artemis (1997) *Adverb Placement*, New York and Amsterdam: John Benjamins.

Alexiadou, Artemis (2001) *Functional Structure in Nominals*, New York and Amsterdam: John Benjamins.

Alexiadou, Artemis (2004a) On the development of possessive determiners: Consequences for DP structure. In Eric Fuss and Carola Trips (eds), *Diachronic Clues to Synchronic Grammar*, New York and Amsterdam: John Benjamins, pp. 31–58.

Alexiadou, Artemis (ed.) (2004b) Adverbs across Frameworks. Special edition of *Lingua*, 114.

Alexiadou, Artemis and Elena Anagnostopoulou (1998) Parametrizing AGR: Word order, verb movement and EPP checking. *Natural Language and Linguistic Theory*, 16, 491–539.

Alexiadou, Artemis and Elena Anagnostopoulou (2001) The subject *in situ* generalisation and the role of case in driving computations. *Linguistic Inquiry*, 32, 193–213.

Authier, J.-M. (1992) Iterated CPs and embedded topicalisation. *Linguistic Inquiry*, 23, 329–36.

Baker, Carl Lee (1991) The syntax of English *not*: The limits of core grammar. *Linguistic Inquiry*, 22, 387–429.

Baker, Mark (1997) Thematic roles and syntactic structure. In Liliane Haegeman (ed.), *Elements of Grammar: A Handbook of Generative Syntax*, Dordrecht: Kluwer, pp. 73–138.

Baker, Mark (2002) Building and merging, not checking: the non existence of (Aux)-S-V-O languages. *Linguistic Inquiry*, 33, 321–8.

Baker, Mark, Kyle Johnson, and Ian Roberts (1989) Passive arguments raised. *Linguistic Inquiry*, 20, 219–51.

Baltin, Mark R. and Chris Collins (eds) (2001) *The Handbook of Contemporary Syntactic Theory*, Oxford: Blackwell.

Basilico, David (1998) Object position and predication forms. *Natural Language and Linguistic Theory*, 16, 541–95.

Battistella, Ed (1995) The syntax of the double modal construction. *Linguistica Atlantica*, 21, 49–65.

Battye, Adrian, Marie-Anne Hintze, and Paul Rowlett (2000) *The French Language Today: A Linguistic Introduction*, 2nd edition, London: Routledge.

Belletti, Adriana (1988) The case of unaccusatives. *Linguistic Inquiry*, 19, 1–35.

Belletti, Adriana (1990) *Generalised Verb Movement: Aspects of Verb Syntax*, Turin: Rosenberg and Tellier.

Belletti, Adriana and Luigi Rizzi (1988) Psych verbs and theta theory. *Natural Language and Linguistic Theory*, 6, 291–352.

Bernstein, Judy B. (2001) The DP hypothesis: Identifying clausal properties in the nominal domain. In Mark Baltin and Chris Collins (eds), *The Handbook of Contemporary Syntactic Theory*, Oxford: Blackwell, pp. 536–61.

Birner, Betty (1992) The Discourse Function of Inversion in English. PhD dissertation, Northwestern University.

Birner, Betty (1994) Information status and word order: An analysis of English inversion. *Language*, 70, 233–59.

Birner, Betty and Gary L. Ward (1992) On the interpretation of VP inversion in American English. *Journal of Linguistics*, 28, 1–12.

Blakemore, Diane and Robyn Carston (eds) (2005) Coordination: Syntax, Semantics and Pragmatics. Special issue of *Lingua*, 115.

Bobaljik, Jonathan (1995) Morpho Syntax: The Syntax of Verbal Inflection. PhD dissertation, MIT.

Bobaljik, Jonathan (2002) Realizing Germanic inflection: Why morphology does not drive syntax. *The Journal of Comparative Germanic Linguistics*, 6, 129–67.

Bobaljik, Jonathan (2003) Floating quantifiers: Handle with care (revised version). In Lisa Cheng and Rint Sybesma (eds), *The Second Glot International State-of-The-Article Book*, Berlin: Mouton de Gruyter, pp. 107–48.

Bobaljik, Jonathan and Diane Jonas (1996) Subject positions and the role of TP. *Linguistic Inquiry*, 27, 195–236.

Borsley, Robert and Richard Ingham (2002) Grow your own linguistics? On some applied linguists' views of the subject. *Lingua*, 112 (1), 1–6.

Borsley, Robert and Richard Ingham (2003) More on "some applied linguistics": A response to Stubbs. *Lingua*, 113, 193–6.

Boskovic, Zeljko (2002) A-movement and the EPP. *Syntax*, 5, 167–218.

Boskovic, Zeljko (2004) Be careful where you float your quantifiers. *Natural Language and Linguistic Theory*, 22, 681–742.

Bowers, John (1993) The syntax of predication. *Linguistic Inquiry*, 24, 591–665.

Bowers, John (2001) Predication. In Mark Baltin and Chris Collins (eds), *The Handbook of Contemporary Syntactic Theory*, Oxford: Blackwell, pp. 299–334.

Bowers, John (2002) Transitivity. *Linguistic Inquiry*, 33, 183–225.

Bresnan, Joan (1994) Locative inversion and the architecture of universal grammar. *Language*, 70, 72–131.

Brown, Keith (1992) Double modals in Hawick Scots. In Peter Trudgill and J. K. Chambers, (eds), *Dialects of English: Studies in Grammatical Variation*, London: Longmans, pp. 74–103.

Camacho, José (2003) *The Structure of Coordination*, Dordrecht: Kluwer.

Caponigro, Ivano and Carson T. Schütze (2003) Parametrizing passive participle movement. *Linguistic Inquiry*, 34, 293–308.

Carnie, Andrew (2002) *Syntax: A Generative Introduction*, Oxford: Blackwell.

Chomsky, Noam (1970) Remarks on nominalizations. In Roderick Jacobs and Peter Rosenbaum (eds), *Readings in English Transformational Grammar*, Waltham, MA: Ginn. Also in Noam Chomsky (1972) *Studies on Semantics in Generative Grammar*, The Hague: Mouton.

Chomsky, Noam (1972) *Studies on Semantics in Generative Grammar*, The Hague: Mouton.

Chomsky, Noam (1975) *The Logical Structure of Linguistic Theory*, New York: Plenum.

Chomsky, Noam (1995) *The Minimalist Program*, Cambridge, MA: MIT Press.

Cinque, Guglielmo (1999) *Adverbs and Functional Heads: A Cross-linguistic Perspective*, New York/Oxford: Oxford University Press.

Cinque, Guglielmo (2004a) Issues in adverbial syntax. In Artemis Alexiadou (ed.), Adverbs across Frameworks, Special edition of *Lingua*, 114, 683–710.

Cinque, Guglielmo (2004b) Restructuring and functional structure. In Adriana Belletti (ed.), *Structures and Beyond: The Cartography of Syntactic Structures*, vol. 3, Oxford and New York: Oxford University Press, pp. 132–91.

Clahsen, Harald (ed.) (1996) *Generative Perspectives on Language Acquisition*, Amsterdam: John Benjamins.

Collins, Chris and Höskuldur Thráinsson (1993) Object shift in double object constructions and the theory of case. *MIT Working Papers in Linguistics*, 19, 131–74.

Coopmans, Peter (1989) Where stylistic and syntactic processes meet: Locative inversion in English. *Language*, 65, 728–51.

Cormack, Annabel and Neil Smith (2002) Modals and negation in English. In Sjef Barbiers, Frits Beukema, and Wim van der Wurff (eds), *Modality and Its Interaction with the Verbal System*, New York and Amsterdam: John Benjamins, pp. 133–64.

Cottell, Siobhan (2002) The Comparative Syntax of Cleft Constructions. PhD dissertation, University of Wales, Bangor.

Cottell, Siobhan and Alison Henry (2004) Transitive expletives, quantifier stranding and subject positions in an English dialect. Paper presented at the Comparative Germanic Syntax Workshop 19, CUNY.

Crystal, David (1971) *Linguistics*, London: Penguin.

Culicover, Peter (1991) Topicalization, inversion and complementizers in English. In Denis Delfitto, Martin Everaert, Arnold Evers, and Frits Stuurman (eds), *OTS Working Papers: Going Romance and Beyond*, Utrecht: University of Utrecht, pp. 1–45.

Culicover, Peter (1993) Evidence against ECP accounts of the *that*-t effect. *Linguistic Inquiry* 24, 557–61.

Culicover, Peter and Robert Levine (2001) Stylistic inversion in English: A reconsideration. *Natural Language and Linguistic Theory*, 19, 283–310.

Davies, William D. and Stanley Dubinsky (1999) Sentential subjects as complex NPs: New reasons for an old account of subjacency. *Chicago Linguistics Society*, 34, 83–94.

Davies, William D. and Stanley Dubinsky (2001a) Functional architecture and the distribution of subject properties. In William D. Davies and Stanley Dubinsky (eds), *Objects and other Subjects*, Dordrecht: Kluwer, pp. 247–80.

Davies, William D. and Stanley Dubinsky (eds) (2001b) *Objects and other Subjects*, Dordrecht: Kluwer.

DeGraff, Michel (1997) Verb syntax in creolization (and beyond). In Liliane Haegeman (ed.), *The New Comparative Syntax*, London: Longman, Addison and Wesley, pp. 64–94.

DeGraff, Michel (1999) *Language Creation and Language Change: Creolization, Diachrony and Development*, Boston, MA: MIT Press.

Diesing, Molly (1997) Yiddish VP order and the typology of object movement in Germanic. *Natural Language and Linguistic Theory*, 15, 369–427.

Dik, Simon (1989) Functional grammar and its relevance to grammar writing. In Gottfried Graustein and Gerhard Leitner (eds), *Reference Grammars and Modern Linguistic Theory*, Tübingen: Niemeyer, pp. 33–55.

Dikken, Marcel den and Alma Næss (1993) Case dependencies: The case of predicate inversion. *The Linguistic Review*, 10, 303–36.

Doetjes, Jenny (1992) Rightward floating quantifiers float to the left. *The Linguistic Review*, 9, 313–32.

Duffield, Nigel (1993) On case checking and NPI licensing in Hiberno English. *Rivista di Linguistica*, 5, 215–44.

Einstein, Albert (1954) *Ideas and Opinions*, New York: Crown.

Emonds, Joseph (1976) *A Transformational Approach to English Syntax*, New York: Academic Press.

Emonds, Joseph (1978) The verbal complex V'-V in French. *Linguistic Inquiry*, 9, 151–75.

Ernst, Thomas (1992) The phrase structure of English negation. *The Linguistic Review*, 9, 109–44.

Ernst, Thomas (2002) *The Syntax of Adjuncts*, Cambridge: Cambridge University Press.

Ernst, Thomas (2004) Principles of adverbial distribution in the lower clause. In Artemis Alexiadou (ed.), Adverbs across Frameworks, special edition of *Lingua*, 114, 755–78.

Fischer, Olga, Ans van Kemenade, Willem Koopman, and Wim van der Wurff (2000) *The Syntax of Early English*, Cambridge: Cambridge University Press.

Frazier, Lynn and C. Clifton, Jr. (1989) Successive cyclicity in the grammar and parsing. *Language and Cognitive Processes*, 4, 93–126.

Friedemann, MarcAriel and Luigi Rizzi (eds) (1999) *The Acquisition of Syntax*, London: Longman, Addison, Wesley.

Friedemann, MarcAriel and Tal Siloni (1993) AgrO is not AgrPart. *GenGenP*, 1, 41–53.

Fu, Jingqi, Thomas Roeper, and Hagit Borer (2001) The VP within process nominals: Evidence from adverbs and the VP anaphor *do so*. *Natural Language and Linguistic Theory*, 19, 549–82.

Gavruseva, Elena (2000) On the syntax of possessor extraction. *Lingua*, 110, 743–72.

Gibson, Edward and Tessa Warren (2004) Reading–time evidence for intermediate linguistic structure in long-distance dependencies. *Syntax*, 7, 55–78.

Ginzburg, Johnathan (1999) Interrogatives: Questions, facts and dialogue. In Shalom Lappin (ed.), *The Handbook of Contemporary Semantic Theory*, Oxford: Blackwell, pp. 385–422.

Giorgi, Alessandra and Giuseppe Longobardi (1991) *The Syntax of Noun Phrases: Configuration, Parameters and Empty Categories*, Cambridge: Cambridge University Press.

Goodall, Grant (1987) *Parallel Structures in Syntax*, Dordrecht: Kluwer.

Goodall, Grant (2001) The EPP in Spanish. In William D. Davies and Stanley Dubinsky, *Objects and other Subjects*, Dordrecht: Kluwer, pp. 193–223.

Graustein, Gottfried and Gerhard Leitner (1989) *Reference Grammars and Modern Linguistic Theory*, Tübingen: Niemeyer.

Grimshaw, Jane (1990) *Argument Structure*, Cambridge, MA: MIT Press.

Haeberli, Erik (2000) Adjuncts and the syntax of subjects in Old and Middle English. In Susan Pintzuk, George Tsoulas, and Anthony Warner (eds), *Diachronic Syntax: Models and Mechanisms*, Oxford: Oxford University Press, pp. 109–31.

Haegeman, Liliane (1994) *Introduction to Government and Binding Theory*. Oxford: Blackwell.

Haegeman, Liliane (1995) *The Syntax of Negation*, Cambridge: Cambridge University Press.

Haegeman, Liliane (ed.) (1997a) *Elements of Grammar: A Handbook of Generative Syntax*, Dordrecht: Kluwer.

Haegeman, Liliane (ed.) (1997b) *The New Comparative Syntax*, London: Longman, Addison and Wesley.

Haegeman, Liliane (2000a) Negative inversion, the NEG criterion and the structure of CP. In Larry Horn and Yasuhiko Kato (eds), *Negation and Polarity*, Oxford and New York: Oxford University Press, pp. 29–69.

Haegeman, Liliane (2000b) Inversion, non-adjacent inversion and adjuncts in CP. In Paul Rowlett (ed.), *Transactions of the Philological Society, Special Issue: Papers from the Salford Negation conference*, 98 (1), 121–60.

Haegeman, Liliane (2003) Notes on long adverbial fronting in English and the left periphery. *Linguistic Inquiry*, 34, 640–9.

Haegeman, Liliane and Jacqueline Guéron (1999) *English Grammar: A Generative Perspective*. Oxford: Blackwell.

Harlow, Stephen (1981) Government and relativisation in Celtic. In Frank Heny (ed.), *Binding and Filtering*, London: Croom Helm, pp. 213–54.

Hegarty, Michael (2003) Semantic types of abstract entities. *Lingua*, 113, 891–927.

Henry, Alison (1995) *Belfast English and Standard English: Dialect Variation and Parameter Setting*, Oxford: Oxford University Press.

Henry, Alison (2001) The direction and motivation of movement: Transitive expletives and floating associates in Belfast English. Paper presented at the Motivating Movement conference, Jordanstown, January.

Heycock, Caroline and Anthony Kroch (1997) Inversion and equation in copular sentences. *ZAS Papers in Linguistics*, 10, 71–87.

Hoekstra, Teun and René Mulder (1990) Unergatives as copular verbs: Locational and existential predication. *The Linguistic Review*, 7, 1–79.

Holmberg, Anders (1986) Word Order and Syntactic Features in the Scandinavian Languages and English. PhD dissertation, University of Stockholm.

Holmberg, Anders (1999) Remarks on Holmberg's generalization. *Studia Linguistica*, 53, 1–39.

Holmberg, Anders and Christer Platzack (1995) *The Role of Inflection in Scandinavian Syntax*, Oxford and New York: Oxford University Press.

Hoop, Helen de, Marco Haverkot, and Maurits van den Noort (2004) Variation in Form Versus Variation in Meaning. Special issue of *Lingua*, 114, 1071–89.

Hooper, John and Sandra Thompson (1973) On the applicability of Root Transformations. *Linguistic Inquiry*, 4, 465–97.

Hornstein, Norbert, Jairo Nunes, and Kleanthes K. Grohmann (forthcoming) *Understanding Minimalism: An Introduction to Minimalist Syntax*. Cambridge: Cambridge University Press.

Horrocks, Geoff and Melita Stavrou (1987) Bounding theory and Greek syntax: Evidence for *wh*-movement in NP. *Journal of Linguistics*, 23, 79–108.

Huddleston, Rodney (1994) The contrast between interrogatives and questions. *Journal of Linguistics*, 30, 411–40.

Jackendoff, Ray (1977) *X′ Syntax: A Study of Phrase Structure*, Cambridge, MA: MIT Press.

Jackendoff, Ray (1987) The status of thematic relations in linguistic theory. *Linguistic Inquiry*, 30, 69–96.

Jaworska, Ewa (1986) Prepositional phrases as subjects and objects. *Journal of Linguistics*, 22, 355–75.

Jonas, Diane and Jonathan Bobaljik (1993) Specs for subjects: The role of TP in Icelandic. In Jonathan Bobaljik and Collin Phillips (eds), *MIT Working Papers in Linguistics: Papers on Case and Agreement*, I, 59–98.

Kayne, Richard (1972) Subject inversion in French interrogatives. In J. Casagrande and B. Saciuk (eds), *Generative Studies in Romance Languages*, Rowley, MA: Newbury House, pp. 70–126.

Kayne, Richard (1984) *Connectedness and Binary Branching*, Dordrecht: Foris.

Kayne, Richard (1994) *The Antisymmetry of Syntax*, Cambridge, MA: MIT Press.

Kayne, Richard and Jean-Yves Pollock (1978) Stylistic inversion, successive cyclicity, and move NP in French. *Linguistic Inquiry*, 9, 595–621.

Kayne, Richard and Jean-Yves Pollock (2001) New thoughts on stylistic inversion. In Aafke Hulk and Jean-Yves Pollock (eds), *Subject Inversion in Romance and the Theory of Universal Grammar*, Oxford: Oxford University Press, pp. 107–61.

Kemenade, Ans van (1987) Syntactic Case and Morphological Case in the History of English. PhD dissertation, University of Utrecht.

Kiparsky, Paul and Carol Kiparsky (1971) Fact. In Danny Steinberg and Lee Jakobovitz (eds), *Semantics: An Interdisciplinary Reader*, Cambridge: Cambridge University Press, pp. 345–69.

Kitagawa, Yoshihisha (1994) *Subjects in Japanese and English*, New York: Garland.

Klima, Joseph (1964) Negation in English. In Jerry Fodor and Jerold Katz (eds), *The Structure of Language*, New Jersey: Prentice-Hall, pp. 246–323.

Koopman, Hilda and Dominique Sportiche (1991) The position of subjects. *Lingua*, 85, 211–58.

Kornai, Andras and Geoffrey K. Pullum (1990) The X-bar theory of phrase structure. *Language*, 66, 24–50.

Koster, Jan (1978) Why subject sentences don't exist. In Jay Keyser (ed.), *Recent Transformational Studies in European Languages*, Cambridge, MA: MIT Press, pp. 53–64.

Kroch, Anthony and Ann Taylor (2000) Verb-order in Early Middle English. In Susan Pintzuk, Georges Tsoulas, and Anthony Warner (eds), *Diachronic Syntax: Models and Mechanisms*, Oxford: Oxford University Press, pp. 132–63.

Kuroda, Sige-Yuki (1986) Whether we agree or not: A comparative syntax of English and Japanese. *Linguisticae Investigationes*, 12, 1–47.

Law, Paul (1999) On the passive existential construction. *Studia Linguistica*, 53, 183–208.

Lehmann, Christian (2004) Data in linguistics. *The Linguistic Review*, 21, 175–210.

Levin, Beth and Malka Rappaport-Hovav (1995) *Unaccusativity: At the Syntax-Lexical Semantics Interface*, Cambridge, MA: MIT Press.

Lightfoot, David (1979) *Principles of Diachronic Syntax*, Cambridge: Cambridge University Press.

Longobardi, Giuseppe (1996) The syntax of N-raising: A minimalist theory. OTS publications, Utrecht University, Research Institute for Language and Speech, OTS-WP-TL-96-105.

Lumsden, Michael (1988) *Existential Sentences: Their Structure and Meaning*, London: Croom Helm.

McCawley, James D. (1988) *The Syntactic Phenomena of English*, Chicago: University of Chicago Press.

McCloskey, Jim (1996) Subjects and subject positions in Irish. In Robert D. Borsley and Ian Roberts (eds), *The Syntax of Celtic Languages*, Cambridge: Cambridge University Press, pp. 241–83.

McCloskey, Jim (1997) Subjects and subject positions. In Liliane Haegeman (ed.), *Elements of Grammar: A Handbook of Generative Syntax*, Dordrecht: Kluwer, pp. 197–235.

McCloskey, Jim (2000) Quantifier float and *wh*-movement in an Irish English. *Linguistic Inquiry*, 31, 57–84.

McCloskey, Jim (2001) The distribution of subject properties in Irish. In William D. Davies and Stanley Dubinsky (eds), *Objects and other Subjects*, Dordrecht: Kluwer, pp. 157–92.

McCloskey, Jim (forthcoming) Questions and questioning in a local English. In Raffaella Zanuttini, Hector Campos, Elena Herburger, and Paul Portner (eds), *Negation, Tense and Clausal Architecture: Cross-linguistic Investigations*, Georgetown: Georgetown University Press.

Miller, Jim (1993) The Grammar of Scottish English. In James Milroy and Lesley Milroy (eds), *Real English: The Grammar of English Dialects of the British Isles*, London: Longman, pp. 99–138.

Miller, Philip (2001) Discourse constraints on (non) extraposition from subject in English. *Linguistics*, 39, 683–701.

Milsark, Gary Lee (1974) Existential Sentences in English. PhD dissertation, MIT.

Milsark, Gary Lee (1979) Toward an explanation of certain peculiarities of the existential construction in English. *Linguistic Analysis*, 3, 1–30.

Moro, Andrea (1997) *The Raising of Predicates: Predicative Noun Phrases and the Theory of Phrase Structure*, Cambridge: Cambridge University Press.

Newmeyer, Frederick (1983) *Grammatical Theory: Its Limits and its Possibilities*, Chicago and London: University of Chicago Press.

Newmeyer, Frederick (2001) Grammatical functions, thematic roles, and phrase structure: Their underlying disunity. In William D. Davies and Stanley Dubinsky, *Objects and other Subjects*, Dordrecht: Kluwer, pp. 53–76.

Nilsen, Øystein (2004) Domains for adverbs. In Artemis Alexiadou (ed.), Adverbs across Frameworks, special edition of *Lingua*, 114, 779–808.

Oirsouw, Robert van (1987) *The Syntax of Coordination*, London: Croom Helm.

Ouhalla, Jamal and Ur Shlonsky (2002) *Themes in Arabic and Hebrew Syntax*, Dordrecht: Kluwer.

Panagiotidis, Phaevos (2002) *Pronouns, Clitics and Empty Nouns*, New York and Amsterdam: John Benjamins.

Panagiotidis, Phaevos (2003) *One*, empty nouns, and θ-assignment. *Linguistic Inquiry*, 34, 281–92.

Penke, Martina and Anette Rosenbach (eds) (2004) What counts as evidence in linguistics? The case of innateness. *Studies in Language*, 28, 4.

Perlmutter, Paul (1971) *Deep and Surface Structure Constraints in Syntax*, New York: Holt, Rinehart and Winston.

Pesetsky, David and Esther Torrego (2000) T-to-C movement: Causes and consequences. In Michael Kenstowicz (ed.), *Ken Hale: A Life in Language*, Cambridge, MA: MIT Press, pp. 355–426.

Pintzuk, Suzan (1991) Phrase Structure in Competition: Variation and Change in Old English Word Order. PhD dissertation, University of Pennsylvania.

Pollock, Jean-Yves (1989) Verb movement, UG and the structure of IP. *Linguistic Inquiry*, 20, 365–425.

Pollock, Jean-Yves (1994) Checking theory and bare verbs. In Guglielmo Cinque, Jan Koster, Jean-Yves Pollock, Luigi Rizzi, and Raffaella Zanuttini (eds), *Paths toward Universal Grammar*, Georgetown: Georgetown University Press, pp. 293–310.

Pollock, Jean-Yves (1997) Notes on clause structure. In Liliane Haegeman (ed.), *Elements of Grammar: A Handbook of Generative Syntax*, Dordrecht: Kluwer, pp. 237–80.

Prince, Ellen (1981) Toward a taxonomy of given/new information. In Peter Cole (ed.), *Radical Pragmatics*, New York: Academic Press, pp. 223–54.

Radford, Andrew (2004) *Syntactic Theory and English Syntax*. Oxford: Blackwell.

Reinhart, Tanya (1981) Pragmatics and linguistics: An analysis of sentence topics. *Philosophica*, 27, 53–94.

Reinhart, Tanya (2000) The theta system: Syntactic realisation of verbal concepts. *OTS Working Papers in Linguistics* (00,01/TL), February. (To appear (extended) in the LI Monographs Series, MIT Press.)

Richards, Norvin (2001) *Movement in Language: Interactions and Architectures*, Oxford and New York: Oxford University Press.

Rizzi, Luigi (1990) *Relativized Minimality*, Cambridge, MA: MIT Press.

Rizzi, Luigi (1996) Residual V-Second and the Wh-Criterion. In Adriana Belletti and Luigi Rizzi (eds), *Parameters and Functional Heads: Essays in Comparative Syntax*, New York and Oxford: Oxford University Press, pp. 63–90.

Rizzi, Luigi (1997) The fine structure of the left periphery. In Liliane Haegeman (ed.), *Elements of Grammar: A Handbook of Generative Syntax*, Dordrecht: Kluwer, pp. 281–337.

Rizzi, Luigi (2001) On the position Int(errogative) in the left periphery of the clause. In Guglielmo Cinque and Giorgio P. Salvi (eds), *Current Studies in Italian Syntax: Essays Offered to Lorenzo Renzi*, Oxford: Elsevier, North Holland.

Roberts, Ian (1985) Agreement parameters and the development of English modal auxiliaries. *Natural Language and Linguistic Theory*, 3, 21–58.

Roberts, Ian (1990) Some notes on VP-fronting and head government. In Joan Mascaró and Marina Nespor (eds), *Grammar in Progress*, Dordrecht: Foris, pp. 386–96.

Roberts, Ian (1993) *Verbs and Diachronic Syntax: A Comparative study of English and French*, Dordrecht: Kluwer.

Roberts, Ian (1998) *Have/be* raising, move F, and procrastinate. *Linguistic Inquiry*, 29, 113–25.

Roberts, Ian (2005) *Principles and Parameters in VSO Languages*, New York and Oxford: Oxford University Press.

Rohrbacher, Bernhard (1999) *Morphology-Driven Syntax: A Theory of V to I Raising and Pro-drop*, New York and Amsterdam: John Benjamins.

Rowlett, Paul (1998) *Sentential Negation in French*, Oxford: Oxford University Press.

Rowlett, Paul (2005) *The Syntax of French*, Cambridge: Cambridge University Press.

Safir, Ken (1985) *Syntactic Chains*, Cambridge: Cambridge University Press.

Schütze, Carson (1999) English expletive constructions are not infected. *Linguistic Inquiry*, 30, 467–84.

Shlonsky, Ur (1991) Quantifiers as functional heads: A study of quantifier float in Hebrew. *Lingua*, 84, 159–80.

Shlonsky, Ur (1997) *Clause Structure and Word Order in Hebrew and Arabic*, Oxford: Oxford University Press.

Sobin, Nicholas (1997) Agreement, default rules and grammatical viruses. *Linguistic Inquiry*, 28, 318–43.

Sperber, Dan and Deirdre Wilson (1986) *Relevance*, Oxford: Blackwell.

Sportiche, Dominique (1988) A theory of floating quantifiers and its corollaries for phrase structure. *Linguistic Inquiry*, 19, 425–40.

Stubbs, Michael (2002) On text and corpus analysis: A reply to Borsley and Ingham. *Lingua*, 112 (1), 7–11.

Stuurman, Frits (1989) Generative grammar and descriptive grammar: Beyond juxtaposition. In Gottfried Graustein and Gerhard Leitner (eds), *Reference Grammars and Modern Linguistic Theory*, Tübingen: Niemeyer, pp. 229–54.

Svenonius, Peter (2002) Subject positions and the placement of adverbials. In Peter Svenonius (ed.), *Subjects, Expletives, and the EPP*, Oxford: Oxford University Press, pp. 201–42.

Szabolcsi, Anna (1983) The possessor that ran away from home. *Linguistic Review*, 1, 89–102.

Szabolcsi, Anna (1994) The noun phrase. *Syntax and Semantics*, 27: *The Syntactic Structure of Hungarian*, New York: Academic Press, pp. 179–274.

Vikner, Sten (1995) V° to I° movement and inflection for person in all tenses. *Working Papers in Scandinavian Syntax*, 55, 1–27.

Vikner, Sten (1997) V to I movement and inflection for person in all tenses. In Liliane Haegeman (ed.), *The New Comparative Syntax*, London: Longman, Addison and Wesley, pp. 189–213.

Ward, Gregory L. (1988) *The Semantics and Pragmatics of Preposing*, New York and London: Garland Publishing.

Wilkins, Wendy (1988) *Syntax and Semantics 21: Thematic Relations*. New York: Academic Press.

Williams, Edwin (1981) Argument structure and morphology. *Linguistic Review*, 1, 81–114.

Zanuttini, Raffaella (1997a) *Negation and Clausal Structure: A Comparative Study of Romance Languages*, New York and Oxford: Oxford University Press.

Zanuttini, Raffaella (1997b) Negation and V-movement. In Liliane Haegeman (ed.), *The New Comparative Syntax*, London: Longman, Addison and Wesley, pp. 214–45.

Zanuttini, Raffaella and Paul Portner (2003) Exclamative clauses: At the syntax–semantics interface. *Language*, 79, 29–81.

Zwart, Jan-Wouter (1997) The Germanic SOV languages and the universal base. In Liliane Haegeman (ed.), *The New Comparative Syntax*, London: Longman, Addison and Wesley, pp. 246–67.

Sources of examples

Newspapers

The Atlanta Journal-Constitution
The Chicago Tribune
The Guardian

The Independent
The Independent on Sunday
The Los Angeles Times
The New York Times
The Observer
San Francisco Chronicle
The Sunday Times
The Times
USA Today
The Washington Post
The Wall Street Journal

Fiction

Dexter, Colin (1992) *The Jewel that was Ours*, London: Macmillan. First published 1991, Pan Books.

Dexter, Colin (1995) *The Daughters of Cain*, London: Pan Books. First published 1994, Macmillan.

Dexter, Colin (2000) *The Remorseful Day*, London: Pan Books.

Francis Fyfield (2001) *Undercurrents*, Warner Books 2001. First published 2001, Little Brown and Company.

Franzen, Jonathan (2001) *The Corrections*, New York: Fourth Estate.

George, Elizabeth (1993/1996) *Missing Joseph*, London: Bantam Books.

Lloyd, Josie and Emlyn Rees (1999) *Come Together*, London: Arrow Books.

McCarthy, Mary (1989) *The Company She Keeps*, Harmondsworth: Penguin. First published 1942, Weidenfeld and Nicolson.

Muller, Marcia (1993) *Edwin of the Iron Shoes*, London: The Women's Press. First published in the US in 1977, McKay Washburn.

Rankin, Ian (2001) *The Falls*, London: Orion.

Spark, Muriel (1963) *The Bachelors*, Harmondsworth: Penguin. First published 1960, Macmillan.

Spark, Muriel (1977) *Memento Mori*, Harmondsworth: Penguin. First published 1959, Macmillan.

Townsend, Sue (1993) *Adrian Mole: The Wilderness Years*, London: Mandarin.

Wharton, Edith (1998) *The House of Mirth*, New York: Berkley. First published 1905.

Non-fiction

Bryson, Bill (1990) *The Lost Continent*, London: Abacus. First published 1989, Martin Secker and Warburg.

Bryson, Bill (1996) *Notes from a Small Island*, London: Swan. First published 1995, Doubleday.

Glendinning, Victoria (1984) *Vita*, Harmondsworth: Penguin.

MacCarthy, Fiona (1995) *William Morris*, London: Faber and Faber.

Shields, Carol (2001) *Jane Austin*, London: Phoenix. First published in the UK 1991, Weidenfeld and Nicolson.

Dictionaries

Concise Oxford Dictionary of Current English (6th edition) (1976), edited by J. B. Sykes. Oxford: Clarendon Press. First edition 1911.

Longman Dictionary of English Language and Culture (1998). London: Longman, Addison, Wesley.

Webster's Third New International Dictionary of the English Language (1981). Springfield, MA: Merriam-Webster.

Index